Ionesco's Imperatives

Ionesco's Imperatives

The Politics of Culture

Rosette C. Lamont

Ann Arbor

THE UNIVERSITY OF MICHIGAN PRESS

Copyright © by the University of Michigan 1993
All rights reserved
Published in the United States of America by
The University of Michigan Press
Manufactured in the United States of America

1996   1995   1994   1993   4   3   2   1

Library of Congress Cataloging-in-Publication Data

Lamont, Rosette, C.
    Ionesco's imperatives : the politics of culture / Rosette C.
Lamont.
        p.   cm. — (Theater—theory/text/performance)
    Includes bibliographical references and index.
    ISBN 0-472-10310-5
    1. Ionesco, Eugène—Political and social views. 2. Theater—
Political aspects—France—History—20th century. 3. Politics and
literature—France—History—20th century. 4. Political plays,
French—History and criticism. I. Title. II. Series.
PQ2617.06Z742   1993
842'.914—dc20   92-43167
                                                           CIP

A CIP catalogue record for this book is available from the British Library.

In memory of Loudmilla's luminous presence

Albertine's Lesson

Dear Albertine, each artist gives one world—
a world unique the artist makes us see.
The novels of Stendhal all have the sense
of altitude: the height of prison walls,
the tower of Fabrice, the guillotine
which severed Julien's head.

                    But you, dear child,
who love the painter's art, and who have seen
some pictures of Vermeer, do you recall
that they are fragments of the same creation:
in each of them a table and a desk,
a painted window glass, a woman dressed
in silk—the center figure of the room—
who reads a book or plays a harpsichord?
                    —Wallace Fowlie *(Characters from Proust)*

Acknowledgments

My greatest debt is to Eugène Ionesco, without whose friendship and endorsement of the term *metaphysical farce* this book would not have come into being.

I owe what I have become as a teacher and scholar to my own teacher and dissertation director at Yale University, Henri Peyre. Those of us who had the privilege and pleasure of maintaining constant contact with his brilliant, witty mind still breathe the air of his immense generosity.

Friends and colleagues provided inspiration and guidance along the way: Doris Abramson, who shared my young enthusiasm for avant-garde drama and invited me to publish in the pages of the *Massachusetts Review,* of which she was and is the theater editor; Jules Chametzky, who carefully edited my essay "Death and Tragi-Comedy" and my long interview with Ionesco; Tom Bishop, the impresario of French culture in the United States, with whom I could always talk about Ionesco and Beckett; Edith Wyschogrod, whose immense erudition and subtle philosophical mind offered food for thought on the subject of mass death and the Holocaust even as she guided my reading of Ionesco's favorite text *The Tibetan Book of the Dead;* Katherine H. Burkman, who encouraged my exploration of myth and ritual in Ionesco's drama; Marcel Mendelson, whose unfailing friendship and love of the arts gave meaning to my endeavor; and Geoffrey Hartman, Elie Wiesel, Saul Bellow, who taught me to hear the ethical pitch under the shimmering aesthetic surface. Carrie Smelser's attentive, loving presence helped me through the completion of the final draft. My undergraduate and graduate students all queried keenly. I am particularly indebted to the members of my spring 1992 seminar at the Graduate School of City University of New York, "Metaphysics, Mystery and Menace: Beckett, Ionesco and Pinter." Much was contributed to the class by Zohra Lampert, one of the rare metaphysical actresses I have seen on the American stage.

I am grateful to the J. S. Guggenheim Memorial Foundation for a fellowship (1973–74) which gave me leisure and freedom to deal with a subject that required both, and to the Rockefeller Foundation for its Humanities Fellowship (1983–84). I also wish to express my gratitude to the Yaddo Foundation for its writing fellowships (1962, 1963, 1966) and the peaceful atmosphere of its gracious estate. Queens College of CUNY assisted me with a Fellowship Research Leave in 1976. Dean John H. Reilly deserves special thanks for his understanding, encouragement, and assistance with travel funds.

My deepest debt is to my parents, who always encouraged me to develop my interests. My mother was a gentle but ardent feminist, a fine musician who knew how to listen to the inner harmony of life and lend an ear to people of all ages and stations in life. My father, who fought bravely in World War II, was a patriot and a gentleman. My husband, Frederick Hyde Farmer, spent many hours reading the manuscript of this book, giving me precious advice and moral support.

Grateful acknowledgment is made to the following publishers and journals for permission to reprint previously published materials.

L'Esprit Créateur for "The Proliferation of Matter in Ionesco's Plays" by Rosette C. Lamont, *L'Esprit Créateur* 2, no. 4 (Winter 1962): 189–97.

French Review for "The Metaphysical Farce, Beckett and Ionesco" by Rosette C. Lamont, *French Review* 32, no. 4 (February 1959): 319–28; and for "Air and Matter: Ionesco's *Le Piéton de l'Air* and *Victimes du Devoir,* by Rosette C. Lamont, *French Review* 38, no. 3 (January 1965): 349–61.

Grove Veidenfeld for material quoted from Grove Press editions of Eugene Ionesco's works.

Louisiana State University Press for "Characters from Proust." Reprinted by permission of Louisiana State University Press from *Characters from Proust,* poems by Wallace Fowlie. Copyright © 1983 by Wallace Fowlie.

The Massachusetts Review for "Death and the Tragi-Comedy" by Rosette C. Lamont, *Massachusetts Review* 6, no. 2 (Winter–Spring 1965): 381–402; and for "Interview with Eugene Ionesco" by Rosette C. Lamont, *Massachusetts Review* 10, no. 1 (Winter 1969): 128–48. Reprinted from *The Massachusetts Review,* copyright © 1965 and 1969 by The Massachusetts Review, Inc.

Modern Drama for "From Macbeth to Macbett" by Rosette C. Lamont, *Modern Drama,* December 1972, 231–53.

Performing Arts Journal for "Ionesco's *L'Homme aux valieses*" by Rosette C. Lamont, *Performing Arts Journal*—1, no. 2 (Fall 1976): 21–36.

Prentice Hall for "Introduction" and "Eugene Ionesco and the Metaphysical Farce," both by Rosette C. Lamont, from *IONESCO a Collection of Critical Essays,* edited by Rosette C. Lamont, pp. 1–10 and 154–83. Copyright © 1973. Reprinted by permission of the publisher, Prentice Hall, a division of Simon & Schuster.

Riverrun Press for material quoted from *Journeys Among the Dead* by Eugene Ionesco, copyright © 1985 by John Calder (Publishers) Ltd., London, and Riverrun Press, New York. Translation from the French by Barbara Wright copyright © 1985 by Barbara Wright.

Undena Publications for *"Journey to the Kingdom of the Dead:* Ionesco's Gnostic Dream Play," by Rosette C. Lamont, *The Dream and the Play: Ionesco's Theatrical Quest,* edited by Moshe Lazar, 93–119. Malibu: Undena Publications, 1982.

Yale French Studies for "The Hero in Spite of Himself" by Rosette C. Lamont, *Yale French Studies,* Fall 1962, 73–81.

Every effort has been made to trace the ownership of all copyrighted material in this book and to obtain permission for its use.

Contents

Introduction

In France, the name Eugène Ionesco is firmly linked to those of Jean Tardieu, Samuel Beckett, and Arthur Adamov, the creators of a dramaturgic mode that characterizes the second half of the twentieth century: Metaphysical Farce. The term is an oxymoron. The ancient Greeks joined *oxys* (sharp, keen) and *moros* (foolish), producing a verbal centaur: pointedly foolish. Thus, an oxymoron is an epigrammatic paradox, a lexical construct issuing from the mind's quest for a third term to combine antithetical states of mind and being that, far from excluding one another, might coexist in the same mental space.

Farce, a popular form of entertainment, characterized by slapstick, bastinadoes, clownish tumblings and fumblings, insults added to injuries, in short all manner of humiliation that flesh is heir to, hardly seems to harmonize with ontological speculations. Yet, in the avant-garde theater that issued from World War II, the Holocaust, the Gulags, physicality is put in the service of that which transcends the physical. The human being's exacerbated awareness of his or her fragile situation as a vulnerable, mortal creature, living out its brief life span upon a dying planet, becomes crystallized upon the modern stage in a series of antinaturalist, apsychological, consciously grotesque comic forms. In fact, it is the form itself that calls attention to the plight of a paltry creature, once viewed as having been shaped in God's own image. The laughter elicited by this incongruity is a jaundiced merriment often turning to black humor.

Although once strictly separated, the comic and the tragic genres have often flowered simultaneously. An epoch rich in tragic drama also produces exhilarating comedy. Violent emotions such as pity and terror, the human being's identification with the protagonist's destiny, need not be purged solely by the tragic apprehension of our human situation; catharsis may also occur by means of the wild anarchy of humor. The French have a wise saying: *"Le ridicule tue."* Indeed, derision may be a powerful weapon, one that can only be blunted by a superior form of humor. If wit is always a battle of wits, humor—a philosophical kind of laugh directed primarily at oneself— is able to deflect the attack of rapier-sharp mockery, and heal the open wound. Our contemporary critics have taken apart the mechanism of purgation; they refer frequently to "catharsis through laughter."[1]

In a world turned upside down by apocalyptic wars and genocide, a universe deprived of heroic models, tragedy—in the Aristotelian sense—seems no longer a viable genre. The tragic view of human existence is tied to a dignified hierarchical order, with an emperor, king, moral ruler at the head of a structured society where lines of command as well as responsibility are clearly drawn. Ours is an epoch in which human beings are often treated as disposable, recyclable things. This reification of humanity is grotesquely sad, closer to comedy than tragedy. However, as the dramatist Friedrich Dürrenmatt points out in his 1958 essay "Problems of the Theatre": "The tragic is still possible even if pure tragedy is not. We can achieve the tragic out of comedy. We can bring it forth as a frightening moment, as an abyss that opens suddenly; indeed many of Shakespeare's tragedies are . . . really comedies out of which the tragic arises."[2] Dürrenmatt believes that it takes greater courage today to live as a Gulliver among the giants, mocking these monstrous, humorless creatures. The artist asserts his freedom by the act of parody. In his book *L'Esthétique du rire,* the modern philosophe Charles Lalo suggests that comedy is the reigning genre in an unsteady, fluid element of shifting values tumbling downward. Like Dürrenmatt, Lalo believes that the comic sense is the life jacket that will save us from sinking in the shipwreck of our values.

Clearly, the traditional masks of comedy and tragedy no longer express our modern attitude in regard to dramatic genres. For us they are not irreconcilable categories. In fact, no one today is able to read Voltaire's definition of Shakespeare as "a barbaric genius" without smiling at the French philosophe's assumption that only an untutored Englishman would mix in one and the same play the tragic and the comic. In our post–World War II era, all masks have been stripped, revealing the grimacing mouth, the lips widening for a grin only to turn down in sorrow. This is the sadly funny face of Rouault's clowns and Picasso's Pierrots. It also happens to be the typical expression of Eugène Ionesco's moon-shaped face, with one eye half-closed, seeming to look inward, while the other stares out in fearful disbelief. The lower part of the face attracts attention to the sensuous, perpetually mobile mouth, chewing words like ripe plums. In old age, leaning on a cane, an escapee from the riddle of the Sphinx, Ionesco begins to look like those ambiguous clowns who make us laugh at death, who die of laughter.

In his essay "Why Do I Write?" composed for *The Two Faces of Ionesco,* the playwright states: "One writes in order not to die completely, not to disappear all at once, although everything must perish in the end."[3] As early as 1932, he consigned to the pages of the intimate journal he started to keep in Bucharest: "I will die without having played a significant role on the European scene. The latter will have to do without me, before sinking into nothingness."[4] Thus, this twenty-year-old budding intellectual foresees the demise of our fragile society. For him, there are two reasons for committing to paper the perishable, evanescent, transitory thoughts and feelings of a human being: "To allow others to share in the astonishment of being, the dazzlement of existence, and to shout to God and other human beings our anguish, letting it be known that we were there."[5]

It took a while for the Franco-Romanian writer, grieving over the fact that his Balkan origins condemned him to play the role of a poor relation within the realm of the European intelligentsia, to become a modern French classicist, a member of the Académie Française. Though his early prophecy failed to materialize, he was thirty-nine years old when his first play, *The Bald Soprano,* was presented on May 11, 1950, at the tiny Noctambules theater on the Left Bank. No one, least of all the author himself, could have foreseen that this perversely funny one-act "antiplay" would make theater history by running at another small house, La Huchette, for forty uninterrupted years, with no end in sight. Some members of the original cast, notably the brilliant actor-director Nicolas Bataille, who presides over a rotating company of Ionesco veteran players, still appear in the play, as well as in its companion piece at La Huchette, *The Lesson.* They play side by side with members of a second generation of actors, some of whom are the children of their erstwhile companions.

Initially, the loosely tied scenes that comprise *The Bald Soprano* were written as an exercise for the acquisition of a new language: English. Using the Assimil conversation textbook, *English Made Easy,*[6] Ionesco found himself in the company of a stuffy British couple, Mr. and Mrs. Smith, who inform one another that "the ceiling is above our heads, the floor under our feet, and the week is made up of seven days, MondayTuesdayWednesdayThursdayFridaySaturdaySunday." As the adult student began to transcribe these sentences into his notebook, it seemed to him that he saw the ambient world for the first time, and that he was no longer able to take anything for granted. Seized by vertigo, he had to lie down. Six characters (the same number as in Pirandello's *Six Characters in Search of an Author*)—Mr. and Mrs. Smith, Mr. and Mrs. Martin, the Smiths' maid, Mary, and a passing fireman—took hold of the writer, dictating to him the rest of the sketch.[7] Ionesco enjoys telling his friends: "I became a dramatist by accident."

Ionesco is not so much a dramatist as he is many dramatists rolled into one. First there is the irreverent debunker who set into motion the mechanism of a new genre, the tragic farce. *Soprano,* initially entitled *The English Hour,* was quickly followed by *The Lesson,* and *Jack or the Submission.* The love of provocation, which marks the early Ionesco sketches, suggests the influence of a compatriot, Tristan Tzara, one of the leaders of the Dada movement. Ionesco readily admits that Tzara played a determining role in his own artistic evolution. Like the dadaists, Ionesco embraces the oneness of contradictory propositions. This is particularly obvious in the essays he wrote in Romania as a twenty-one-year-old budding literary critic. These were first published in various reviews, then collected in a volume entitled *Nu* (No).

At first glance, *No* appears a sophisticated joke played on established Romanian critics of the thirties, and also on a number of respected poets and novelists of the time: Tudor Arghezi, Ion Barbu, Camil Petresco. It is all the more daring since these texts are the utterances of an unknown, albeit promising, youth, who treats his elders as though he were enthroned on Mount Olympus. Claiming that no intellectual endeavor ought to be taken seriously, the young writer proceeds to demonstrate that the revered "geniuses" of his country are pompous windbags or sentimental fools, none of whom ought to be considered as writers of world stature since Romania is "the poor relation of western Europe's intelligentsia."[8] The critics who sing the praises of these inferior writers do so in loosely impressionistic prose, utterly devoid of any objective standards of judgment. However, establishing such standards is a waste of time anyway, according to the young iconoclast, a futile activity.

The absurdity of judging a work of literature is given an eloquent demonstration as Ionesco produces two companion pieces written about a novel of his close friend Mircea Eliade, the student of the history of religions. Taking as an example the latter's book about India, *Metrayi,* the future inventor of the antiplay proves that it is possible to write with equal passion an enthusiastic and a negative review of the same work. This can mean only one thing: the work itself does not have an absolute value. Which judgment is one supposed to believe? Where does the truth lie? The author of *No* would answer: "Nowhere and everywhere. It doesn't matter since literary criticism is nothing but a game."

In an essay that concludes the 1986 French edition of *No* (Non), the critic Ileana Gregori points out that Ionesco's nihilistic stance must be taken as a form of self-dramatization. Not yet a playwright, but a lycée teacher of French and an avant-garde essayist, Ionesco embarked on a demystification of the endeavor of writing about writing. This attack on the whole profession must also be viewed as self-destruction. If no one is able to judge the quality of a work of literature, least of all that provincial human, a Romanian, then what is the significance of his perverse joke? Should he give up before even trying? One can hardly speak of an attitude, Gregori suggests, but of "an anti-attitude,"[9] an all-embracing irony.

Ionesco's irony is close to the Socratic undermining of existence, that "infinitely bottomless, invisible, and indivisible spiritual state" diagnosed by Kierkegaard in *The Concept of Irony*.[10] This process of derision must be situated in a zone one might call "the between," an "empty space," a "nothingness"[11] that conceals what is perhaps most important. Just as Socrates questioned the knowing subject in order to demonstrate gradually that the latter knew nothing at all, so Ionesco puts in question the authority of established critics, holding them up to ridicule. Nor does he fear being crushed under the weight of the structure he pulls down. Kierkegaard draws a comparison between Socrates and Samson when he writes: "Here we have irony in all its divine infinity, which allows nothing to endure. Socrates, like

Samson, seizes the columns bearing the edifice of knowledge and plunges everything into the nothingness of ignorance."[12] Yet this ignorance must be viewed as a kind of triumph over "the sum total of phenomena."[13] It suggests a dizzying kind of freedom, a divine unreason bordering on the illumination of the dream state.

In Ionesco, the oneiric universe surfaces quite soon after the first neosurrealist plays. Although the dramatist retained his love for language games—clichés, mock proverbs, maxims, intertextual allusions, absurd syllogisms, all of these tinged by planned lacunae, inversions, substitutions—his plays grew metaphysical. In *Amédée* and *The Chairs,* the proliferation of matter (mushrooms for the first, empty chairs for the second) translates an obsession with being de trop. Although resolutely anti-Sartrian, Ionesco admires the existentialist philosopher's early novel *Nausea,* where metaphysical horror is diagnosed as a malady. Perhaps Ionesco's direct literary ancestor is the French symbolist poet Stéphane Mallarmé, whose uncanny ability to make absence palpable, thus lending a haunting presence to the void, became the basis of the peculiar form of *The Chairs,* a play in which empty chairs, brought onto the stage at an ever-quickening rhythm, represent imaginary guests received by an aged, solitary couple.

With *Victims of Duty,* a confessional dream play, Ionesco's dramaturgy takes a new turn, one that will surface again in the last two oneiric stage poems. *Victims,* Ionesco's favorite work, depicts the confrontation between a man and his father's ghost. Although it owes a great deal to Kafka's preoccupation with the Primal Sire, it is also the dramatist's first openly autobiographical composition.

The relationship between Ionesco and his father was a difficult one from the start. A Romanian attorney, Eugen Ionescu moved to Paris in 1911 with his French wife Thérèse Ipcar and their two-year-old son. He spent a good part of the day away from home, supposedly to prepare for his doctoral examinations. In 1916, following Romania's entry into World War I, he returned alone to Bucharest. There, he divorced his wife in absentia, leaving the care of two small children (Eugène and his younger sister Marilina) to the mother. These were years of great financial hardship. The young mother was not informed of her status, nor of her husband's second marriage in 1917. In 1922, he demanded that the two children join him and his new wife, thus bringing about a painful separation between them and their mother. Ionesco never stopped harboring a deep resentment of his father's deception and cowardliness, characteristics that also surfaced with the rise of fascism in Romania, a situation that elicited from the highly adaptable lawyer chameleonic political adjustments. *Victims* is steeped in this personal drama; on one level, it is a bold public confession enclosed in the form of self-psychoanalysis, while on the other, it constitutes a lucid meditation on the vagaries of contemporary European history.

A fuller orchestration of the latter theme is achieved in *Rhinoceros* and *The Killer*. In these plays we witness the emergence of Ionesco's Everyman, his courageous antihero, Bérenger. Bérenger's passive resistance to evil shows him to be a spiritual brother of Mahatma Gandhi.

Two fundamental apprehensions are found at the core of Ionesco's weltanschauung: lightness and heaviness, air and matter. There are moments of bliss, when one feels that levitation is possible, that a human being might rise from the mortal flesh weighing him or her down. In *Amédée* and *A Stroll in the Air* the protagonist experiences a joyous liberation. Yet, these moments of wonder are of short duration. At the end of *Stroll* the unencapsulated astronaut returns from circling the earth on winged feet only to bring terrifying news: beyond our verdant planet lie deserts of fire or ice. This fragile world is our only paradise, one we must learn to appreciate for the brief time allotted us. Yet, Ionesco writes, the longer we live, the greater our attachment to "the warm slime of the living."[14] When he was a young man of twenty, Ionesco committed to his journal this anguished cry: "Someday I shall die!"[15]

It is this knowledge that informs *Exit the King* and *Killing Game*, two somber tone poems on the subject of individual mortality and mass killings. The first is profoundly metaphysical, echoing in its imagery the poems of John Donne, as well as those of Ionesco's favorite French poet, Charles Baudelaire. The second is no less philosophical. It owes its central image to Daniel Defoe's *A Journal of the Plague Year*, as well as to Poe's "The Mask of the Red Death," and Artaud's horrifying description of the bubonic plague in *The Theater and Its Double*. However, *Killing Game* also possesses a complex political subtext, showing that death is no respecter of power or wealth. Both of these works use the comic genre to instill fear and horror, urging the human creature to face nature's cruelty and the absurdity of its mortal condition. In these stage poems on death and dying, Ionesco shows himself as a moralist, an heir of Montaigne, Pascal, La Bruyère.

Another Ionesco is the political cartoonist, or creator of stage *bandes dessinées.*[16] *Macbett,* a caricature of absolute power in the modernist tradition of Jarry's *Ubu Rex,* is an exposé of human blood lust. Another work that belongs to this genre is the short film scenario *Anger.* It shows how a trifling incident unleashes a world conflagration.

The film begins with a sentimental vision of an all-sweetness-and-light society: the small square of a typical country town with a Sunday crowd coming out of church, nodding amicably to acquaintances or exchanging formal handshakes. An old lady hands a coin to a beggar. Ionesco suggests that the filmmaker might add "two or three other edifying scenes of a similar nature."[17] The protagonists are a young married couple. The husband is seen coming home for lunch, once a sacrosanct custom in France. His wife brings in a steaming soup tureen. A series of cross-fading shots show other hands, other tureens being brought to the table, thus suggesting that the ritual of the midday meal is going on in every part of the city, in fact, of the country. Suddenly, the young man scowls: he has discovered a fly in his soup. The other husbands are equally upset with flies in their tureens. Their wives are guilty of a crime of *lèse-majesté,* or *lèse-mariage.* Marital quarrels break out. The first husband tips the tureen over his wife's head. She shrieks, "Murderer!" Domestic tiffs turn into brawls, and the police vans roll in. Ionesco makes a point of stating: "The scuffle between the police and the local population spreads through the whole district."[18] At this point, the dramatist-screenwriter suggests, there ought to be a montage of newsreel shots showing riots, and various dictators' impassioned proclamations. "Then all hell breaks loose, with floods and earthquakes . . . which finally lead to a shot of the atom bomb exploding."[19]

Thus, in a brief sketch, the playwright has encapsulated the ever present possibility of utter destruction, the threat of an apocalyptic end of life as we know it. The veneer of civilization is exposed as thin, ready to crack at the smallest provocation. The scenario ends with a warning: "Final shot: the planet exploding."[20] *Anger* has much in common with Voltaire's *Candide;* it is a cartoon of the absurdity of wars and human cruelty. It is the vision of a philosophe, a humanist rather than a philosopher, steeped in political awareness.

Surveying this considerable body of work, one is overwhelmed with its variety in form and content: plays, short sketches, ballet and movie scenarios, short stories, a novel, fairy tales for small children and childlike adults, five volumes of memoirs, and a work of dramaturgic theory, as well as numerous important articles of a polemical, political nature. Nevertheless, it is possible to integrate these various works into a single, steadily developing worldview, a philosophy of art and life.

This study seeks to combine the chronological approach with the thematic. It also hopes to bring some clarification to a confusion about Ionesco due to his reiterating throughout his life that his oeuvre is apolitical. Lately, however, he admitted that being virulently apolitical is in itself a political attitude. In *Notes and Counter Notes* he insists that his early plays should be viewed as abstract, architectural constructs, free of content. However, a careful perusal of his early plays, such as *The Lesson*, reveals a powerful political parable imbedded in what appears, at first, a light farce about the process of education based on the archetypal fairy tale "Little Red Riding Hood." The time has come to do a revisionist study of Ionesco's oeuvre, to decode the presence, at almost every turn, of the forces of history and politics. Nor is it surprising to find this parable in the work of a man who could be considered a living icon for the twentieth-century predicaments of European men and women, people deeply marked by tragic events. A stranger among his own people, particularly when they fell prey to a fascist regime, a foreigner in the midst of a nation estranged from itself when occupied by an enemy power, Ionesco is the eternal wanderer, interrogating the world, and plumbing his own psyche.

Now that Ionesco has reached the end of his career as a writer, it is clear that even his neosurrealist beginnings were tinged with the apprehension of global catastrophe. On August 13, 1932, he records the following thought in the pages of his journal: "I'm afraid of looking through my window at the gaping holes. I close my eyes. I ask you humbly, I implore you not to force me to open my eyes on the void. Everything will crumble. It is all crumbling at this very moment. My shouts, my cries sound like a sigh."[21]

From the very beginning, Ionesco has been a thinker, a poet-philosopher. There are echoes from Pascal in this early apprehension, and they will continue to resound throughout the plays, even in the seemingly light one-act *The Gap*. Ionesco is both an artist and a true intellectual, that is, one who lives for thought. His writings bear the imprint of his voracious readings in the history of religions, mythology, the European classics, gnostic and Byzantine mystic texts, and his favorite book on the process of dying, *The Tibetan Book of the Dead*.

For many years Ionesco was misunderstood and misinterpreted in Europe, and particularly in France. Reading the press clippings from the fifties and sixties, one is amazed to see that he was taken for a satirist of bourgeois society, a pessimist, a decadent cosmopolitan. Those who dismissed him in the haughty manner of academics or establishment journalists labeled him an enfant terrible, a *farceur* (practical joker), and suspected him of being a *fumiste* (blowhard). Before the publication of his theoretical essays, *Notes and Counter Notes* (1962), few critics had an inkling of the writer's dramaturgic program, of the lucidity of his views on art, culture, and politics. Gradually, a sprinkling of enlightened journalists, such as Jacques Lemarchand of *Le Figaro*, began to point out to the public the dramatist's underlying seriousness, the poetic power of his astonishing stage images rising from the depths of his subconscious, and the liberating effect of his anarchic humor. It took twenty years for Ionesco, who made a late start as a dramatist, to find his way into the pantheon of France's *classiques modernes*, a consecration fully achieved in 1991, when his publisher, Gallimard, brought out his *Théâtre Complet* in the elaborately annotated, highly prestigious Pléiade edition.

One wonders what accounts for the many misinterpretations Ionesco has suffered. Some of it is due to his own prankish perverseness. Not unlike Baudelaire, Ionesco reveled in sending people on the wrong path, in confusing the issue even as he granted numerous interviews and pretended to explicate his work in great detail. He wished to keep his audience off balance, shaking them out of their smug self-assurance. Logic, he suggested, can only bring one to a certain point, perhaps a point too certain to allow for ambiguity. Again and again, he advised the reader to give up his or her cherished Cartesian longing for rationality. Life and the human psyche, he hinted, are irrational. Thus, to reproduce total truth, art must probe the deeper *vérité* hidden under surface *réalité*.

Another unsettling feature of Ionesco's art is its amalgamation of the real and the surreal. For Ionesco surrealism *is* reality, superior to the flat surface we are taught to accept as real. He always says with mock amazement: "But I am a realist, you know!" He then explains that when we dream, what we see and feel appears to us as real as what we experience in a waking state, even more so. When we wake, we carry with us images of our dream life; they are part of us, as are our remembrances of past events, and reveries on a possible future. By reaching deep within himself, Ionesco believes he is able to rejoin the collective subconscious, to issue from the confines of the self and finally be at one with all humanity.

Ionesco's journey as an artist is not linear; it is a spiral along which he descends into the depths of his private inferno, or climbs toward the dazzling heights he has glimpsed on rare occasions. He has been called "a failed mystic," but his "failure" lies in the high expectations of his spirit, whose "hunger and thirst" can never be assuaged.

Chapter 1

Ionescoland

Marcel Proust once stated that every artist is the citizen of a foreign country whose topography, moral landscape, climate, and customs he or she interprets in his or her works. This land, governed by its own laws, exists within each artist as his or her private universe.

Eugène Ionesco takes Proust's assertion a step further when he claims that every writer creates an autonomous world parallel to the one we believe is "real." For Ionesco, the writer must not hold a mirror up to nature, as nineteenth-century realists proclaimed, but represent the life of those who inhabit the space on the other side of the looking glass. Yet, Ionesco considers himself a modern realist since the suprareality he crystallizes on the stage is a complete kind of reality that comprises both the conscious and the subconscious worlds.

How do we, readers and viewers of his plays, approach this bizarre world? Proust might have advised us to become travelers, open-minded tourists. Certainly we must be ready to wander and wonder, to proceed like people who enter an unfamiliar house. We go from room to room, floor to floor, often in the dark. Gradually, we discover where the hallway leads, what lies behind each door. If the house is sensibly constructed, the novelty of its architecture shall not prevent us from dwelling in this habitation. In fact, its peculiar charm will grow on us, make us feel that this intriguing house is a home.

If, like Lewis Carroll's Alice, we step through the looking glass into Ionescoland, we will find a gray, muddy soil, an overcast sky. Everywhere there are fissures in the ground, treacherous crevices, holes that open upon the void. Marshes await the unwary traveler.

Occasionally, one happens upon an isolated village, one of those untouched rural communities bypassed by so-called technological progress. There, the daily round of activities is dictated by traditional occupations: farming, cooking, religious holidays. These rare outposts are oases in the wasteland, mirages, places out of time, crystallizations of things past.

More often than not, Ionesco's characters are city dwellers. They inhabit basement apartments that slowly sink into the slimy soil beneath. Rain falls steadily with no sun breaking through the low clouds. And, in the winter, the snow turns sooty. However, once in a while, an amazing illumination occurs, an epiphany: a wall of one of these dank lodgings grows transparent, revealing a hidden garden. The flowers, shining brightly in the grass like scattered precious stones, the single tree at the center, are magical. But, like those of the Cluny tapestry depicting the Unicorn and the Maid, these mystical apparitions are doomed to fade.

Haunted by this momentary lifting of the veil, Ionesco's protagonists set out in search of perfection. Sometimes, after climbing to great heights, they catch a glimpse of a dazzling sky, its unblemished azure teasingly out of reach. At other times, the wanderer reaches an orderly city neighborhood, a technological paradise. The light created by the engineer of this utopia is reminiscent of the glow experienced on the solitary heights, yet there is nothing spiritual about it; it is an ersatz, machine-controlled illumination. This urban marvel may be free of the vagaries of climatic alterations but not of evil, crime, and death. In fact, it is in these very places that killers tend to go on a rampage, as though this perfect setting elicits the surfacing of the monsters of the subconscious. In Ionescoland, the utopian dream is synonymous with dehumanization. Like Dostoyevsky's jaundiced "underground man," Ionesco harbors a strong dislike of Crystal Palaces.

The citizens of Ionescoland tend to be middle-aged, or even very old. Their careworn faces are deeply lined; their hair is the gray of the sooty snow covering the pavement of city sidewalks. More often than not, couples are childless, staying together out of habit, or an anguished, tender pity for their life companions. The wives slowly become mothers of their childlike husbands. Together they wait for death that comes inexorably, entrapping and crushing them. In the meantime, they huddle in tiny rooms crowded with heavy pieces of furniture. Outside these paltry havens there is nothing but silence and darkness.

In this peculiar country people are objects, while things seem endowed with a kind of independent existence, a will of their own. Mushrooms proliferate on the floor of a damp room under the growing legs of a corpse who has mysteriously taken over the couple's bedroom, and the conjugal bed. The rhythm of disaster is marked by the hysteria of matter. Objects multiply, like the cells of a cancerous growth, overwhelming, entombing the frantic protagonists: empty chairs carried in at a dizzying pace by the Old Woman *(The Chairs),* who must keep up with the delirious expansion of the imaginings she and her husband share; pieces of furniture piling up to form a kind of Egyptian pyramid around "the new tenant" trapped by his possessions; coffee cups brought in at breakneck speed by the over-hospitable wife of a man cross-examined in his own home by an unexpected detective *(Victims of Duty);* monstrous eggs hatched by a young husband who watches with amazement a progeny of things and people, chaotic matter doomed by future wars to become a mass of scrambled eggs *(The Future Is in Eggs).* Thus, we are made to witness the triumph of a brutal technology crowned by the looming of the atomic mushroom.

According to Ionesco, the Enlightenment's vision of limitless progress was a dangerous illusion. He recognizes within himself two fundamental states of consciousness that make up the polar principles of a personal dialectic: a feeling of heaviness due to the oppressive presence of matter, and a sense of airiness, lightness, freedom. The drudgery of daily existence weighs upon human beings, plunging them into opaque, viscous matter. At rare moments of grace everything seems easy, light, transparent. When this occurs, Ionesco's protagonist experiences a miraculous recovery of the state of childhood. The dazzling glow he espies is not of this world; it is similar to the light into which Dante, led by Beatrice, ascends when they scale the sublime region of Paradise. Most of the time, however, Ionescoland is overcast by the somber shadows that characterize our all too solid and sullied world.

There are some avenues of escape. The protagonist might discover that he possesses the wondrous gift of levitation. Bursts of optimism propel him upward to the level of tree tops, then still higher, into the galaxy. Encapsulated in his longing for freedom, this self-sufficient astronaut, whose envelope of flesh is his only flying machine, is able to explore space by walking through the skies around the planet earth. The character's short triumph, however, proves illusory since, as he looks down upon the universe, he sees hellish regions where biological life cannot endure. How does one continue living with such dreadful knowledge? Ionesco believes that laughter, a sense of humor—the distinguishing human characteristic—may tame anguish. Wit and lucidity are powerful weapons in the struggle against all-devouring time, power-hungry tyrants, and even the forces of our subconscious. In the hands of an artist and a poet, wit becomes a rapier, humor a shield.

Ionescoland rises from the moist, intimate, sexual substratum, the watery principle associated with the female. It is a difficult birth. Once expelled from the visceral crib of the womb in which humans would like to linger, the inhabitants of Ionesco's country dream of escaping to ethereal regions. However, they are unable to forget that they issued from the depths. Descent is the attraction of the abyss, a longing to be unborn, uncreated, a desire for annihilation. The opposite dream of flight, of a positive escape, is associated, as Gaston Bachelard points out in *L'Air et les songes,* with a philosophy of the will. Therefore, the protagonists of Ionesco's plays are driven simultaneously in two polar directions, attracted to God and Satan at once. This is what Baudelaire calls in one of his essays "the simultaneous pull" downward and upward.

Ionesco was deeply influenced by Baudelaire's fundamental duality. The future playwright, who returned to France from Romania on the eve of World War II, owed his escape from fascism to a fellowship granted him for a projected doctoral dissertation on Baudelaire's treatment of the theme of death. Both in Ionesco's plays and in his private journals one hears echoes from the nineteenth-century poet's ironic, unfinished, moral autobiography, *My Heart Laid Bare.* Baudelaire and Ionesco are equally aware of the ascensional/descensional human impulse. Although double-edged, it stems from the psychic need of transcendence. One of Baudelaire's finest prose poems bears the English title "Anywhere Out of this World." The text presents a speaker and a listener. The first offers his friend various remote places where he might find peace of mind and discover amazing sights. The second does not react in any fashion to these suggestions, until, at the very end, he bursts out with the desperate, bitter exclamation: "Anywhere out of this world." Ionesco's antiheroes share this sentiment.

Ionesco is a poet of the four elements, a cosmic visionary. For him, as for many of the poets he admires, earth is the most alien of the four elements, a place of exile. Below the thin crust of our globe burns the fire that threatens to consume the universe. Fire, air, and water haunt the poet-dramatist's imagination while he must sojourn on this earth.

Fire is intimately tied to an apocalyptic vision. In *The Bald Soprano,* a universal fire is prophesied by the maid. In fact, she recites a comic poem announcing the end of the world; it is written in honor of her lover, the Fire Chief. At the end of *Killing Game* flames spread through the plague-ridden city, destroying those few people spared by the epidemic that ravaged the community. Although this tragicomedy follows closely Daniel Defoe's *A Journal of the Plague Year,* culminating in events that evoke the great fire of London, the conflagration engulfing the unnamed city acquires cosmic dimensions since the flames spread from town to country, engulfing the entire planet.

Fire in Ionescoland is akin to the unearthly illumination that breaks into the life of the mystics that the dramatist studied and continues to read: St. John of the Cross, the Neoplatonists, Plotinus, the Hesychasts, the Hassidic story tellers. In his first published volume of memoirs, *Fragments of a Journal,* Ionesco tells the following story culled from Martin Buber's *Tales of the Hassidim:* "Rabbi Dov Baer, the maggid of Mezritch, once begged Heaven to show him a man whose every limb and every fibre was holy. Then they showed him the form of the Baal Shem Tov, and it was all fire. There was no shred of substance in it. It was nothing but flame."[1]

In his essay "Eugène Ionesco and 'La Nostalgie du Paradis,'"[2] Mircea Eliade detects an influence on the dramatist of the Byzantine mystics. Eliade explains that like many Romanian writers of his generation Ionesco was attracted by the Byzantine spirituality of the Eastern Orthodox tradition. In the Balkans, as in Russia, there has always been a pull in two geographic and cultural directions: the West, particularly French culture, and the Orient. Ionesco attempts to fuse the philosophies of East and West, but his aversion to Cartesianism, to classical logic, reinforces the mystical influences of Buddhism, Neoplatonism, and Gnosticism.

Ionescoland may be a kind of no man's land because it is situated at the crossroads of various cultures. It is a place where people of the most varied backgrounds live side by side, where one expects to hear seven or eight languages, or perhaps a composite tongue made up of all of these. "I'm just a peasant from the Danube!" Ionesco likes to quip. He comes from a part of Europe where there are Turks, Sephardic Jews (what's left of them), Greeks, Albanians, Armenians, Gypsies. Ionesco, a French Romanian, is what the American painter R. B. Kitaj calls, when describing himself, "a Diasporist." As such, he is a man with a hundred eyes, half of them behind his head.

What the eyes see the tongue must express. For Ionesco, the absurdity of being can still be put into words, although language itself has become fractured, and discourse deconstructed. Ionesco claims that he writes and speaks in order to find out what he thinks. Perhaps because the dramatist divided the first part of his life between France and Romania, he never took either one of his two native languages for granted. In fact, he harbors a tender feeling for his mother tongue, which was indeed his mother's tongue. The French he writes is characterized by classical purity, even when his word games betray his multilingualism, which brings him closer to James Joyce, and to a number of his contemporaries: Samuel Beckett, Arthur Adamov, Fernando Arrabal—an Irishman, a Russian, and a Spaniard, all writing in French. Like the prophet Abraham, they are "strangers and sojourners."

The language of Ionescoland is intentionally made up of clichés. Like proverbs, the latter reflect popular wisdom, but, as they pass from mouth to mouth, they lose their initial pungency. The trite expressions used and misused by the concierges and the petty bourgeois of Ionesco's plays weave an aural tapestry, the monotonous music of popular culture. The protagonists of the plays are surrounded by these flat utterances. Although they themselves do not use clichés, they are being used by them, manipulated by ambient platitudes. The subsidiary characters who come in contact with the protagonists are embodiments of hackneyed thoughts. Yet this language, "weary, stale, flat, and unprofitable,"[3] has nevertheless terrifying power. Events seem shaped by words. As Richard Schechner states: "Words are no longer the vehicles of thoughts and feelings; they are themselves actions—the initiators of dramatic events."[4]

In Ionescoland, linear discourse becomes dislocated. No inner logic governs the sequence of words; the rules of syntax have evaporated. Words float like bits of wreckage, coming together as though magnetized by sound alone. Signifier and signified fall apart, broken asunder. Some of these techniques stem from surrealist free association, but Ionesco's intentions are not playful. As Leo Spitzer demonstrated, neologisms may be rooted in the known, but they journey toward the new, the unknown, perhaps the unknowable.[5]

Ionesco intends to shake our faith in what lies behind the word, what is hidden at the core of so-called civilized discourse. He mounts a concerted attack on language because he intends to shake his reader, his audience, out of a natural propensity to lethargy, to the unquestioning acceptance of certain values or premises. The dramatist's fantastic isomorphisms, grotesque onomatopoeias, enumerations, numerologies, pseudo-Pythagorean calculations, mock-logical constructs and syllogisms constitute an intellectual circus act of great elegance and daring. It is a verbal walk on a tight rope stretched over the Void. As he peers down, he exclaims:

> What a flood of images, words, characters . . . symbolic figures, signs, all at the same time and meaning more or less the same thing, though never exactly the same, a chaotic jumble of messages that I may perhaps in the end understand but which tells me no more about the fundamental problem: what is this world?[6]

Ionesco created Ionescoland to question that "chaotic jumble." His "country" may look familiar at first, but it is actually teasingly, disturbingly *other*. The untranslatable French word the dramatist favors is *insolite* (the dictionary offers the translation *unwonted*). What Ionesco means to suggest is his desire to introduce the reader, or audience, into a strange universe, to create a positive, stimulating sense of estrangement. He wishes to lure us into his diasporic state by flipping open his refugee's suitcase full of trinkets from various epochs and cultures. Like Kitaj, this "man with bags" refuses to be caught in amber. In fact, he welcomes a creative misreading, for the gathering he envisions is that of the dispersed.

For Ionesco, the literary artist is the sum of his or her dreams, and of the expression these dreams are given in the work. By creating a new literary form, the writer attempts to race against time. For time will uncreate the artist since death is unavoidable; but, in the brief interim passage between birth and the ultimate dissolution, one is able to shape a world in one's own image. Thus, by degrees, the disappearing human being, Ionesco, becomes absorbed in his creation, Ionescoland.

Chapter 2

The Wonder-full Enfant Terrible

Découvertes, Stories for Children under Three
Years of Age, Journaux

One of Ionesco's most enduring perceptions has to do with the sense
of wonder that infuses the developing consciousness of the child. His
untranslated, self-illustrated journal, *Découvertes*, testifies to the
writer's ever-renewed longing for a state of beatitude, the feeling of
oneness with the universe. He claims to have experienced this natural
joy as a very young boy. *Découvertes* (Discoveries) is a fragmentary
journal in which Ionesco, much like Nathalie Sarraute in her *Enfance*
(Childhood), goes back to his infancy to recover the pristine amazement he once felt so keenly, but which faded from his life as an adult.
Ionesco's Klee-like illustrations are another device used to recapture
the naïveté of early years.

Like Wordsworth, Ionesco believes that "the Child is father of
the Man."[1] However, unlike the speaker of "My heart leaps up when
I behold," he is no longer moved by the sight of a rainbow in the
sky. He might well exclaim:

There was a time when meadow, grove and stream,
The earth, and every common sight,
To me did seem
Apparelled in celestial light,
The glory and the freshness of a dream,
It is not now as it hath been of yore;—
Turn wheresoe'er I may,
By night or day,
The things which I have seen I now can see no more.[2]

For Ionesco, as for the mature Wordsworth, "there hath past away a glory from the earth."[3]

In his "Intimations of Immortality from Recollections of Early Childhood," Wordsworth sought to record the vividness and splendor that invest with a special light objects of sight in early childhood. He recalls that, walking to school, he would at times clasp a tree as if to become one with nature. For him this was a time of "absolute spirituality . . . of 'all-soulness.'"[4] Ionesco says much the same thing in *Découvertes;* it is revealing to realize that the writer, whose work is considered one of the salient examples of high modernism, is deeply rooted in Romanticism. Once this filiation is established we are able to read him anew, to decipher the literary substratum of his absurdism. In fact, nothing is less "absurd" than his joyous acceptance of being. He knows that a child questions the world in a different way than an adult and writes:

> When I happen to recapture the virginal newness of childhood, my questioning brings me back to a sense of wonder and joy. The child's "why?" does not really seek an answer; the fact that this question arises provides its own answer.[5]

What is the nature of the catastrophe that severed the ties between the child and nature, the child and its profound joy of being? Ionesco believes that the break took place when, at the age of four, he became aware that he was mortal, that all those he loved were doomed to die someday. Perhaps because love and wonder were so swiftly followed by the discovery of human mortality, the child Ionesco grew up to become a dramatic poet of loss, death, longing.

In his journals, Ionesco returns repeatedly to the moment when he was told by his mother that everyone must die. The scene of this revelation is imprinted on his mind: he was sitting on the floor, playing with his toys. A secret fear flitted across his mind, making him question his mother about death. She did not avoid the question, nor did she lie to her child. When he heard her say that death was unavoidable, it was as though something irreversible had occurred: a world of innocent ignorance lay on one side, the real universe filled with the horror of universal death on the other. The four-year-old sat on the floor, pierced by this revelation, his heart wrung with anguish, less for himself than for this woman, the mother he deeply loved. Someday, they would both be gone from this earth, but at that moment they were still together, sharing an awesome truth. A couple of seconds earlier a boy was playing, unaware of what lay before him. Suddenly, that same child was projected into a tragic universe from which there was no escape.[6]

In *Fragments of a Journal,* Ionesco explains that, although he acquired much information after what the French call "the age of reason" (seven years of age), this learning was of little value compared to the metaphysical illumination that penetrated his mind when he realized that mortality was built into the human condition. However, death's dark shadow did not altogether obscure the luminous, ecstatic spaces of childhood. Ionesco never forgot his early years at La Chapelle-Anthenaise, a small village in the Mayenne, where he boarded with a family of kind peasants while his mother was struggling to make ends meet. At the Old Mill, where the child lived with Père Baptiste and Mère Jeannette, "everything was joy . . . presentness."[7] It was a miraculous kind of existence, "outside of time, in a sort of Paradise."[8]

With its central village square, its church steeple that could be seen from the surrounding small farms and fields, La Chapelle-Anthenaise was a self-contained world. It was human-sized, even child-sized. Although he had experienced moments of boredom in Paris, the boy Eugène never tired of exploring the village and its environs. Away from his mother, he was no longer obsessed with the thought of death. He loved the simple farmers, and trusted his country teacher Monsieur Guéné. It was a manageable universe with its little gardens, low houses, gentle hillsides, and the Mill standing in a hollow, a kind of natural nest. World War I was a distant rumble. The children sang patriotic songs as they walked around the school yard during recess. The boy with a foreign name yelled the words at the top of his voice: "Long live our flag, the glorious flag of France!" Monsieur Guéné admonished him: "Not so loud, Ionesco, you're singing out of tune. Let the others sing, they do it better."[9]

There were some two hundred soldiers billeted with the peasants in the village. The war was drawing to a close, and the U.S. troops were waiting to be returned home. In the meantime, some of the men organized a bit of merrymaking. There was a U.S. soldier in residence at the Mill, a dance master in civilian life. In the evening, his friends gathered by the hearth: a singer, who accompanied himself on a guitar, and a pastry chef, who would bake cakes with chocolate filling. There would be enough custards and pies to distribute throughout the village. In the memory of the aging writer, this vision of a safe, warm, loving, prelapsarian universe acquired a fairy-tale quality. Unlike Pagnol, who kept this untainted remembrance whole, letting it infuse his oeuvre, Ionesco contrasts this earthly paradise with the desolate reality of our modern existence. However, his warm feelings in regard to Americans were only strengthened when the latter returned to Europe once again as allies and saviors during World War II. Yet, because of his naïve memory of these grown-up men bent on music making, pie baking, and dancing, they retained something touchingly childlike.

The passages that deal with the blessed time at La Chapelle-Anthenaise, both in the journals and as subtextual references in the plays, are perfect examples of the writer's fundamental romanticism. If they seem to echo the odes and ballads of Wordsworth, they might well be illustrated by the painting of the British landscape painter John Constable, who learned to translate the fresh colors of nature by working out in the open a century before this became common practice with the Impressionists. Constable's idyllic *The Cornfield* could be a paradigm for Ionesco's remembrance of things past.

The painting depicts a path through the woods, along which a flock of sheep is escorted by a shepherd's dog. In the dappled shade a schoolboy is stretched out, face down, drinking from a clear brook, the very source from which the painter drew water on his own way to school and, indeed, the clear fount of his art. Just beyond the line of trees lies a dazzling cornfield, golden in the sun. The painting plays with contrasts of light and shadow. It conveys a sense of harmony, as though everything within that world knows its rightful place. It is framed by graceful, tall trees.

In *Découvertes,* Ionesco paints his own Constable.

> I grew up . . . reached the age of two, then three, and made amazing discoveries. I saw admirable things as well as terrifying ones. First, I'll mention the lovely ones: the sky, the daylight, a market with its fruits and vegetables, the summer glow filtered by the green foliage of tall trees, that same light streaming through closed shutters. . . . What were some other sights that dazzled me then? At the end of a dark, hollow path, a bright cornfield

dotted by red poppies under a sky of intense blue which seemed to touch the golden corn. Yet there was also the grayness of winter. At the age of four, I found out about death and howled in despair.[10]

Death is the heavy cloud drifting over the cornfield of life. Ionesco's shimmering Constable soon grows as dark and menacing as the Goyas of the "Deafman's Farm."

The dramatist's own illustrations for *Découvertes* are not in the Romantic mode. They have some of the playfulness of Dufy, and the ingenuous wit of Klee. The hieratic figure of a king appears, looking much like a character from *Alice in Wonderland*'s game of cards, as well as Ionesco's own Bérenger Ier. Brightly colored objects, like pieces of a puzzle, seem to be blown across the page by a strong gust of wind. They are carefully scrutinized by an eye, perhaps the poet's "I." Ionesco confesses:

> I am endowed with the faculty of astonishment which makes it possible for me to emerge from the turmoil of life and reintegrate my true place in immobility. The ability to experience astonishment is what made me into a writer. Writing is the only thing I know how to do.[11]

What is this "immobility" the writer mentions? It may be the state of serene detachment gained through transcendental meditation. The motionless floating described in the text, and depicted in the drawings, is not unlike that achieved in shamanic trance. It approximates the ecstatic state of grace that the dramatist recalls as "the blessed oneness with the universe."[12] But after the threshold of adolescence is crossed, the joyful glow fades, and finally vanishes. The writer wonders: "How can one go on living without grace? Yet we do go on."[13]

In his essay "On Being Very Surprised . . . Eugéne Ionesco and the Vision of Childhood," Richard N. Coe explains that transmitting a mystic experience of the highest order "through the paradoxical medium of comedy . . . has given Ionesco the status of one of the most influential dramatists of the present century."[14] It appears that Ionesco believes very deeply that to receive "intimations of immortality" one must proceed "by way only of childish things."[15]

The time is ripe to acknowledge that what was assumed to be a neosurrealist game of antilogic, played for the sake of a perverse form of contradiction and provocation, requires reassessment. Ionesco's epistemological and ontological pursuit is embodied in a series of spiritual exercises aimed at dispelling the opaqueness of adult thinking processes. Thus, his use of nonsense is calculated to drill a hole in the thick wall of common sense—the quality that Descartes proclaimed as the best apportioned and most universal of all human attributes. Once it breaks through the protective enclosure, the hole or gap is barely wide enough to admit a small child. To follow the young explorer we would have to take a sip from Lewis Carroll's tiny bottle that invites us to "Drink!" Only then could we follow the White Rabbit, and gain access to the tiny garden full of "beds of bright flowers and cool fountains."[16]

Late in life, when his only child, Marie-France, was already a grown woman, Ionesco composed four mock-naïve tales "for children under three years of age." This time frame is not chosen at random; it precedes by one year the child Ionesco's discovery of mortality. As to the tales, they could be called the poet-dramatist's "Songs of Innocence."[17]

At the "Décade Ionesco" at the Centre Culturel International de Cérisy-la-Salle (August 3–13, 1978), the playwright, who arrived in time for the final couple of days, referred jokingly to his fairy tales as a "collaborative work" composed with his daughter's assistance. He did not mean that his coauthor was the mature woman who had accompanied him to Cérisy, but rather that, in his imagination, he had returned to the time when he was the father of a girl child. Also, by recalling his only child's questions and feelings, he had traveled back to his own forgotten childhood. By means of this double voyage back in time, Ionesco was able to compose irreverent and provocative stories. As all fairy tales, they hold a good deal of terror and expose the workings of the human subconscious.

Ionesco possesses a rare gift of empathy, at least in relation to two women: his mother and his daughter. In *Present Past Past Present,* he evokes a violent quarrel between his parents that took place when he was a very young child, too young to grasp the subject under debate. He realized, however, that his mother was crying like an inconsolable child. Next, she seized a vial of iodine, emptying its contents into the silver goblet that had been given to her son on the day of his baptism. It seemed to Ionesco that he and his beloved mother were united in a sacrilegious act, the desecration of the baptismal cup. The dramatist recalls his father rushing over to the desperate woman, wresting the poison from her. This melodramatic scene, which would not be out of place in a Pirandello play, never stopped haunting the writer. (It reappears in his last dream play.) In his journal he confesses:

> The cup, which I still have, is indelibly stained. Every time I look at it, it reminds me of this scene. My pity for my mother goes back to this day. I must have been astounded when I perceived that she was merely a poor, helpless child, a puppet in my father's hands and the object of his persecution. Ever since, I have pitied all women, rightly or wrongly.[18]

Clearly, the child Ionesco recognized another child in his bewildered, weeping mother. He felt that they were two lost children in an alien world peopled by monstrous adults. He was never able to identify with these heartless grown-ups. He chose to remain an eternal child, perhaps a victim but never an executioner.

The second entry in *Present Past Past Present* deals with the writer's infant daughter. Although obviously written long after the fact as a remembrance of a significant moment, it is strikingly vivid in all its details. Ionesco describes carrying the infant into the room of someone living with them on rue Claude Terrasse, possibly a relative. This person, Régine, was indisposed, and the child seems to sense the danger of a life-threatening illness. The writer imagines that his daughter detects the nearness of death, making a discovery parallel to his own when he was four. His entry shows to what extent he identifies with the frightened child, lending her his own anguished apprehension.

> Standing in the doorway, we spoke to Régine as she lay there. We wished her pleasant dreams. Then I turned out the light before leaving. Régine and the entire room disappeared in the darkness. My daughter began to scream in terror, as if Régine, the bed, the furniture in the room had suddenly ceased to exist.[19]

The last sentence attributes to an infant a vision of the void, of the boundless dark whence all life issues and to which it must return. This entry is preceded in the journal by one that highlights a parallel discovery on the part of the girl's father. At approximately the same age, he was taken on a trip by his parents (undoubtedly the 1911 move from Romania to France). Ionesco describes the train suddenly entering a long tunnel. The two adults—his parents—vanished from his sight. He was gripped by an overwhelming anxiety, a foreshadowing of irretrievable loss. This first entry ends with a shout: "I cry out."[20] It will be echoed in *Découvertes:* "At the age of four I found out about death and howled with despair."[21]

The long corridor in the rue Claude Terrasse apartment, and the dark tunnel that swallowed the train with all its passengers are one and the same place. The experience is the same: terror and the knowledge of mortality. Judging by the first two entries in *Present Past Past Present,* it appears that the memoirist intends to show how his own past flows into his child's present, how that child's past ("when my daughter was two years old") is a reenactment of her father's enlightenment. The Proustian title of the volume constitutes an aesthetic program, a reader's guide. The writer's remembrances are to follow a meandering path that will take him back to his own past and, further still, into that of his parents, his ancestors, then return him to the present, his own and that of his growing daughter. Yet, the link he establishes with his child is through the shared state of childhood, as though that condition of helplessness—being carried in one's father's arms, the unveiling of a terrifying fact—made him and his daughter contemporaries, kindred spirits. Just as Ionesco realized, as a child, that he and his mother were children, lost in a cruel world, so he shares what he imagines to be his daughter's realization of life's brevity. By inviting his reader to enter with him the spiral of time, he removes us from chronological linearity, leading us into the cosmic cycle of primitive, archaic humanity, into dream time.

In *Cosmos and History,* Ionesco's friend Mircea Eliade writes that primitive humans felt a need to suspend profane time.[22] Archaic human creatures, Eliade states, had no tolerance for the linearity we call history. In fact, the historical dimension, with its emphasis on cause and effect and on the logical sequence of facts, is antithetical to an instinctive apprehension of the world. The memory of primitive people is collective, ahistorical; it lifts the individual experience onto the archetypal plane.

Ionesco's journals reveal the writer's dislike of the Hegelian divinization of the historical process. Even Marxism should be viewed as grounded in myth rather than history. As Ionesco explains:

> The hidden meaning of revolution is liberation, the desire for a virgin world, the rediscovery of purity through the liberation of man's energies. The Communist revolution is the most painful attempt to liberate and transfigure the world; it is painful and tragic because it is a failure.[23]

He quotes Lenin's cynical "History is crafty."[24] History is shrewd when used or rather abused by crafty tyrants in love with power, but it also has a way of turning against them, of eluding their best laid plans. In the section "Bucharest before 1940 and around 1940" of *Present Past Past Present,* Ionesco declares:

> I believe that our ideas are not "historical," that they do not represent a certain historical moment, or that they do not represent only their respective historical moment; I believe that they express profound historical tendencies which go beyond us and lie below the surface of History, that come to us from far, far off. Ideas . . . are the expression . . . of metaphysical temperament.[25]

The creator of Metaphysical Farce envisions his art as archetypal, even when it represents "a certain historical moment." Ionesco's images spring from his subconscious as well as from the collective dream world. "To be oneself does not prevent one from being universal," he observes.[26] Yet, in order to be fully oneself, one ought to preserve within one's inner recesses the child one has been. It is that child's encounter with the world, his or her *découvertes,* that forms the basis of a work as new and fresh as the dawning day.

The antilogic of Ionesco's early plays is a step in the direction of greater spiritual freedom. Once this becomes clear, it is easy to grasp why an aging writer, the father of a grown, unmarried, childless daughter, composed four poetic *Stories for Children under Three Years of Age*. Nor is it surprising that, having written them separately, he should have incorporated them into his confessional journal *Present Past Past Present*. The stories belong to the same time spiral that dictates the journal's form. As meditational exercises the stories allow an aging man to recapture the wonder of childhood, his own as well as that of his middle-aged daughter.

Story Number 1 is a cosmological fable about the victory of the faculty Baudelaire privileged above all others: imagination. We are introduced to thirty-three-month-old Josette (the number thirty-three suggests the perfect age of the human being, that of the crucified Christ). Josette confronts the tightly shut door of her parents' bedroom. Impatient to join them, she would like to awaken them. Their slothful sleep suggests a vaguely guilty condition: they stayed out late and are hung over. While their child bides her time—clearly her time is not that of the adults—the maid bustles in, balancing the breakfast tray. She proceeds to inform the parents of their offspring's expectations. However, Daddy and Mummy are not ready to face either food or child. The maid, who is Josette's accomplice, will help her gain access to the space where the sleepers lie snoring, like the unconscious inhabitants of Sleeping Beauty's castle.

"Daddy, tell me a story," begs Josette.[27] While her mother is asleep, the daughter captures her place as well as her father's undivided attention. He in turn weaves a tale about a little girl called Jacqueline, like the family maid, who multiplies, forming a family of Jacquelines. Whether the tale is true or not, the teller is a demiurge who unleashes the forces of nature together with those of the creative mind.

The exponential proliferation of Jacquelines is reminiscent of the multiplications of cups in *Victims of Duty*, or of mushrooms in *Amédée or How to Get Rid of It*. As to a universe in which everyone has the same name, it is not unlike the weird exchange between Mr. and Mrs. Smith *(The Bald Soprano)* about a husband and wife who are both named Bobby Watson. It is, in fact, impossible to tell men from women and the living from the dead when all bear the same name, a perfect metaphor for the faceless, interchangeable human beings who inhabit prefabricated homes in dormitory cities.

Story Number 2 again features the father-daughter couple, linked by the complicity of story telling. In the second story they are alone, two naughty children left to their own devices by Mummy, who went off to the country to visit her mother. With her rival out of the way, Josette once again begs Daddy to tell her a story. This time, the tale will assume the character of a familiar singing game: "Who's Afraid of the Big Bad Wolf?"

In the game, the Wolf (played by one of the children participating in the game) is out of sight but not out of hearing. He is ready to pounce out of his hiding place at any moment to devour one of the players. In Ionesco's story, Daddy/Wolf is actually in the bathroom, getting ready for a busy day ahead. In the meantime, he is sending Josette on a wild goose chase to look for him in all the places he cannot be found: under the table, on the living room couch, behind the bookcase, at the window, inside the closet, behind the mirror, under the rug, in the kitchen, and even in the garbage can. Josette would much prefer to watch Daddy washing all over, but he sends her scurrying in absurd pursuits, thus safeguarding his privacy and private parts, yet arousing to fevered pitch the girl's longing to be admitted into the intimacy of his secret ablutions. In fact, Josette's desire for Daddy keeps on growing as she reports to him that there is no trace of his presence in the places he told her to look.

Ionesco's story is not only comically absurd, it is redolent with cruelty. It culminates when the bathroom door swings open, and Daddy emerges washed, shaved, and fully dressed. On the surface he is an ordinary businessman and Josette's loving father, but under this thin veneer he is every man in his subconscious desires and dreams: a Big Bad Wolf and his daughter's sole lover. Seeing him emerge at last from his place of hiding, Josette jumps into his arms. This is the moment Mummy returns, perhaps in the nick of time. As Josette inquires whether they will be going soon to visit "Granny," we catch a final ironic echo of "Little Red Riding Hood."

Ionesco's perverse pastiche of fairy tale and singing game fused into one gives off a strong whiff of incest. The sophisticated writer is of course well aware of contemporary psychiatric interpretations of the function of stories, that is of the story's power to defuse the secret fears of childhood and bring to the surface dormant emotions, thereby purging them of their ability to thwart human personality. Even without the assistance of Bruno Bettelheim's *The Uses of Enchantment*, the reader is able to detect Ionesco's awareness of what he is doing. The naïve surface of the tales is a mask; the inventor of the antiplay is also, late in his life, the creator of the anti–fairy tale. But these stories are not meant for children, before or after the age of three; they are winks directed at the adult reader of Freud, Jung, and Lacan.

Cruelty also informs *Story Number 3*. Once again Daddy is telling Josette a story. This one is about the two of them going for a plane ride above Paris, and then above La Chapelle-Anthenaise (the village where Ionesco spent some of his sweetest childhood years). The ride begins like a pleasant dream, then quickly turns into a nightmare. As the imaginary plane flies over a zoo, Daddy suffers a metamorphosis: he becomes one of the lions and threatens to devour his little girl. Josette is both terrified and fascinated by this new game. However, the danger is averted when the flying machine reaches the moon, and father and daughter feast on a piece of the planet often compared to cheese. The next stop in this interplanetary voyage is the sun, where the climate is as hot as a blazing summer. Clearly the intertext of this story is Savien Cyrano de Bergerac's romance *L'histoire comique . . . contenant les états et empires de la lune* and his *Histoire des états et empires du soleil*. Mummy, who in Ionesco's traditional, bourgeois setting is not an educated woman, does not catch Daddy's literary references. She simply voices her disapproval: "You're going to ruin her mind with your silly stories."[28] This comment also echoes the reactions of the broad audience to Ionesco's "silly" plays, particularly those depicting imaginary voyages, levitation, the space walk of a self-styled astronaut.

Story Number 4 is a parable of the intellectual activity of designation. The process of naming turns the One into the Many, thus breaking the wordless harmony of Creation. As Daddy names the familiar objects in the apartment, he shifts their definition and perverts their function: "The chair is a window. The window is a pen. The pillow is bread. The bread is the rug by the bed. Feet are ears. Arms are feet. A head is a derrière. A derrière is a head. Eyes are fingers. Fingers are eyes."[29] Josette is enchanted by this realization of the familiar. Soon she begins to use this new vocabulary and the quiet milieu of the family home is subverted by this unnaming and renaming, which serves to put in question the world we accept as a given (much as the Assimil method acted upon Ionesco when he tried to learn English). Thus, a connection can be established between this story and *The Bald Soprano*. The daddy of these imaginative, perverse, often cruel tales is none other than the writer Ionesco.

At the end of *Story Number* 4, Josette's mother walks in at last,
carrying in her arms a huge bunch of wild country flowers. In "her
flowered dress, her eyes like twin flowers, her mouth like a flower,"[30]
she is an archetypal figure, the Roman goddess Flora. Struck with
awe at this lovely sight, the child exclaims: "Mama, you opened the
wall."[31] Although she is now using the absurdist vocabulary taught
her by her father, this substitution of wall for door conveys poetically
the child's emotion. She has learned to look at the world with wonder, to see it as poets do, and to express her feelings in a language at
once familiar and new. Indeed, it is this way of seeing and speaking
that allows people to transcend the every day acts of opening doors
and windows. In Ionesco's world, walls that usually hide from us the
richness of the world outside become transparent, disappear; one can
also walk through them as though they were made of water or fog.
Ionesco suggests that it is the power of imagination that helps us
"open the wall."

In the fairy-tale world of the wonder-full enfant terrible there are
no doors. Poets and children, childlike poets, possess the magic gift
of splitting open the walls of convention in order to allow the spirit
of inspiration to step in and take over. These days we have witnessed
that political action can operate poetic miracles as the Berlin wall was
literally torn down by young people.

Literary critics who have surveyed Ionesco's oeuvre as well as his
political stance have often wondered what constitutes his immunity
to the malady of conformity that he calls "rhinoceritis." It seems clear
that the antibodies his system produces are the direct result of his
faculty of ecstatic, childlike astonishment. No inquiry into the
writer's philosophy, aesthetics, or political attitudes can begin without taking this into account. Although these epiphanies dimmed with
age—as they did with Wordsworth—they were not forgotten; they
have remained the touchstones of his personal method. In his *Conversations* with Claude Bonnefoy, Ionesco explains:

Everywhere there's a cause for amazement: in language, in picking up a glass of something, in draining it at a single gulp, in the
mere fact of existing, of being. Going for a walk, not going for

a walk, it's astonishing. Doing something, not doing something; astonishing. Having revolutions, not having revolutions; astonishing. Once people have accepted existence, once they've moved inside it, everything stops being amazing or absurd.[32]

For Ionesco, habit is lethal for the life of the spirit. Bourgeois coziness protects one from seeing the abyss of nothingness (that infinite space that haunted the philosopher Pascal), but it is also a deadener. Coziness is the bread distributed by Dostoyevsky's Grand Inquisitor. Walls are erected with the stones of the desire for safety. Ionesco knows that nothing is more dangerous, politically or spiritually. What he seeks is an intense experience of being, the one he describes in *Present Past Past Present:*

> It is being that fills me with joy and amazes me, being astonishes me much more than existing. I am stronger than nothingness. All the rest is insignificant. . . . I exist, I am, and when I think of that everything falls silent and anything else becomes nonsense.[33]

To this day, Ionesco has remained true to this discovery. On May 7, 1989, when he was handed the prestigious Molière Prize on the stage of the Théâtre du Châtelet in honor of a restaging of *The Chairs* at the newly created Théâtre National de la Colline, he echoed this apprehension in his acceptance speech:

> At the beginning there is astonishment: the awareness of being, a joyful, pure, dazzled amazement, devoid of judgmental attitudes. Next comes discernment, the knowledge of the existence of evil, or simply of the fact that things are not going well. . . . As a writer, universal misery is my personal, intimate concern.
>
> I have a friend, a philosopher of despair [Emil Cioran] who lives with pessimism as his natural element. He speaks a good deal, eloquently, and is merry. "Modern man," he claims, "dabbles in the incurable." That's what he does also. Let's be like him since there's nothing else to do, since we are all doomed to die. Let's be merry. Yet, let's not be fooled.
>
> There is perhaps one way out, and that's contemplation, amazement in regard to the existential fact of being.[34]

The numerous critics who have called Ionesco a pessimist have overlooked his fundamental love of life. It is a love grounded in his refusal to become a "grown-up." By nurturing within himself the "Child of Joy,"[35] he grew into something better than a reasonable adult: a poet-dramatist.

Chapter 3

The Surrealist Prankster

The Bald Soprano, The Lesson, Jack, The Future Is in Eggs

It all began with a grown man becoming a schoolboy again.

Ionesco told the story of the birth of *The Bald Soprano* many times, but never as clearly as when he lectured at the French Institute in Italy in 1958. A decade before that talk, and two years before writing his first play, Ionesco decided to study English, a useful tool for the business world. At that time, shortly before World War II, the Ionesco family was living in near poverty in Paris. Ionesco contributed articles to prestigious Romanian journals, such as *Viata Românească* (Romanian life), edited by the philosopher Mihaï Ralea. With his academic career interrupted by the war, he was never able to complete his thesis, "The Theme of Sin and Death in French Poetry from Baudelaire to Valéry."

Having fled the fascist regime in Romania, Ionesco and his wife spent the years of the German occupation in hiding. Their only child, a daughter, was born on the day of France's liberation in 1944; she was named Marie-France. Life was not easy for anyone in postwar France, and although Ionesco was bilingual and the son of a French mother, his status was still that of an impoverished, struggling refugee.

In Romania, Ionesco belonged to a literary community. He taught French at the Bucharest Lycée Sfântul Sava, and wrote essays for the leading reviews of the capital: *Azi, Floarea de Foc, Viata Literara, Facla*. He was also the author of a slim volume of poetry, *Elegy for Miniscule Beings,* and a highly controversial collection of essays, *Nu* (No), which contained a tongue-in-cheek attack against established figures of Romanian letters such as T. Arghesi, I. Barbu, C. Petrescu. In *Nu* one is able to catch a glimpse of the future Ionesco—a witty, irreverent rebel.

The French literati had never heard of the minor poet and intriguing literary critic Eugène Ionesco. Their knowledge of Romanian culture was minimal, with the exception of the inventor of dadaism, Tristan Tzara. They would have recognized in the timid exile Tzara's heir had they been able to read *Hugoliade,* an antibiography of Victor Hugo, which held up to ridicule France's leading Romantic poet, exposing him as a pompous, egotistical versifier, but this early composition (1935) did not become available in French until 1982.

Hugoliade reveals Ionesco's fundamental distrust of literary monuments. He picked on Hugo as the perfect representative of an inflated, bombastic style both in daily life and in his oeuvre. He demystifies and demythifies France's literary giant by depicting him as a vain, vulgar womanizer who talked incessantly about himself in clichéd rhymed verse, even on the occasion of his favorite daughter's tragic death by drowning. According to Ionesco, French poetry evolved in the sense of *dehugolization* with Baudelaire, Mallarmé, Valéry, who preferred to whisper their deepest feelings with modest reticence rather than shout and proclaim their ideas and ideals as though perched on some eternal tribune. Verlaine suggests in his "Art Poétique" that poets ought to "twist the neck of eloquence." This is just what Ionesco does to Hugo. *Hugoliade* is a serious prank, not unlike the mustache Marcel Duchamp painted over the much too famous smile of the Mona Lisa.

The reader of *Hugoliade* will discover the seed of Ionesco's aesthetic, as well as some of his obsessions. There is a revealing passage in praise of "negative intelligence," which can never enjoy success because of its propensity to derision. A striking passage about the finality of death has little to do with Hugo's grief over the loss of his daughter Léopoldine, but it is pure Ionesco. The young man who makes the metaphysical statement: "We do not allow our dead to die"[1] is already the dramatist who will compose at the very end of his career the magnificent, somber dream play *Journeys among the Dead.*

In 1948, Ionesco was still unknown in Paris, He himself never imagined he would become a playwright. In 1945, he embarked on a translation of the Romanian poet Urmuz, whom he considered a precursor of Surrealism. He also kept a journal. Mostly he made ends meet by proofreading legal and medical material for Les Editions Administratives, a labor he despised, but which, in retrospect, taught him to focus his attention on textual precision while sensitizing him to the clichés used in daily communication. This was also the time when he thought he should study the English language, which led to the composition of *The Bald Soprano*. Ionesco revels in the story of what he considers a happy accident. He writes:

> I bought an English-French conversational manual for beginners. I set to work. Conscientiously I copied out phrases from my manual in order to learn them by heart. Then I found out, reading them over attentively, that I was learning not English but some very surprising truths: that there are seven days in the week, for example, which I happened to know before; or that the floor is below us, the ceiling above us, another thing that I may well have known before but had never thought seriously about or had forgotten, and suddenly it seemed to me as stupefying as it was indisputably true.[2]

What happened next made literary history. Suddenly flat cartoon characters emerged, speaking the sentences from the conversation manual and dictating others. Ionesco's first play was born.

Unlike Pirandello's six characters, Ionesco's do not possess colorful individual traits. They are merely illustrations that slipped from the pages of the textbook, cutout dolls, or animated cartoons. Their literary ancestor is not the Italian modernist, but the turn-of-the-century inventor of a grotesque, expressionist *théâtre en guignol*, Alfred Jarry.

As a child, Ionesco was taken by his mother to the Luxembourg garden's puppet show, the *guignol*. In his *Notes and Counter Notes*, he recalls sitting spellbound, "watching those puppets talking, moving, and cudgeling each other."[3] For him this was life itself, truer than everyday existence.

Great theater, whether tragic or comic, is always wider and deeper than daily life; it is life, but with an added dimension. Ionesco did not learn this lesson from the large stage—he claims to dislike going to the theater—but from the tiny box stage of his childhood's guignol. Thus, when he came to compose his first dramatic piece, the images that surfaced and crystallized upon the inner theater of his mind were the naïve enactments that were buried all those years in the depths of his subconscious. They were summoned by the exercises of the language textbook. Perhaps this could never have occurred had the future dramatist failed to put himself in the receptive, almost passive attitude of a child, a schoolboy. The "accident" of becoming a writer was actually a process of self-hypnosis.

For Ionesco, to become a schoolboy again means a reprieve from death. For example, when King Bérenger Ier in *Exit the King* realizes that he must part with life "at the end of the play," as his physician and wife inform him, he expresses the longing to repeat all his classes, as though he had failed every subject. To go back to school would mean to start life all over again, to fool nature. This is Bérenger's way of echoing the profoundly tragic exclamation of Madame du Barry on the scaffold: "Another minute, please, Sir Executioner!" Moreover, the study of a new language signals a rebirth, almost another incarnation. Yet, in Ionesco's case this second chance actually took place as the Romanian refugee, the alienated man, the bored professional proofreader became a highly original creative artist, the originator of a new dramaturgic mode.

As the would-be student of English began to transcribe the obvious truth contained in the Assimil text, he felt the ground under his feet—the ground he was supposed to notice and name—begin to move. He was seized with such vertigo that he had to lie down. The once familiar world of his room dissolved. Once his attention was drawn to the objects whose presence he had always taken for granted, there seemed no reason for their being there, nor, in fact, for their being. His own existence in the world was put in question. Not unlike Jean Paul Sartre's Roquentin, the melancholy antihero of *Nausea,* Ionesco sensed that both he and the ambient world were *"de trop"* (in excess of being).

Despite the fact that at that fateful moment Ionesco suffered a metaphysical vision of the absurd, an existential revelation, it is inaccurate to call him an absurdist playwright. As was pointed out earlier, he is inherently an optimist, albeit a somber one. He is a writer of comedies; even though he subtitles them "tragic farces." An artist who celebrates the childlike wonder of constant renewal and fresh discoveries, he is torn by conflicting emotions: angst, self-doubt, a sense of guilt, indignant political commitment, humanist compassion for his fellow human beings, murderous fits of rage, tender dependence in regard to those he victimizes (his loyal wife, his daughter), hatred of tyrants accompanied by tendencies to tyrannize, modesty coupled with boundless pride and ambition. In other words, this metaphysical thinker is no saint. His weaknesses and failings serve him in good stead for the composition of his tragicomic drama made up of farcical slapstick, vaudeville acts, and circus tricks. And no one has analyzed better than he his particular blend of the tragic and the comic:

> I have called my comedies "anti-plays" or "comic dramas," and my dramas "pseudo-dramas" or "tragic farces": for it seems to me that the comic is tragic, and that the tragedy of man is pure derision.[4]

On May 11, 1950, when *The Bald Soprano* was presented by Nicolas Bataille on the experimental stage of the tiny Théâtre des Noctambules, the one-act sketch was received as a prank. In his preface to Ionesco's *Théâtre I,* Jacques Lemarchand, the drama critic of *Le Figaro* and a life-long champion of avant-garde theater, recalls with amusement people's bewilderment as they issued from the theater: "Why bald soprano? What a strange title? No soprano ever appeared as far as I could see. And why 'bald'? Did you see anyone bald on the stage, dear? And what about the fireman? What was he doing there anyway? Who do they think we are, assuming we'll fall for this nonsense?"[5]

Later, Ionesco was happy to reveal how, in the course of rehearsal, one of the actors slipped up in the recitation of a nonsense soliloquy and substituted "the bald soprano" for some other group of arbitrarily assembled words. It was decided then and there to change the title from *English Made Easy* (the title of the conversation textbook) to *The Bald Soprano,* opting for one of those chance events favored by the surrealists. Thus, if Ionesco became a playwright "by accident," one might well say that the actor's accidental substitution proved providential.

To allow for chance to enter and modify one's life or art, to dictate art's form, was one of the key devices of Surrealism. André Breton and his followers believed that one's chief attribute is free-

dom, and that it is essential to leave oneself available to all manner
of adventures of the flesh and spirit. Although by the middle of the
twentieth century Surrealism was a movement of the past, Breton's
Manifestores exercised a profound and lasting influence on all the arts.
Their optimism served as an antidote to Tristan Tzara's dadaist manifestoes. Ionesco is heir to both these seminal movements that ushered
in the era of modernism.

It is curious to see that French critics failed to identify Ionesco's
literary roots at the start of his career. Their blindness proved almost
total for many years to come. After the premiere of *The Bald Soprano,*
both *Le Monde* and *Combat* attacked the play. *Combat*'s Renée Saurel
had to admit that it was witty and well acted, but her tone remained
condescending as she advised her readers to see if they could get to
the theater "between downpours"[6] (May, 1950, must have been a
particularly wet month in Paris). Saurel pointed out that the characters talk without the slightest hope of being listened to by their inter-
locutors. In this analysis she demonstrates much perspicacity, particularly in her evocative phrase describing the dramatis personae as
"inhabiting transparent, vertical coffins."[7]

The characters of Ionesco's first play are indeed the living dead.
As Richard Schechner states in his essay "*The Bald Soprano* and *The
Lesson:* An Inquiry into Play Structure," "In *Soprano* the characters
are dying and language is the true protagonist."[8]

Ionesco imagined he had written "something like the tragedy of
language."[9] He was surprised when he heard the audience laughing.
Although most critics saw the humor of the piece, they made the
error of considering this comedy as social satire, a way of poking fun
at bourgeois French society by means of a cartoon version of the
British middle class. Many years later, Ionesco would say in conversation, "Why should I make fun of the bourgeoisie when I'm a good
bourgeois myself!" Indeed, if any joke was intended, it was at the
expense of Henri Bernstein–type boulevard melodrama. Nicolas
Bataille, Ionesco's first director, claims to have imitated Bernstein's
approach in directing his actors, while using for his set the decor of
Hedda Gabler.

Ionesco does not deny a satirical intent, but he points out that his
first play is not a caricature of the bourgeoisie but one of bourgeois
mentality. He carefully explains the difference between the two: "It
is above all about a kind of universal petite bourgeoisie, the petit

bourgeois being a man of fixed ideals and slogans, a ubiquitous conformist: this conformism is, of course, revealed by the mechanical
language."[10]

Thus, in writing *Soprano*, Ionesco is neither making fun of British mores (or the English temperament) nor deriding the French under the mask of another nationality. He seeks to represent what he
calls "a ubiquitous" type, one that can be encountered just as easily
in Latin America as in the former Soviet Union. Such people do not
enter into conversation with one another; a particular kind of discourse—the French call it *la langue de bois* (a wooden language made
up of clichés or shaped by propaganda)—filters through them, running from their mouths like a dribble of saliva. Such talk is not used
to say anything, but to emit a signal. When Mrs. Smith raves about
the English meal they just had, she is saying: "We're a happy English
family. Everything's all right with our world. It may be true that our
son loves 'getting tiddly,'[11] just like his father, but on the whole we're
nice and safe, and superior to the rest of humanity. So, let's count
our blessings." Her husband is well aware that she does not expect
an answer, only some animal sound in response to this peroration,
an affirmation of their status in the world; he contents himself with
clicking his tongue from behind his "English newspaper."[12] The only
disquieting element in this cozy middle-class interior comes from the
clock when it "strikes seventeen English strokes."[13] If the audience is
led to believe time is out of joint, the Smiths do not harbor such
Hamletian doubts. In fact, despite the extra strokes, Mrs. Smith announces cheerfully: "There, it's nine o'clock."[14] Her time may not
be ours, but we are invited to enter the play's time space.

When the reader follows Alice through the looking glass, she or
he finds a world similar to ours but reversed. In Lewis Carroll's
mirror-structured universe we acquire the ability to tell time by the
White Rabbit's pocket watch, to converse with a solemn, pompous,
giant egg, and have tea in the company of a dormouse. The other
inhabitants are flat playing cards or chess pieces. There are many rules
of their games to be learned, but one must not make the mistake of
calling a spade a spade.

Ionesco likes to compare himself to an architect. For him theater
is a mobile form of architecture. It conforms to laws of its own, but
these have nothing to do with conveying a message, an ideology, a
philosophy, or even the so-called realities of life. In reply to Kenneth

Tynan's article, "Theatre and Life," Ionesco raised the following argument:

> What is the point of a temple, a church, a palace? Can we find any realism there? Certainly not. Yet architecture reveals the fundamental law of construction: every building testifies to the objective reality of the principles of architecture.[15]

As Schechner states so cogently: "Ionesco wants to reveal the structure by sucking out the contents."[16] Indeed, for the dramatist "theatre can be nothing but theatre."[17]

Ionesco has said repeatedly that his first play remains his best. *The Bald Soprano* is pure theater, pure dramatic structure. Musically speaking it is nothing but rhythm. Below its neosurrealist surface lies a postmodern skeleton that invites us to join an ecstatic dance of death, which is led by the only two Dionysian characters in the play: the Fire Chief and his maenad, the Smiths' maid, Mary.

Mary is the only character in the play who knows the whole truth: "Elizabeth is not Elizabeth, Donald is not Donald."[18] The Martins, who have just played to the hilt the typical recognition scene, with its gradual unveiling of forgotten facts, have based their discovery that they are man and wife upon a flawed piece of evidence: the fact that their daughter has one red eye and one white. However, they have overlooked an essential clue: "Whereas Donald's child has a white right eye and a red left eye, Elizabeth's child has a red right eye and a white left eye."[19] Mary's superior reasoning powers undermine the careful structure erected by Donald. The marriage therefore is null and void, and the Martin couple, now dozing in the Smiths' living room, is illegitimate. Thus, Mrs. Smith's self-satisfied babble and the Martins' accord proclaim a fake order, one ready to collapse at any moment when genuine energy is released.

When Mary claims she is Sherlock Holmes[20] Ionesco does not suggest, like his character Choubert in *Victims of Duty,* that "Every play's an investigation brought to a successful conclusion."[21] He is well aware that there is no such thing as a successful conclusion, or perhaps any conclusion. He makes fun in fact of this naïve idea, and of the fact that one can arrive at the truth. But he introduces into his first play an ambiguous, androgynous Tiresias figure. Indeed, Mary's role parallels that of the prophet of *Oedipus,* at least in its comic rendition in Apollinaire's surrealist farce *Les Mamelles de Tirésias* (The paps of Tiresias).

Ionesco's Thérèse/Tiresias is also the Bacchante of Dionysus the Fire Chief, whom she celebrates in a paean to the power of fire:

> The polypoids were burning in the wood
> A stone caught fire
> The castle caught fire
> The forest caught fire
> The men caught fire
> The women caught fire
> The birds caught fire
> The fish caught fire
> The water caught fire
> The sky caught fire
> The ashes caught fire
> The fire caught fire
> Everything caught fire
> Caught fire, caught fire.[22]

Any poem starting with a neologism (*polycandres* in the original text, *polypoids* in translation) is disquieting and suspect. The prefix, meaning the many, opens it to a variety of explications, yet reminds us of Ionesco's interest in the aesthetics of nonsense. In his chapter entitled "Le Discours du Spectacle Nouveau," Michael Issacharoff makes some sense from the nonsensical neologism *"polycandres."* If the prefix ushers in Ionesco's favorite device, endless proliferation, "andres" suggests the Greek *andros* (man). In the center of the word lies the *k* sound, which the critic compares to Jarry's added *r* in Ubu's resounding "MERDRE." Thus the signifier becomes a microcosm of Mary's poem. The *k* sound spreads its contagion all over the text of the play, erupting with great violence in the finale:[23]

> Mrs. Smith: Such caca, such caca, such caca, such caca, such caca, such caca, such caca, such caca, such caca.
> Mr. Martin: Such cascades of cacas, such cascades of cacas, such cascades of cacas, such cascades of cacas, such cascades of cacas, such cascades of cacas, such cascades of cacas, such cascades of cacas.[24]

There is also a very precise echo in this apocalyptic explosion, one that allows us to read into this ditty a powerful political subtext. There was a song, composed on the eve of World War II that in retrospect appears strangely prophetic. It had a jolly tune and an ironic refrain: "Tout va très bien, madame la marquise." It told a whole story: a butler, speaking on the telephone, informs the lady of the house, the marquise, who has gone off for a short trip, that disaster has befallen her château as well as her entire household. As he lists deaths and destruction by fire, he keeps on repeating the hollow reassurance: "Tout va très bien, tout va très bien!" (Everything's fine, just fine and dandy). Indeed, as in Mary's paean, fire engulfs everything, reducing it to ashes. During the war, the news bulletins from the front, or even the home front, sounded much like the butler's song. Mary's absurdist poem makes a good deal of sense. It tells us that the fire that started in the castle grew to cosmic proportions, reached the heavens and burned up the whole planet. Humanity is wiped out, and even the water is covered by flames. This is the atomic mushroom before the bomb was invented. Mrs. Martin's reaction is that of a generation afflicted by the very same political associations: "That sent chills up my spine..."[25] Of course, this cliché is particularly grotesque in connection with a conflagration. This early image of total destruction by fire reappears in a number of Ionesco plays, in particular in his late tragic farce *The Killing Game*.

Mary's lover, the Fire Chief, is enchanted by her celebrating his "conception of the world."[26] His present concern is that the fire business is doing poorly. He expresses the hope that a small fire might be burning out of control in the Smiths' attic or cellar. When he is told that nothing is burning, he turns to the Smiths' guests with the same inquiry. Once again he receives a disappointing answer tempered by the promise that he will be notified at once in case of any catastrophic developments. Since he cannot exercise his particular skill, the Fire Chief suggests that he might tell stories, providing no one listens. Moved by this modest request, the Smiths and Martins crowd protectively around the young man, kissing him and calling him "a boy," "a sweet child."[27] This ludicrous scene suggests a rite of passage, a progression from adolescence to adulthood. However in this case we have a reversal of the natural process, a regression to the state of childhood.

From the moment the Fire Chief assumes the role of story teller he becomes a child again (one of Ionesco's principal themes). Strange tales erupt from his fiery mind. These bizarre tales may have suggested surrealist prose poems to the 1951 audience, but, as we survey Ionesco's oeuvre, they appear as prefigurations of his *Stories for Children under Three Years of Age*. Indeed, verbal associations, peculiar inversions of meaning, *lapalissades* (truisms presented as something new and astonishing), and mock moralisms characterize both Ionesco's *Stories* and the Fire Chief's strange fables.

One of the Fire Chief's fables, "The Headcold," presents in capsule form a burlesque tableau of the marriages, alliances, and family relations parodied in *The Bald Soprano*. The text is a single, immensely long sentence held together by relative pronouns. It could be a pastiche of the Proustian sentence, winding itself over many pages. (Proust is one of Ionesco's favorite writers.) A burlesque family tree emerges, reminiscent of the paragraph in *Candide* in which Voltaire traces the line of descent of Doctor Pangloss's venereal disease. However, even without these literary echoes, this vaudeville set piece within the play ridicules a certain kind of empty everyday conversation, as people drone on names and family ties. Of course, like the gratuitous mention of "the bald soprano," the "headcold" of the title appears only at the very end, when the meandering talk about paternal and maternal in-laws and their friends and acquaintances reaches the priest's grandmother, who catches an occasional cold in the winter. The Fire Chief's monologue is a veritable tour de force, a mockery of human communication, and perhaps of literary realism.

Mary's fiery paean to her lover and his fables constitute the dynamite charge that brings down the walls of convention. The play's rhythm intensifies, grows delirious. In the final scene, the sentences ejaculated by the players have no meaning; they are cries, shouts, imprecations, implorations. One recognizes sentences lifted from the language textbook, some in English. It is as though the writer, a former lycée teacher, had turned against all learning, subverting the very process, transforming it into a barbaric, highly erotic dance.

Initially, Ionesco wished to end his play with something violent, something outrageously menacing: the maid was to appear, announcing that dinner was served, and the two couples would leave the room; hecklers, planted in the audience, would shout catcalls; this would be followed by the appearance on the stage of armed police-men, pretending to open fire on the unruly audience. Ionesco also envisaged an alternate finale: the author himself would rush onto the stage, shake his fists at the audience, and shout invectives: "Bastards, I'll get you!" It was Nicolas Bataille, the director who also played Mr. Martin, who suggested that there be no end. It would all begin anew, but with the Martins becoming the first couple, and the Smiths their visitors. This device attracts the viewer's attention to the fact that the two couples are interchangeable, and that the form of the play is circular. Perhaps this fine bit of stage business was suggested by a line in the text: "Take a circle, caress it, and it will turn vi-cious."[28]

Having witnessed the developmental process of Bataille's stag-ing, Ionesco realized that his "accidental" antiplay was a lampoon of theater, perhaps the ultimate compliment one can pay a literary genre. It revealed the mechanism of dramatic tension, free of any plot line, or even a subject. Yet this abstract theater, conveyed emo-tionally, by means of a gestural language, the basic violence of human nature. Ionesco's laughter does not disguise the revelation of some-thing monstrous at work. It is in this sense that the playwright is clearly a descendant of Jarry and Artaud. Later, this disquieting mon-strosity will be linked to political themes and subtexts, yet its incipi-ent, pervasive presence in what appears to be an absurdist neosurreal-ist farce may be due to the fact that Ionesco is stamped by History's pain, that he is a true child of our century.

His first play, *The Bald Soprano,* has become one of the great modern classical works in France, recommended viewing for lycée classes. It is ironic that Ionesco, an enfant terrible, is now enthroned in the pantheon of assigned authors. No play has had a longer run, nor been performed in so many countries. Once considered difficult, it has proved that its appeal is universal.

"The Lesson," Ionesco states in conversation, "is the story of rape, or rather of a whole series of rapes." The Pupil is impaled on a word, pierced by the invisible, phallic knife of her teacher. It is an intensely violent piece of theater that illustrates the headiness of absolute power, and the attraction this power exerts over the weak and the meek.

There are three characters in the play, a number suggestive of the circularity of the piece. The Professor is a middle-aged man; the Maid, an older woman (initially played by a man), fills the theatrical "function" of mother or older wife; and the Pupil is a pretty eighteen-year-old. When the curtain rises, we hear the imperious ring of the doorbell. The Maid shuffles across the stage, drying her hands on her apron. She opens the door, admitting the Pupil dressed as a schoolgirl and carrying a satchel full of books and notebooks. She is full of eager anticipation and the irrepressible vitality of a natural force, eros.

The Maid is a slovenly, grumpy frump. She announces the Pupil's presence with reluctance, conveying some kind of disapproval and secret fear. The Professor answers from a great distance in the house, saying that he is coming. As the Maid leaves, the girl is left to her own devices. She surveys the place with a happy expression on her young face.

When the Professor enters, he does so cautiously, timidly. He is dressed like a twentieth-century Molière caricature of an academic: all in black, with a detachable, starched white collar. He is balding and wears glasses. His expression is also eager, but in an entirely different way from the girl: Ionesco writes in his stage directions that there is "a lewd gleam in his eyes."[29] His body language is that of a stealthy jungle animal, ready to pounce upon its prey.

The erotic connection between the older man and the girl is established at once. The Professor circles around her, like an old dog sniffing a young bitch in heat. She is aware of being the object of his scrutiny, and her whole healthy body quivers with pleasure. Their initial remarks are full of double entendre:

Pupil: I know my seasons, don't I, Professor?
Professor: Yes, indeed, miss . . . or almost. But it will come in time. In any case, you're coming along. Soon you'll know all the seasons, even with your eyes closed. Just as I do.[30]

Richard Schechner, who directed the play in Provincetown (1961), speaks of having the actors go through a kind of mating dance, a series of gyrations that increase in intensity and amplitude. He explains: "These dances are sometimes introductory, sometimes titillating, sometimes climactic.[31] The director-critic likens them to the "scalp dance" with its frenzied rhythm culminating in murder.

The Pupil's ambition is not modest, or limited; she has come to this master in order to prepare herself for "the total doctorate."[32] The girl's hunger for knowledge is symbolized by a prop: a bulging satchel. As she fingers it, examining its contents and playing with its lock, the reader of Freud's "Dora" case is reminded at once of the psychiatrist's deciphering of telltale signs. As Dora fingered her reticule, the analyst eagerly explained to the young analysand the significance of these subconscious gestures: the small bag represented her private parts, unlocked by masturbation. As to the patient's symptoms—a nervous cough coupled with breathlessness—Freud assumed they were related to her attraction to Herr K., her father's friend, and the husband of her father's mistress. Ionesco's Professor, like Freud, is keenly aware of the Pupil's fidgeting, of her hugging a tumescent briefcase. He inquires whether she has brought her books and notebooks. Her immediate answer is unambiguous: "Certainly. I have brought all I need."[33] This affirmation is followed by total acquiescence: "Yes, Professor, I am at your disposal."[34] As he echoes this statement, the excited man rises from his seat, then, falling back as in a sexual swoon, sighs: "Oh, Miss, it is I who am at *your* disposal. I am only your humble servant."[35] The initial steps of the courtship game have been completed; we witness the Hegelian master-slave relation, with its profoundly erotic undertones. The rest of the play will reveal who is the true master in this contest to the death.

The teacher-student or analyst-analysand relation serves as a cogent parable for the complex network of controls established by a tyrannical ruler over his people, and the nations this ruler is driven to conquer. Ionesco, who always claimed to be an apolitical writer, has at last admitted in a lengthy interview, reproduced in his untranslated journal *Un homme en question* (A man questioned), that to declare oneself apolitical is in fact a political act. Although many critics in France are opposed to this kind of reading, preferring to study the abstract patterns of the play, a thorough study of the text, together with Ionesco's precise stage directions, reveals that his second play contains a powerful political statement enrobed in the burlesque trappings of the nature versus culture dialectic.

Proof of this political reading is offered by the dramatist at the end of his "comic drama," when, following the Pupil's murder-rape (she is the fortieth victim of the day), the Maid slips an armband around the Professor's sleeve. The stage directions indicate that the insignia on the band could be "the Nazi swastika."[36] (For some reason, perhaps the author wishes not to be too explicit, this important sign was left out of the French production.) The motherly servant, who is willing to assist her "naughty boy" in carrying the coffins through the streets, explains: "wear this, then you won't have anything more to be afraid of. . . . That's good politics."[37] (Unfortunately, the translation deadens the impact of the original phrase, *"c'est politique,"* which means "it's prudent, wise.") The Maid's cynicism is a reminder that no one questioned mass murder while the Nazis were in power. As to the number forty, which Peter Hall reduced to four for his 1955 production, it is not to be taken literally; it is symbolic, like that of the days and years in the Old Testament. This ironic echo of the Book's numerology represents in the form of a modern parable the millions carried in cattle trains to the concentration camps. The point is clearly made in one of the exchanges between the Professor and his maid:

Professor: There's a chance we'll get pinched . . . with forty coffins. Don't you think . . . people will be surprised. . . . Suppose they ask us what's inside them?

Maid: Don't worry so much. We'll say that they're empty. And besides, people don't ask questions, they're used to it.[38]

So were those who lived on the edge of the camps of Buchenwald, Belzec, Majdanek, Treblinka, Birkenau. No one questioned the arrival of locked cattle cars, nor seemed to smell the stench of burning flesh rising from the chimneys of the crematoria. Like the Professor's maid, they were silent accomplices.

Today, after a careful reading of Ionesco's journals, and of numerous references in his plays, in particular those in his final dream drama, *Journeys among the Dead,* we are beginning to see an unexplored aspect of the comic dramatist's apprehension. He is one of the Holocaust writers of our tragic age. Nor do we have to wait to discover this in his late plays. Is the Fire Chief the innocent, charming young man admired by the Smiths and the Martins, or is there something threatening about his passion for smoking chimneys? His whereabouts are dictated by a strict schedule. For example, he lets everyone know that he must rush to the other side of the city since a fire has been planned there in three-quarters of an hour. This oxymoronic situation (a planned chimney fire) may elicit a smile on the part of the audience or reader, but for some it is a reminder, one that sends chills up our spines, as it does for Mrs. Martin. Even more than the Fire Chief, the Professor is anything but "a naughty boy" (except for his maid). He is a tyrant and, ultimately, a killer.

The Lesson is a "comic drama" whose darkly glowing image of inhumanity culminates in the total destruction of society. However, it is presented as entertainment, enclosed in the colorfully decorated pill box of language, one of the *sileni* described by Monsieur Alcofribas Nasier (the anagram for François Rabelais). This is how the learned Renaissance doctor of medicine explains the sileni's appearance and their function:

> Sileni, in the days of yore, were small boxes such as you may see nowadays at your apothecary's. They were named for Silenus, foster father to Bacchus. The outside of these boxes bore gay, fantastically painted figures of harpies, satyrs, bridled geese, hares with gigantic horns, saddled ducks, winged goats in flight, harts in harness and many other droll fancies. They were pleasurably devised to inspire just the sort of laughter Silenus... inspired.[39]

Like Rabelais, Ionesco wishes to elicit a healing laughter. He encloses the bitter pill of his message within the apothecary boxes of his plays, as weirdly decorated with winged beasts and satyrs as were these ancient receptacles. It is easy to overlook what he is trying to achieve, to turn a deaf ear to the truth he prefers to whisper through his subtext. If this avid reader has a model, it may well be the Socrates described by Alcibiades in *Gargantua:*

> [Socrates] was ill-shaped, ridiculous in carriage, with a nose like a knife, the gaze of a bull and the face of a fool. His way stamped him a simpleton, his clothes a bumpkin. . . . Yet had you opened this box, you would have found in it all sorts of priceless, celestial drugs.[40]

The Professor may be far more subtle than a rhinoceros, but he is a dangerous monster, deadly and yet weirdly comical. At first, he seems to be a caricature of pedantry, trying to instruct a particularly dumb student, but as the play progresses he emerges from behind this mask, revealing a sadistic, wrathful face.

The play is structured on the two "scientific" subjects the Professor teaches in order to prepare the Pupil for the "total doctorate": mathematics and philology. Both subjects turn the teacher on. The Maid warns him: "Arithmetic is tiring, exhausting."[41] The Professor grows indignant, as though his virility were in question. Indeed, the encounter between the middle-aged man and the girl shows the depletion of age in contrast with a tireless vitality. This may explain why the Pupil is able to add to "infinity."[42] However, she is unable to subtract and divide. Division is an attribute of the Devil, a fallen being composed of fractured units. As Ionesco's favorite poet, Baudelaire, puts it in his short book of *pensées, My Heart Laid Bare:* "What is the Fall? It is unity become duality."[43]

The Pupil's utter impermeability to the process of division turns the teacher into a raving lunatic. The absurd problems he throws at her also reveal his wolfish nature. He is in fact an avatar of the hypocritical, masked devourer of "Little Red Riding Hood," the creature that rears its ugly head in *Story Number 2.* Here his cannibalistic blood lust takes the form of arithmetical calculations, culled from the textbook used by Ionesco's seven-year-old daughter, but raised to the level of unbridled violence.

The first "problem" has to do with the girl's nose. The Professor begins almost mildly: "Let's take a simpler example. If you have two noses, and I pulled one of them off... how many would you have left?"[44] The next one concerns the girl's ears. The wolfish nature of this man surfaces clearly in the following exchange:

Professor: You've not understood my example. Suppose you have only one ear.
Pupil: Yes, and then?
Professor: If I gave you another, how many would you have then?
Pupil: Two.
Professor: Good. And if I gave you still another ear. How many would you have then?
Pupil: Three ears.
Professor: Now, I take one away... and there remain... how many ears?

Pupil: Two.

Professor: Good. I take away still another one, how many do
   you have left?

Pupil: Two.

Professor: No. You have two, I take away one, I eat one up,
   then how many do you have left?

Pupil: Two.

Professor: I eat one of them . . . one.

Pupil: Two.[45]

The Pupil's only successful subtraction occurs in this passage. It may
be due to the fact that she goes from the surreal example of having
three ears to a natural state, that of a girl with two ears. She refuses,
however, to submit to any further mutilation. The devouring passion
of the Professor propels him to sadistic excesses: he speaks of tearing
off her nose, a symbolic castration.

Driven up the wall by the girl's incomprehension, the teacher
begins to shout his philosophy of life. It is pure nihilism: "It's not
enough to integrate, you must also disintegrate. That's the way life
is. That's philosophy. That's science. That's progress, civilization."[46]
Subtraction here is the abstraction of murder, the Professor's main
occupation. The Pupil, unable to acquire the negative aspects of culture, will have to content herself with "a partial doctorate."[47]

The next subject to be studied is linguistics and comparative
philology. Once again the Maid intervenes. This time her warning is
full of gloom and doom: "Professor, especially not philology, philology leads to calamity."[48] The tragic end of Ionesco's "comic drama"
is in sight.

Never is Ionesco more clever than in his caricature of linguistics,
even when his bias against the reductive quality of the scientific approach is clearly visible. Substituting Spanish for Indo-European, the
Professor declares that "Spanish is truly the mother tongue which
gave birth to all the neo-Spanish languages."[49] As part of this group
of tongues that includes his native Romanian, Ionesco introduces the
invented "Sardanapalian," derived from the name of the proverbially
cruel *débauché,* Sardanapalus, King of Assyria. Thus, under the guise
of a made-up language, the dramatist reemphasizes the theme of
cruelty and mass death inflicted upon all the women of the king's

seraglio. Clearly the Professor identifies with a tyrant who never questioned the exercise of unchecked power.

Tongue in cheek, Ionesco develops an outrageous, dadaist linguistic theory: all neo-Spanish languages have one characteristic in common; they cannot be distinguished from one another. In fact, they take "years and years to learn to pronounce."[50] The description of phonetic exercises is amusingly close to reality, yet tinged with sexuality. Here the mouth becomes the archetypal *vagina dentata:*

> In order to project words, sounds and all the rest, you must realize that it is necessary to pitilessly expel air from the lungs and make it pass delicately, caressingly, over the vocal cords, which, like harps and leaves in the wind, will suddenly shake, agitate, vibrate, vibrate or uvulate, or fricate or jostle against each other, or sibilate, placing everything in movement, the uvula, the tongue, the palate, the teeth.[51]

The word *teeth* reawakens in the Pupil the psychosomatic symptom she began to experience from the start of the philology lesson, "a toothache."[52] As the girl's pain rises in response to the Professor's fevered discourse, she is no longer able to listen to him. The more he bullies her, the less she hears. Occasionally, when he forces her to repeat something, she echoes mindlessly half a phrase. The irony of the situation is deepened by the fact that the Professor's main point is that people of various nationalities understand one another because each speaker and listener possesses an instinctive knowledge of the thing described. Thus the word for *homeland* for a Frenchman or Frenchwoman is *France,* which translates for the Portuguese into *Portugal.* On the other hand, the word *rose* is the same in each and every language. The very diversity of tongues is expressed by their wholly identical characteristics. This pseudoscientific theory springs from Ionesco's early essays collected in *Nu.*

To put his theory to the ultimate test, the Professor rummages through a drawer of his dresser, whence he extracts a huge knife. According to Ionesco's stage directions, this weapon may be "invisible or real."[53] The Pupil is urged to call it by its "Spanish, neo-Spanish, Portuguese, French, Oriental, Romanian, Sardanapali [once again the dramatist introduces the mythical image of Sardanapalus,

presiding over the sacrificial death of his wives and concubines],
Latin" and, coming full circle, once again "Spanish"[54] names. No
doubt an ironic Gertrude Stein might have commented: a knife is a
knife is a knife. This one, however, is a Freudian phallus, erect and
angry.

Yet, as Elizabeth Klaver carefully points out in her essay "The
Play of Language in Ionesco's Play of Chairs," words in *The Lesson*
are anything but innocent. Indeed, they "go beyond discourse, performing dramatic action on the stage in the form of suggested rape
and murder."[55] It is the word "knife" rather than the actual weapon,
be it visible or imaginary, that lacerates the Pupil's limbs and pene-
trates her sexual parts. As feminist criticism explains, the mastery of
discourse allows men to establish their rule and enforce their control
over the rest of society. No one is more aware than an academic that
words may constitute a formidable arsenal.

The Professor is a caricature of the tyrannical academic, as well
as an avatar of the fairy tale Big Bad Wolf. He is about to gobble up
Little Red Riding Hood. A far from innocent victim, the pubescent
maiden feels her toothache spread to her whole body: shoulders,
arms, breasts, stomach, hips, thighs. As the girl names every part of
her anatomy, she writhes with pain or/and desire. The Professor
stands with his back to the audience, hanging over the Pupil with her
rag doll legs spread limply apart. The spasmodic movements of the
man's back and pelvis, his muffled cries and heavy breathing leave
no doubt as to the sexual nature of this scene. It culminates with a
spectacular thrust of the knife/phallus. Both the expiring victim and
the triumphant rapist cry out in their different ways "Aah!" As a
final, orgasmic convulsion shakes the man's entire body, he mumbles
in ecstatic anger: "Bitch . . . Oh, that's good, that does me good . . .
Ah! Ah! I'm exhausted . . . I can scarcely breathe."[56] He seems to have
forgotten that his Maid warned him that teaching is tiring. Comic
and highly erotic, the philology lesson demonstrates the ambiguous
overlapping of sex and politics.

The Professor should have heeded his maid's warning about philology leading to calamity and criminality. When at last the old servant shuffles back into the room, she finds the girl's inanimate body
sprawled in a chair. Her assassin pretends complete innocence. It was
all the Pupil's fault; she was disobedient, a bad student. When the
Maid calls him a liar, he slinks toward her, his knife behind his back,

ready to do away with this part of his own conscience. Well aware of his sneaky nature, she parries the attack, disarms him and deals him two resounding slaps. The killer/rapist is now reduced to the state of a repentant child, whining and begging for her assistance. It is she who now assumes complete control as she plans the funeral arrangements. For Ionesco, the Maid represents the Wife/Mother who will allow her spouse/child to have his fling so long as he returns home. United in their common goal, the Maid and the Professor lift and carry out the body of the fortieth victim of the day.

The play does not end here. After a brief interval, the doorbell rings again, just as impatiently as it did when the curtain rose. Clearly, the next victim has arrived. This time we do not have the *Soprano's* "vicious circle," but an equally vicious Möbius curve. The murders, the processions of coffins go around and around ad infinitum, without us being able to determine where the process begins or ends. Lust for power and love of evil are as endless and eternal as Satan, whose ironic laugh sounds throughout this bitter comedy.

Composed in June, 1950, *The Lesson* was presented in Paris at the Théâtre de Poche on February 20, 1951. The director, who also played the Professor (his daughter now plays the Pupil), was Marcel Cuvelier. The Pupil was Rosette Zucchelli. And the Maid was played by a man, Claude Mansard, the Mr. Smith of *The Bald Soprano*. Cuvelier's decision to have a man interpret a female role was one of the elements that took the play away from realism. It lent it a grotesque and disquieting character and highlighted the final struggle in the play, a duel for mastery between two men, one masked by false humility, the other by cross dressing. As in *Soprano,* the problematics of language lie at the core of the enactment. However, in *The Lesson* it is clear that power will be held by the one who controls the use of language. But, if at first culture kills nature, power is ultimately wrested by the uneducated servant whose physical strength, greater cunning, and practical mind insures his or her mastery over his or her master. Ionesco's subtly subversive sketch is haunted by Hegel's philosophy of war, and the dialectic of the master/slave relation. The bitter medicine of the text is enrobed by the sugar coating of the nonsense wit Ionesco admires in the works of Carroll and Lear. Freud's gallows humor also appears at the end of the play, when, as the two accomplices carry out the body, the Professor cautions: "Be careful. We don't want to hurt her."[57]

Although the play was not initially well received by the audience, the critics were enthusiastic. Having seen this play, Guy Dumur expressed his regret at having missed *The Bald Soprano*. In his piece for *Opera* (2/28/51), he compared Ionesco to Chekhov and Raymond Queneau. Theater history was made when in October, 1952, *The Lesson* and *The Bald Soprano* were paired at La Huchette where they can be seen to this very day.

Perhaps the most genuinely surrealist of all of Ionesco's plays is *Jack or the Submission,* subtitled "A Naturalist Comedy." Written in 1950, it is contemporary with *The Lesson*. However, it is usually assumed to have been composed after *The Chairs*, because it was not performed before October, 1955, when Robert Postec staged it at the Théâtre de la Huchette on a double bill with *The Picture*. Jean-Louis Trintignant, who was to make a brilliant career in film, played Jack. Some of the actors were Ionesco "regulars": Tsilla Chelton as Jacques Mère and Paul Chevalier as Jacques Père (the original Old Woman and Old Man from *The Chairs*); Claude Mansard as Robert Père; the lovely Reine Courtois played Roberta of the three noses. The play was a success despite the attack of Jean-Jacques Gautier, *Le Figaro*'s critic. Those critics who were favorable to the play compared Ionesco to Labiche and Feydeau. The play's sequel, *The Future Is in Eggs,* written a year later (1951), was not given until June, 1957.

Ionesco's ironic subtitle for *Jack* signals the dramatist's intention to parody family drama. This is Ibsen gone wild. The problem of the Jack family is a rebellious son, whose heretical behavior manifests itself in his violent rejection of the traditional French peasant dish *pommes de terre au lard* (hashed brown potatoes).[58] Jack spends his days sulking and moping. What is worse still is the fact that he has not evinced the slightest interest in the opposite sex. Clearly he is unnatural, un-French, a "mononster" who must be reined in and brought to the state of complete submission. In order to accomplish this reprogramming, his family embarks upon a search for the right girls. It is assumed that were his sexual, reproductive instincts awakened, the young man might be saved, that is, reclaimed by the bourgeois order.

The Jack family is a comic daguerreotype: Mother, Father, Sister Jacqueline, the "octogeneric"[59] grandmother, and her husband, a generic "dirty old man." Mother Jack is horrified at having "brought a monster into the world."[60] Sister Jacqueline keeps on scolding the "naughty boyble."[61] As to Father Jack, he wreaks the ultimate bourgeois vengeance on his heir by disowning him.

The young man protests that he is misunderstood. His superior attitude, a caricature of the Byronic pose, is deflated by his sister when she reminds him that he is "chronometrable."[62] There is no escape from this existential situation; Jack is caught on the treadmill of time and history. He is ready to proclaim at last: "I adore hashed brown potatoes!"[63] Clearly, he is also ready for the final step in submission, matrimony.

Almost instantly a potential fiancée is brought in by her family, the Roberts. In this play, the family name is dictated by the Christian name of the children. Thus, Jack's family is known as the Jacks, and Roberta's family as the Roberts. The two families unite in chanting her attributes: "truffled feet, a hand for scouring pots and pans, armpits for turnpits, green pimples on a beige skin, red breasts on a mauve background, an illuminated navel, a tongue the color of tomato sauce, panbrowned square shoulders, and the meat needed to merit the highest recommendation."[64] This is a delectable morsel: the perfect Pop art housewife/courtesan, a modern icon worthy of being painted by Picasso, or even Andy Warhol.

This paragon exhibits a fatal flaw once her veil is lifted: she is endowed with *only* two noses. Jack states that he will accept a bride on the condition that she have at least three noses. His rejection of Roberta I is scandalous, yet all is not lost; the Roberts have a second "only" daughter, "completely equipped with three noses."[65] In fact, she is "trinary in everything, for everything."[66] This promises an ecstatic romp, an orgiastic feast.

Even then, Jack is not satisfied: the girl is not "homely enough."[67] Ionesco's addiction to contradiction manifests itself clearly in this passage. There is also a poetic riddle to be deciphered. For "homely" we must read its antithesis, "beauteous." Ionesco explained in conversation that beauty, when it first appears, is always astonishing, and often strikes the viewer as monstrous. Gradually, we become used to this new concept of the beautiful, accept it, and it becomes part of the new canon. This is certainly true of most avant-garde forms. Thus, Jack the rebel, is also Ionesco the creator of antiplays, "mononstrous" creations, shocking at first, but perceived now as a new form of classical drama. In fact, artists bring into

being the kind of beauty Baudelaire calls "Monstre énorme, effray-
ant, ingénu" (enormous, frightful, ingenuous monster).[68] If Roberta
II is to win Jack, a rebel and a poet, she must become for him the
essence of beauty and poetry, a creature full of mystery and strangeness.

Roberta II, whose mask (designed by Jacques Noël, the stage
designer of many Ionesco productions) made her look like a Picasso,
lives up to Father Jack's parting admonition: "Truth has only two
sides, but it's the third side that's best."[69] Roberta's third side is that
of an inspired storyteller. Her bizarre tales—not unlike those of the
Fire Chief—prove her to be a Sheherazade, able to enchant her reluctant lover with an oneiric reality, the third side of truth.

Roberta's first fable deals with a bathtub filled to the brim. In the
water, she sees a white guinea pig whose quivering snout repels and
fascinates her. As she stares at the seemingly dying animal, she no-
tices two growing bulges on its forehead; the cells proliferate, suggesting cancerous cysts. They prove, however, to be "his little
ones . . . coming out there."[70] Roberta's fearful attitude is obviously
a virgin's fear of sexual initiation, followed by procreation. The watery element suggests amniotic fluid. Jack interprets the image as
cancer. While she is moved by *eros,* he is in the throes of *thanatos;* the
love and death impulses will now fuse.

Jack also finds the weird story liberating. He embarks on a
monologue of a confessional nature. His life, since he was born at the
age of "almost fourteen,"[71] has been a series of disappointments. All
is deception. He tells his bride: "They all had the word goodness in
their mouths, a bloody knife between their teeth."[72] Jack's indignation with cruelty and political machinations mirrors that of Ionesco,
particularly the latter's reaction to his father's life in Romania.

Is there a way out of this ugly world? Roberta II claims to know
all the trapdoors, although she never makes it clear whether they lead
in or out. She is, after all, a tender trap herself.

Her next tale is far from tender; it is about death by drowning.
The story deals with a miller who drowned his infant son accidentally
when intending to dispose of a litter of puppies. A pyramid of absurdisms is erected by Roberta II as she states that the miller feared he
had drowned the foals instead of the pups. The oedipal infanticide is
thus twice removed from its original intentions, but the murderous
design has clearly turned against the man, undoing his progeny.

Again, Ionesco's coded language addresses his father, a man who abandoned his French family, only to claim his children many years later.

Roberta's second fable reverses the first. Taken together, the two stories constitute a diptych of life and death, birth and murder. As to the teller of the tales, she takes on the dual aspect of the Great Mother and a multiarmed (here multinosed) Hecate. The trapdoor might be the archetypal womb of death, destroying what it has conceived.

Intoxicated by her "foals" and "puppies," Jack begs his fiancée for another story. She obliges with one about a horse "engulfed in the marsh."[73] Sirenlike, she chants:

> Come on . . . don't be afraid. . . . I'm moist. . . . My necklace is made of mud, my breasts are dissolving, my pelvis is wet, I've got water in my crevasses, I'm sinking down. . . . In my belly there are pools, swamps. . . . I've got a house of clay, I'm always cool. . . . There's moss . . . big flies, cockroaches, sowbugs, toads. . . . I wrap my arms around you like snakes; with my soft thighs . . . you plunge down and you dissolve . . . in my locks which drizzle, drizzle, rain, rain. My mouth trickles down, my legs trickle, my naked shoulders trickle, my hair trickles, everything trickles down, runs, everything trickles, the sky trickles down, the stars run, trickle down, trickle . . . [74]

The flaming stallion of Roberta's final tale can only put out the fire that consumes it by plunging into the marsh. With this paean to female wetness, Roberta of the three noses, the snakelike arms, and the enveloping thighs wins herself a husband. The life cycle is about to continue. After so many seductive stories, a single word is essential to start the process of procreation: *chat* (pussy). There is no longer any need for language, for conversation. "Everything is cat,"[75] cries out the priapic Jack as he clasps in his embrace the archetypal woman.

As the happy pair mews and hisses all kinds of words containing the word cat, Jack's cap slips off, revealing he has green hair (like the Jeunes France of the nineteenth century, or a contemporary punk poet), while Roberta shows him her nine-fingered hand, which she had kept hidden under her gown. Two "mononsters" in heat are about to be joined. The triumphant families come slinking in, like feline creatures. Everyone squats, clawing, meowing. The play ends on a highly comical, sexually explicit scene of total submission to the animal nature of humanity.

In the sequel to *Jack or the Submission, The Future Is in Eggs,* cats are metamorphosed into chickens. The feline world of premarital sexuality becomes, after marriage, a vulgar barnyard. In French a word for a fecund wife is *une pondeuse* (one who lays one egg after another). Here, however, a role reversal takes place; if the husband does not lay the eggs, he is the one to hatch them.

The play opens with the sensual purring of the happy pair. Yet, according to their bourgeois families, the marriage is a failure: no offspring has been produced over a period of three years. (The Ionescos' only child was born eight years after their marriage.) This sterile bliss will not do. The couple must be awakened from their erotic trance and reminded of their obligation to society. Father Jack clamors: "The future of the white race is in your hands. It must go on, go on and extend its power more and more!"[76]

The Future Is in Eggs is a play of social and political satire couched in surrealist language and form. The central image is worthy of Guillaume Apollinaire: huge baskets of monstrous eggs are brought in, and Jack's parents order their son to proceed to the hatching. The Roberts intervene, their dignity is at stake: it is their daughter's duty to perform this function. Father Jack retorts: "In our family it's the man's job!"[77] This statement echoes Mrs. Smith's bizarre declaration in *The Bald Soprano:* "Men are all alike! You sit there all day long, a cigarette in your mouth, or you powder your nose and rouge your lips, fifty times a day, or else you drink like a fish."[78] Ionescoland is full of peculiar inversions and gender reversals. However, our so-called real world is not immune to these confusions.

Perhaps *The Future*'s central image owes something to Maupassant's pathetically comical peasant story "Toine." It describes a fat, bedridden farmer who is turned into a human incubator by his hag of a wife. Since he is unable to move, she brings him a batch of eggs, placing them next to his paralyzed body sprawled under an eiderdown. Toine is reluctant at first, feeling used and feminized, but when the chicks appear one by one, hopping all over the bed, he feels joy and pride, as though he were newly delivered of a babe. Like Toine, Jack assumes the role of a mother hen, a further sign of his "submission."

What is strongly suggested by Ionesco's ironic short play is that the harnessing of the sex drive leads not only to reproduction, but to societal controls culminating in agricultural and industrial mass production. Father Jack chants: "Long live production! Still more production! Produce! Produce!"[79] He sounds like a good Communist commissar, or the director of a Toyota factory.

Soon we realize that the monstrous eggs indiscriminately yield human beings and things: turnips and onions, bankers and pigs, policemen, firemen, diplomats, employers and employees, officious officials, radishes and radicals, Marxists and marquesses, aspirin, pencils, matches, Jansenists and existentialists, intellectuals, friends and enemies. It is all a huge mass of matter to be destroyed by wars, beaten into a gigantic, frothy omelette, mushrooming like an atomic explosion over our planet. Children are produced in order to become cannon fodder, cannons to be destroyed as they destroy in order for production to start all over again. To manufacture, destroy, and recreate one indistinguishable mass of nothingness in which human beings, consumed and replaceable, are products on the same level as manufactured objects, such is the supreme achievement of our modern civilization. Ionesco is no Marxist, but his grim picture of our world is the result of his witnessing two world wars, the Holocaust, the exponential growth of atomic and chemical weapons, the constant poisoning of our air and water. Such, in fact, is the message of one of his most recent articles in Le Figaro, "Aveuglement sur l'essentiel" (Our blindness to what is essential).[80]

The proliferation of matter on the stage is one of Ionesco's typical scenic devices, but, as this play reveals, it is not simply a mechanism, a question of rhythm. There is a philosophical reason for this theme, so that, although Ionesco has been compared to Feydeau, whom he acknowledges as one of his masters in stage craft, he is much closer to the creator of the word surrealism, Guillaume Apollinaire, the poet who described with horrified fascination the fireworks of the battlefield. The latter is the author of an ironic comedy that, together with Jarry's Ubu Rex, must be considered seminal to avant-garde theater. It is the intertext of The Future Is in Eggs. Indeed, Les Mamelles de Tirésias (1917) pretends to be "a thesis play," written to encourage the French to make love more frequently and repopulate their depleted country. It presents a "modern couple": Thérèse, the wife, has decided she will have a career instead of children. Opening her blouse, she allows her two breasts (two balloons, one red, one blue) to escape so she can explode them. She is now fashionably flat-chested, and male enough to take the name of Tiresias, the hermaphroditic seer. It will therefore be up to her passive husband to save his country. Metamorphosed into a self-made baby factory, he produces 40,049 babies in a single day, a more than adequate "production." Ionesco has certainly taken a page from Apollinaire's text, but where *Les Mamelles* is irreverently optimistic, Ionesco uses a similar situation to travel to the tragic core of the second half of the century. In his play, the proliferation of the monstrous eggs symbolizes the cancerous growth of consumer goods, with their built-in obsolescence, and of weapons of war. It appears that when men do the hatching they create "a hell of a mess" (the title of one of Ionesco's later plays).

Within Ionesco's oeuvre, *The Future Is in Eggs* marks a shift from the playful surrealism of the early plays to political cartooning. Paradoxically, this shift occurs in one of the wildest, and seemingly most surrealist, comedies of this first phase. Despite the banter, and the vaudeville imagery, the short sequel to *Jack* is the more far-reaching of the two plays.

Chapter 4

Metaphysical Farce

The Chairs, The New Tenant

At the midpoint of our century, an ethical theater of ideas evolved in France, the offspring of an ironic consciousness shaped by the German occupation. It was a time when a whole people felt estranged within the confines of their own land. Their enemies were not solely the occupying foreign forces, but some of their nationals who sided with the enemy. Deeply divided, France was no longer one country but two: the collaborationists and the Resistance fighters.

The writers who emerged during the German occupation, and made their reputation in the post-World War II era, used their plays as a platform to deliver messages or convey their philosophy. They also mastered a coded language that helped them avoid censorship. A number were primarily what the French call philosophes (social thinkers in the tradition of the Enlightenment), political ideologues, reformers. Some, like Albert Camus, started out as actors and theater directors, so it was natural for them to turn to the stage in order to make their point. Others, like Jean-Paul Sartre, came to the dramatic art later in life, seeing it as the ideal platform to air their views and reach a wide public. For Sartre, the stage became a natural extension of the university amphitheater, another space for the informal teaching he carried on at the café terraces of the Deux Magots and the Flore. This is where he enjoyed holding intellectual court, much as Socrates did in the streets of his beloved Athens.

Never had there been a greater need to address a large audience of one's compatriots than in the aftermath of the Nazi occupation. For many years the French lived under the pall of censorship. The presence of the enemy in their capital, and even within their homes, where officers were billeted, had imposed a heavy silence on an articulate, lucid, free people. The Liberation meant more than political freedom; it was a time for regaining a sense of self as well as the feeling of belonging once again to a nation.

During the time of their imprisonment, French playwrights made a fine art of speaking indirectly, in coded language, in parables. They skirted censorship regulations by rereading and rewriting familiar classical texts. Of course, intertextual allusions, the sophisticated play between the original classical text and the neoclassical interpretation, was an integral part of seventeenth-century dramaturgy. The same can be said of the witty, ironic plays of the period known in France as *l'entre deux guerres* (between two world wars). On the surface, the drama composed during the German occupation seems to echo some of the devices used by Cocteau in *The Infernal Machine,* or by Giraudoux in *Tiger at the Gates.* However, the new theater had a secret agenda: to lend a voice to a gagged people, to speak to them and for them above the heads of the collaborators, the police, and the leaders of the occupying forces. These highly political plays are parables, disguised orations, secular sermons. They are informed by the highest moral purpose: to lend the imprisoned nation strength, convey hope, teach patience, courage, and tenacity.

Thus, Anouilh's *Antigone* does not portray the growing tragedy of Creon—as does Sophocles' tragedy, a play subtly balanced between two equally valid points of view—but the resolve of a rebellious young princess, who, like a Resistance fighter, defies authority and chooses death over tyranny. However, like the classical heroine, this movingly childlike, life-loving girl is ready to give her whole being for what she views as the honor of her race. She becomes a martyr to a higher law, except that it is not a law wrought by the gods, but dictated by the moral precepts each and every one must forge for oneself in times of crisis. The same can be said for Sartre's *The Flies.* It is a retelling of *Electra,* but also with an essential change of focus. In Sartre's play Electra is the weak, frightened sister of the new existential hero Orestes. The young prince, who has returned to a vitiated state, knows that he must assume the matricidal act as a crime necessary to purge his country of what Sartre calls *"mauvaise foi"* (bad faith). In a scene in which the avenger defies Zeus, severing all pre-established ties with a higher law, he affirms his own freedom

as the supreme lawmaker, a man who knows the corrupt world must
be bled and refashioned. Again, Sartre's modern rereading is an exploration of the deeper meaning of Sophocles: Orestes must renew
the *dikê* (justice) disturbed by Clytemnestra when she murdered
Agamemnon. Sartre's audience was ready to receive this ancient message: wrong action provokes reaction, retribution is part of the force
of nature.

Although of the same generation as the late Jean-Paul Sartre and
Albert Camus, Eugène Ionesco and Samuel Beckett went further in
their exploration of despair, that sickness of the void that the Existentialists call "angst" or, in Sartre's case, "nausea." Unlike Sartre and
Camus, Beckett and Ionesco offer no solution to problems in their
work. Their literature neither teaches nor preaches; it is not didactic.
They did not feel they could express their apprehension by way of a
conventional form, a well-wrought play. Instead, they invented a
dramaturgy suited to the crystallization on the stage of images from
their inner world. As Ionesco explained in a talk that inaugurated the
Helsinki Debates on the Avant-Garde (June, 1959),

> A work of art and a dramatic work too . . . must be a primary
> instinct, profound or vast according to the talent or genius of the
> artist, but a truly primary instinct which owes nothing to any-
> thing but itself. But in order that it may rise up and take shape,
> one must let the imagination run free above external and second-
> ary considerations such as those of its future, its popularity or its
> need to express an ideology. In this flowering of the imagination,
> meanings emerge by themselves and they are eloquent for some
> and less so for others. . . . Besides which a creative work of art is,
> by its very novelty, aggressive, spontaneously aggressive; it
> rouses indignation by its nonconformity which is, in itself, a
> form of indignation.[1]

What then is this "spontaneously aggressive" new form? Both
for Beckett and Ionesco, the philosophical, intellectual concerns of
humanity must be couched in the rough-and-tumble language of the
most primitive kind of comedy. The physical needs and foibles of the
human animal are grotesquely emphasized. However, although human beings seem at times to be Yahoos, they are also capable of fine
feelings, and of a longing for perfection. It is this discrepancy be-

tween their lowly instincts and lofty aspirations that tickles the funny bone.

Jean Tardieu, Arthur Adamov, Samuel Beckett, and Eugène Ionesco are the creators of a new dramatic genre or mode, one I call *Metaphysical Farce*.[2] In this type of theater, philosophic thought is never expounded, nor even dramatized, as it is in the plays of the Existentialists. Rather it is introduced under a mask, that of the explosive, subversive, liberating anarchy of laughter. The originality of this theater lies in the paradoxical amalgam of the broadest kind of comedy with the most refined meditation upon the human condition.

In a world turned upside down by devastating wars and the Holocaust, a universe in which the vision of the heroic life is preempted and desecrated by the theoreticians of mass murder, tragedy, in the classical sense, is no longer a viable form. According to Friedrich Dürrenmatt, tragedy presupposes "guilt, despair, lucidity, vision, a sense of responsibility."[3] However, these can exist only within the framework of a hierarchical order. In such a society there are clear, incontrovertible differences between the "the higher type" of person, the one whose every act is based on an inner moral vision, and the average human being, content to drift from day to day.

Our epoch no longer views the moral world in clear-cut fashion. Ruled by mass production, societies that equate people and things as products to be consumed and discarded have lost their hold upon physical and moral reality. Thus, in the twentieth century, the boundary line that used to divide the tragic view from the comic is no longer clearly drawn. Self-appointed charismatic leaders moved by a distorted sense of historical mission proved lethal and in retrospect appear grotesquely funny. In dire circumstances—on the field of battle, in political prisons, concentration camps—it was the modest, self-effacing antihero who cut a selfless, courageous figure. Thus, the traditional comic type took on some of the aspects of the tragic hero.

As a result of this radical transformation of life and sensibility, the postwar dramatists faced a dilemma: they realized they could not pour their new weltanschauung into an antiquated mold. Ionesco's first step was to distance himself from the tyranny of aesthetics by subtitling his pieces "antiplays."

What is the nature of this new dramaturgic mode? It stems from the need to convey the tragic apprehension of life—universal and eternal, yet exacerbated by the upheavals of war—by means of the most democratic of forms, a lowly, popular kind of entertainment, farce. By so doing, the writer does not set an artistic self above the audience (or reader). Nor does he or she address the audience as an elite group, superior to the struggling, ridiculous creatures portrayed on the stage. These are fellow human beings, even when, as in Beckett's *Waiting for Godot,* they are homeless tramps, concerned with their aching feet, weak bladders, smelly breath, tight boots. Like the Medieval poet-felon Villon, writing his "Ballade des Pendus" for his *"frères humains"* (human brothers), the poet-dramatists of our time assume that their audience is composed of people who will identify with these humble protagonists. Their concerns, like those of the characters on the stage, are the basic ones of survival.

Our modern farces are classical because they are infused with the sacred spirit that informed the earliest enactments. To purge human beings of the sin of pride by reminding them that they are like the antiheroes of the modern stage is to bring about their salvation. In ancient Greece to engage in a performance known as the *komos* was far more than merrymaking; it was a joyous religious ritual characterized by disguises, animal masks, ribald ridiculing of the god in whose honor the play was being presented. No blasphemy was intended. The revellers enjoyed a release from the restraints of daily life. Today's transcendental humor assumes the salvational function of tragedy. "Catharsis through laughter"[4] aims to effect a cure. The new theater is still tragic, but it is "tragedy coming out of comedy."[5]

The Ontological Void: *The Chairs*

One of the most striking examples of a contemporary tragi-comedy is Ionesco's one-act play *The Chairs.*

It was first presented on April 22, 1952, at the Lancry theater in Paris. The director was Sylvain Dhomme, who also played the silent Orator. Except for this brief appearance, there are only two characters: the Old Man (Paul Chevalier) and his wife, the Old Woman (Tsilla Chelton). The rest are invisible, imaginary visitors represented by forty empty chairs that are carried onto the stage at an ever-increasing speed by the Old Woman.

Ionesco likes to tell the amusing story of how, when the play was taken on tour to the conservative city of Lyons, the audience stormed out in indignation. People were heard grumbling: "These

Parisians take us for fools. They've sent us three out of their forty-
three actors, and one of the three is mute."

At the beginning of the play's run, the number of people in the
audience matched that of the actors on the stage. There were evenings
when the three actors faced an audience of three: Ionesco, his wife,
and their eight-year-old daughter.

The author of *The Bald Soprano, The Lesson, Jack or the Submission*
began to attract the attention of his peers. About twenty of them
attended the premiere of *The Chairs*. Yet the critical reception was
guarded. J. B. Jeener of *Le Figaro* wrote that "the author himself
succumbed under the weight of the incoherence he decries."[6] *Libéra-
tion, Combat, Arts, La Croix* were puzzled by the absurd, interminable
dialogues. One of the rare exceptions was Renée Saurel of *Lettres
Française*. She praised the work, calling it "hauntingly beautiful and
perfectly structured under its surface of incoherence."[7] In May, Jacques Lemarchand declared in the pages of *Le Figaro Littéraire* that
Ionesco was one of the truly important new writers, "a true poet of
the stage."[8]

The same month, the weekly *Arts* published a page of *témoignages*
(testimonies). These reactions of some of the best known critics and
writers of the time point to a considerable breakthrough in regard to
Ionesco's reputation among the *cognoscenti*.

The poet Jules Supervielle voiced his admiration for "the miracle
of the multiplications of chairs." Raymond Queneau, who had cham-
pioned *The Bald Soprano* in which he had not failed to recognize
echoes from his own *Exercises de style,* pronounced himself in favor
of the new play. Samuel Beckett addressed Ionesco directly in an
open letter: "I have just seen *The Chairs*. I wish to let you know that
I was deeply moved." Arthur Adamov revealed some of his personal
anguish in his declaration: "Ionesco uncovers something most people
do not wish to acknowledge about themselves: the image of decrepitude. We owe him at least our respect for his courage in exposing
himself in his nakedness."[9]

A month earlier (April 23, 1952), Ionesco published an analysis
in *Combat* of what he was tackling in his new play.

I've tried to express the moral decomposition of my characters,
their incoherence. This had to be achieved by means of an appropriate language, one which reveals their progressive deteriora-

tion, although at times it is able to restructure itself. . . . I wanted this farce to be dramatic, yet remain farcical. Creatures lost in incoherence, imprisoned in a meaningless universe, wrenched from any kind of essential reality, cannot be purely tragic. . . . Above all, I attempted to convey my own feelings as to the unreality of the world.[10]

In 1956, when the play was recreated at the Studio des Champs-Elysées under the direction of Jacques Mauclair—who was to prove himself Ionesco's most loyal, most faithful interpreter—Jean Anouilh, whose own play was being given next door, wrote a generous article for *Le Figaro,* stating, "Every Parisian who loves theatre (and I do not mean those who only run to avant-garde productions) will blush one day (ten or twenty years hence) when he'll have to admit at a social gathering that he missed seeing *The Chairs*. The play can wait, for it has all the time in the world. I myself believe it to be superior to Strindberg; it is a dark comedy, in the style of Molière, a madly zany black comedy, scary and quizzical, poignant and always true. . . . It ought to be called a classic."[11] Ionesco also tells the story of how the same Anouilh approached people unable to purchase seats for his sold-out play with the following recommendation: "Why don't you go next door. It's far better than what I do."

Combat asked Ionesco to compare and contrast the two stagings of *The Chairs*. He wrote:

Sylvain Dhomme directed the play in a sharp, abstract, cerebral fashion. . . . He stressed the metaphysical meaning of the work: evanescence, absence, the unreality of the real, the ontological void, also the absurd. . . . He created a time out of time, a spaceless space. . . . With the arrival of the chairs, the stage was filled with absence. . . . On the other hand, Mauclair humanized the inhuman.[12]

In a letter addressed to Sylvain Dhomme while the play was in rehearsal the dramatist stressed that "everything ought to be exaggerated, excessive, painful, childlike, a caricature stripped of refinement."[13] These directives echo those offered by Cocteau in his famous preface to his *Marriage on the Eiffel Tower*. Cocteau was one of the first dramatist theoreticians to point out that "poetry *of* the theatre" (stage effects) is different from "poetry *in* the theatre" (poetic language). Poetic language is a fine lace, he explained, while the poetry woven of gestural language, the set, lighting, makeup, or masks is thick lace woven with the kind of rope used on sailing vessels. It must be visible from a great distance, and therefore blownup, exaggerated. In his own notes to *The Orator* (the original title of *The Chairs*), Ionesco jotted down: "To express the void by means of language, gesture, acting and props. To express absence. To express regret and remorse. The unreality of the real. Original chaos."[14]

The Chairs presents an aged couple (the Old Man, 95 years old, and the Old Woman, 94 years old), living in complete isolation in a building surrounded by water, a watchtower or lighthouse. The Old Man, the "janitor" of this tower, calls himself Quartermaster General. His wife entertains him in the illusion that he is a man of genius who might easily have become president, doctor of medicine, or field marshal, had circumstances beyond his control not turned him into the failure that he is. The Old Woman is both wife and mother to her husband. She rocks him in her lap, fondles him, sings him popular songs, lullabies, and blows his nose when he gets weepy. When he whines that he is motherless, an orphan—Ionesco suggests that we never forget the loss of parents we loved, that time does not heal—his wife whispers that she is now his mamma. As he lies limply across her lap, we are presented a cartoon version of the Pieta.

Having played the mother role, the Old Woman turns into a respectful wife. She encourages her husband to tell her a story she has heard a hundred times but, much as children do, enjoys listening to all over again. Now it is she who plays the role of a small child, one who needs to be pacified.

Ionesco draws for his audience a devastating picture of dependency. He does not spare any of the grim details that render marriage an association of two helpless, self-indulgent, egocentric individuals, who try to find in each other their own image and the comfort they lost in growing out of childhood. However, his protagonists are in the state of second childhood; they have come full circle.

Time in *The Chairs* is some kind of vague future; the landscape suggests a catastrophe that might have annihilated most of the planet, drowning the mainland under some gigantic tidal wave. The Old Man tells the Old Woman the story of a great city of which nothing remains save a popular tune: "Paris Will Always Be Paris." The title is in itself an ultimate irony since obviously Paris has disappeared. In fact, so much time has elapsed since the city's annihilation that the Old Man is no longer certain whether this place called Paris was a small village or a great metropolis. It was known, he recalls, as "la Ville Lumière" (the city of lights), but this light was extinguished "four hundred years ago."[15] Nothing has survived, not even ruins as in Persepolis. The destruction seems as complete as that of the great pyramid of the mysterious Pharaoh Radedef at Aby Rawash. The glorious capital of France, the jewel of the world, has suffered the fate of Carthage and Byzantium. No doubt Ionesco's audience recalled with a shudder the Germans' master plan to blow up their city before retreating, as they did in Warsaw. Paris came close to being nothing more than a dot on a map.

With the game of story telling over, as well as that of sipping imaginary tea from invisible china cups, a new subject is introduced by the Old Woman, Semiramis. The old hag is endowed with a grotesquely ill-suited name, that of the Assyrian princess who supposedly founded Babylon. The ancient name may go with her wrinkled face and mummylike body, but it emphasizes the passing of a glorious epoch. However, the Old Man and his wife have kept a sense of history, a desire to leave a trace of their passage on this earth. Since they cannot build pyramids or plan suspended gardens, they will turn to oratory, that off-shoot of philosophy that flowered as a conscious art from Gorgias to Aristotle. Since the Old Man is no Demosthenes, he wonders whether he will be able to acquit himself of this task. His admiring, tirelessly supportive wife tries to build his self-confidence. Her comment furnishes us with the perfect illustration of one of Ionesco's typical stylistic devices: the seemingly throwaway line enclosing a key concept, indeed an aesthetic principle.

It's easy once you begin, like life and death. It's enough to have your mind made up. In speaking, ideas come to us, words, and then we, in our own words, we find everything again, the city, the garden. Then we are no longer orphans.

Ionesco starts with a joke: What is easy about "life and death"?[16] Then we recognize the writer who likes to quip: "I write to find out what I think," the dramatist who dictates his plays to a secretary, writing them as he speaks. The passage culminates in a moving praise of the art of oratory and of writing. Through this activity we find what was lost in the depths of our memory: "the city, the garden." Better still we encounter our dead parents, our relatives, and friends. "Then we are no longer orphans." Thus, the Old Woman's injunction is also the writer's statement about the nature of his art. Ionesco, who always says that he cannot imagine for himself any other life than the one of man of letters, says that it is in literature that as readers and writers we find our true home.

Because the Old Man is full of self-doubt he will take no chances: he has invited a professional orator to deliver his message. Like the ancient Greeks, he believes that "the orator" is the prose artist par excellence, the one able to make the *written* word *heard*. For this momentous occasion a great crowd has been summoned. Ionesco draws up one of his absurd lists held together not by meaning, but by rhyming words, alliterations, rhythmic patterns. Since there is no rhyme or reason for this grouping of people, the effect is of a chaotic mob.

> The property owners and the intellectuals . . . the janitors, the bishops, the druggists, the tinsmiths, the violinists, the delegates, the presidents, the police, the merchants, the buildings, the pen holders, the chromosomes . . . the post office employees, the innkeepers, the artists . . . the proletarians, the clerks, the military, the revolutionaries, the alienists and their alienated.[17]

It is a mad hodgepodge of opposites, of people and objects, much like the "production" line in *The Future Is in Eggs*.

The guest list drawn, a sound is heard outside; a boat glides through the water, comes to a stop at the bottom of the lighthouse. This sound is followed by a doorbell ringing. The Old Man and his wife rush out of one of the many doors at the back of the stage. They can be heard speaking to someone in the wings. Slowly, they back into the room, talking with animation to their first visitor. Finally, they separate, allowing the guest to pass. This is the moment when the audience realizes that all the visitors will be invisible, imaginary.

The first invisible guest is a woman. The space she is imagined to occupy is framed by her excited hosts. The Old Man walks out to fetch an extra chair since, at the start, there are only two downstage.

In the meantime, the visitor and her hostess occupy these two. When the Old Man returns, he sets his chair on the other side of the empty one, the guest's chair.

Soon the bell rings again. From this time on there will be a steady flow of new arrivals. The Old Man rushes to open the door, while his wife fetches the chairs. Her comings and goings become so precipitous that it is hard to imagine that the same person is performing all the exists and entrances. Tsilla Chelton, who was a young woman when she played the role, achieved the speed of an automaton, a marionette gone wild. Her act echoed the comical assembly-line scene of Chaplin's "Modern Times." No wonder; Ionesco stated a number of times that his sources must not be sought in dramatic literature but in the circus, the cabaret, and above all silent films. He jokes in all seriousness: "I belong to the cabaret school of drama. My ancestors are Charlot [Chaplin], the Marx Brothers, the Keystone Cops, Buster Keaton, Laurel and Hardy, and the cartoon characters, Les Pieds Nickelés." Tsilla Chelton is a clown in this tradition. Tall, gaunt, made up to look ashen, she literally ran in breathless circles behind the set to reappear almost instantly upon disappearing. She created the visual illusion that there were two of her on the stage at once. It was an unforgettable tour de force as breathtaking as watching an acrobat walking a tight rope. She lived up to Bergson's definition of the comic in Le rire, "le mécanique plaqué sur du vivant" (something mechanical superimposed on something alive).[18] Exhilarating and comical, her performance captured the very essence of Metaphysical Farce.

As the stage becomes peopled with an invisible, yet not inaudible crowd (Ionesco calls for sounds that suggest a room filling up with people), empty chairs are placed in neat rows, their backs to the audience. The effect is of another theater orchestra, the mirror image of the real one below. Clearly the "show" is to take place upstage, where a huge double door dominates the back wall. Meanwhile, the Old Woman, who has become an usher, circulates up and down the aisle selling popsicles, candy, cigarettes, and cold drinks, just like the ouvreuses in French movie houses.

All of a sudden the doors at the back soundlessly swing open. A hush falls over the room as the Old Man and the Old Woman stand petrified, awestruck at the apparition. It is the supreme moment of a lifetime: the Emperor, as invisible as the rest of the guests, has arrived.

The audience in the theater is caught in the magic make-believe of the moment; yet, instantly a cruel realization dawns on the public: nothing has actually happened, there is no one there. The Emperor's entrance is part of a dream, or a rehearsed game played by the couple on many of their solitary evenings. This time, however, it is an endgame.

At the Centre Culturel International de Cérisy-la-Salle in Normandy, where Ionesco arrived for a "Décade Ionesco" (ten days devoted to his work in August, 1978), he was questioned about the meaning of the Emperor in *Les Chaises*. Did he mean a real emperor, like Napoleon? For the French, "l'empereur" has a specific ring. However, the dramatist grew indignant: "It would be a mistake to reduce this apparition to the arrival of a temporal leader." Then he went on calmly: "There is an indication in my stage directions about a strange, supernatural light. You don't see anything, but the light changes. There is the suggestion of an emanation. My emperor is not human; he is the King of Kings."

Ionesco's mystical bent comes to the fore in this statement. The scene, however, is more ambiguous, leaving the audience with many questions. Is God absent, hidden, or dead? Is faith nothing but illusion? Why is the light described in the stage directions as "cold, empty"? Ionesco is adept at playing games, seeming to answer questions while reserving part of the truth. There is no denying that the old couple experiences a moment of illumination, of bliss. Semiramis fails to understand at once what has happened, but her husband prompts her and she echoes his awed greeting, adding to it a note of tenderness: "Ah! yes, the Emperor! Your Majesty! Your Majesty! *(She wildly makes countless grotesque curtsies.)* In our house! In our house!"[19]

This visitation of a deity, albeit an invisible one, honoring a humble, tenderly united old couple, has been compared to that of Zeus and Hermes receiving the rustic hospitality of Philemon and Baucis.[20] Ionesco's Old Man and Old Woman are much like the Philemon and Baucis of Goethe's *Faust II*. They have been bypassed if not crushed by the modern world, making of their isolation a virtue. Like Goethe's victims of so-called progress, they will have nothing to do with the "clever masters' minions."[21] However, whereas Goethe's Emperor was based on Maximilian I, Ionesco's radiant "King of Kings" is neither the Roi Soleil, nor Bonaparte; he issues from myth, not history. The Old Man, however, is utterly taken in by his self-made illusion. Perched on twin stools placed at opposite sides of the room, now crowded with empty chairs, the two old people act like kids at a parade.

> Old Man: . . . I want to see . . . move aside . . . I want . . . the celestial gaze, the noble face, the crown, the radiance of his Majesty. . . . Oh! I caught sight of him clearly that time. . . . I caught sight.[22]

Claiming he is "at the height of joy,"[23] he stands on his toes, ready to fly up. Perhaps he would do so, had the ironic writer failed to perforate his hot air balloon with his wit's rapier. The moment of pathos is demystified when the Old Man remembers that he is not a general at the imperial court, but merely a "simple general factotum,"[24] a euphemism for janitor or, at best, lighthouse keeper. He must do any kind of work at "the little court"[25] he sweeps and tends.

Ionesco's ambiguous text gives rise to a multiplicity of questions: Do we know one another, even in the most intimate of human associations, marriage? Is love free of the possibility of betrayal? Is everything in daily life a matter of illusion if not deceit? The dramatist does not believe in offering answers, and he has structured his text in such a way that it is a tapestry of unanswerable queries.

At the start of the play, the Old Man and his wife are close to one another, tied to each other by a child-parent relation in which each is alternately parent and child. However, as soon as the imaginary guests begin to arrive, the couple's unity is broken. The Old Man welcomes a former lover, a woman he has not forgotten and who has come with her husband. In a series of broad asides, the former beau tells his lady love that she was the only woman he ever cared for, and that his wife, whom he calls "Semiramis, ma crotte" (Semiramis, my little turd),[26] has assumed the place of his dead mother. During that time, the Old Woman, back to back with her spouse, is flirting with the lady's husband. Whereas the Old Man is sentimental, Semiramis is grotesquely lustful, lifting her skirt to reveal a bright red petticoat, and inquiring whether "one could have children at any age."[27] She wriggles obscenely under the imaginary touch of her companion, and backs reluctantly, begging her "lover" to show some respect for her husband's poor mother, that is, herself.

As they stand back to back, the spouses are pursuing their parallel adulteries. This is no Philemon and Baucis marriage, but a caricature of the typical bedroom farce couple. Thus, the marriage relationship that appeared warm, tender, and real, although disturbing in its dependency, is built on water, like the watchtower inhabited by the old spouses.

Nor is marriage the only lie in Ionesco's devastating picture of human conduct. In fact, it is impossible to tell when one of the characters is lying, and when he or she is telling a deeper truth. In this sense, the play is indebted to Pirandello. Like his predecessor, Ionesco sets about confusing his audience. Lies crisscross in intricate patterns, weaving the web of illusion, or revealing the depths of the characters' subconscious. The obvious conclusion is that there is no single truth, that the notion of such a truth is the supreme illusion.

One example is that of two contradictory stories: the Old Man tells his first love that he always wished he could have had a son, while his wife confesses to that woman's husband that she and her husband had a son, a perfect, pure child, who ran away because his parents had killed a bird. Next, the Old Man proceeds to accuse himself of having left his mother alone, to die in a ditch. On the contrary, Semiramis states that her husband has been a model son to both his parents. How does one puzzle out the truth? Could it be that the Old Man is obsessed with feelings of guilt in regard to his treatment of his mother, feelings that have no basis in reality? Is he lying when he speaks to the woman he used to love, or has he been lying to his wife all along? Does he speak in humility and sudden understanding, touched by the vivifying renewal of love, or in masochistic self-abasement? Did he and his wife actually have a son, or did the Old Woman's longing for an offspring create this pure boy out of thin air—the very air from which the man she is talking to is made. Ionesco's contrapuntal treatment of lies, illusions, ancient guilts, and broken dreams illustrates effectively the insubstantial basis on which people erect their lives.

Reality is dream, dream reality. We live among shadows, ghosts. For the old couple, the illusion of receiving guests acquires greater reality than any event in their personal past or present. The writer's skillful dosage of farce and pathos lends his antiplay a modern quality of atonalism; the discordant sound of a sob stifled in an outburst of mirth.

But what of human dignity, quite apart from the lies and illusions that make up the fabric of daily existence? Could there be after all an untouched core of being?

The Old Man's story is not unfamiliar: his friends betrayed him when he needed them most; his enemies tried to destroy him with an almost fatal efficiency. When he wished to travel, he was refused a passport; when he tried to cross a river, he found the bridges blasted; when he decided to climb the Pyrenees, the mountain chain had crumbled into dust. No one listened to him, no one invited him. Sick, he was sacked; well, he was kicked. Most of the time he was simply ignored.

This is the list of grievances he presents to the Emperor. The moment of rehabilitation has come at last; he will put the world on trial, denounce it to the supreme moral authority. The Emperor has the power to confer on the Old Man the dignity he has been denied throughout his life. In fact, the very presence of this august being confirms that dignity. Yet the supreme affirmation is still to come. The hired Orator's appearance should dispel all doubts and set things right.

Although the Orator's arrival is announced by the old couple in the form of a duet—"He will come, he will come. He is coming, he is coming . . . he is here . . ."[28]—one senses that the old people are not certain of succeeding in summoning his presence. When he materializes all of a sudden, it is as though the thick air of incantation had thickened into a presence. Ionesco's stage directions are explicit: "He is a real person . . . a typical painter or poet of the nineteenth century; he wears a large, black felt hat with wide brim, loosely tied bow tie, artist's blouse, mustache and goatee, very histrionic in manner, conceited; just as the invisible people must be as real as possible, the Orator must appear unreal."[29]

The two old people greet him with amazement:

Old Man: Here he is!
Old Woman: It's really he, he exists. In flesh and blood.
Old Man: He exists. It's really he. This is not a dream!"[30]

Turning then to the invisible audience on the stage, the Old Man begins his farewell address. It is meant not only for those who have assembled in this theater space—the one on the stage, as well as the theater orchestra below—but for society at large, "the paper manufacturers and the painters, proofreaders, editors to whom we owe the programs."[31] This is a writer's leave-taking.

Addressing himself to the ghostly Emperor, the Old Man exclaims: "Your Majesty, my wife and myself have nothing more to ask of life. Our existence has come to an end in this apotheosis."[32]

Can something real be created out of passionate longing? The stage directions do not foster this way of thinking. The Orator looks like an old ham actor; if he spoke he would undoubtedly spout fractured alexandrine verse like Hugo's Hernani. The supreme irony lies in the Old Man's blindness, his willingness to die, entrusting his message to this relic of a bygone era. He says with a flourish worthy of Cyrano de Bergerac: "I count on you, great master and Orator."[33]

The two old people are ready for their planned double suicide. They have signed a pact to cast themselves out of the two windows opening upon the waters that surround their tower. However, they are not meant to share "the same sepulchre . . . the same worms."[34] as did Tristan and Isolde. Rather, like the dead of Hugo's "Oceano Nox," they will dissolve in "an aquatic solitude."[35]

The Old Man's final speech is purple rhetoric, pitiful and grotesque. It is the kind of bombastic eloquence ridiculed by the young Bucharest dadaist in his *Hugoliade*. This discourse mirrors perfectly the nineteenth-century dress and aspect of the Orator, it is delivered in the tone he might have used. Thus, the death of the caricatural Philemon and Baucis spells the disappearance of a certain kind of Romantic sensibility, of an antiquated culture. Ionesco is aware of how ridiculous they were, yet he also mourns their passing. He knows that it marks the end of language.

It is no wonder then that after the couple's final splash into the watery waste, the Orator stands in dumb silence. Slowly he opens his mouth to deliver the message, but what comes out is a gurgle, the dying rattle of a drowning man. Seeing that he cannot make himself understood, this paltry Isocrates grabs a piece of chalk to scribble on the blackboard (the use of the blackboard is often omitted in production, but this takes away from the strange reality of the school teacher/orator). Among the meaningless letters written in large capitals, two words appear: ANGEPAIN (ANGELFOOD) and ADIEU.[36] If the final farewell echoes that of Philemon and Baucis, it also suggests that only God knows the answer, or at least the text of the message. In the beginning was the Word, in the end only a rebus.

In a series of letters written to the first director of *The Chairs,* Ionesco stresses his theme, "the ontological void."[37] He asks Sylvain Dhomme to time carefully the departure of the Orator, the murmuring of the invisible crowd of people, that is the audience occupying the empty chairs, and finally the slow closing of the curtain. He explains that the audience will not then be tempted to give some easy, psychological interpretation.

> They must not be able to say, for example, that the old couple are mad or senile and suffering from hallucinations; neither must they be able to say that the invisible characters are only the old couple's remorse and memories. This may perhaps be true up to a point, but it has absolutely no importance; the interest lies elsewhere . . . [38]

What is this "elsewhere"? It is *an* elsewhere, the ontological void, the abyss all around us, the unknown whence we came and where we are heading. What Ionesco is saying is that he is a metaphysical dramatist "trying to express the void by means of language, gesture, acting, and props. To express absence. . . . The unreality of the real. Original chaos."[39] *The Chairs* is Ionesco's first metaphysical farce, a tragicomic meditation on the human confession, and a whispered confession of his sense of guilt and fear of failure. The image of the empty chairs makes eternal absence palpable, but it also reminds us that "all the world's a stage."[40] If Shakespeare's feeling for the absurdity of life and death informs this text, the poet who is Ionesco's direct forerunner is Stéphane Mallarmé. Like his predecessor, Ionesco proved himself the stage poet of Non-Being.

A Pyramid of Possessions: *The New Tenant*

Ionesco's plays are often born from an image, one that comes to him before he has a clear notion of what he is going to write. Thus, in the case of *The Chairs,* he first saw a dim and ghostly light playing over "empty chairs on an empty stage decorated with streamers, littered with useless confetti, which would give an impression of sadness, emptiness and disenchantment such as one finds in a ballroom after a

dance."[41] The image of the detritus after a celebration is picked up
again in *Amédée or How To Get Rid of It*. Written after this play, *The
New Tenant* also presents the detritus and clutter of our civilization.
It suggests the overwhelming weight of matter.

Like Beckett's *Act without Words, The New Tenant* is a play whose
language is that of gestures and props. Not that all four characters are
silent. The two movers puff and groan, voices rise from the street
and the courtyard, and the concierge speaks nonstop. What she says,
however, should be qualified as nothing more than noise pollution.
Her discourse is a tapestry of clichés, as though the language of the
street and the marketplace had risen to the sixth floor, bursting
through the lips of this vulgar woman. In fact, this tidal wave of
common speech threatens to engulf the silent man, the new tenant.

Dressed in black, or shades of gray (dark coat, black hat, sun
glasses), the gentleman cuts a foreboding figure. He is the embodiment of nay-saying. His deathly pallor, monosyllabic answers, delib-
erately slow movements contrast with the concierge's jolly singing
and prattling, her shouts to some invisible acquaintance from across
the courtyard, her ceaseless agitation. Oblivious to everything except
her own busybody world, she remains unaware of the tenant's with-
drawal, of his stubborn refusal of all she has to offer: advice on how
to arrange the pieces of furniture being brought up by the movers,
possible future house cleaning. It soon becomes obvious that the
silent man needs no human contact; he has come to seek refuge on
this top floor from the triteness and bourgeois coziness this woman
symbolizes. An inveterate loner, the new tenant is a prefiguration of
Ionesco's "hermit," the central character of the dramatist's only
novel, *Le Solitaire* (The hermit).

The play starts in the manner of a naturalist comedy. The set is
a bare room, recently vacated. A din is heard offstage: voices, the
fracas of children running up and down the stairs, laughing and
shouting, loud hammering, snatches of popular music. The light is
bright and sunny as it bounces off brightly painted walls. Everything
suggests the richness of life, of new beginnings as well as comforting
continuity.

The concierge enters humming and rattling a bunch of keys. She
is middle-aged and not unattractive in a plump, healthy-looking way.
She walks to the open window, leans out, shouting something in the
direction of someone called George. He must go see Bill to let him

know that Mr. Clarence is waiting for him. From this first sentence a human chain is established. Out there, in the world, connections are being made, social intercourse goes on.

The silent Gentleman who comes in conveys at once something profoundly disquieting. He stands at the door for a while, staring at the woman's broad back, then addresses her in a quiet voice: "Excuse me, are you the caretaker?"[42] The concierge is visibly startled. She puts her hand to her heart, begins to hiccup. It is as though she had come in contact with something threatening, an apparition from the antiworld. The man's cold expression and atonal voice suggest a force far more powerful than the life force.

The concierge's verbal flow is cut short by the Gentleman's polite request that she close the window. He has to repeat it four times before his demand is heeded. The shutting of the window muffles the sounds of the world outside; it signals a severing of social ties, a separation from people and life. When the obtuse, chatty woman insists that she would like to serve him, to help him with some domestic chores (not an unusual arrangement between a single male tenant and a concierge) the Gentleman turns her down: "I shan't be needing your services, I'm afraid."[43] The words have an ominous ring; they are spoken with finality. However, the simple-minded woman does not catch this nuance; she merely feels rejected.

From this point on, the Gentleman concentrates his attention on the furniture movers, who have started to bring up his pieces. Ionesco's stage directions indicate that all pretense at realism has now been dropped. The first objects are small and light (low stools, vases), yet the movers are puffing and straining. Gradually, the pieces of furniture grow larger, heavier, more cumbersome, yet, paradoxically, the movers shed their fatigue, coming and going up and down the stairs at a rhythm that rises exponentially. The small room fills with an odd assortment of possessions: tables, chests of drawers, screens, wash basins, umbrella stands, chamber pots, pictures, piles of books. Meanwhile, the Gentleman has drawn a circle on the floor with a piece of chalk. He indicates to the movers that they are to set the furniture on the periphery. He himself selects a box and some small items to take within the circle. As his possessions begin to clutter the room, the Gentleman gains assurance; he gives clear orders: "There . . . there . . . there. . . ."[44] He is beginning to organize his space. Ancestor portraits are hung high on the wall, by means of a ladder. Then a sideboard is pushed against the only window, partially blocking the light. As though this were not enough, a winter landscape is set on top of the sideboard. Ionesco indicates: "This time the window is completely masked."[45] The movers and the Gentleman contemplate this effect until the first suggest that they turn the bleak landscape around, with the back facing the room. Now the audience sees the backs of the three men, and the blank back of the painting. The Gentleman is satisfied with this arrangement: "Much nicer, more restrained."[46] This is echoed by the second Furniture Mover, and re-echoed in all seriousness by the tenant. The humor lies in the fact that the back of a canvas is discussed in the same terms one uses to speak of a work of art when walking through a gallery. "Restrained" is also the supreme compliment of the average buyer who backs away from anything original, compelling, passionate. Nothing could be more restrained than nothing, and here we have nothingness, life's obverse side. Under the comic effect of these clichés of art criticism lies something terrifying; the new tenant will have no need of a landscape painting, indeed of any landscape, since he is embarking on a voyage into the Void. We are being shown a grotesque, modern Pharaoh, supervising the erection of his pyramid, his tomb.

At last the Gentleman is ready for his armchair; it is wide and high-backed, a throne. At his request, the movers set it at the very center of the chalked circle. However, the flow of the furniture has not abated. New objects invade the cramped quarters: wardrobes, wicker baskets, settees, and even "strange furniture never seen before."[47] The set designer is free to create bizarre futuristic forms, or postmodern amalgams of the ancient and the new. One piece is rejected by the tenant until he is reassured that it does not work: a radio. It is quite obvious from his first encounter with the Caretaker that he will not maintain contact with the outside world. Clocks are another distraction, but since human time will not matter after death they are waved in. The clutter makes it impossible to step or breathe. One of the movers ventures: "There'll be no room left."[48] At this point the Gentleman enters the circle and sits down solemnly upon his throne-chair saying: "Like this there will be."[49] This position prefigures that of Bérenger Ier at the end of *Exit the King,* when the frightened monarch, who has spent the time of the play refusing to face his mortality, accepts the fact of his dying. Here also we are made to realize that the Gentleman is ready to embark upon this final voyage. The main difference lies in that the "tenant" will go with all his belongings, like an Egyptian sovereign, whereas Bérenger is instructed by Queen Marguerite to open his hands and let everything go.

Created in Finland in a Swedish translation (1955), *The New Tenant* was presented a year later in London at the Arts Theatre. The first French production, directed by Robert Postec, took place on September 10, 1957, despite the play having been written as early as 1953.

In spirit and form, *The New Tenant* is close to both *The Chairs* and *The Future Is in Eggs*. Like these two, it is a one-act play written in the delirious style of farce, yet intent on making an enduring universal statement. It has less to say about the Void than about the way in which we fill this emptiness with absurd objects, the result of an ever-accelerated production. We seem to accumulate things in order to bury ourselves under them. The play is a metaphysical farce about death and dying, but it also satirizes social ills. In a larger sense it is replete with political implications. These days, the pale "tenant," his eyes covered by dark glasses, reminds us of Ceaucescu at the end of his tyrannical regime. Romania's strongman, however, was not buried with his gold bathroom fixtures, stolen art works, and packs of hunting dogs; dispatched summarily without a trial, the *conducator* was taken into a blind alley and shot like a dog.

In 1953, the year in which *The New Tenant* was composed, Ionesco turned to the problematics of a theater stripped of all accidental qualities: plot, social character, historical background, dramatic conflict, justifications, explanations. He arrived at the following definition:

> Pure drama, or shall we say tragic action, is then the following: an action of universal significance, serving as a pattern or prototype, which embraces and reflects all the particular stories and actions that belong to the same category as the model action represented. . . . What we need is mythical drama: that would be universal.[50]

In his hauntingly disturbing short play Ionesco transposed to modern times the image of the Pharaohs, living gods who, while yet alive, supervised their priests' and architects' work on the underground chambers and corridors where "herds of concubines, dwarfs and eunuchs, bodyguards and masters of the court"[51] would be walled in after their sovereign's demise. The furniture brought up to the final abode of the "tenant" is not unlike "the royal barges discovered buried in deep rock-cut slots around the mighty pyramids at Giza."[52] Yet, Ionesco carefully banalizes this solemn ritual, uncovering at the same time its infantile character: the hope that all one treasures can be taken into the afterlife. Is this not the hope of all power-mad tyrants, whether dying in their bunkers or strung up to hang, head down, amid a jeering crowd?

Although Ionesco banalizes the situation, reducing the Egyptian priests to common furniture movers, he also widens the everyday situation of becoming "a new tenant." Taking the play even further away from realism, he lets us know that the house stairs are jammed with huge pieces of furniture, and that traffic has come to a standstill, paralyzing the city. It is as though the gradual stiffening of the dying man had infected his town. However, there are still some objects to fit in; they will have to be lowered into the room through the sliding ceiling. Once again this suggests a tomb, one that can finally be sealed.

Now that everything, including the occupant, is in its final resting place, one of the two movers calls out: "That's it. Sir. Are you nice and comfortable? Has the move gone off to your satisfaction?" The man's muffled voice reminds them: "Ceiling. Close ceiling, please."[53] The movers' final gesture is to relieve the Gentleman of his hat, which can be seen "appearing from within the enclosure."[54] This is followed by the pious gesture of tossing in a bouquet of flowers. As the movers prepare to leave, one of them inquires: "Is there anything you want?" A sepulchral voice whispers in the semidarkness: "Put out the light." At this point all the stage lights are killed, and the audience shares the utter darkness with the Gentleman. His last words are "Thank you."[55]

The "new tenant" is a very ancient tenant.[56] As in the later *Exit the King,* a monarch is simply Everyman, a human being, particularly when he must face his ultimate departure from this world. Ionesco presents on the stage a human being's dignified acceptance of his end, as quietly planned as a stoic's suicide. Yet this man's dignity and silence are subverted by the contrapuntal huffing and puffing of the busy movers, and the ridiculous proliferation of useless things. The protagonist's existential situation is oxymoronic: he is renouncing contact with fellow human beings, erecting a wall within walls, yet this very enclosure is composed of material possessions. No sermon could be more persuasive than this crystallization on the stage, reminding us of how hard it is to strip ourselves bare, to face our mortality without the encumbrance of the past. In this short, deeply moving stage poem, tragedy and farce are intimately interwoven; they are one and the same. With *The Chairs* and *The New Tenant* Ionesco moved away from his dada-surrealist beginnings to create an entirely new dramaturgic mode.

Chapter 5

Matter and Air

Victims of Duty, Amédée, A Stroll in the Air

In a talk delivered in Lausanne (November, 1954), Ionesco defined two fundamental states of consciousness in which his plays originate: "an awareness of evanescence and of solidity, of emptiness and too much presence, of the unreal transparency of the world and its opacity, of light and thick darkness."[1] The dramatist suggests that a feeling of airiness stems from the remembrance of the lost paradise of youth, whereas the proliferation of matter constitutes a concretization of human beings' imprisonment in the material universe. Evanescence may be experienced as an estrangement *(un dépaysement),* or bring about a sense of euphoria. Yet there are also times when "anguish suddenly turns into release."[2] The immaterial boundary lines that separate one psychic state from its opposite can be crossed as a result of a leap of the imagination. The experience of joy, however, is a rare occurrence, one that tends to fade with aging. More commonly, what was once sensed as light grows opaque. The "wonder of being alive"[3] is replaced by the density of the world, and of one's flesh. Ionesco mentions fighting "a losing battle."[4] Perhaps the only possible victory over our existential condition can be achieved—ever so briefly—through the exercise of humor. One may not be able to laugh off anguish and terror, but the very act of laughing constitutes the human being's testimony to being. Pascal put it succinctly in the *pensée* in which he compares humanity to a delicate reed: "L'homme n'est qu'un roseau, le plus faible de la nature; mais c'est un roseau pensant" (man is but a reed, the weakest plant in nature, but he is a reed that thinks).[5]

Two of Ionesco's plays express these polar states of being: *Victims of Duty* (1953) and *A Stroll in the Air* (1963). Although a decade separates the two, *Amédée or How to Get Rid of It,* presented a year after *Victims,* skillfully balances the two contrasting apprehensions.

Victims of Duty, Ionesco's favorite, is a self-searching autobiographical tragic farce, his earliest confessional play. The drama's central image is that of the protagonist's gradual sinking into the slimy, marshy soil of the subconscious, a descent into his past and the recesses of his psyche. This probing is elicited by a young detective who enters, unannounced, the Choubert family home. His close questioning suggests simultaneously a police investigation and the process of psychoanalysis. For Ionesco both of the above were intimately connected with his life. As a foreign refugee during the German occupation, he lived in fear of being discovered, a dread that did not even dissipate with his naturalization in May, 1950. In fact, in the fifties he was suffering from insomnia and anxiety attacks. He turned to a Jungian psychoanalyst who practiced a therapy based on "waking dreams," in the course of which the analysand outlined an imaginary journey. His friend Mircea Eliade also suggested "an integration technique" based on his own study of shamanism. In his *Conversations* with Claude Bonnefoy the dramatist offers some revealing details of this process.

> When I was suffering from insomnia, a friend advised me, in order to get to sleep, to imagine that I was climbing a mountain. It's really just a question of an integration technique. I tried it. I would imagine climbing up a mountain that I could see in my mind. It was very difficult at first, very painful, it was almost impossible; but then suddenly, at a given moment, near the top of the slope it becomes quick and extremely easy. I'm climbing, taking large strides, in my imagination. Larger and larger strides: a tiny effort is enough. And I fall asleep, completely relaxed. Actually, the climb that this friend, Eliade, advised me to imagine is an archetypal dream.[6]

This is a key passage to the understanding of the symbolic action in *Victims of Duty.* After a brief moment of ascent, escape, and flight, the protagonist is forced by the analyst/detective, in partnership with the man's wife, to go down and down "where it's deepest,"[7] down where the mud reaches his chin, his mouth, so far down he will drown. The search is on for a missing man by the name of Mallot.

The protagonist's name, although it is spelled in a French style, sounds suspiciously foreign, echoing that of the Austrian composer Franz Schubert. Nor is the choice of the Romantic composer accidental. There is much in common between Ionesco's weltanschauung and that of the creator of "Death and the Maiden." The lines Schubert wrote to his friend, the painter Leopold Kupelweiser (March 31, 1824), could have been spoken by Choubert/Ionesco:

I feel myself to be the most unhappy and wretched creature in the world. . . . Imagine a man whose most brilliant hopes have perished, to whom the felicity of love and friendship have nothing to offer but pain . . . whom enthusiasm for all things beautiful threatens to forsake, and I ask you, is he not a miserable being?

Although *Victims* is a metaphysical cartoon of Jungian psychoanalysis, the play also possesses an early political dimension. It deals with the growth of tyrannical power, what Ionesco calls *libido dominandi,* that is the many ways in which dictatorial governments establish their hold on the people.

Early in the play Choubert discusses with his wife the government's recommendation that citizens learn political detachment. This attitude, which is consonant with spiritual exercises, is cynically offered as a viable solution to economic crises. Deeply wary of this pseudomystical vocabulary, used and abused by a secular authority, Choubert imparts his doubts to his wife. He believes that this suggestion will turn into an order.

In *Victims,* the politics of food are used as a metonymy for the wider struggle of freedom. Food and its obverse, the refusal to be fed (force fed), can be applied to exercise control or—in the case of some dissidents—to elude it. Ionesco's play culminates in a violent scene in which Choubert's mouth is crammed with crusts of dry bread. The protagonist's tormentor is the Chief of Police, who, not unlike Eichmann or Klaus Barbie, defines himself as a soldier, a pawn, a "victim of duty." Later in the play, the questioning is taken up by a failed poet turned literary theoretician. Both these bullies are assisted by Madeleine who, having swallowed the official propaganda line, cooperates with her spouse's torturers. Ionesco's bitter derision demystifies the clichéd notion that there is something noble about being an unquestioning victim of duty.

However, domination may assume various aspects. It starts with the power exercised by parents over a child. Ionesco recalls his daughter refusing to eat when she was a baby. Scolded and coaxed by an over-anxious mother, she would store unchewed food between her cheek and jaw. Ionesco suffered at the sight of the baby forced to swallow the cud it had cunningly hidden. In his vivid imagination this banal family scene was translated into a sadistic exercise of power over the individual, the forced feeding of hunger strikers, the silencing of suffragettes.

It would be a mistake to reduce Ionesco's stage images to allegories. The political subtext is always present, ready to be decoded, but it is subservient to a wider philosophical vision. The politics of food exposes human beings' disconcerting dependence on the material world. On a biological level, Ionesco views ingestion as a sign of the mortal creature's clinging to life, a cowardly, obsessive process. In *Fragments of a Journal,* he describes watching a fellow patient in the sanatorium's dining hall gobbling his food as though every morsel stood between him and his inevitable demise.

> In this dining-room . . . opposite me is a bald old man with a white beard, a healthy old man, what's known as a fine old fellow: fresh-looking, pink-cheeked, he eats with conviction; he chews his food slowly, his walnuts and hazelnuts, in the way he's been told is good for him. He's quite revolting. He knows, or he believes, that what he eats is giving him life; by the end of the meal he's sure he has won another week of life . . . that dogged determination to live, the way he clings to life and won't let go, seems to me tragic, frightening and immoral. . . . It's myself I hate in him.[8]

To take matter into oneself in the form of food is to add to one's own matter. For Ionesco, this is the antispiritual act par excellence. He puzzles over how one "can kiss a mouth that eats, eats, keeps on masticating? Unlike a maw, a human mouth is greedy, unclean." In another volume of his journals he writes:

The longer I live, the more tied I feel to life. I sink deeper into it, I am caught in it, bogged down in it, trapped by it. I go on eating, eating, eating: I feel heavy, torpid, comatose. . . . How hard it will be for me to tear myself away! I have grown used to it; grown used to living. I am less prepared to die.[9]

In his novella "La Vase" (Slime), which was made into a film in which Ionesco himself played the central role, the dramatist depicts a modest traveling salesman who peddles his wares from village to village. He is no longer young and his legs find it increasingly arduous to carry his thickening frame through the countryside. Back at the inn where he has taken up residence, he is served huge meals. In the film, the camera lingers over the laden table, and almost peers into the chewing mouth. The salesman has grown sluggish, his liver is overtaxed, his tongue coated, his stomach bloated. He is nothing but matter, full of more matter.

One day, as he sets out on one of his expeditions, he loses his way. The road leads to a marsh. After stumbling through high rushes, the man falls into the damp, soft soil and begins to sink. Gradually his body disintegrates: his limbs detach themselves from his trunk, his mind from his flesh. He watches one of his hands float away from him as though it had never been part of him. The plump, quivering fingers remind him of fat, white worms. At the end, the head separates from the neck, like a bloom on a rotting stalk; it sinks in the stagnant water. Only a single, staring eye remains for a while on the swamp's surface. It sees, high above the slimy earth, an infinitely remote blue sky, as out of reach as the unsullied "azure" that filled the poet Stéphane Mallarmé with longing and despair. In the novella, the dying man wonders whether the sky he has noticed at last was always there? Had he failed to notice it because of his heavy, lumbering flesh that kept him staring at his feet, at the road he had to tread? Like the wounded Prince Andrei in Tolstoy's *War and Peace,* Ionesco's protagonist glimpses for the first time a universe that has nothing to do with matter, a cosmos of open space, light, and freedom.

So long as we remain attached to our bodies, to our life, we are indeed doomed to being "victims of duty." Perhaps, like Hamlet, Ionesco would like to see flesh "melt / Thaw and resolve itself into a dew."[10] It is through our fear of pain and death that tyrants maintain their hold upon us, use us for their purposes. Ionesco, who perused Hegel in 1931, absorbed this lesson well. The play shows the protagonist reduced to a state of infantilism as his mother/wife and his police tormentors chant: "Chew! Swallow! Chew!"[11]

Victims of Duty: Sinking and Choking

Victims of Duty introduces us into the dull, quiet life of a middle-aged couple leading the kind of existence in which nothing untoward is supposed to happen, least of all the intrusion of a policeman. When this man makes his appearance, he seems a timid, young inspector, who has entered the building in order to track down a certain Mallot (spelled either with a final *t* or *d*). (Incidentally, Mallot with a final *t* would make him French, a final *d* might brand him as a foreigner, although both final letters are not sounded.) The couple is cooperative, inviting the young man to step into their apartment. However, no sooner is he ensconced there, than his attitude suffers a transformation: from the shy youth he was at the start, he turns into a self-assured, threatening presence.

The Detective's arrival does not proceed from the plot of the play; it is absurd because nothing calls for it. Ionesco's antiplays do not follow Aristotle's dictates that "the incidents and the plot are the end which tragedy has in view."[12] In fact, it seems that this character has been summoned by Choubert's remarks to Madeleine, with whom he has been discussing a subject she calls scornfully his "obsession": the theater.

> All the plays that have ever been written, from Ancient Greece to the present day, have never really been anything but thrillers. Drama's always been realistic and there's always been a detective about. Every play's an investigation brought to a successful conclusion.[13]

This passage is replete with inside jokes. There is the ludicrous situation of a seedy couple sitting in their shabbily cozy living room, discussing drama in the style of salon small talk. However, the fact that Choubert, who is not a playwright, is accused by his wife of harboring a pathological passion for the theater is an indication of the autobiographical component of the action to follow. The Detective's materialization out of the blue seems the result of the preceding definition: "There's always been a detective about." He is clearly a character created by words and ideas, not a real person. This dramaturgic device turns the investigation into a play within the play.

The inner play, as has been noted by a number of critics, is patterned on *Oedipus Rex*. In his chapter, "Eugene Ionesco: The Existential Oedipus," Hugh Dickinson, the author of *Myth on the Modern Stage,* states: *"Victims of Duty* consciously borrows one of the most famous of all classic myths, that of King Oedipus, to embody the existential dilemma of modern man and to exemplify the kind of theatre that Ionesco believes must supplant the theatre of the past."[14]

The search for Mallot, conducted upon an inner toy stage, much like that of the guignol Ionesco loved as a child, might be viewed as the absurdist reflection of the quest for Laius' slayer.

Like his ancestors the ancient Greek dramatists, Ionesco wishes to show the particular turning point in an individual existence that brings one face to face with the irrevocable. There may be no sphinxes in Ionesco's modern play, no crossroads where a man, unknowingly, kills his "real" father, but, when the pudgy Choubert invites the Detective to step into his home, he commits a similar rash act. There will be no turning back; it is in fact a "no-exit" situation. Ionesco's final joke on the subject of theater becomes apparent when a disquieting character materializes in the wake of the Detective, the cruel drama critic Nicolas d'Eu (pronounced, in French, Nicolas II), whom the dramatist defines as "the ectoplasmic projection of Choubert's anguish."[15]

Indeed, terror will invade the Chouberts' household as soon as the protagonist asks the fatal question: "Can I help you, Monsieur? Perhaps I can tell you what you want to know?"[16] Indeed, this is a "go-ahead" signal for the policeman to take over and embark on a rampage.

The young man starts out by flirting brazenly with Choubert's frumpy wife, while pursuing his investigation of Mallot's whereabouts. In the process, both Madeleine and the Detective assume various masks. He acts in turn the parts of a doctor, a psychiatrist, the protagonist's father, and a judge. Madeleine undergoes parallel metamorphoses: from aging shrew to sensuous vixen, then, in a reverse movement, from a caricature of the femme fatale back to a slovenly housewife/servant.

Ionesco's characters are neither psychological portraits nor social types; they are universal archetypes. They move through the spacelessness of the oneiric universe in which past, present, and future shift, blend, interweave. In this no man's land of the subconscious, they reveal themselves as figments of the dreamer's memories and obsessions.

Twelve years before Dickinson's study was published, Richard N. Coe wrote, "*Victims of Duty* can be taken as a dramatic illustration of Freud on dreams, or a satire on the Oedipus complex."[17] Although Ionesco views himself as a Jungian rather than a Freudian—he underwent a Jungian analysis with the Zurich-trained psychoanalyst Doctor Ziegler—his first autobiographical dream play stages the classical situation of depth analysis, albeit in caricatural form. The analyst is a double-headed monster, Detective Madeleine, a bizarre father-mother team. The analysand is the tortured offspring made to delve into his past. The play transcends this obvious model, as indeed did Ionesco when he took Freud in the direction of Buddhism. In *Fragments of a Journal,* the dramatist states that Freud listed three obstacles to human freedom: anxiety, pity, and aversion. However, the "threefold chain that binds us" is in reality a "fourfold or even fivefold" one. "Hatred or aggressiveness are equal hindrances to freedom. . . . Desire is the most serious obstacle to our deliverance." Ionesco concludes that "Freudianism can thus, to some extent, be reconciled with Buddhism." The connection exists in Freud's own preoccupation with *thanatos,* the death instinct, and the human longing for rest, "the 'Nirvana instinct.' "[18]

One of the recurrent images of Ionesco's oeuvre is the confrontation between the dead father and the son. Ionesco's rejection of his father, and everything the latter stands for, is connected to the dramatist's profound identification with his abused, betrayed, abandoned mother. On the other hand, after his father's death, Ionesco realized that he was much like him in looks and temperament—though politically and philosophically an abyss lay between the two.

In his journals, Ionesco accuses the clever attorney of collaborating with every passing regime, including the Fascists and the Communists. Because of his father's authoritarian stance, Ionesco associated his progenitor with the police states he eagerly served. Yet, the young man's scorn was mixed with a sense of guilt, the secret awareness that their differences masked fundamental similarities. Choubert cries out to his father's ghost:

> Look at me, look! I take after you. . . . If you would only look at me, you'd see how alike we are. I've all the same faults as you. Who will have mercy on me, I who have been unmerciful! Even if you did forgive me, I could never forgive myself.!![19]

The man unable to forgive himself is also heeding his mother's haunting injunction, echoed in Madeleine's imploration: "The time for tears will come, the time for repentance and remorse, you must be good, you'll suffer if you're not and if you never learn to forgive . . ."[20]

The key to deciphering *Victims of Duty* lies in this overwhelming sense of guilt. Choubert's journey into the self is presented as a spiralling descent into a bog. Heedless of the danger to her husband, Madeleine urges him to sink deeper and deeper. On the stage, the scene reeks of sexuality and violence. The wife sounds like a woman in the throes of desire, a woman calling her man to penetrate her body, sink into her moist flesh. Yet there is a murderous intent in her luring call. Like two accomplices in a Hitchcock movie, Madeleine and the Detective are getting rid of their choking victim by pushing him into the marsh. He is about to disappear, with only a few tufts of hair remaining on the surface (an image that will permeate Ionesco's Kafkaesque novella, "Slime"). The Detective clasps his accomplice in his arms, whispering passionate clichés about being alone at last, just the two of them.

Who is this happy pair, glad to find itself alone at last? It could be Jocasta and Laius, after they ordered the infanticide of their newborn son Oedipus, who, as the oracle foretold, is fated to kill his father and marry his own mother. It might also be Oedipus and his mother/bride, Jocasta, when, following the killing of Laius at the crossroads, the triumphant Sphinx-killer entered the city. When Madeleine cries out: "What have we done! But we had to, didn't we? It's all quite legal?"[21] she echoes Jocasta's double concern over the planned murder of her newborn babe and her doubts over her marriage to a young stranger. Indeed, Dickinson is right when he speaks of the dramatist consciously borrowing the famous classic myth.

However, Coe's definition, "a satire on the Oedipus complex," comes closer to the strangely bitter humor of a play subtitled "pseudodrama." This is the Oedipus myth recreated in the modern context of the Oedipus complex. The Ionesco of *Victims* is the heir of Cocteau's *The Infernal Machine*.

As feelings of remorse intensify, the sensual connection between the two accomplices is vitiated. Choubert, who has reappeared, witnesses a violent quarrel between the pair. The woman threatens suicide, lifting a vial of poison to her lips. Choubert stands powerless, wringing his hands and moaning, "Father, mother, father, mother."[22] Readers of Ionesco's journals cannot fail to recognize a poignant personal recollection: the mother's melodramatic suicide attempt.

Cruelty is given center stage in this autobiographical play. Hugh Dickinson states that Ionesco believes "we are members of one another through hate, not love," and that "a demonic reversal [operates] at the heart of things."[23] This is an irreversible process whereby good intentions become their opposite. To his friends John and Vera Russell the playwright admitted that he found cruelty and hatred "dominant factors in human affairs. A foreigner and a stranger, [he observed that] people are out to kill one another; if not directly then indirectly."[24]

There are, however, moments of relief, avenues of escape. As Choubert is forced to resume his quest of Mallot, he emerges from the depths to scale a steep mountain. All at once, he is filled with a sense of well-being. "It's a morning in June. The air I breathe is lighter than air. *I* am lighter than air. . . . I can float through solid objects. All forms have disappeared. I'm going up . . . and up . . . I can fly."[25] We have here a prefiguration of *A Stroll in the Air*.

However, ecstasy is never long lasting. Choubert comes down with a bang, landing in the wastepaper basket like a rejected manuscript. The gravitational pull is far too strong for beings compounded of matter.

And matter proliferates wildly in *Victims of Duty*, as though some mechanism had started to run on its own. Madeleine, whose lover now treats her as a servant, brings in coffee cups at an exponentially growing pace. She moves like a wound-up automaton, one of the sorcerer's apprentices. The scene is played *en guignol*, Jarry-style. A caricature of the good hostess, Madeleine is much like the Old Woman of *The Chairs*. Here, the cups and saucers pile up on the sideboard forming a miniature pyramid, or perhaps a maquette of atomic stockpiling.

Nothing is more dangerous than the energy of matter propelled in the direction of Non-Being. Ionesco meditates upon the Cains of this world, the tyrants willing to give up their own life at the price of taking everyone with them into the abyss. Obversely, by killing their fellow humans, people may feel that they have some control over their own mortality. Ionesco writes in *Fragments of a Journal:* "The greatest crime of all is homicide. Cain kills Abel. That's the crime *par excellence.* And we keep on killing. . . . By killing I exorcise my own death; the act of killing is part of a magic ritual."[26]

A bizarre Cain figure in *Victims* is that of Nicolas d'Eu, the unexpected guest who materializes out of thin air, much like the Orator in *The Chairs.* With his tousled hair and rumpled clothing, he seems to have emerged from the collective nightmare of our planet's secret prison cells and torture chambers. His name, with its noble sounding *particule* (handle) can also be taken for the number two. Unlike Nicholas II, the hapless last czar of Russia, this Nicolas is not weak willed or uninterested in political matters. He acts in imperious if not imperial fashion when he takes over from the Detective the questioning of his "friend" Choubert. We find out that he is a failed poet, one suffering from writer's block. Since he cannot create he has become a drama critic (one of Ionesco's little jokes against establishment criticism). Like Bartholomeus I, II, and III of *The Shepherd's Chameleon,* he enjoys theorizing, pontificating, thus asserting his superiority. In his view, theater does not reflect the cultural tone of the modern period for it fails to take into account a new kind of psychology. As he crams pieces of dry bread into Choubert's bleeding mouth, this inquisitor of stage craft shouts aggressively an aesthetic that caricatures that of the philosopher Lupasco, and even Ionesco's own dramaturgy: "I should introduce contradiction where there is no contradiction, and no contradiction where there is what common-sense usually calls contradiction. . . . We'll get rid of the principle of identity and unity of character and let movement and dynamic psychology take its place. . . . We are not ourselves. . . . Personality doesn't exist. Within us there are only forces that are either contradictory or not contradictory. . . . By the way, you'd be interested to read *Logic and Contradiction,* that excellent book by Lupasco."[27]

Nicolas d'Eu's fellow torturer claims Aristotelian logic. After all, a policeman cannot afford the luxury of believing in the absurd or sounding the clarion call of the avant-garde. Caught between these rival theories, Choubert is nothing but a passive sufferer. Since a writer needs bread to continue living and creating, he will be gagged with inedible pieces of what used to be the staff of life. The simple nobility of bread has suffered a terrible transformation: its very function has been subverted.

This witty attack on dramatic criticism, and the dryness of pure theory does not disguise the fact that *Victims of Duty* is a powerful political parable. Indeed, Mauclair's 1953 production, in which he played the role of the Detective, must have stirred in the audience painful memories of the German occupation. Today the play continues to speak to us of present concerns: the erosion of individual freedom throughout the world.

Victims works simultaneously on political and mythical levels. The central metaphor, the psychoanalytic process, is appropriate to a confessional dream play written in the modern idiom. It suggests that the uses and abuses of analysis have led to thought control. Choubert, the analysand, is a neophyte forced to take part in a bizarre initiation ritual. He reaches the realization that there is nothing to do except endure *la question* (the French word for both *torture* and *questioning*). The audience witnesses the protagonist suffering the physical torment of forced feeding combined with the mental torture of delving into painful, repressed memories. It is interesting to note that the penultimate volume of Ionesco's intimate journals is entitled *Un homme en question* (A man being questioned).

Victims of Duty is the first panel of a triptych, the other two are Ionesco's final dream plays, *Man with Bags* and *Journeys among the Dead*. In all three, the author weaves his own myths, echoing the voyages to the Kingdom of the Dead undertaken by Odysseus and Aeneas. The model for these explorations is that of the Jungian analysis Ionesco underwent in a disintoxication clinic in Switzerland. The writer's preference for Jung over Freud lies in the fact that "Jung does not ban religion."[28] Like Martin Buber, and Hassidic thought, Jungianism teaches that the way to enlightenment begins with the exploration of one's heart, which is an alembic wherein the archetypal, the personal, and the historical are fused. In this sense, the timid Choubert becomes an avatar of twentieth-century humanity.

The audience may laugh at first at his predicament, but these smiles fade as they realize that his destiny is their own.

Amédée or How to Get Rid of It: Liberation

A year after the creation of *Victims*, Jean-Marie Serreau staged *Amédée* at the Théâtre de Babylone (April 14, 1954). Serreau was to become one of Ionesco's favorite directors, and he was asked twelve years later to stage the dramatist's first play to enter the repertoire of the Comédie Française, *La Soif et la faim* (Hunger and thirst).

Amédée reverses the downward movement of *Victims*. Where the atmosphere was heavy with oppression in *Victims*, Ionesco's new play culminates in the hero's euphoric escape from his stifling home, and from the planet earth; it shows the apotheosis of the comic hero.

Like a number of his subsequent plays, Ionesco's *Amédée* is based on a previously written short story. These tales are collected in *La Photo du colonel* (The colonel's photograph). *Amédée*'s original title was "L'Oriflamme."

Written three years prior to its translation into dramatic form, "L'Oriflamme" describes the existence of a threesome: a married couple and a young corpse, which may be the wife's lover. Did Amédée murder him? No one recalls how he died or why he came to occupy the conjugal bed. Ten years elapsed without the spouses reporting the death to the police. The presence of the body is poisoning the marriage relationship. Amédée recalls the love he and his wife felt for one another, how it suffused the universe with light and warmth. Now they exist in stifling bleakness. The unhappy husband realizes that he must get rid of the body. He proceeds to drag it by the hair to the window, lifts it out, and lowers it onto the street. As the body spills out, the pull is so strong it seems to wrench the apartment's entrails and the fabric of the married pair's life is torn asunder. The act of ridding the family of the corpse reverses the process of birth as it signals the rebirth of the comic hero, Amédée.

Having tossed the corpse through the window, Amédée rushes out into the street. Something has to be done with the cumbersome corpus delictis. The body, however, has suffered an astonishing metamorphosis: it has become weightless. Winding itself around Amédée's body, like an umbilical cord, it buoys it up. Amédée's rise in the world, and above it, is applauded by all the neighbors. His wife, however, shouts for him to turn back, claiming that he has not risen one bit in her esteem.

Shortly after the premiere of the play based on this story, Ionesco was interviewed by *Combat* (4/8/54). He stated that he was trying to depict with maximum realism, even naturalism, the tragic life of a married couple, while preserving something of the mystery that pervades all human relationships. He also added a significant statement: "I try to discover within myself a forgotten universe, lost archetypes, myths which express man's deepest desires."

In a 1953 article written for *Arts,* Ionesco analyzes the way in which the artist views the world, its inexplicable absurdity, the gratuitousness of the *thereness* of objects, people, and language. He then adds:

> But when, on the other hand, one lets one's apparitions blossom into life, still faintly bearing the dark traces of violent, incoherent passions, one knows that these rival forces will tear one another in their vehemence, finally giving birth to a work of high drama.[29]

The married couple in *Amédée* may be average, even petty bourgeois, but the "traces of violent, incoherent passions" are visible everywhere. The shabby apartment to which they have been confined throughout their married life is convulsed by the intrusive presence of the huge legs of a corpse, projecting from the bedroom into the only other room, a combination of living room, dining corner, and work space; it is a veritable microcosm. Madeleine, a switchboard operator, has installed the instrument of her trade in a corner of the room, between the window and the door. When she goes off to work, she merely removes her housewifely apron and shawl, sets aside her broom and duster, and, after donning a hat, sits down at the switchboard. Unlike her husband, an unsuccessful dramatist—Ionesco cruelly satirizes himself and his *ménage*—Madeleine maintains contact with the entire planet. She is the breadwinner, while feminized Amédée, with the feminine looking first name, shops for food by lowering a basket out the window. The couple has given up stepping beyond the confines of their cramped quarters.

Of course their home has grown unbearable on account of the

corpse's relentless geometric progression. Not content with occupying the only bed in the offstage bedroom, it requires constant care, like a plant, or a pet. Madeleine trims its finger nails and the toenails that shoot through its shoes. Amédée dutifully picks the poison toadstools sprouting in the shade cast by its huge legs. Once short of stature—like the Ionesco couple—the dead man has grown monstrously tall, acquiring the long, white beard of a patriarch. *Amédée* tries to calculate his age: he was twenty when he wandered in (this may mean that Amédée and Madeleine were that age when they first fell in love), and since that time fifteen years have elapsed; the corpse is thirty-five years old. "Not really old . . . ," the husband suggests. Madeleine replies with perfect absurdist logic: "The dead grow old faster than the living."[30]

Indeed, nothing seems more ancient and dead than a dead love. The body in the bedroom is the perfect concretization of *désamour* (the falling out of love). And yet, perhaps because it represents a love that once illumined the couple's modest interior, this corpse is endowed with a strange kind of beauty. A green glow issues from its eyes, which are wide open, casting a strong beam into the living room. As this strange flesh grows and multiplies, it emits a weird, enchanting music. Both Amédée and Madeleine are fascinated by these phenomena, although they find the corpse's presence repellent.

A fervent reader of Baudelaire, Ionesco translates into dramatic terms the magnificent imagery of "Une Charogne," one of the poet's most striking metaphysical poems. In the poem, a narrator (the poet himself) describes a walk he takes with a woman he loves. On the road, they come across the putrefying corpse of an animal, probably a dog. The poet describes the carcass, alive with buzzing flies and crawling worms. The dead flesh seems to move, rise, multiply.

> Tout cela descendait, montait comme une vague,
>   Ou s'élançait en pétillant;
> On eût dit que le corps, enflé d'un souffle vague,
>   Vivait en se multipliant.
>
> Et ce monde rendait une étrange musique,
>   Comme l'eau courante et le vent,
> Ou le grain qu'un vanneur d'un mouvement rythmique
>   Agite et tourne dans son van.[31]

These two stanzas convey the completion of the cosmogonic cycle. Like Paracelsus, Baudelaire (who held poetry to be verbal alchemy) believed that decay is the start of rebirth. A poem, a play, a work of art are all aspects of the *vas* (the alchemist's vessel) wherein the process of transubstantiation takes place. At the end of "Une Charogne," the poet addresses his mistress in an envoi, reminding her, much as Ronsard did his ladies, whether real or invented, that a woman's flesh is doomed to decay and putrefaction; in the end, she will be like the dead bitch spreading obscenely in the sun her wide-open belly. However, the woman's flesh, preserved within the mold of the poem, will rise again glorious and pure, transformed by art into an object of beauty.

Perhaps it is to contemplate the decomposition of an emotion once vibrant and life-giving that Madeleine keeps on sneaking into the bedroom. There she spends hours contemplating the luminous, humming corpse. However, though graced by a strange, otherworldly beauty, the dead body is afflicted by cancerous multiplication. Not content with its own growth, it contaminates the whole apartment so that mushrooms sprout under its huge feet. These are the visible signs of hidden guilt.

One recognizes in *Amédée* the Oedipus myth, as basic to this play as it was to *Victims of Duty*. Amédée does not recall having murdered a man. Was his victim a young man whom he surprised with his wife, or a baby entrusted to them by a neighbor? He now looks so ancient that the infanticide could be taken for a parricide. Is the corpse that of the infant Oedipus, formerly asleep in a crib next to his parents' bed? Or is it the body of King Laius, slaughtered at the crossroads? Are Madeleine and Amédée ever to be forgiven for having killed this baby, or this grown man?

Guilt and fear are forcing the couple with the foreign-sounding surname (Buccinioni) to live behind closed shutters. They are in hiding, much like the Ionescos during the German occupation of France. In fact, when a postman delivers a letter to Amédée, the recipient is so terrified that he denies his identity. The postman's regulation uniform may have suggested to the writer, and to his 1954 audience, that of Maréchal Pétain's police in the so-called free zone. As for Amédée denying his identity, it is phrased in the neo-Spanish of the Professor's philology class in *The Lesson:* "I am not A-mé-dée Buccinioni. I don't live at 29 Generals Road, but at 29 Generals

Road. . . ."[32] The postman seems convinced he has the wrong party, but his bureaucratic zeal drives him to require a signature. Quaking with fear, Amédée refuses. Finally, the postman retrieves the unwanted letter, muttering under his breath that in this case the signature is "purely optional."[33]

Today, Ionesco's audience finds this scene absurdly comical, yet no one who has lived through the German occupation of France, or as a foreign refugee under a dictatorship, would do so. The importance of anonymity under such conditions is critical. Losing one's anonymous status might mean arrest and deportation. Ionesco's sensibility is that of an Eastern European, an archetypal stranger and wanderer deeply marked by the trauma of fascism. When he speaks with some irony of being a realistic writer, he might well be referring to this disturbing scene.

This is only one of the passages in the play that is written in coded language. Another such passage awakens echoes that have to do with secret documents or letters. As in the case of dissident literature, one must learn to listen to certain lines with the help of an inner ear in order to decipher the subtext. Here, for example, is a conversation between the spouses about the cumbersome corpse, which is a growing embarrassment that endangers their existence:

Amédée: He's growing faster and faster!

Madeleine: Do something, can't you!

Amédée: (appalled, desperately) There's nothing to be done, nothing. There's nothing left for us to do, I'm afraid! He's got geometrical progression.

Madeleine: Geometrical progression!

Amédée: Yes . . . the incurable disease of the dead! How could he have caught it here with us!

Madeleine: (losing control) But what's to become of us! Good God, what's to become of us! I told you this would happen . . . I was sure of it . . .

Amédée: I'll fold him up . . .

Madeleine: That won't stop him getting bigger. He's growing all the time in all directions at once! Where are we going to put him? What are we going to do with him? What's to become of us![34]

The verbs *fold* and *roll up,* when speaking of a human body, particularly of "a stiff," send the attentive reader or listener on an unexpected track. At first glance this description is comical, but it also suggests written matter: a manifesto, a tract, perhaps a dissident text, or an underground publication. Viewed in this light, Madeleine's anguish takes on a somber coloring, and her "What's to become of us!" suggests a familiar political situation.

Because the oedipal motif in *Amédée* has been stressed to the detriment of the others, it is important to decipher the play's historical and political code. The Ionescos were political refugees in France when the country was overrun by the very forces they had fled. In the provincial backwaters where they lived in hiding their Romanian name would have made them suspect. Despite its claim to liberalism, France has always suffered from a dose of chauvinism. A foreign sounding name is defined as *un nom à coucher dehors* (a name that condemns you to having all doors barred against you). The Buccinionis' cloistered existence, their phobia of the postman, their concern with what their neighbors might think are reminders of a situation brilliantly exposed in Ophuls's film *The Sorrow and the Pity.*

Amédée and Madeleine know that their situation is precarious, their life at stake. One of their guilty secrets is that they are foreigners. In occupied France, people often said of foreigners or even refugees from Paris: *"Ils viennent manger notre pain!"* (They've come to eat our bread!). The closing lines of act I resonate with this precise memory:

> Amédée: We've still got some food in reserve, Madeleine! Macaroni, mustard, vinegar, celery . . .
> Madeleine: (collapsing) We shall go a long way on that. . . . I don't care, I can't stand it any more, it's too much.[35]

The foodstuffs listed by Amédée belong on the whole, with the exception of celery, to the staples one could stock up for future use. However, one cannot exist on a diet of pasta. During the German occupation meat, butter, eggs were rationed, and people were constantly devising ways in which to purchase them from farmers in the country or black marketeers. Thus, Madeleine's exclamation: "We shall go a long way on that!" is bitterly ironic. In this passage, the heaviness of matter (stocks of provisions) is of little use. It is rather the weightiness of circumstances that seems beyond one's control, the more unbearable when there is "no one to turn to for help or advice."[36] The isolation suffered by such people as the Ionesco couple, refugees and foreigners in a country held by a ruthless enemy, is eloquently conveyed by this line.

Structurally, *Amédée* could be called a well-wrought play. It is Ionesco's first drama in three acts, with a steady progression from one act to the next. The play has a typical comic ending, the joyous escape and liberation of the hero, which also symbolizes the liberation of France at the end of World War II. Were it not for the surrealist strangeness of the central image (the growing corpse), one would be inclined to agree with Ionesco when he says, with perverse wit, that he is the true representative of realism in art.

However, his realism takes the form of well-worked-out, precise weirdness. In act 1, for example, the huge feet protruding into the living room are said to advance "about eighteen inches on the stage."[37] However, despite this presence, life goes on almost as usual. Act 2 shows a cluttered living room, with many pieces of furniture that have been moved from the bedroom into the only space left to the couple. Like the New Tenant, Amédée and Madeleine are walled in by their belongings. Here, however, the atmosphere does not have the somber grandeur of the short sketch. Husband and wife dart about, trying to avoid the legs of the corpse that extend further and further into their space. The atmosphere is that of a bomb shelter, or of an improvised dwelling under the condition of exodus.

Her nerves frayed, Madeleine launches an attack on her husband: he is a congenital dreamer, incapable of taking any kind of action. She has lost her job as switchboard operator, and there is no money coming in. Amédée promises he will get rid of the corpse tomorrow. His wife cries out she can no longer tolerate his *mañana* philosophy; the deed must be performed this very night.

While the couple waits for the fading of the light, Amédée has a vision, Ionesco's play within the play. Amédée II and Madeleine II appear before the dreamer's eyes; the dream couple is young; it is their wedding day. The bridegroom moves eagerly toward his veiled bride. Throughout the scene he conveys a sense of ecstasy, a lyric state of mind. Still true to her nature, the young Madeleine is a whining realist. She takes her poet-husband for a simpleton. This scene is directly culled from the story "L'Oriflamme." Although the couple plays this sketch "quite naturally,"[38] it is less about two human beings than about two diverse ways of apprehending the world: poetic versus disenchanted realism. The first term of the dialectic is characterized by a feeling of airiness, of dazzlement, the second by murky darkness, cold, the wetness of rain-soaked earth. In alchemical terms, the poet is the embodiment of *aurum philosophicum, aurum mercurialis, aurum volatile* (philosophic; mercurial, light gold; not common gold), while his wife is still plunged in the *massa confusa* (undifferentiated primal matter).

Ionesco, the poet-playwright, illustrates two ways of being and seeing in the brief exchanges between the two young people. The bridegroom intones joyously: "Madeleine, wake up, let's pull the curtains, the spring is dawning.... Wake up... the room is flooded with sunshine... a glorious light... a gentle warmth!" However, her response is: "night and rain and mud!... of, the cold!... I'm shivering... dark... dark... dark! You're blind, you're gilding reality! Don't you see that you are making it beautiful?"[39] This last statement is a reproach, not a compliment. While the poet believes they dwell in "a house of glass, a house of light," Madeleine echoes a distortion of this illumination: "House of brass, house of night!"[40]

Through the long years of marriage Amédée has changed, losing his enthusiasm, catching from his wife the malady of practicality and sadness. From his armchair, Amédée moans: "Time is heavy. The world dense. The years brief. The seconds slow.... Nothing but holes... the walls are tottering, the leaden mass subsides."[41] Has he sunk in *prima materia*?[42] Somewhere within this slow-moving, reticent, disheartened, failed writer lives the young Amédée II; it is he who will be able to eventually fly into the sky.

It is also Amédée the poet who breathes in the fragrant night air as he opens the window to cast out the dead body. This is one of the magic moments in Ionesco's play. The stage directions are as explicit as those of Chekhov. Here Ionesco becomes a painter, a set designer, and a lighting specialist; he reveals that for him the stage vocabulary is as important as the text. He indicates: "There is a striking contrast between the sinister room and the dazzling light effects. The mushrooms, which have not stopped growing, are now enormous and have silvery glints... the atmosphere of the married couple's

room . . . must suggest the mingled presence of horror and beauty."[43]
This last statement is an aesthetic program.

Amédée's soliloquy at the window is written in the lyrical mode.
The protagonist's gaze is directed up, above the tops of acacia trees
in bloom. The heady odor wafts into the room, rising like incense.
Once again the earthbound poet is able to forget his environment and
dream of wide-open spaces. The heavens are remote and yet infinitely
tempting. Ionesco's cosmic evocation echoes the visionary language
of *The Book of Revelations:* "The Milky Way is like creamy fire. Hon-
eycombs, countless galaxies, comets' tails, celestial ribbons, rivers of
molten silver, brooks, lakes and oceans of palpable light. . . ."[44]

However, the dreamer must be brought back to earth; there is a
job to be done. The stifling room is bulging at the seams with the
corpse's growing frame. As Amédée begins to pull the body across
the floor, it unrolls with a tremendous crash, plaster falls from the
ceiling, the whole set shakes. Madeleine is doing her best to assist her
husband, but she is actually hampering the process. Amédée moans:
"He's harder to pull out than an old wisdom tooth . . . tougher than
an oak."[45] The grand simile from nature is undermined by the comical dental one. The latter may be a key to the murder mystery, the
couple's guilty deception. In French you say *"mentir comme un ar-
racheur de dents"* (to lie like a puller of teeth). As the couple pushes the
body out the window, their secret life will be exposed for all to see.

Eventually the husband runs out into the street to continue pull-
ing on the body, which hangs like a bed sheet put out to air. Inside
the room, Madeleine regrets their decision, yet begs Amédée to go
faster. Her heaving, the body's progress through the room (womb)
suggests a painful parturition. At last the deed is done. To complete
the final steps of this second murder, Amédée must cast the corpse
in the nearby Seine. This Hitchcock operation is orchestrated by the
woman who sounds as though she is shouting from childbed:
"Pul-l-l. . . ." The curtain falls on this painful delivery.

Act 3 takes places outside, in little Torco square. For the first
time in fifteen years Amédée finds himself in a crowd. To be sure
this is not high society, but the atmosphere is celebratory. American
jazz music escapes from a brothel bar in which shadowy figures can
be seen dancing. American soldiers are everywhere, filling the bars,
the streets, ambling through the square. Ionesco has clearly tied his

play to a precise historical moment: the epoch of France's liberation, the end of World War II. But this image is also colored by his child-hood recollections, that of seeing for the first time U.S. soldiers in the tiny village of La Chapelle-Anthenaise at the end of World War I. His love for everything American can be traced back to this experi-ence. These happy memories of an eight-year-old child, combined with the relief felt by Eugene and Rodica Ionesco when they were able to emerge from hiding, constitute the joyous climate of the third act.

Indeed, the U.S. soldier Amédée bumps into while dragging the corpse in the direction of the river is jolly and helpful. After all, a corpse to be disposed of holds no surprise for a man who has just returned from the front. The soldier asks no questions; he simply solves a physical problem with pragmatic common sense. "Taking hold of Amédée by the shoulders and winding the body around him, the American spins [him] like a top."[46] Amédée becomes a living gadget, a musical toy. He and the corpse are now one, a whirling, humming flying machine.

By now, the French police are in hot pursuit of the criminal. Ionesco treats us to a classical silent flicks chase scene right out of the Keystone Cops. The dramatist who claims to belong to "the cabaret school of literature" is the true heir of the artists of "the Banquet Years," particularly Jarry and Erik Satie. For him, as for these in-spired practical jokers, "humor . . . [is] a method and a style."[47] Yet, mockery and the art of clever pastiche do not mask an underlying, ever-present commitment to serious thought. *Amédée* speaks on many levels: the mythical, the psychoanalytic, the literary, and the political. For a complete reading of the play these various levels must be considered at one and the same time. An Ionesco play acts like a symbolist poem that addresses the mind, the heart, the senses, and the memory.

At the end of this play it is clear that the Americans are the liberators, the allies, whereas the police are reminders of Vichy France. To escape from the fascists, Amédée will have to flee and fly. Ionesco writes careful stage directions, as detailed as those of a film script: "The body wound round Amédée's waist seems to have opened like a sail, or a huge parachute; the dead man's head has become a glowing banner. . . . Amédée is flying out of reach of the policeman."[48] The word *parachute* adds still another dimension; it harkens back to the time when British and Free French paratroopers were dropped behind enemy lines.

As Amédée begins to rise, there are joyful exclamations. People crowd the balconies, hang out the windows, wave handkerchiefs. There is music, dancing in the street, fireworks. (In conversation, Ionesco explained that he wanted to recreate a Bastille Day celebration.) Below, the people celebrate the freedom they have regained—all except the abandoned Madeleine—while above, we are treated to a cosmic "astral carnival."[49]

A sense of total jubilation informs the end of the play. One is reminded of the days when De Gaulle's Free French troops, walking side by side with their U.S. allies, entered Paris to be greeted with flowers and kisses. It seemed then that the very fabric of life could be changed, that this had been the war to end all wars.

Amédée is neither a historical play, nor a political allegory, at least no more than Aristophanes' *Peace*. However, both of these comedies hint at a set of circumstances that were familiar to their contemporaries: the peace of Nikias and the liberation of France. Although neither play is tied to its particular situation, both have in common an irreverent kind of wit and a boundless zest for living. The comical apotheosis of Ionesco's failed playwright, "a caricatural self-portrait,"[50] is as provocative as Trygaios' straddling of the dung-beetle, the grotesque war horse he uses to invade the Olympian heights. Aristophanes' Common Man is successful in bringing down to earth the sweetest of all deities, the young goddess Peace. In the Ionesco play, peace may not come down in person, but her spirit is everywhere once the heroic antihero emerges from his stifling home. His escape into the heavens shows that repression is over, at least for that time. In the spirit of new beginnings, Ionesco's antihero achieves the kind of *gloire* associated on the French classical stage with the heavenly enthronement of an Alexander the Great, the seventeenth-century symbol for Louis XIV, the Sun King.

Ionesco's protagonist flies up because of the spirit of freedom that fills his whole being; it is the triumph of soul over matter. As he sheds his suit jacket, letting his cigarettes and shoes fall to the ground, together with the corpse's hat and beard, we witness the protagonist's decisive victory over subconscious feelings of guilt and fear. This is one of the rare plays by Ionesco in which we are treated to a happy ending—perhaps because the ending is not merely personal, but suggests one of those rare utopian moments when people and peoples are united in a single aspiration for freedom and peace.

A Stroll in the Air: Flight

"To fly is indispensable to man . . . it is as natural as breathing. Flying is an innate faculty . . . luminous and childishly simple."[51] With these words, Ionesco's Bérenger—his Everyman—proceeds to test his newly acquired gift of levitation. Leaving his earthbound wife and daughter among the British strollers—the locale of the play is an idyllic image of the English countryside—the protagonist rises like an astronaut without a spaceship. The air that fills his lungs is the breath of inspiration.

In an article written in New York at the time Ionesco arrived in the United States to supervise the rehearsals of *Rhinoceros,* the dramatist discusses humanity's dream of flight:

> I declare . . . that the world lacks boldness—and that this is the reason for our suffering. And I affirm that dreams and imagination, rather than a routine existence, require courage and reveal fundamental, essential truths. As a matter of fact (this is the concession I am making to those who believe only in the useful and the practical), if nowadays planes fly across the skies, it is because we conceived the dream of flight long before we succeeded in flying.[52]

Ionesco's poetic intuition is paralleled by the great naturalist Loren Eisley in his book *The Immense Journey.* The scientist describes waking up at dawn in New York and looking out of his hotel window. High above the streets, among the spires and cupolas of the metropolis, white-winged birds glide soundlessly. At this early hour the city belongs to them. They respond to a radiant light that has not yet reached the canyons and alleys below, a light imperceptible to the human eye. Eisley's vision is akin to a poet's revelation:

> As I crouched half asleep across the sill, I had a moment's illusion that the world had changed in the night, as in some immense snowfall, and that if I were to leave, it would have to be as these other inhabitants were doing, by the window. I should have to

launch out into that great bottomless void with the simple confidence of young birds reared high up there among the familiar chimney pots and interposed horrors of the abyss.[53]

The poet-dramatist reflects upon our modern inventions while the scientist muses in the fashion of the artist, envisioning casting himself out of the window to try his imaginary wings. Both share a common longing for communion with the cosmos, and a knowledge that this kind of thought is an act of defiance that requires physical and intellectual courage.

A scientist in thematics, a poet among literary critics, Gaston Bachelard is the author of a series of books on the poetics of the four elements. *L'Air et les songes, essai sur l'imagination du mouvement* is particularly relevant to *A Stroll in the Air*. Bachelard states that "air is a matter of our freedom."[54] It liberates us from our attachment to matter, to the material world. King Lear warned his daughter Cordelia that "Nothing will come of nothing,"[55] but he was wrong both on philosophical and practical grounds. There is great value in nothing, in self-induced detachment. Thus, in poetry, whenever we encounter the image of air, we find ourselves close to "dematerialization."[56]

The dream of flight is such a common occurrence that many have reported that upon awakening they could not believe this faculty was not within their powers. Bachelard brings numerous examples to bear upon these affirmations, particularly from the poetry of the English Romantic poets. He reaches the conclusion that "air is a kind of metaphysical hormone which allows us to grow psychologically."[57] When we dream of rising, the horizon expands, the sky stretches out; we are aspired by infinity. One does not fly in order to ascend to heaven, one ascends to heaven because one is able to fly. Nor is this done by means of wings affixed to human shoulders. Most often, Bachelard argues, flight is related to giant steps, winged feet. In order to retain his or her humanity, even in the process of entering another sphere of existence, the dreamer enhances an existing human feature. To walk vertically at first, the progress along a high curve, is to be at once a human being and a demigod.

Bérenger's self-achieved ascent begins with a light-footed stroll in the company of his beloved wife and daughter. The idyllic setting is that of Wordsworth's ballads, but illustrated by *le douanier*

Rousseau. There are pear and cherry trees in bloom, a tiny white cottage (not unlike Dove cottage)—the house Bérenger rented in the English countryside—children at play, and neatly dressed strollers moving slowly, hieratically, as though they had just stepped out of Georges Seurat's *Sunday Afternoon at the Grande Jatte*. In the distance one catches sight of a toy cable car going up a gentle hill, so that the scene is an amalgam of England and Switzerland, two of Ionesco's favorite vacation sites. Later, a toy train runs across the stage as tiny lights blink, and all kinds of Lilliputian props are set in motion by stage machinery. There is something delightfully childlike about this bucolic first scene that suggests that life on our planet could be peaceful, gracious, civilized. This vision is rooted in Ionesco's childhood years at La Chapelle-Anthenaise and the cult of childhood established by the Romantic movement. It suggests that a revaluation of the concept of maturity is needed, that we must not put off the naïve, trusting attitude of the child in favor of being reasonable adults. As Roger Shattuck explains in his *Banquet Years:*

> The history of the modern movement begins with a reaffirmed innocence of all attitudes and techniques that have made the arts beautiful and instructive and adult. Rousseau, unconcernedly starting his career at the age of forty, painted himself back into the years he had lost; in that lies his greatness and his modernism. The atavistic-prophetic monstrosity of *Ubu Roi,* a play that Jarry wrote at fifteen, and Satie's limpid piano pieces "for tiny hands," composed when he was over fifty, show a similar response to an earlier self. But Rousseau's entire career was devoted to creating the universe of a grown-up child.[58]

One can see from the above the extent of Ionesco's debt to Jarry, *le douanier* Rousseau, and Erik Satie. Indeed, one could also say about him that having started his career late in life, he sought to reproduce the green paradise of his childhood years in a French village. He is, like Rimbaud, a "child-man." The universe of *A Stroll* is a make-believe one, stilted, stiffly polite, but profoundly reassuring. For Ionesco, a passionate Anglophile, England represents a haven; it is the blessed isle that, during World War II, managed to preserve its distinctness from the continent thanks to the narrow Channel, which was still not easily crossable. England is the hallowed ground Hitler was unable to invade.

However, London was not spared cruel bombings. A reminder of these raids occurs early in *Stroll*. A plane literally comes out of the blue, cloudless sky, and drops a bomb on Bérenger's modest cottage. The house is totally destroyed, but the writer escapes with his life, if not his manuscript. The plane is not contemporary; it is a ghost bomber from World War I, an absurd tiny engine of destruction lost in time and space. In the dramatist's private mythology it is a reminder of the death of his father-in-law, killed in that war. Indeed, Ionesco introduces into his play a moving encounter between Josephine, Bérenger's wife, and her father's ghost. We recognize in this encounter between the living and the dead the seed of Ionesco's final dream play, *Journeys among the Dead*.

As to Bérenger, despite the loss of his material possessions or perhaps on account of being bereft of the weightiness of ownership, he experiences a dizzying, irrational joy. As a result, his steps get increasingly lighter, turning into childlike skips. Every jump takes him a bit higher, off the earth's surface. His wife is embarrassed by his undignified behavior, particularly among the staid population. She fears that they will never obtain a renewal of their visas—again a reminder of the Ionescos' precarious situation in occupied France. Josephine is not wrong; the Britishers find this display of high spirits (so literally expressed) quite shocking. No proper gentleman walks in such a manner. However, Bérenger's exalted mood remains undampened. He senses that something is buoying him up. Now that he treads air, the mature writer—Bérenger is a successful artist, unlike Amédée—recaptures the wonder he knew as a boy.

Jean-Louis Barrault's 1963 production of the play was a masterpiece of the genre. Barrault, who played Bérenger, recaptured the body language he used to enact the mime Debureau in the film *Children of Paradise*. It was hard to believe he was lifted by thin cables; he seemed to float naturally, convincing his audience that a human being can free himself or herself from the gravitational pull. He rose on a circus bicycle, which promptly disintegrated, allowing the cyclist to pedal in air. Next, Bérenger/Barrault made his way up along an invisible tree, one as high as Jacob's ladder. The performance suggested a joyous, daring circus act, a *salto immortale* rather than *mortale*.

Ionesco's principal intention for the play was to set images and characters in motion. He was excited by the prospect of scenes in which the set would slide, props materialize and dematerialize. One can find the seed of this fascination in his 1959 "Talk about the Avant-Garde":

> I would like to bring a tortoise onto the stage, turn it into a racehorse, then into a hat, a song, a dragoon and a fountain of water. One can dare anything in the theatre and yet it is the place where one dares the least. I want no other limits than the technical limitations of stage machinery. People will say that my plays are nothing but music hall or circus. So much the better; let's bring in the circus.[59]

Ionesco, the would-be aerialist and prestidigitator, was magnificently served by the theater magician and mime Jean-Louis Barrault.

In theater history the form best suited to fulfill Ionesco's wish is the *féerie,* or machine play, whose origins can be traced to the Italian ballet troupes favored by Catherine de Médicis. They had been the centerpieces of the *grandes festes* given on the occasion of a princely or royal entrance into a city. Thus, the dolphins and griffins of Jacques Callot's engravings, faithful records of these happenings, found their way from the parade ground onto the royal stages. As stage techniques improved, the Italian entertainers moved from the Louvre into a theater Mazarin had erected at the Tuileries for the performance of these popular machine plays. Both Louis and the Sun King called on their favorite dramatists to write and stage *féeries.* The leading master of this genre was Jacques Torelli, who accompanied a troupe of Italian players in 1645 to the theater of Le Petit Bourbon. For his *Stroll,* Ionesco chose to recreate this Renaissance form, adapting it to the epoch that witnessed space travel.

Bérenger circles the earth in a delirious space walk. One of the Englishwomen counts more than two hundred complete circles. The strollers no longer see Bérenger, who has risen too high; for the earthbound he has become a luminous ball of fire, a comet. Finally impressed by her husband's feat, Joséphine admits: "He really is someone after all!"[60]

Unlike Amédée, Bérenger will finally float down to earth. This Odysseus returns home to a sarcastic Penelope, but the tidings he brings are of doom. From all the way up, at a point where space and time meet and mingle, he has glimpsed deserts of fire and deserts of ice. They are slowly moving toward the planet earth. For a while longer (in cosmic time), it will remain verdant, but one day all life shall perish. This apocalyptic vision will also inform Ionesco's later play *Exit the King*.

Nor is our planet the best of all possible worlds. A scene in *Stroll* reveals that Ionesco is haunted by the Holocaust, a fact that became incontrovertible after the publication of his first opera libretto, *Maximilien Kolbe*.[61] At the core of Ionesco's seemingly light-hearted *féerie* we have a Massacre of the Innocents.

This brutal scene is introduced by Joséphine's appearance before a court of law composed of grotesque, gigantic puppets, seven to ten feet tall. The Judge is dressed in a long, crimson robe, and his enormous doll's head is topped by a square red hat. He is flanked by two assessors, also dressed in red, but not as tall as he. The court of law sits on a platform that glides forward on rails. Joséphine is terrified and she protests her own innocence: "I haven't done anything wrong, your Honor. . . . Why do I have to appear before you? What am I accused of? I haven't done anything. . . . I've nothing to hide, I swear I haven't. . . . Why make *me* the scapegoat? . . . Do you want to punish me because I've been unhappy?"[62] Marthe, her daughter, keeps on assuring her that this apparition is nothing but a nightmare, a figment of her imagination, so that, were she to refuse acknowledging it as a reality, it would vanish. However, this nightmare is only too real, as was that of the death camps. Some words in Joséphine's text clearly suggest Hitler's genocidal program: *scapegoat* and *unhappy*. The last word is not an allusion to persecuted peoples (Jews, Gypsies), but an autobiographical hint that the abandoned Josephine is Ionesco's mother, the victim of a Romanian court of law that granted her husband an uncontested divorce.

The grotesque Judge and his Assessors are, under their masks and robes, average citizens who practice unhesitatingly what Hannah Arendt called "the banality of evil." As though to disprove Marthe's assertion that they are phantoms, the second Assessor removes his hood; it is John Bull, John Arbuthnot's personification of the average Englishman. However, this common man is carrying a machine gun that he aims at children accompanied by their mother. This group of innocent people is followed by the undertaker's man and a doctor.

The children are shot as a measure of "preventative mercy-killing."[63] Although there is much talk about the advantages of preventive medicine, we wonder what preventive euthanasia might be. The answer can be culled from the pages of Lucy Dawidowicz's *The War against the Jews*. She lists the following facts: "In spring 1939 Hitler regularized [a] procedure of killing mentally deficient and physically deformed children. . . . Having set in motion the official destruction of 'racially valueless' children, Hitler turned to the murder of the adult insane."[64] Panels of experts were convened to decide whether the practice of euthanasia ought to be regularized, and in regard to which groups. Dawidowicz states that five thousand children were put to death, and that the installations erected to carry out this program were later used for the mass gassing of Jews in death camps. "Preventative mercy-killing" is a euphemism, like "the final solution."

In *Stroll,* Joséphine is horrified to see her own uncle, a doctor, among the murderers. He explains to his niece that he never ordered these killings, but is merely going along with what has been sanctioned. Ionesco is exposing in his play the misuses of science as practiced by Nazi doctors. In *Present Past Past Present* he states: "Anything can be supported, anything can be proven by the sciences. People do what they please with science."[65] The most horrifying of all Nazi crimes were those committed against small children and infants. These children were the first taken to the gas chambers, together with their mothers, or burned alive in the crematoria. Others were used as guinea pigs in so-called scientific experiments, such as the ones conducted on twins by Doctor Mengele. The short scene in *Stroll* is a devastating sketch of these practices:

> John Bull: Doctor, will you verify that these children are well and truly defunct.
> 2nd Lady: I protest, It's absolutely disgraceful. It shouldn't be allowed. (To the Doctor-Uncle) You call yourself a doctor, and you accept it all just like that?
> Doctor-Uncle: I don't accept it. I'm resigned to it.
> Joséphine: What, is it you, Doctor-Uncle? You're not in this too?
> Doctor-Uncle: (To Joséphine) This way, you see, I shall avoid being judged myself. . .

. . . .

Joséphine: I'd never have thought you could behave so contemptibly.

Doctor-Uncle: What do you expect, my poor Joséphine? We all acquire wisdom in time. Besides, it's better that way. In any case it was bound to happen. It's all over much quicker this way. It's better sooner than later, much better to be thirty years early than two seconds too late.

Joséphine: You, you who've saved so many human lives, thousands of children . . .

Doctor-Uncle: This is how I redeem myself.[66]

This short final statement is one of the most bitter and pessimistic in Ionesco's entire oeuvre. Men such as the doctor-butchers of Auschwitz had not only perverted the Hippocratic oath, they turned against life itself. Such men were in the service of death.

In *Fragments of a Journal* Ionesco expresses repeatedly his amazement at the virulence of anti-Semitism. He also offers a philosophical meditation on its roots:

The greatest crime of all is homicide. Cain kills Abel. That's the crime *par excellence*. And we keep on killing. I have to kill my obvious enemy, the one who is trying to put me to death, in order that he shall not kill me. In killing him I find relief, for I am obscurely aware that I have killed Death. By killing I exercise my own death; the act of killing is part of a magic rite. When the Germans killed the Jews they did so with a clear conscience, for they "killed in self-defence."[67]

This myth, springing from ancient superstitions, seems all the more monstrous and unaccountable for a man who believes that the Jewish people "invented love, the love of others, fatherly love, divine love."[68] He concludes that this must be the reason for accusing them of hatred, and in turn for despising them.

As for Joséphine, in her nightmarish vision she finds herself condemned to death despite her claim to a clear conscience, and there is no one to protect her from harm. She exclaims sadly, giving voice to Ionesco's own despair: "My father's dead, my mother's dead, all my family are dead. The neighbors who used to know us have left

the town where I was born, and scattered all over the world. . . .
Once I had my parents who were big and strong. . . . I've never got
used to them not being there. And I never shall. Never, never. . . ."[69]
Why has she been condemned? The mendacious explanation she is
offered is that since she is bound to die sooner or later—mortality
being humanity's common fate—it might as well be now. Not convinced by this line of argument, she pleads for a tiny delay, using the
famous words of Madame du Barry on the scaffold: *"Encore un moment, Monsieur le bourreau!"* (Give me a little longer, Monsieur Hangman).[70]

A Stroll in the Air appears at first glance as a light-hearted *féerie*
on the subject of interplanetary explorations, but it is actually an
extension of the autobiographical dream play that preceded it, *Victims
of Duty*.[71] It bears the imprint of Ionesco's own fears and sense of
guilt, as well as the haunting images of absurd genocidal extermination. When Joséphine begs: "Punish the wolves, if you like, but *I'm
a lamb*,"[72] she speaks for all those who entered the portals of the
Nazi camps.

There are of course numerous light touches, such as the bizarre
appearance of the Visitor from the Antiworld, who makes his way
through the strollers, smoking an upside-down pipe. This is no
ghost, simply a casual passerby from another planet. Bérenger believes that "negatives of our universe"[73] exist, spaces where people
have "antiheads."[74] One has only to consult language to have ample
proof, for instance the expression "The world turned upside
down."[75] There are also "in jokes," winks addressed by the playwright to his audience as when one of the children, a girl, "produces
a series of trills, just like a mechanical nightingale."[76] She is exposed
as "the little bald prima donna"[77] when an impish playmate lifts the
wig off her bald head. This self-quotation is in the tradition of Molière's *L'Impromptu de Versailles,* the model for Ionesco's future *Improvisation or the Shepherd's Chameleon*. But this airiness is a shimmering veil cast by the ex-dada prankster upon the unbearable naked
truth.

In *Journeys among the Dead,* two women discuss the philosophical
question at the core of the playwright's apprehension.

> Madame Simpson: God is great, but greater than what? I say
> "My God," but I don't know who he is.

Arlette: Maybe he's Matter—but then we don't know what Matter is either.[78]

Perhaps not to know is a way of knowing.

Chapter 6

Bérenger: Birth of an Antihero

The Killer and *Rhinoceros*

The dramatic character Bérenger, Ionesco's Everyman, is born in *The Killer*. Although he loses his life at the end of the play, he rises again in *Rhinoceros*. The protagonist of *A Stroll in the Air* is also called Bérenger, and is possessed of personality traits similar to those of his predecessors. The king in *Exit the King* is Bérenger Ier, a tragicomic sovereign, a petit bourgeois tyrant. From one play to the next, Bérenger remains true to himself, a recognizable Ionesco type.

Unlike Amédée Buccinioni, with his foreign-sounding name, Bérenger is one hundred percent French. In most of the plays in which he appears he does not have a Christian name, except in *A Stroll* where his wife Joséphine calls him "Herbert." There is nevertheless one element in common between Buccinioni and Bérenger: their surnames begin with the second letter of the alphabet. This suggests that Ionesco wished to establish a continuity between his protagonists, but with a marked, consciously chosen emphasis on the latter's Frenchness.

For the French, Bérenger echoes the name of a well-known nineteenth-century song writer, Pierre Jean de Béranger. His satirical poem "Le Roi d'Yvetot," an attack on Napoleon, was sung all over France. Nor did his rebellious spirit endear him to the Restoration. He was imprisoned twice for his dissident compositions. Shortly before his death, Béranger began working on a treatise he was not to complete, *Social and Political Morality*. His funeral in 1857 brought the Parisians down into the streets. They stood, heads bare, watching the procession and shouting: "Glory and honor to Béranger!" This minor bard was one of the lucid and courageous political dissenters of his day. The name Ionesco chose for his protagonist rings with echoes of liberalism and defiance. It is an indication of the playwright's political orientation.

What type of man is Ionesco's Bérenger? What did the dramatist have in mind when he created him? First and foremost, he is what Ionesco calls "a specialist in survival," an essential quality for the twentieth-century human being. He is of course a self-portrait. Although Bérenger is not usually a writer—in *Rhinoceros* he is a modest office clerk, not unlike Ionesco himself at the time he wrote *The Bald Soprano*—he has the kind of sensibility associated with the artistic personality. He reacts deeply to the beauty of nature, and is possessed with an extraordinary capacity for experiencing the emotions of love and friendship. There is something oddly old-fashioned, romantic about this man. This makes him vulnerable, touching, perhaps slightly ludicrous but also very dear. Despite his real affection for his fellow men and women, he is basically a loner. Some might consider this a fault in his character, but this failing will serve him in good stead, preserving him from a wide-spread epidemic: rhinoceritis. In every play in which Bérenger appears, he retains his modest humanity to the end.

Bérenger may seem a passive kind of person, but his very reluctance to make decisions, to be a leader, protects him from getting involved in ideological struggle. Crowds frighten and repel him. He is certain of one thing only, that a human being ought not impose his or her goals and programs on fellow citizens. Thus, Bérenger's outward passivity becomes the source of a gentle kind of strength. An eccentric, he believes that people ought to be allowed to live according to the dictates of their individual conscience. In short, Bérenger is a humanist, albeit a comical one.

Many critics have called Ionesco a pessimist. Nothing could be further from the truth. His plays do not leave us with a feeling of despair, for the protagonists are often full of hope, trust, human kindness; they are ready to fight for what they believe. Art, for Ionesco, is one of the ways in which we oppose the dark forces of the irrational, and affirm the spiritual dimension.

The haunting theme of death in Ionesco's work is not proof of a neurotic personality as much as it betrays the meditative attitude of a poet-philosopher. Ionesco never stops feeling amazement at the knowledge that the world in which he lives, and which also lives in his person, will be obliterated. In order to preserve this particular universe, at once private and universal, he feels that he must put together the many fragments that constitute it. In *Present Past Past Present* he states: "I am trying to restore a world by putting its bits and pieces together again so as to bear witness that there has been such a world."[1] In his private journals (some pages of which remain unpublished), he claims a victory over time: "Yet this will have existed. No one can prevent this from having existed."[2] To bear witness to what has existed, to that little world of the self, is all we can achieve, yet it is enough to justify one's whole life.

Bérenger is Ionesco's witnessing self. He is both a type and an individual. He is a structural entity, separate from society. Ionesco has often stated that he is profoundly suspicious of the structural form of groups, and of mass psychology. For him it is the self, not society, that is "a complete self-evident truth."[3] Groups do not possess consciousness; they either obey blindly, or lead as a pack. Higher consciousness always transcends group thought. When he created his Bérenger, Ionesco brought into being a character who is nothing if not a questing, questioning self, a hero of thought, and even, in spite of himself, a hero of action.

Based on his short story "The Colonel's Photograph," *Tueur sans gages* (The killer) was written in London in 1957. It was staged two years later by José Quaglio in the small Salle Récamier (600 seats). The director, Jean-Marie Serreau, played the role of the Architect. Nicolas Bataille, the creator of *The Bald Soprano,* was the ambiguous, disquieting Édouard, and Claude Nicot played Bérenger. The premiere was attended by many celebrities: Albert Camus, Jean Tardieu, André Rousseaux.

Interviewed for *Le Monde* by Claude Sarraute, Ionesco spoke jokingly about his new drama: "It's a detective play written in the pure classical tradition of this genre, or rather the falsely classical tradition of fake detective plays. . . . It's a mystery plot dreamt by someone who has turned it into a nightmare."[4]

The press was far from unanimous. Robert Kemp of *Le Monde* was negative, with the exception of the final monologue, which he found interesting.[5] Pierre Marcabru of *Arts* called it Ionesco's best play to date.[6] *Carrefour* compared Ionesco to Dostoyevsky. The critic

(M. L.) wrote: *"The Killer's* intention is to reduce all of us to the condition of peaceful, stupidly happy sheep."* Although this is hardly complimentary, he went on to say: "Ionesco's theatre is making *entre-deux-guerres* drama obsolete. We are made to enter a kind of inverted tragedy where man no longer addresses the gods from below, but, setting himself in their place, gazes at himself as though he were one of them. His laughter is the divine chuckle of the Olympians."[7] Even Gabriel Marcel of the Institut, who always attacked Ionesco in the *Nouvelle Littéraires* had to concede that *The Killer* was the dramatist's "most intriguing play."[8] However, he claimed to not understand the significance of the character Mother Peep. In the *Express,* Robert Kanters compared Ionesco to Beckett and Kafka, calling the play "a theological parable."[9] The most stimulating essay was written by Jacques Lemarchand for *Le Figaro Littéraire.* He entitled his piece "A Dramatic Symphony," and summed up the theme with his customary lucidity: "The theme of *The Killer* is the abysmal lack of responsibility of society in regard to the presence of evil in its midst, an evil that aims to destroy its very fabric."[10] With this play, Ionesco's reputation began to reach the English-speaking world. Orson Welles intended to bring *The Killer* to Broadway. What a pity this did not come to pass!

In *Present Past Past Present* Ionesco writes these bitter words: "People like killers. And if one feels sympathy for the victims it's by way of thanking them for letting themselves be killed."[11] Danton could not have spoken more eloquently from the scaffold.

The Killer is an inadequate translation for *Tueur sans gages,* a poetic oxymoron invented by Ionesco. A literal translation would be "the unhired gun." The French title suggests that this assassin is not a *"tueur à gages"* (a hired killer), but a being who derives a kind of perverse pleasure from the gratuitous, serial murders he perpetrates. At the time Ionesco wrote this play (London, August, 1957), terrorism had not yet proliferated. Today, this play is more timely than ever, much like Jules Feiffer's *Little Murders.*

Although no one has seen the Killer, it is known that he uses a device to lure his potential victims: he shows them "the Colonel's photo," and while they are engrossed peering at this brutal face, with its Stalin-type mustache and lurid grin, he pushes them into the fountain in the public square where they drown. Why people should drown in a shallow fountain is never explained, it is part of the absurd situation. As for the Colonel, with his uniform and military medals covering his chest, he is the embodiment of oppression and war. The fact that so many are fascinated by his picture suggests that the masses are subject to overwhelming masochistic impulses, to the death wish that Freud saw as underlying most of our patterns of behavior. They admire ruthless power, and endure dictation.

The Killer's criminal activities take place in a technological utopia, "the radiant city." The name suggests one of Le Corbusier's projects, but it transcends concrete references by alluding to the New Jerusalem. When Bérenger reaches this neighborhood by accident (he stayed on the street car to the end of the line), he finds himself in a place so perfect, so pleasing to the eye and all the senses, that he is filled with euphoria. The district is bathed in an even, gentle light, the sky is a dazzling blue, the flowers are all in bloom. It is an environment that reproduces the mythical memory of paradise. For the readers of Proust, there are hawthorn bushes. Everything is perfect, perhaps a bit too manicured, like condominium communities for the aged. On second look, however, there is also something amiss. The streets are deserted, the shutters of the rose-covered cottages closed tight. If this is the Garden of Eden, then a worm seems to be feeding on the fruit of the Tree of Knowledge.

The creator of this ersatz Garden of Eden, a modern bureaucrat, is also the technocrat par excellence. He is only one of the cogs in a complex hierarchy of faceless executives. At first, Bérenger is full of awe for this efficient, clearheaded scientist, but soon he discovers that the Architect has studied a variety of subjects and filled various positions, all of them having to do with science: medicine, psychiatry, sociology, surgery. He is the embodiment of the New Man, practical and efficient.

In one of the play's most ironic scenes, we are shown the Architect/Psychiatrist listening with one ear to Bérenger's confessional outpourings, while his other ear is glued to the telephone receiver. He explains: "Don't let it upset you too much. I have two ears; one for duty and the other I reserve for you. One eye too, for you. The other's for the borough."[12] As Bérenger, a latter-day romantic, speaks rapturously of "those reasonless reasons for living and loving,"[13] the Architect shouts into the receiver: "Hullo, the supplies have run out!"[14] Deeply moved by his own confession, the analysand echoes: "Yes, I'm afraid they have, Monsieur."[15] This is a perfect example of quid pro quo: Bérenger is assuming that the psychiatrist (the Architect's function at the moment) is referring to the waning of vital powers, whereas the bureaucrat is simply discussing with an invisible interlocutor some technical matter. As he himself explains: "I wasn't saying that to you, it's about my files."[16]

When the Architect takes Bérenger on a stroll through the radiant city, the two men come upon a shocking sight: three corpses are floating in the lovely public fountain. At this point, the technocrat assumes still another public function, that of police inspector. As such, he is unruffled by murder, inured to it.

As a municipal civil servant, the policeman is not in danger, nor is Bérenger, so long as they are together. In the bistro located at the edge of the district, the Inspector launches into a lengthy description of all the crimes and disasters he has witnessed. Bérenger, however, is not able to reconcile himself to the misfortunes befalling humankind. He exclaims that he plans to make use of all his powers of "unreason" to track down the assassin who has turned this replica of Paradise into a breeding ground for evil and death.

Ionesco will not allow us to forget that great crimes have had their theoreticians. The Killer's plan, a minute by minute schedule comprising the complete list of past and future victims, his visiting card, and a stack of the Colonel's photos, is found by Bérenger in a most unexpected place: his friend Édouard's briefcase.

When we first see Édouard (act 2, scene 2), he is a weak, mysteriously ailing man, who has found his way into his friend Bérenger's apartment where he is awaiting the latter's arrival. Bérenger is puzzled by his friend's presence, and even more by the fact of his entry into his locked quarters. Éouard reminds his reluctant host that the latter handed him a key to his apartment, encouraging him to make use of it whenever he felt the need for it. Bérenger is hard put to recall any such arrangement, and so Édouard's presence remains a mystery. It is, however, deeply disturbing, suggestive of the fact that people must not count on privacy, that the sanctity of their home may be broken. A European audience would no doubt be reminded of police searches and confiscated possessions during the German occupation of its neighbors. Édouard, the faceless clerk, is not unlike the unexceptional youth Heinrich Himmler, who took over the *Schutzstaffel* (Defense Corps), converting it into a brotherhood formed along racial lines. When the Nazis came to power, the SS numbered fifty thousand members. Their mandate was to be the unremitting guarantors of the internal security of Germany, sniffing out the subhumans who might pervert the order of the Reich with their Jewish-Bolshevistic conspiracies.

Faced with the fait accompli of his friend's infiltration of his home, Bérenger tells him of his discovery. However, Édouard does not share his friend's indignation, which upsets Bérenger further. He cries out: "Your indifference makes me sick."[17] These words also awaken familiar echoes: they remind us of the world's indifference in regard to the atrocities committed in concentration camps. The question we must ask ourselves is whether Édouard is truly unmoved. He seems so ill, so close to fainting that one can hardly expect him to have any strength left for compassion. Bérenger becomes aware of his visitor's predicament and, setting aside his righteous indignation, grows solicitous: "When you're ill yourself, when you're really a sick man . . . it's hard to get carried away by something else. . . ."[18] This apology revives the spectral intruder, who suggests a stroll in the fresh air. Always amenable, the exhausted Bérenger consents to step out. The cadaverous Édouard picks up his briefcase and sets it upon the table. As he does, the case springs open, spilling its contents all over the tiny room.

The stage business that follows is a terrifying piece of black humor presented in vaudeville form. Objects tumble out as though the case were a magician's trick box, its bottom part open upon the yawning gulfs of Hell. First to fall out is a whole set of the Colonel's photos. It is followed in quick succession by the bric-a-brac of our civilization: pins, pens, pen holders, boxes, sweets, children's watches, clothes, crutches, toys, brushes. In Jacques Mauclair's revival of the play there were artificial flowers and skull caps. It looked as though the contents of the glass display cases of the Auschwitz Museum had been emptied all over the stage. The clothing in particular suggested the confiscated belongings of prisoners sent to the gas chambers. The children's toys were heart-rending, mute metonymies of genocidal murder.

Édouard denies any knowledge of these contents, particularly of the documents found by Bérenger. Buried under the flotsam and jetsam of pathetic things, once cherished personal possessions, lie the

Killer's diary and his master plan: "January 13th: today I shall kill . . . January 14th: yesterday evening I pushed an old woman with gold-rimmed spectacles into the lake . . . January 23rd: nothing to kill today. January 25th: nothing to get my teeth into today either. . . ."[19] If the first date is not chosen at random—it is connected with the popular superstition about the number 13—some of the others are even more revealing. A month after Christmas day the monster's desires and designs have become exacerbated. Clearly, this is one of those creature spawned by modern urban life. Ionesco's murderer is the archetypal criminal of the tabloids raised to the level of natural disasters such as earthquakes and floods.

Édouard, faced with this incriminating evidence, can only stammer: "I'm ashamed . . . I can't explain . . . I don't understand. . . ."[20] He sounds about as innocent as Eichmann in the Jerusalem courtroom. In fact, the Killer's plan, accompanied by detailed maps and a hit list, suggests Hitler's *Mein Kampf*. The comparison is reinforced by Édouard's statement that these papers were handed to him with a possible publication in view. However, he is unable to say who left them with him, and in what manner they found their way into his briefcase. His vagueness is typical of the world's blindness in regard to Hitler's rise to power, and his mysterious malady symbolizes Europe's disarray in the face of ruthless determination.

Bérenger, however, will not allow himself to be paralyzed by Édouard's evasiveness. He has made up his mind to find the Killer and bring him to justice, even if he has to do it single-handedly. His search is not merely a personal crusade; it is paradigmatic of all human longing to eradicate evil.

Not that this is an easy task. In act 3, the loss of Édouard's briefcase in the midst of Mother Peep's political rally, followed by the realization that it now seems to belong to the monstrous concierge-queen, suggests that evil infiltrates every strata of society. Mother Peep, an avatar of Jarry's Mère Ubu, feeds her followers, a mob of goose-stepping geese, the kind of double-talk they expect:

> We won't persecute but we'll punish and deal out justice. We won't colonize, we'll simply occupy the countries we liberate. We won't exploit men, we shall make them productive. We'll call compulsory work voluntary. War shall change its name to peace, and everything will be altered thanks to my geese.[21]

This grotesque *Magna Mater* (the archetypal Great Mother) figure is a terrifying amalgam of Hitler, Mussolini, Stalin, the Argentinian generals, Pol Pot, Den Xiaoping, and Saddam Hussein rolled into a single, fat, blood sausage.

The crowd at the rally is getting high on Mother Peep's pep talk. There are loud shouts of "Long live Mother Peep! Long live the geese!"[22] Predictably, Édouard joins in, echoing the enthusiastic response to these slogans. There is a lone dissenter, a man in top hat and tails. Dead drunk, he nevertheless clutches a briefcase. For a moment, Bérenger hopes he has found Édouard's missing case, the evidence he plans to take to the police. However, when he gets hold of it, he discovers it contains nothing but half-empty wine bottles.

Paradoxically, the dipsomaniac is the only member of the crowd to raise the subject of heroism. As he stumbles in, he is shouting that what is needed is "the rehabilitation of the hero."[23] In the meanwhile, Mother Peep is promising to force the intellectuals to parade in perfect goose step. Thus, the stubborn determination of the tyrannical leader is opposed only by the hiccuping ravings of a sot. Édouard questions the drunk, asking him what he means by hero. The answer is lucidly phrased: "A hero? A man who dares to think against history and react against his times."[24]

Might this be Ionesco's own definition? If it is, he has thrown us off the track by having it delivered by a tipsy dandy. Toward the end of a longer discourse, the dissenter takes a swig from one of the bottles in his attaché case. Thus, the whole speech ends in a visual joke, a circus clown act. As for the questionable Édouard, the fellow traveler par excellence, he sums up the spirit of the times when he remarks: "It's heroism to think against the times, but madness to say so."[25]

According to the above definition, Bérenger is undoubtedly a hero. He certainly "thinks against [his] times," but he is not afraid to say so. There is a touch of sublime madness about this modest, self-effacing man who looks like Sancho Panza but is possessed of the daring of Don Quixote. This comical character may not have set out to be a hero, but gradually he reaches the realization that, since no one else will move a finger, it is up to him to act. In the course of the play, he will become a Molieresque clown: the hero in spite of himself.

Caught in the goose-stepping mob, Bérenger is delayed reaching in the police station. Dusk is thickening. The traffic cops, assigned to control the crowd, mock the frantic man instead of assisting him. Clearly these bullies would not listen or do anything beyond their circumscribed duty. They merely send the protagonist on his way.

Their guidance leads him to a deserted neighborhood, chilled by a glacial wind; it is a kind of no man's land. As Bérenger walks on and on, the set behind him moves so that that the audience gets the feeling that he has wandered far and lost his bearings. Suddenly, he catches sight of a puny man sitting astride a low wall. There is nothing distinctive about the man's appearance, nothing frightening either, except for a way of holding himself, and a sneer accompanied by an inane chuckle. This is the Killer, and he is the incarnation of "the banality of evil."

Ionesco's play ends in a long monologue-dialogue. Bérenger is the only speaker, the one able to manipulate language, to use it as a weapon and a shield. Yet, it will prove a useless tool against the Killer's conscienceless indifference; his sole response is a soft snicker. The stage directions indicate that it is up to the director to use an actor for the Killer, or simply to have the audience imagine him. Essentially, Bérenger is arguing with himself, or with an aspect of himself. Shot through with blinding moments of ontological apprehension, the final monologue is a profoundly metaphysical *Grand Guignol*.

Bérenger's initial reaction when he catches sight of the Killer is a mixture of amazement and amusement. The dreaded murderer is so small, weak, pale; like Édouard, he looks as though a flick of someone's fingers would make him keel over. Could this ratty runt be the relentless force that has annihilated so many? Today, as we watch old newsreels showing Hitler gesticulating and ranting, we find it difficult to imagine that this grotesque puppet was the charismatic leader who unleashed the demonic machinery of a world conflagration, and that of the death camps. In this play, with its political and metaphysical subtexts, Ionesco has caught a deeply puzzling truth.

When Bérenger tells the Killer: "I could put you in my pocket,"[26] he is not merely referring to the man's puny size. Although this phrase is meaningless in English, it is a French colloquialism to state that one has complete control over a person, that the latter, be he or she a high ranking bureaucrat or politician, will do one's bidding. It implies that this person has been "bought," that he is in the pay of the one who controls him. Thus, Bérenger assumes at first that the *"tueur sans gages"* (the unhired killer) might be a regular *"tueur à gages"* (a hit man). It is difficult for men and women of good will and sound common sense, people such as the protagonist, to fathom the irrationality of evil. Ionesco's Bérenger is constantly looking for causes, for reasons and reason: "I want to understand. You're going to answer my questions. After all you are a human being."[27]

To pursue this line of inquiry is both futile and dangerous. Bérenger would have been wiser had he made his escape in time. It is useless to enter into philosophic argument with terrorists or even narrow ideologues. But Ionesco's hero makes the typical mistake of all humanists: he tries to solve the enigma of the murderer's psychology. Does this man wish to destroy all human beings indiscriminately? What might his view of personal happiness be? Since the only answer Bérenger receives is an idiotic snicker—the sound of Satan's laugh in the desert—he tries to provide his own answers. Thus, he is drawn gradually into the criminal mind. He ventures: "I don't suppose you believe in happiness. You think happiness is impossible in this world, don't you? You wish to destroy the world because you think it is doomed."[28] The bizarre monologue-dialogue has veered, become a colloquy between Being and Non-Being, Life and the Void.

To take an innocent life is an absurd, mindless act, but to enter into argument with the absurd is to deliver oneself into the hands of its blind, grinding power. Bérenger may have started to argue *against* the murderer's act, but he ends up speaking *for* it, mustering reasons for killing: "Perhaps you think the human race is rotten. Answer me! You want to punish the human race, even in the person of a child, the least impure of all creatures. . . . We could debate the problem publicly if you like, defend and oppose the motion, what do you say?"[29]

The idea of establishing a miniature United Nations made up of two members facing one another in a vacant lot, would be pitiful and grotesque were it not for the many useless debates of the Security Council. These charades are often played out by representatives whose minds are made up in advance because they have received directives from their governments; no one can convince anyone under such circumstances. In a passage that must have been written in the late thirties, the author of *Present Past Past Present* speaks up in the sorrowful tones of a wrathful Jeremiah:

Just look at them; just listen to them. They do not avenge themselves, they punish. They do not kill; they defend themselves:
defense is legitimate. They do not hate, they do not persecute;
they render justice. They want neither to conquer nor to domi-
nate; they want to organize the world. They do not want to drive
out tyrants but to take their place; they want to establish real
order. They wage holy wars. They have hands full of blood,
they are hideous, fierce, they have animal heads . . . [30]

These "hideous," "fierce" creatures with "animal heads" are already
the herds of rhinos of Ionesco's future play. Like his Bérenger, the
dramatist started wondering early in life whether the human race was
worth saving. As a member of this vicious tribe, he asks himself a
terrible question: Is he worthy of the gift of life? He is filled with
doubt as to his own intentions. He might be a martyr aspiring to
become a hangman. The dialogue of the Killer and his victim goes
on within the dramatist himself.

The dialectic movement of Ionesco's thought can be analyzed in
his journals where he explores a number of paradoxical behavior
patterns. Some people, he says, commit suicide because they are
driven by a fear of death so overwhelming that they anticipate its
inexorable coming; others kill in order to conjure that same fear,
redirecting it onto the Other who is also Oneself. Heroes are privileged; they may kill in good conscience, with the total approval of
their society. Of course they also sacrifice themselves, giving up their
life for the society whose model they are, or the god that society
worships. Thus, all heroes are "half in love with easeful death."[31]
On the contrary, antiheroes wish to destroy within themselves this
nihilistic love and fear of death that drives men of action to impart
annihilation. This purgation can be achieved only by facing with
complete frankness and courage this hidden terror. Thus, in the final
monologue of *The Killer,* Bérenger is psychoanalyzing both himself
and society.

As Ionesco's protagonist tries to persuade the Killer not to kill,
tries to convince him that life is not absurd, he is sinking deeper and
deeper into nothingness. It is as though the gaping silence, interrupted only by the murderous snicker, absorbs his whole being. In
the midst of this moral quest, a strange idea surfaces; it is formulated

as a question: "Perhaps you kill all these people out of kindness! To save them from suffering!" Mercy killing for Ionesco, as we have seen in the preceding chapter, is a disguised form of legal murder. Bérenger exclaims: "You think like others before you that man is and always will be the sick animal in spite of all his social, technical, or scientific progress, and I suppose you want to carry out a sort of universal mercy killing."[32] We are reminded of the experiments of Doctor Mengele, or of Doctor Kurt Heissmeyer, who inoculated Jewish children with tuberculosis at the "clinic" of the Neuengamme camp, on the outskirts of Hamburg. At the Magdeburg trial, Heissmeyer stated that he could not perceive any basic difference between "Jews and guinea pigs."

Bérenger suggests that the Killer ought not to hasten the inevitable end. Time passes quickly and people will have "a whole eternity of *not* suffering."[33] Does the Killer despise all mankind? Perhaps no more than Bérenger/Ionesco does his own flesh, cringing nevertheless at the thought of its dissolution. As he stares into the glittering eye of the Killer, he sees mirrored within it his own emotions: fear, hate, self-hate. He does not see, however, his own kindness, nor his ability to forgive and forget.

After such knowledge, how can anyone believe the Killer could be talked out of his purpose? Clearly, not a single word spoken by Bérenger has had any effect; they are a form of derision, one that echoes the Killer's snicker, and is echoed by it. In vain will the protagonist pile up humanity's arguments against Non-Being: the religious, the philosophic, the sociological. Finally, at his wit's end, Ionesco's antihero proclaims himself a nihilist. The European intellectual has given up, allowing the murderers, the terrorists, the tyrants to take over. Bérenger's final point is an argument *ad absurdum:* "When you know everything is dust and ashes, you'd be a fool if you set any store by crime, for that would be setting store by life."[34] Life and crime are at last equated. The Killer has persuaded Bérenger, not the other way around.

Deprived of all his powers of persuasion, Bérenger begins to laugh, mocking the Killer. He tells the speechless snickerer that everyone will take him for a fool, "a crank who 'believes' in crime."[35] The protagonist's hollow laugh suggests that the murderer's demonic derision has penetrated the soul of the lone crusader, corrupting his thinking, and issuing from his lips as though projected by a medium. Bérenger is laughing at himself, for it is he and no one else who is "the idealist . . . the simpleton."[36]

As the Killer takes out his pocket knife and begins to toy with it, Bérenger is brought back to the reality of present danger. He sees his enemy in all the latter's beastly ugliness. He can no longer afford the luxury of identifying with his would-be murderer. Now he must fight to the end. Slowly, a hero emerges, slightly ludicrous perhaps with his antiquated pistols, but also the last of the humanists. The antihero must now become a true hero.

It would be too simple, however, if Bérenger could shoot his assailant. Although Ionesco's protagonist aims his pistol at the criminal, he is unable to carry out his intention. This is not out of cowardice, or weakness, but for a very obvious reason: unlike his opponent, he is not a killer. Slowly, solemnly Bérenger lays down his weapon on the ground. With head bent and kneeling, as though in expectation of the *coup de grâce,* he stammers a final question: "There's nothing we can do. What can we do . . . What can we do?"[37]

A person of good will, brought up in the tradition of humanistic Western thought is no match for a terrorist, or an asocial psychopath. Determined killers, Ionesco suggests, always ruled many part of the world, and will continue to do so. But it would be a mistake to read *The Killer* as a simple political allegory. The political dimension is present, awakening echoes of our present and our recent past, yet Ionesco is principally a metaphysical dramatist, and he is dealing here with our universal anguish at the thought of mortality. Even killers must die. When their time comes, how much dignity will they be able to muster. By depersonifying death, mass killers unveil the nakedness of dying, and by imparting death, they must face their own unavoidable demise.

The Bérenger of *The Killer* is the representative of an age in which people still believe in one's ability to control destiny, and one's own manner of dying. It was once a noble illusion. Perhaps this is why the dramatist shows his protagonist armed with antiquated weapons. He is not the New Man. In fact, Ionesco has much to say against the latter:

It is as though there were two human races: Man and New Man. The New Man seems to be different from Man not only psychologically, but physically. I am not a New Man. I am a Man. Imagine that one fine morning you discover that rhinoceroses have taken power. They have rhinoceros ethics, a rhinoceros philosophy, a rhinoceros universe. The new master of the city is a rhinoceros who uses the same words as you and yet it is not the same language. The words have a different meaning for him. How can we understand each other? . . .[38]

From this imagery the next play was born. In the meanwhile, *The Killer* shows the nobility and grace of one who remained nothing but "a Man." Bérenger's bowed head and kneeling posture suggest prayer rather than imploration. He knows something his murderer does not, nor ever will, namely that it is useless to kill the Other for you are only killing yourself, not your fear of death. As the Killer draws closer and closer, raising his knife, the antihero-hero accepts nothing more but also nothing less than what Ionesco calls "a human permanence."[39]

One afternoon, in the winter of 1960, as I sat discussing *Rhinoceros* with Eugène Ionesco, who had arrived for the New York performance of his play, we started talking about the concept of the antihero as it applies to Bérenger, both in *The Killer* and the newer play. Ionesco was in a relaxed mood and he began to explain:

My hero, if indeed he can be called that, is not so much an antihero as a hero in spite of himself. We must go back to the time when I was a young man in Romania. I was amazed to witness the total conversion to fascism of everyone around me. It did not happen overnight of course; it was a gradual process. Little by little, everyone—the professional men, the intellectuals, the so-called liberals—found sufficient reason to join the party in power. You would run into an old friend, and all of a sudden, under your very eyes, he would begin to change. It was as if his gloves became paws, his shoes hoofs. You could no longer talk intelligently with him for he was not a rational human being. Then again, there were those who rationalized their chameleonic transformations, men like my father. His legal training enabled him to justify all his shifts of allegiance. He was an instinctive Hegelian; to him History was Truth and Truth History. I left home just as soon as I could, but there were still my colleagues at the lycée where I taught, my literary friends and acquaintances. All of them had swallowed Codreanu's propaganda. Later they transferred their allegiance to Hitler's ally, General Antonesco. I could see the handwriting on the wall: I was to remain alone with my opinions. I often felt that I was the last human being left in the world, among creatures of some other genus. Not that I belonged to a superior kind, or race, but that a strange responsibility had befallen me, the most insignificant of creatures, that of remaining who I was, a human. It was frightening to think that it was somehow up to me to do something, in fact, to do *everything*. Just by retaining my humanity, I was opting for something difficult, so unlivable. Such is, I believe, the plight and the privilege of the modern hero. His strength stems from what may be taken for weakness. In my early journal entries, written while I was still in Romania, I said that all around me men were metamorphosed into beasts, rhinoceroses. I forgot these notes, jotted down in an old notebook. After I completed the short story on which the play is based, and then this play, I happened to come across this ancient entry. I was astounded to discover that the central image had come to me in 1940.

In *Present Past Past Present,* published in France in 1968, one finds the echoes of this early apprehension:

I have been present at mutations. I have seen people transformed beneath my eyes. It is as if I had come across the very process of metamorphosis, as if I had been present at it. I felt them becoming more and more strangers. I felt them withdrawing little by little. I felt how another soul, another mind germinated in them. They lost their personality, and it was replaced by another. They became other.[40]

In the same book, Ionesco actually uses the word rhinoceros, as well as hyena and dog.

The dehumanization he witnessed is translated in various ways in his oeuvre. In his first play, *The Bald Soprano,* the characters are flat, as though they had emerged from a cartoon. The same is true, in varying degrees, of all his dramatis personae. Ionesco always says: "I don't write psychological plays. My theatre is apsychological, and the characters in it are types, even archetypes."

Rhinoceros, a political allegory on the first level, is also a fable, even a fabliau. This accounts for its peculiarly innocent charm. Nevertheless, it deals with what Ionesco calls "a pernicious disease of epidemic proportions." When questioned further, he says with an impish smile:

> People always wish me to spell out whether I meant the rhinos to be fascists or communists. Rhinoceritis is not an illness of the Right or the Left; it cannot be contained within geo-political borders. Nor is it characteristic of a social class. It is the malady of conformity which knows no bounds, no boundaries.

Rhinoceros was first staged in German by Karl Heinz Stroux at the Düsseldorf Schauspielhaus (October, 1949). On January 22, 1960, it opened at the Odéon in Jean-Louis Barrault's famous production. Barrault played Bérenger. It was to become Ionesco's most highly praised and frequently performed play, and the first of his works to receive a Broadway production (January, 1961).

The play's universality is no doubt due to the fact that it transcends the simplistic code of the allegory. A French boy in Romania, a Romanian in France, its author could never adhere to any national group, or political party. He was a man of no place and every place, but his true homeland was literature.

For Ionesco, the most treacherous element is History. It is characterized by tidal waves. Some of the most eloquent pages in *Present Past Past Present* deal with this fluid, unpredictable sphere.

> It is necessary . . . to soar above one's time, to go beyond it so as not to disappear with it. It is perhaps because I am weak, or because I am strong, for what appears to be a weakness may be a strength, that I am going to be able to resist the crises, the currents, the ebb and flow of time, not outside of my time but struggling with my time and expressing it through this very opposition to it. This opposition does not manifest itself in ideologies, for ideologies are only waves that are destined to disappear. I will not be another wave, but a rock . . . that is to say a

human permanence, a sort of universal consciousness, something covered up by the waves, but still there nonetheless.[41]

Ionesco's apprehension is not that of a Western European. In many ways it is closer to Buddhism. A Western education does not favor this state of passive resistance, of stubborn endurance: One is taught to improve oneself by doing. A very important and over-looked aspect of *Rhinoceros* is the opposition between two fundamental attitudes, the Eastern and the Western. They are embodied in two characters, Jean and Bérenger.

Jean is a so-called responsible citizen. He feels superior to his friend Bérenger because he has a well-organized existence. He is punctual and hard working. In fact, he takes pride in the minute-by-minute program he has put together to guide him through the days, and he urges his lackadaisical friend to follow it:

Get yourself up to the mark.
Dress yourself properly, shave every day, put on a clean shirt.
Keep abreast of the cultural and literary events.
Don't let yourself drift.
Work eight hours a day . . . but not on Sundays, or evenings, or for three weeks in the summer.
Spend your free time constructively . . . by visiting museums, reading literary periodicals, going to lectures.

The end result of this self-improvement will be: "In four weeks you'll be a cultured man."[42]

Bérenger is not in the least tempted by Jean's plan to refashion him into the ideal social being. It is clear from the start that the self-righteous Jean, so proud of his appearance—hat, tie, well-cut suit, polished shoes—is rhinoceros material, whereas the timid loner, Bérenger, a dreamer, is a flawed but endearing human being. He confesses to one fault: he enjoys the occasional lift he gets from a drink. As presented by Ionesco, it is a comic defect, one that testifies to the character's modest humanity. Although Jean is going off to a cocktail party, he maintains that, unlike his friend, he is not a drunkard because "there's moderation in all things," and he is "a moderate person."[43] This statement will soon be contradicted by his behavior after the first rhinoceros crosses the small public square.

Early in act 1 there is a very amusing scene of slapstick comedy when Jean orders Bérenger to set his glass back on the table without drinking, while he, himself, takes a gulp from his own *pastis*. Bérenger, made nervous by the scolding tone and the arrival of Daisy, the pretty office secretary on whom he has a crush, spills the contents of his full glass upon Jean's trousers. Jean grows enraged. This bit of stage business is in perfect keeping with the farcical mode of the play, but it also serves to emphasize the Chekhovian helplessness, clumsiness, and timidity of the protagonist.

As Bérenger attempts to explain to his domineering friend that he does not drink because he likes the taste of alcoholic beverages, but in order to lighten the burden of everyday existence, Jean grows impatient and scornful. Bérenger's confessional tone is much like that of his predecessor, the Bérenger of *The Killer*.

> I drink not to be frightened. . . . I feel out of place in life, among people, and so I take to drink. . . . I've been tired for years. It's exhausting to drag the weight of my own body about. . . . I'm conscious of my body all the time, as if it were made of lead, or as if I were carrying another man around on my back. I can't seem to get used to myself. I don't even know if I *am* me. Then, as soon as I take a drink, the lead slips away and I recognize myself, I become me again.[44]

It is of course a waste of time to take into his confidence a third-rate conformist who poses as a well-meaning friend. However, what Bérenger describes goes to the very core of the dual feelings the dramatist considers central to his work: heaviness and lightness, air and matter. The important aspect of Bérenger's minor fault—as it is presented by Ionesco, one not foreign to this kind of indulgence—is that this tippling may be a way of momentarily escaping from the existential condition, yet at no time would Ionesco's antiheroic hero exchange his vulnerable human skin for the heavy hide of a beast. Unlike his dreamer of a friend, Jean is embedded in the here and now, and takes pride in being "normal." This assumption is the Achilles' heel of the future rhino who, unlike the sensitive, intelligent Bérenger, does not realize that life "is an abnormal business."[45]

The "abnormal business" that the town will be faced with is the appearance of one rhinoceros, then another (or could it be one and the same, escaped from a nearby zoo?). Excited, slightly frightened, people begin to debate whether the creatures had the same number of horns. Jean, who views himself as a cultured man endowed with a disciplined mind—all Germanic traits—states unhesitatingly: "No, it was not the same rhinoceros. The one that went by first had two horns on its nose, it was an Asiatic rhinoceros; this one had only one, it was an African rhinoceros." Bérenger calls Jean "a pedant who's not certain of his facts because . . . it's the Asiatic rhinoceros with only one horn on its nose, and it's the African with two. . . ."[46] Scientific definitions turn to pure venom as the two friends come close to blows.

> Jean: I'm not betting with you. If anybody's got two it's you! You Asiatic Mongol!
> Bérenger: I've got no horns. And I never will have . . . I'm not Asiatic either. And in any case, Asiatics are people, the same as everyone else . . .
> Jean: They're yellow! Bright yellow!
> Bérenger: Whatever they are, you're bright red![47]

If every French person knows that a reference to "horns" means that a man is being labelled a cuckold (*le cocu* is traditionally a farcical type), calling a man an "Asiatic Mongol" is both redundant and redolent of racism. Yet, during the German occupation of France, a Romanian refugee might well have been the butt of such an insult. Seen in this light, the farcical attack acquires a deeply sinister coloring, reminding those who lived through that period of the clichéd image of Jews as horned men, subhumans in the image of the Devil. The mild Bérenger bristles at these words. When he shouts that he will never have horns, he may also point out a basic difference between himself and the potential rhinoceros. The latter is a racist through and through, one who judges people by their color. However, in so doing, he has turned "bright red" with rage. Finally, he storms off, shouting that he will not see his friend again: "I'm not wasting my time with a fool like you."[48]

If Jean's propensity to conform, together with his choleric nature, make him the perfect would-be rhinoceros, intellectualism is no guarantee against catching the fatal disease. On the contrary, the intellectual and the middlebrow, convinced as they are of being superior people, are best equipped to rationalize their metamorphoses: neither Botard, the former school teacher, nor Dudard, the deputy-head of the firm in which Bérenger is employed, will escape turning into beasts.

Act 2 begins in the office of a publishing company specializing in law books (much like Durieu where Ionesco was employed between 1948 and 1955). The employees are discussing the latest headlines about the town being overrun by herds of rhinos. Botard is vehement in his rejection of the facts. He will not even yield to the testimony of an eyewitness, Daisy. This rigid man, as proud as Jean of his methodical mind, lives by clichés, albeit liberal ones. He fulminates against the church; his temple is the union. When his colleague Mr. Boeuf (the word means "ox" in French) returns to the office's foyer in the shape of a rhinoceros, Botard's principal concern is that he not be denied the support of the organization. However, faced with this creature, who is even recognized by his wife, Botard can no longer deny the obvious. He proclaims that a conspiracy must be afoot, suspecting Dudard, his superior, of being a traitor. He must expose the deputy-head in order to "get to the bottom of this fake mystery."[49] Ionesco shows in this scene the pattern of "patriotic" denunciations basic to the mechanism of dictatorships; that is, spying on one's friends, business associates, and even members of one's own family.

This is a masterful caricature of the rancor of semieducated masses, lashing out at phantoms of their making, but refusing to recognize present danger. They are dangerous because they are supremely convinced that reason is on their side. Since they have spent a lifetime grazing on platitudes, it is easy to force feed them. Nor are bovine creatures necessarily peaceful; they trample the unwary. Thus, it is the most natural of transitions for a Mr. Boeuf to turn into a rhinoceros. As to Botard, he is a Boeuf to the nth degree.

As act 2 unfolds, the audience witnesses the process of the metamorphosis so eloquently described by Ionesco in his journal. It takes place before our very eyes on the occasion of Bérenger calling on his sick friend Jean.

Bérenger has come to apologize, although the quarrel showed that Jean was in the wrong. It is a mark of the protagonist's generosity that he is willing to forgive and always doubts himself. As he enters Jean's small studio apartment, he finds his erstwhile friend in bed. The man's pulse is regular, but he is suffering from a ravenous appetite. His complexion is turning green (not a sickly pallor, but the greenish-gray of a rhinoceros hide), and a strange bump is rising in the center of his forehead, right above the nose. With every trip the man makes to the bathroom, the bump grows larger, looking at last like a horn. As Bérenger informs the ailing man of Boeuf's transformation, Jean begins to utter hoarse, nasal cries, huffing and puffing from the heat. In an unrecognizable growl, he exclaims: "Well, whether he changes into a rhinoceros on purpose or against his will, he's probably all the better for it."[50]

Ionesco insists that masks are essential to the production. In Barrault's staging, Jean became gradually more and more like a rhinoceros with the addition of certain elements to his face. He seemed to wear a shamanic mask that allowed him to coincide with a savage deity. No doubt Ionesco must have discussed this scene with his lifetime friend Mircea Eliade, the author of *Shamanism, Archaic Techniques of Ecstasy*. In this study Eliade discusses "the shamanic imitation of the actions and voices of animals," or rather the shaman's "taking possession of his helping spirits." Eliade concludes: "Each time a shaman succeeds in sharing in the animal mode of being, he in a manner re-establishes the situation that existed *in illo tempore,* in mythical times, when the divorce between man and the animal world had not yet occurred."[51] Thus, Jean's metamorphosis may be grotesque, even laughable, but it also has a mythical dimension.

When Zero Mostel played Jean on Broadway, opposite Eli Wallach's Bérenger, the great clown refused to wear a mask. At a pre-opening cocktail party, Mostel demonstrated to Ionesco how he would create the illusion of metamorphosis by expression and gesture alone. On the stage, Mostel moved with lurching steps; it was the dance of a primitive in a state of trance, the dancer became his totem animal. The actor rushed and glided, lunged and drew back. He seemed to grow larger, as though able to inflate his huge form, yet he retained a disquieting grace. He made you understand why, at the end of the play, Bérenger wonders why he opted for retaining his puny human shape. The U.S. production was less like a child's story book than that of Barrault; it was awesome, terrifying, and utterly convincing.

The second metamorphosis we witness is both more subtle and more frightening since it takes place on a moral plane. The gradual shift of Dudard's attitude in act 3, when he comes to visit Bérenger, suggests the pernicious infiltration of the virus, its hold upon a fine intelligence.

Dudard begins by voicing his doubts as to what constitutes good and evil. The trained jurist, the impeccable employee is hardly the man to question the fundamental codes of civilized society, yet he wonders: "Evil! That's just a question of personal preference."[52] He is obviously afflicted with the intellectual's malaise: bad faith. In drawing this portrait, Ionesco had in mind a man he admired in many ways, with the exception of his politics, Jean-Paul Sartre. "Dudard is Sartre," he said in New York in the course of a private conversation. For Ionesco, Sartre's failure to denounce the existence of the gulags smacked of rhinoceritis of the Left. As recently as on April 19, 1990, in an article written for *Le Figaro* entitled "When 'they' suddenly discover Havel," the dramatist accuses Sartre of having corrupted the French intelligentsia. He goes on with profound bitterness, and a sense of having at last been justified: "These Leftists were well aware of the immense misdeeds of the Stalinists. They had been warned by men such as Arthur Koestler, Raymond Aron, Jean-François Revel, and myself. We were right, but they vilified us, calling us despicable fascists, cowards, scoundrels." Surrounded by former Communists, Maoists, Castro supporters, assembled at the Ministry of Culture to greet Czechoslovakia's new president, Ionesco reports that he was nevertheless able to raise two fingers in sign of victory.[53]

In *Rhinoceros* Ionesco demystifies the cult of rationalism, Descartes's legacy to Western culture. He shows that this philosophy can serve as blinders at a time of murderous violence. In the scene between Dudard and Bérenger, the latter may appear as hypochondriacal, even cowardly, but his anguish is a positive reaction to the germ of rhinoceritis. This angst is a symptom, like fever, suggestive of the fact that the sick body's struggle must begin before recuperation can occur. On the contrary, Dudard's superior attitude covers a wavering, ailing conscience.

True heroism for Ionesco is a quality of the heart rather than of the mind. It is the reaction of a modest man who wishes to remain true to himself. While the intellectual wavers, weighing abstract good against abstract evil, and letting real evil overtake him, the intuitive man rejects intuitively what he senses as destructive. Some intellectuals, such as Vaclav Havel, have been able to combine the qualities of the spirit with those of the mind. Despite polar conditions of life, neither Havel nor Ionesco have ever deviated from their path.

The final pages of *Rhinoceros* allow the reader and the audience to follow the tracing of this path. The penultimate scene is that between Bérenger and Daisy. The pretty secretary enters her colleague's room, a basket on her arm. She has brought him lunch. However, this innocent has witnessed a general panic in the office and the streets. M. Papillon (Mr. Butterfly), the head of the department, has joined the herd. Names from one of Ionesco's time capsules are added to that of the flitting creature: Cardinal de Retz, Mazarin, Saint-Simon. "All our great names!"[54] exclaims Bérenger, who seems to have forgotten that they are those of political plotters, dishonest ministers, and literary gossips.

Bérenger and Daisy will also be caught in a time capsule. We are invited to travel through a telescoped future. The couple's conversation goes from a declaration of love to planning a family. However, the presence of rhino heads all around them is oppressive. Ionesco and his bride, Rodica Burileanu, must have felt much the same way in July, 1936, when they were married. Unlike Rodica, however, Daisy is not a true companion in days of misfortune. She wonders whether the rhinoceros world might not be in the right. As her fiancé speaks of their love, she exclaims: "I feel a bit ashamed of what you call love—this morbid feeling, this male weakness. And female too. It just doesn't compare with the ardour and tremendous energy emanating from all these creatures around us."[55] Incensed, Bérenger slaps her face. They have come to the parting of ways. As Daisy says: "In a space of a few minutes we've gone through twenty-five years of married life."[56] The life of the couple has been poisoned by the surrounding climate of opinion. As Daisy makes her escape to join the beastly mob, Bérenger remains alone, defiant yet terrified. He is the last human left on the face of this planet.

What makes Ionesco's protagonist fully human is the fact that he is racked by self-doubt. There is a moment in his soliloquy when he experiences a profound revulsion in regard to his weak body, pallid skin, hairy limbs, smooth brow. He cries out: "Oh, I'd love to have a hard skin in that wonderful dull green colour."[57] The latter is a reminder of the Nazi uniforms.

No one who has seen the Nazi armored vehicles forging forward overrunning the nations they were determined to subjugate, will ever forget it. They seemed undefeatable, a Master Race, Wagnerian demigods. Their propaganda machine rolled in with their tanks, telling the conquered nations that they were weak, corrupt, sinful, and had brought this misfortune upon themselves. Many, like Bérenger, felt a kind of servile admiration for the discipline of people intent only on maintaining their well-oiled war machine. In the death camps, they took superhuman strides, in their greenish uniforms, shiny black boots, always accompanied by sleek attack dogs. The lice-covered, shivering prisoners were faced at every moment with the image of their inferior condition. Yet, those who came to doubt their right to exist were done for; they would not survive the camps.

Nor was there a way of communicating with these automatons. They shouted orders in a language many did not know, and if these orders were not instantly obeyed their whips spoke eloquently. Listening to their "Heils!" and military music, Bérenger wonders whether their raucous song may not have charm. He even tries to bellow as they do, but realizes he is incapable of learning their tongue. But what is the protagonist's language? What is he saying since he is the last creature to utter these sounds? He even wonders whether he understands what he is saying.

It is in this reflection that we may find a key to Ionesco's problematics of style and expression. Following this experience, it was no longer possible for Ionesco to entertain easy relations with the common tongue. As Elie Wiesel said at one of his public lectures: "Words in camp did not mean what they mean outside: 'hunger,' 'thirst,' 'bread.'" When Ionesco denies being an avant-garde writer, it is his way of saying that he does not experiment for the sake of experimentation. However, he is unable to take language for granted. The returning deportee, or exile, sees the once familiar world with the eyes of a stranger. Only then, when we come back among the living having visited the kingdom of the dying and the dead, do we have a chance to exist again.

The last man is much like the first. Alone among rhinoceroses, Bérenger is as grotesque as Adam among the animals of the newly fashioned planet. "I'm a monster, just a monster!" he shouts. Yet, there is no going back. The protagonist states defiantly:

I'll take on the whole of them! I'll put up a fight against the lot of them, the whole lot of them! I'm the last man left, and I'm staying that way until the end. I'm not capitulating![58]

These last words have a Churchillian ring.

Bérenger, the shy dreamer given to fits of exaltation and spasms of anger, a fearful and yet audacious man, ineffectual at work, ill-adapted to society, often dependent on the small comfort of drink, flabby, paunchy, pallid, essentially kind and well-meaning, turns out to be our only champion. Unlikely as it seems—Ionesco wishes us to be aware of the paradox—when this man opposes evil, his act of defiance constitutes the triumph of each and every one of us. We are able to identify with this "man for our time," who has kept his decency among the mob of monsters. He is the emblem of our troubled epoch, an antihero who is a true hero, because he must.

Chapter 7

Death and Dying

Exit the King and Killing Game

To experience every moment of existence as though it were one's last breath, to stand at every instant, in joy or sorrow, in pride or modest self-awareness, on the brink of dissolution, to be eternally condemned to capital punishment, reprieved at every second only to be condemned again, such is the state of mind of one of the philosophic clowns of contemporary European literature. Even as a child, Ionesco found himself unable to taste the present's full-bodied joys without thinking that these were bound to melt away.

"What's got to finish one day is finished now,"[1] cries out Bérenger the First, king of the mythical realm of *Exit the King*. He has been informed by the elder of his two queens, as well as by his court physician, that he is to die at the end of the show, in an hour and a half. In this way, Ionesco reminds his audience that it is looking at a play, and that the protagonist, a tragicomic marionette, is doomed to disappear as the lights begin to dim. As Shakespeare reminded his public, we are all merely players on the stage of life. King Bérenger's predicament is our common lot, as in the French children's song: "Ainsi font, font, font les petites marionnettes / Ainsi font, font, font trois petits tours et puis s'en vont" (The little puppets do this and that and this / They circle thrice and disappear").

Ionesco's *Exit the King* is one of the great stage poems on the process of decay and dying; it invites the public to experience "an apprenticeship in dying."[2] Actually the play offers a double apprenticeship: Bérenger faces the fact of mortality, which he refused to do while in good health, and he discovers, on the brink of personal dissolution, that life is infinitely precious, that every moment, however trivial it may seem, ought to be noted, treasured, savored, as though it were to be the very last one.

Nascentes morimur, says the poet, an apprehension echoed by Beckett's Pozzo when he declaims: "They give birth astride of a grave, the light gleams an instant, then it's night once more."[3] King Bérenger, however, is unable to accept the fact that this common fate, or rather the fate of the commoner, should also be his. Much like the patient of Elisabeth Kübler-Ross's "First Stage," he builds a protective shell of denial. Kübler-Ross explains in chapter 3 of *On Death and Dying:* "Denial functions as a buffer after unexpected shocking news, allows the patient to collect himself and, with time, mobilize other, less radical defenses."[4] Ionesco's protagonist, however, will not come to terms with reality, except at the very end, when he can no longer speak and is gradually led into nonbeing by his wife, Queen Marguerite. Death, as he first sees it, is guilty of the crime of "lèse majesté."[5] He informs his doctor, who is simultaneously the surgeon, hangman, bacteriologist, and astrologer of the kingdom, that he, the King, will die only when he has decided to do so, "in forty, fifty, three hundred years."[6] He simply cannot consider dying while he is busy attending to affairs of state. Yet, as he is making these statements, his strength is clearly ebbing, his legs are giving way, his body going to pieces; he is no longer in control, neither of the world nor of himself. The rest of the play, until Queen Marguerite's final monologue, is a tragicomic outcry of rage and despair. Unlike his creator, Ionesco, the King refuses to acknowledge that "nous sommes des moribonds qui n'acceptent pas de mourir" (we are all of us dying men who refuse to die).[7] He will have to travel through the stages carefully outlined and analyzed by Kübler-Ross in her study, published seven years after the premiere of *Exit the King* at the Théâtre de l'Alliance Française in Paris (December 15, 1962):

> First Stage: Denial and Isolation
> Second Stage: Anger
> Third Stage: Bargaining
> Fourth Stage: Depression
> Fifth Stage: Acceptance

It is important to keep in mind that Ionesco is writing from an ancient tradition of comedy. Bérenger Ier is no more cowardly than the great poltroons of literature: Falstaff, Panurge, Sancho Panza, Molière's Argan, or, closer to our time, Jarry's King Ubu. Like all these antiheroes, Bérenger the First is not merely ridiculous; he embodies fear stripped bare. Even in the act of laughing at him, we cannot help but identity with him, just as we do with the fate of tragic heroes; we are laughing at ourselves, cathartic laughter par excellence.

Bérenger's disintegration may be the result of the sinful, frivolous life he led with the voluptuous young Queen Marie, his "favorite," more of a mistress than a consort. Though she appears loving and generous, she is Eve, the temptress, despite her holy name. Marguerite, the shrewish older queen, attacks her for having led the King astray with her "fun and games, dances, processions, official dinners, winning ways and fireworks displays, silver spoons and honeymoons!"[8] For the King, Marie is the life force, to be enjoyed while one has sufficient health. But the philosophic mind will no doubt recognize in her the allegorical figure of Pascal's *divertissement*.[9]

Queen Marguerite's *Ars Moriendi* also owes much to the writer of the *Pensées,* but it is rooted in St. Augustine's "First Dialogue" and Bossuet's *Oraisons funèbres.* Marguerite would not favor Montaigne's statement that one ought to meet death like the unquestioning peasant, planting his cabbages, indifferent to his ultimate demise. Since to be human is to be aware of the brevity of life, it is advisable, the old queen suggests, to spend time in meditation, staring into the blinding light of impending death. Thus, she scolds Bérenger for having been taken unawares, and provides him with a retrospective program. "You were condemned and you should have thought about that the very first day, and then day after day, five minutes every day. . . . Then ten minutes, a quarter, half an hour. That's the way to train yourself."[10] Quite a regimen!

In this early passage, Marguerite assumes the function of Ionesco's mother, who told her young child that everyone must die someday. Although as a mature man and artist, Ionesco appreciated her honesty and courage, he was, at that time, struck with horror. His sweetly familiar mother became a terrifying Magna Mater. This is also the meaning of Marguerite's metamorphosis at the very end of the play, when she reveals herself as the divinity of the Ultimate

Passage, one of the guides of Ionesco's favorite book, *The Tibetan Book of the Dead*.

King Bérenger is more than a man, he is Man. Ionesco kept the name of his antihero to indicate that this ruler is still the Everyman of his previous works, not a mighty sovereign. If anything, we witness the democratization of power in his person, a lie-a-bed petit bourgeois waited on by a kind but slovenly maid, Juliette. If his biblical and literary ancestors are Job and Shakespeare's Richard II, his own name sounds as ludicrous as would Jourdain Ier.[11]

When we first see him shuffling in, letting Juliette put slippers on his swollen feet, Bérenger is a living ghost of the ruler he used to be. Once he was an amalgam of Caligula, Ivan the Terrible, and Stalin, but now he's just a doddering old fool. On his death throne—he dies sitting on his throne—he is reminded of his deeds of valor as well as of his greatest crimes. Queen Marie may remember him as "a hero,"[12] but the Doctor reminds him of the executions he ordered. To this the King retorts: "It was all euthanasia to me."[13] Marguerite, sounding much like Stalin's wife, lists his unnatural acts: "You had all my parents butchered, your own brothers, your rivals, our cousins and great-grandcousins, and all their families, friends, and cattle. You massacred the lot and scorched their lands."[14] This speech raises the ghosts of the mighty leader's blood bath: the systematic decimation of personal friends and political allies, that of the members of Alliluyeva's family, barbarous acts that drove the tyrant's wife to take her own life. The reference to land scorching strengthens the association with Russia. Twice this policy defeated invaders: Napoleon and Hitler.

Was the King a hero or a brutal assassin? Perhaps Ionesco suggests that all heroic endeavors culminate in mass death. Ambitious rulers, who wish to be remembered as heroes, bring about immeasurable suffering, be their names Alexander, Napoleon, Hitler, Pol Pot, Saddam Hussein. When they fall they wish to take everyone down with them. The King shouts: "Let it all die with me! No, let it all stay, let it all die, stay, die!"[15] The more one reads Ionesco, the more prophetic his plays appear.

The political level in these plays is never far from the surface, but Ionesco's vision transcends history; it is cosmic. King Bérenger is all of humanity. Like us, he is trapped on a planet doomed to destruction at some future time. Thus, all dreams of immortality are tinged with the knowledge that everything is temporary: books crumble to dust as surely as human flesh and bones. When all human life has disappeared this cold star will continue to spin, with no one to remember the achievements that made us proud. There will be no eyes to see paintings and sculpture, no ears to hear music, no minds to feel nostalgia.

Since Ionesco is surveying the history of the human race, what appears absurd is perfectly rational. The King has been living for thousands of years. It was he who invented steel, balloons, airplanes. He built Rome, New York, Moscow, and Geneva. He *founded* Paris and was responsible for revolutions and counterrevolutions. By writing the *Iliad* and the *Odyssey* he created the art of literature. It was he, not Bacon, who composed the tragedies and comedies performed under the pseudonym of Shakespeare. Not too long ago, he added to his accomplishments the splitting of the atom. Now, a dying man, he is too weak to even switch off the light.

Once upon a time, this powerful monarch had but to issue an edict for everyone to instantly spring to his command. Even Nature followed his dictates. He could make trees sprout from the floor, order leaves to grow, and he held a thunderbolt in his hand, like Zeus.

Ionesco, whose fundamental aesthetic belief rests on the writer's ability to connect with archetypal images is reproducing in this play some of the features of the ancient ritual connected with the Vegetation Spirit, or King of the May. In *From Ritual to Romance,* Jessie L. Weston brings together early Aryan Drama, and Babylonian and Classic ritual to show the survival of ancient practices. In the wake of Mannhardt's *Wald und Feld-Kulte* and Frazer's *The Golden Bough,* Weston speaks of a surviving custom, that of the burial of the vegetation spirit, attended by mourning women. The figure carried on a bier may be resuscitated by the Medicine Man. The King, a representative of God, must not be allowed to become feeble, "lest, with the diminishing vigour of the ruler, the cattle should sicken, and fail to bear increase, the crops should rot in the field and men die in ever growing numbers."[16] Indeed, as Weston states: "The woes of the land are directly dependent upon the sickness, or maiming of the King."[17]

We hear that King Bérenger's realm is turning into a wasteland. Now, although the sovereign shouts in the style of Lewis Carroll's

Red Queen—"Off with the guard's head, off with his head!"—the man's pate no longer topples from his shoulders, it merely "wobbles a bit."[18] With the ruler's imminent demise, intimations of an apocalyptic end fill the earth and heavens. The Doctor/Astronomer reports: "Snow is falling on the North Pole and the sun. The Milky Way seems to be curdling. The comet is exhausted, feeling its age, winding its tail around itself and curling up like a dying dog." The grass is wilting, the earth cracking. Giant fissures open onto the Void. "The sun has lost between fifty and seventy-five percent of its strength."[19] Huge spiders have invaded the palace, weaving cobwebs in the throne room. Juliette, the maid-of-all-works, cannot keep up with this proliferation. One need not suffer from arachnophobia to realize that, as in Elsinore, "all is not well."[20] Indeed, King Bérenger's realm is strongly reminiscent of Baudelaire's "Spleen" poems. As in "Spleen 77" of *Les Fleurs du mal,* the King's blood is turning into icy lymph, the same green Lethe waters that circulate through the veins of Shakespeare's melancholy prince.

However, these waters of forgetfulness have not yet worked their magic. Bérenger is conscious of his state. Realizing at last that there is no escape, the sick man rushes to open a window, shouting: "I want everyone to know that the King is going to die. My good people, I am going to die! Hear me! Your King is going to die!"[21] Fear has obliterated dignity. The sovereign's physician tries to shame him into decorum: "Your Majesty, think of the death of Louis XIV, of Philip II, or of the Emperor Charles V, who slept in his own coffin for twenty years!"[22] Bérenger is deaf to these entreaties. His wild thrashing corresponds to Kübler-Ross's second stage: "Anger." She writes: "In contrast to the stage of denial, this stage of anger is very difficult to cope with from the point of view of family and staff. The reason for this is the fact that this anger is displaced in all directions and projected on to the environment at times almost at random."[23] Bérenger's behavior could serve as the perfect illustration of this study. He exclaims like a naughty child: "Off with Marguerite's crown! Knock it on the floor."[24] However, it is his crown that falls; it rolls on the floor and is picked up by his wife.

In Kübler-Ross's book, the stage of "Anger" is followed by that of "Bargaining." Once again, *Exit the King* proves the soundness of the pattern traced by the thanatologist following the two years she spent interviewing dying patients. Ionesco uses the device of *bargain-*

ing as one of his most pathetic and comical effects. For example, when the young wife wishes for time "to turn back,"[25] Bérenger picks up this suggestion to deplore the time he wasted and lost. This is Proust's narrator before he found his vocation. Now the King demands to travel back in time so he may become a schoolboy again. "I'd like to re-sit the exam,"[26] he sighs. Even this unpleasant task would be welcome since it would mean recapturing one's youth, having a whole future ahead. The King feels he needs "a whole century"[27] since he "came into the world five minutes ago," married "three minutes ago," and "came to the throne two and a half minutes ago." He "never had time to get to know life."[28]

Bérenger's obsessive counting is the perfect caricature of what Kübler-Ross means by *bargaining*. With the dying man's anxiety spiralling up, *bargaining* is tinged with *anger*. Kübler-Ross points out that "most bargains are made with God."[29] This is true of Bérenger's plea, except that it is highly public, and utterly shameless. He proclaims his readiness to see everyone he knows die, provided he might live forever, "even alone in a limitless desert." He would not mind solitude in the Void, in "a vast and airy wasteland," and concludes: "It's better to miss one's friends than to be missed oneself."[30] This comically cynical bargaining is followed by a bitter appraisal of friendship: one is never missed anyway. Each and every one dies alone.

The desirable stage the dying must reach is the one Kübler-Ross calls "Acceptance." This is what Ionesco means by "the apprenticeship of dying."[31] It is a rite of passage, or rather of a series of passages. Turning in his mind to the crowd of the invisible dead, Bérenger cries out:

Come back from the other side a while and help me! Assist me all of you who were frightened and did not want to go! What was it like? Who held you up? Who dragged you there, who pushed you? Were you afraid to the very end? And you who were strong and courageous, who accepted death with indifference and serenity, teach me your indifference and serenity, teach me resignation![32]

Following this address to the dead, the two queens, the doctor, the guard, and the maid form a chorus. Their chanting is like that of

Tibetan monks, instructing the dying man in the stages of his final
liberation. Indeed, the King is in that state of suspension called the
bardo (the gap) in *The Tibetan Book of the Dead*. He must learn to travel
from the space of life to the space of death. This also suggests the way
of the neophyte of the Orphic cults, led into the Netherworld by a
mystagogue. The women surrounding him could be Demeter, Persephone, and Tyche (the goddess of fortune). The doctor might be
said to play the role of Lord of the Abyss. Ionesco echoes here many
Occidental and Oriental myths, yet he also creates his own mythical
universe. In this initiation scene, Ionesco's sacred chant lends a voice
to the figures of the Orphic Sacramental Bowl that was discovered
near the Romanian town of Pietroasa, in the Buzau area. As Joseph
Campbell explains, the sixteen figures of the bowl represent "the
sequence of initiatory stages of [the] inward search."[33] This is the
quest Bérenger must undertake as the voices of his retinue blend into
a solemn requiem.

> Juliette: You statues, you dark and shining phantoms, ancients
> and shades . . .
> Marie: Teach him serenity.
> Guard: Teach him indifference.
> Doctor: Teach him resignation.
> Marguerite: Make him see reason and set his mind at rest.[34]

These are wise injunctions, but the King is not quite ready to receive
them. He implores the dead to teach him "lassitude."[35]

Before being instructed by the dead, Bérenger Ier receives a lesson from the most humble of the living, one whose presence and
work went unnoticed, or taken for granted: the maid. While he was
happy and in good health, the King never bothered with her. What
could this servant girl tell him that he did not know? And yet, it is
she who, unbeknownst to herself, reveals to him the most essential
of all truths: the fact that every moment of life is precious, that each
ought to be experienced as the very first and the very last.

At the core of a play about dying, lies this extraordinarily moving scene about feeling oneself alive. Not that the maid Juliette experiences this happiness; her life is one of endless chores, exhausting
labor. But, by listening to her tale of woe, the spoiled man, who
thought of himself as the center of the world, reaches the knowledge

that the most modest of existences is far better than no life at all. He discovers that he ought to have paid attention to simple things, such as breathing, moving, walking. He learns from this natural Zen master the lesson imparted by the ghost of Achilles to Odysseus when the latter visits the Underworld: "Don't bepraise death to me, Odysseus, for I would rather be a plowman to a yeoman farmer on a small holding than lord paramount in the Kingdom of the Dead."[36]

From his hospital wheelchair—he is moved from his throne to this modern conveyance—Bérenger questions the servant. He is not really interested at first in her answers. He wishes to gain a bit of time before dying, to give himself the illusion that things still matter, that he belongs in some way still to the world where people wear shoes, sew on buttons, darn socks, patch clothes, go to market, cook, and eat. Juliette represents the kind of life everyone takes for granted. Bérenger inquires: "Tell me how you live. What sort of life do you have?" "A bad life, Sire,"[37] is the maid's answer. Bérenger waves off this comment impatiently. How can life be bad, "life is life."[38] As to back-breaking labor, it is so wonderful to be reminded that one has a back. The dying man cries out ecstatically, as though he had just made this discovery: "That's right! She has a back! We've all got backs!"[39]

The spoiled, self-involved man, who had never given a moment's thought to another human being's problems, understands for the first time what life means. He speaks in wonder and longing. Now that he is on the brink of losing the most precious of all gifts, the most squandered of possessions, he knows that life is not parades and fireworks, not even sensual love—the kind he shared with Queen Marie—but the light of early dawn, or the riot of colors on the stalls of an open air market. Joy is to set one's foot on the ground, the ability to walk out of one's house, to go up and down the stairs, to turn the key in the lock. If you walk it means you have feet, and as you slowly turn the key, you may notice that you have fingers. If something aches, the ache will eventually subside, and while you enjoy health and youth there is the assurance of convalescence, the pleasure of restorative sleep, the return to a state of no pain. How can one complain about the weather, working hard, rising early? Everything is a feast and a blessing. While there is breath to draw, eyes to see, hands that feel, all is, or ought to be, joy and gratitude. Juliette moans about her chores: "There's no end to it!" while Bérenger evokes "an endless celebration."[40] They are not speaking of the same endlessness; Juliette refers to an existence in which there is no respite from pain and fatigue, the dying King dreams of a world without the finis of death.

When Hamlet learns from the lips of the dying Laertes of the poisoned épée whose venom is circulating in his blood, he exclaims: "I am dead, Horatio" (*Hamlet* [V.ii.322]), and again, a little later in the same speech, "Horatio, I am dead" (V.ii.327). He is filled with amazement at the realization that one may move, breathe, still address a friend, yet know that "there is not half an hour's life" (V.ii.304). Hamlet does not say: "I am dying!" or "Soon, I shall be dead!" He speaks of the unavoidable, imminent future in the present tense, suggesting that he, the creature on the stage, as well as all the spectators (those present at Claudius's games, and those in the theater audience) are pregnant with mortality.

Ionesco's Bérenger Ier, who describes in loving details every step of an ordinary life, is, at last, filled with Hamlet's truth: he knows that he *is* dead. This newly gained apprehension may divest him of the superiority of rank, making him in the most fundamental way the equal of his maid, and of each and every living, and dying, creature, but it also confers on him the only superiority there is, that of wisdom. Unbeknownst to him, he has become a poet-philosopher, like Ionesco, a metaphysician and an artist.

For one who has learned to perceive life keenly, the ill-named *nature morte* is a *nature éternellement vivante* (nature eternally alive). King Bérenger's conversation with the maid is a genre painting, immortalizing a ray of light upon the table cloth, a piece of bread and a knife resting on a cutting board, a modest interior. Life, Ionesco suggests, must be held up to attention, and art is the sublime, humbly faithful instrument whereby we may worship physical and spiritual reality.

Tibetan Buddhism teaches that the fundamental principle of birth and death recurs constantly in this life. In his comments on *The Tibetan Book of the Dead*, Chögyam Trungpa, Rinpoche, states that the book ought to be renamed *The Tibetan Book of Birth* since it is not "based on death as such, but on a completely different concept of death."[41] It is in fact a book of space, perhaps of spaceless space.

This spaceless universe is evoked by Queen Marguerite in her mesmerizing final monologue. At the end of *Exit the King,* the shrewish wife reveals herself as a female shaman who will assist in achieving her dying spouse's redemption by bringing him to superconsciousness. As he nears death, all the unnecessary people and props vanish. Lovely Queen Marie falls through a trap in the floor since her usefulness is defunct. All the other dramatis personae vanish, and the palace walls are either lifted up, or deflated. At the very end, the King remains alone in a gray void, with only Marguerite's voice to guide him into the hereafter.

The old queen, seemingly a shrew, emerges as an archetypal figure, an anima embodying the instinctual world of the unconscious. She is an avatar of Demeter, the goddess of transformation. While Bérenger Ier was a young man, he was surrounded by a magical whole, Demeter and Kore. Their conjunction represents the Eternal Feminine, a guarantee of fertility and the survival of life. Now that Kore (Queen Marie) has vanished underground, the King is left with Demeter. She is the Dark and Terrible Mother, "the womb of the earth become the deadly devouring maw of the underworld."[42] As a student of Jung, and an analysand who underwent a form of Jungian therapy, Ionesco wishes to concretize on the stage the monstrous side of the unconscious. One will find it clearly described in the work of Jungian analyst Erich Neumann. In his study *The Great Mother: An Analysis of the Archetype,* Neumann writes:

> In the myths and tales of all peoples, ages, and countries—and even in the nightmares of our own nights—witches and vampires, ghouls and specters, assail us, all terrifyingly alike. The dark half of the black-and-white cosmic egg representing the Archetypal Feminine engenders terrible figures that manifest the black, abysmal side of life and the human psyche.[43]

Marguerite is also Sophia, the goddess of wisdom and the transformative Great Round. According to Erich Neumann, the elementary character of the Feminine appears as the beginning and end of spiritual transformations. At first, the feminine principle is associated with the night sky and the darkness of the underworld. The unconscious is the mother of all things. However, Sophia transcends the earth/night/unconscious; she is the vessel of rebirth. Thus, she must be viewed in her double aspect, as a healing and a destructive force.[44]

The apprenticeship of dying performed by Queen Marguerite

upon her husband is more akin to Eastern philosophy than to any Occidental image of salvation. Become egoless under the guidance of the goddess, Bérenger Ier becomes a Bodhisattva, one whose being *(sattva)* is enlightened *(bodhi)*. A perfect knower of the world, he will enter the realm of infinite space, infinite consciousness, and nothingness. Eventually, he will be able to abandon the perception of perception. Thus, whereas Juliette brought him in touch with himself and the world's reality, Marguerite guides him to Nirvana.

Ionesco acknowledges his "kinship with Oriental thought."[45] An Eastern Christian by upbringing, he admits to the influence of Byzantine mysticism, and of the Hesychasts. Mircea Eliade, the Ionescos' closest friend before his death, explains that in the thirties the dramatist was attracted by the spirituality of the Eastern-Orthodox tradition. Eliade detects in Ionesco's entire oeuvre the imprint of the Greek Fathers, Cusanus, Buber, the *Upanishads* (in particular the *Brhadaranyaka-Upanishad*). He is careful to point out that one ought not speak so much of "influence" as of "the renewal of Ionesco's imaginary universe through the creative encounter with exotic and traditional religious worlds."[46]

Within the brief time of a play, we are shown a man instructed in the deep meaning of the humble life, and in the process of giving up life in order to enter Nirvana. Before our eyes, a man shakes off his terror of death to enter with dignity into the All. We watch him vanish "into a kind of mist"[47] wherein our planet, spinning into stillness, must also eventually dissolve.

Exit the King was originally written as a ballet scenario. When Jacques Mauclair staged it, also playing the role of King Bérenger, he retained the dance aspect of the piece. The dying man's stumbling steps, swooning, slow-motion falls, his faltering, tottering gait, and guignol-style mock resurrections formed rhythmic patterns, a staccato progression. In contrast to these farcical, clownish missteps, the final scene of the play followed a single, fluid curve. Steered by the queen's hypnotic voice, the dying man groped his way through imaginary brambles, avoided clutching hands, skirted a precipice, and did not listen to the babble of a brook. With the wounded dignity of a blind Oedipus led by Antigone, he made his way toward an elevated throne. His winding, spiralling motion suggested planetary circling. Once seated, the King froze, assuming the hieratic pose of a great ruler's immortal bust. His eyes closed to the world of history, Ionesco's King evokes a cosmic realm, an empire that suggests a New Jerusalem with its twin suns and moons, and then still other suns rising. "As one sun sets, others are rising . . . dawn and twilight all at once. . . . Beyond the seven hundred and seventy-seven poles."[48]

Even this dazzling, mystic vision must be given up. The Queen/ Goddess of Death tells the King to throw away the flower he smelled for the last time. He needs no words, no heartbeat, no breath. His blind eyes must look through this woman, an "unreflecting mirror."[49] Life will then leave every part of his body: "Give me a finger! Give me two fingers . . . three, four . . . five . . . all ten fingers! Now let me have your right arm! Your left arm! Your chest, your two shoulders and your stomach!"[50] All worldly pursuits appear at last as nothing but wasted energy, meaningless agitation. The throne itself glides into the smoky grayness of time and space that swallows both the King and his realm.

Exit the King may well be the most perfect example of Metaphysical Farce. With the exception of *The Chairs,* Ionesco never achieved a more sublime amalgam of the tragic and the comic, the philosophic and the poetic. The press was unanimous in acclaiming the play as the dramatist's triumph in a genre of his creation. Even an old enemy like Jean-Jacques Gautier of *Le Figaro* speaks of "a very simple and authentic resonance" (12/24/62). Jean Paget of *Combat* calls the play "an oratorio of the fantastic" (12/24/62); Georges Lerminier of the *Gazette de Lausanne* describes it as a "ceremonial parade" and compares it with the *danses macabres* of the Renaissance (1/13/63). The ever faithful Jacques Lemarchand declares in *Le Figaro Littéraire* (1/5/63) that "nothing is more difficult than to speak of death, which, like the sun, defies a steady gaze." For Lemarchand, Ionesco gives new expression to our most disquieting meditations. The journalist waxes poetic when he writes: "This king is the innocence of childhood, the light of the sun, and all the humble and virtuous things of life which are doomed to vanish."

Like Samuel Beckett's *Rockaby, Exit the King* is a concentrated stage poem on the passing of life. It is also a meditation on the eventual cooling of our planet, the fading of human consciousness and therefore of memory. The comparison with Beckett does not stop here. It can be found in the title itself, which, according to

Emmanuel Jacquart, echoes the Persian *shâh mat* (checkmate), which translates as "the king is dead." Jacquart wonders, "Was the dramatist aware of this?"[51] If so, one could establish through the moves of the game of chess, basic to *Endgame,* a link with Beckett's metaphysical tragicomedy. However, the French title, *Le Roi se meurt,* does not mean "the king is dead" but "the king is dying." Syntactically, the ancient *se meurt* springs from one of the most famous *Oraisons funèbres* of the great seventeenth-century court preacher Bossuet, bishop of Meaux, who deplored the sudden passing of Henriette-Anne d'Angleterre in the following words: "Ô nuit désastreuse! ô nuit effroyable! où retentit tout à coup, comme un éclat de tonnerre, cette étonnante nouvelle: Madame se meurt, Madame est morte!" (Oh disaster-filled night! Oh frightful night! When all at once, like a thunder clap, burst the astonishing news: Madame is dying, Madame is dead!). The magnificent *Grand Siècle* rhetoric of Bossuet emphasizes the process of dying, from being "about to die" to the fait accompli. There is no doubt that these famous lines inspired Ionesco's poetic and antiquated title, one that harkens back to the epoch of Louis XIV, the Sun King. But, what is more important still, it encapsulates Hamlet's metaphysical apprehension that human beings may be moving, speaking, as though they were fully alive, and yet carry within their bodies their imminent demise. Who has not experienced this bewildering realization when visiting a loved one in the hospital, or speaking with one afflicted with terminal cancer? Ionesco made his intentions clear when he stated that his play is "the apprenticeship of *dying.*"

Exit the King strips away, layer by layer, all conventional and illusory consolations. Even before Queen Marguerite becomes the great deity of the final passage, she forces the King to hear the undisguised, unsoftened truth: "Sire, we have to inform you that you are going to die." The court doctor confirms this diagnosis: "Your Majesty, Queen Marguerite has spoken the truth. You *are* going to die."[52] If we, the audience, started the evening by laughing at a pompous, self-involved, self-indulgent man, the smile quickly fades from our lips as we realize that Bérenger Ier's fate is our fate too. Eventually he gives up his useless thrashing and, with nobility, stares into the face of death. Thus, we discover that this farce is a classically structured tragedy, and that Ionesco, the former prankster, is one of the great classical writers of our century.

Killing Game: Mass Death

Ionesco did not succeed in exorcising his fear of death by writing *Exit the King*. In 1970, he represented an allegorical figure of Death in the form of a Black Monk going on a rampage through a community. In his *Jeux de massacre* (Killing game), the dramatist, not content to show the dying of an individual, albeit one symbolic of the human race, presented the terrifying spectacle of a town decimated by a nameless plague. As the epidemic gathers momentum, dead bodies proliferate through the streets, pile up inside houses, hospitals, prisons. Terror and chaos pervade the city, destroying the fabric of civilized life. People revert to the savage state, looting and eventually turning to cannibalism. Ionesco's original title for the play was *The Cannibals*. The images of mass death evoke the ravages of world war and genocide. In writing *Killing Game,* Ionesco became an important Holocaust writer.

The subject of the play issued from the source used by Albert Camus for his novel *La Peste* (The plague): Daniel Defoe's *A Journal of the Plague Year*. Some of the language and imagery also echo Antonin Artaud's powerful description of the unravelling of a plague-ridden community. Artaud's *The Theater and Its Double* became one of the bibles of twentieth-century dramatists and directors. As to the figure of the Black Monk, it emerges from Medieval sources with additional reminders of the Gothic novel and the tales of Edgar Allen Poe.

The action of the play is not set in a remote past. The dramatist specifies in his opening stage directions that the town is neither ancient nor modern, noting that a suitable style of architecture should evoke a city "between 1880 and 1900." Thus, a Medieval mystery play atmosphere is avoided, yet the action is also removed from the immediate present. Despite numerous political references, the tableau brushed by Ionesco acquires the dimension of timelessness.

Killing Game is structured as a series of quick-moving vignettes, themes and variations that add up to a polyphonic work, as musical as it is visual. Exclamations, shouts of despair, whispered confessions, longer speeches, intertwine and even overlap. It is not always essential to make out what people are saying since the tonalities of discourse, together with gestural language, convey an atmosphere of growing horror. The air is thick with tragic happenings, as though human fear and tears rise as a thick vapor, a putrid fog. Yet, as in all of Ionesco's comic dramas, the tempo is that of farce, or even of a circus performance.

Watching the play, one might assume that, like *Exit the King,* it started out as a ballet scenario. Actually, the very opposite is true. Ionesco's play was staged in 1970 by Jorge Lavelli for the Théâtre Montparnasse. A couple of years later, Flemming Flindt choreographed the work for the Royal Danish Ballet. Set to music by Thomas Koppel, "The Triumph of Death" faithfully preserves Ionesco's vision. Flindt's tasteful use of nudity proved appropriate to convey the frantic, orgiastic moments in the dance, scenes in which the entire population of a great city, believing everyone doomed, indulges in Bacchanalian revelry veering to anthropophagical acts. Flindt's "translation" of the plays takes it in the direction of raw emotions. Lavelli's staging was equally evocative. Not content with emphasizing the musical aspect of the text, the Argentinian director carefully brought out the play's painterly quality. The chiaroscuro of many scenes suggested a hospital painted by Rembrandt.

Ionesco's recurrent rhythmic pattern, the proliferation of matter, is much in evidence in *Killing Game.* The ubiquitous presence of the Black Monk stalks everyone. As he passes through the crowd, bodies keel over, like the paper-mâché figures of a country fair's game of "Hit-the-Baby." The effect is both frightening and farcical, like that of a Punch-and-Judy show for adults.

An admirer of Gordon Craig's Über-Marionette theory, Ionesco specifies in his stage directions that he wants live actors mixed in with life-size puppets. Possibly, this device might have been inspired by Jean Tardieu's 1954 "ballet comique sans danse et sans musique," *Les amants du métro.* It serves to create an eeriness, a guignol and Grand Guignol atmosphere. Long before Ionesco, the Polish dramatist-director Tadeusz Kantor used the same association between actors and wax figures, or "doubles," for his "Theater of Death." Ionesco wanted to create the same disquieting atmosphere, one that has its roots in an epoch in which people were treated as objects or, worse still, used to make things (soap, burlap from women's hair). Ionesco writes: "At the conclusion of the first scene, these puppets can be made to turn about and face the public, motionless, with an aspect of taut, anxious waiting."[53] Thus, the full meaning of the title is illustrated since, in the singular, *un jeu de massacre* is what the English call "Aunt Sally" ("Hit-the-Baby" in the United States). The plural used by Ionesco, *Jeux de massacre,* is appropriate to the spectacle's architecture: each of the vignettes might be viewed as one fairground stall.

Killing Game opens on a scene showing a bustling town square. The many windows of the house façades are like eyes, staring out, or like small, curtained puppet-theater stages. Below, men and women are going about the business of the day: shopping, wheeling baby carriages, exchanging greetings and observations. There is no jollity, however, no sense of an easy social intercourse. This city can be found only on the map of Ionescoland. Here, the natural order is reversed: men walk about knitting and pushing perambulators. Since Ionesco is a traditional European man, these signs represent the outward manifestations of an antiworld, or at least a universe infected by a fundamental kind of malaise. Certainly in 1900 (the characters are dressed in turn-of-the-century, Proustian-looking costumes) this would not be a usual sight. The signs must be decoded by the audience as heralds of the terror to come.

Meanwhile, the separate groups of men and women indulge in a bit of conversation. The "disease" is mentioned. Housewives stop to debate whether it is confined to animals or spread by human carriers. The psychic character of the illness is alluded to by the Third Wife when she ventures: "My husband says that those people live in total confusion, no morals, no tradition. In fact they say that's what they die from . . . confusion." Thus, the epidemic might have a social and a moral aspect; it is but the symptom of decadence. For those who lived through World War II, the woman's clichés echo the propaganda of Marshal Pétain's "Free Zone," which was based on the Nazis' explanation of their swift conquest of France: the French were spoiled by good living, rotten to the core, and had become cowardly. The collaborationist press echoed these sentiments. "Liberté, Égalité, Fraternité" was replaced by a new motto: "Travail, Famille, Patrie." French women, in particular, had to emulate the German hausfrau's three holy duties: church, children, cooking. Although Ionesco's *Killing Game* is not overtly political—much less so than *Rhinoceros*—politics and history are subtly present between the lines or in the vocabulary used by the characters; these subliminal hints color the entire fabric of the play.

The group of women is followed by that of "effeminate" males

pushing prams. Their talk, however, is of a philosophical nature and
also deals with political affairs. Displeased by their government, dis-
couraged by the conditions of life, they suffer from a kind of diffuse
spleen. The Sixth Man admits to having suffered a nervous break-
down that made him view the whole world as though it were "a
distant planet, unreal, ice cold, shut tight."[54] The Fifth Man ponders
whether they might not be "better off dead."[55] Deep depression followed by a death wish seems to summon the presence of the Black
Monk.

The first strange death strikes newborn twins, wheeled in a dis-
quietingly large, black baby carriage, much like a small hearse. A
moment earlier, everyone had been admiring their healthy rosiness;
now they have turned blue. Could someone have strangled them?
The unhappy father suspects his usual *bête noire,* his mother-in-law.
A man voices a deep-seated prejudice: "Old women have always been
a danger to society."[56] The witch hunt begins as the hapless father
rushes toward some woman shouting: "Murderess!"[57] She falls dead
on the spot. The accuser is now a killer, or at least is so defined by
the angry mob. A climate of violence is unleashed, much as in Ionesco's film scenario "Anger." The scene culminates in a paroxysm of
self-accusation, breast-beating, public confessions, all reminiscent of
an occupied country's state of mind. One by one, the members of the
crowd drop dead after experiencing the symptoms of the plague: a
burning sensation at the pit of the stomach, excruciating pains in the
limbs, the darkening of skin pigmentation. Suspicion and wrath seem
to be responsible for the spread of the lethal disease. Mounting panic
reaches epidemic proportions.

The next scene is a soliloquy, an address by one of the City
Fathers. The gist of this man's speech is that the malady strikes at
random, absurdly, with no discernible cause; it is a scandal, as is the
very fact of human mortality. Rumor has it, the speaker declares,
that two remote cities have been experiencing the same phenomenon: Paris and Berlin. Obviously the dramatist selected his cities
carefully. The specific references awaken memories of the past two
world wars. The City Father goes on to say that due to the spread of
the sickness, all public assembly will be forbidden and a curfew imposed. This state of martial law is as contemporary as our newspaper
headlines.

Scene 3, "In a house," is weirdly comical, Molieresque. A rich man, attended by numerous servants, is having his home and his person thoroughly fumigated. A kindred spirit to the "Imaginary Invalid," he hopes to erect a barrier between himself and the raging epidemic. His servants must wear white gloves, not only to serve food, but to prepare it. No expense has been spared, yet wealth cannot insure its possessor against mortality. The servants may have sealed all the cracks in the walls, and stored sufficient provisions for a long siege, but although they recite a litany affirming that their abode is "impenetrable,"[58] words will not make it so. The maniacally careful master is stricken. When his servants attempt to flee the infected dwelling, they are stopped by the police who tell them they will be shot if they try to escape. This is a no-exit situation.

There are no privileged places where death may not enter. Doctors cannot protect their patients in the hospitals. Prisoners who dream of escape realize with horror that a successful scaling of the prison walls would only take them to the invisible dangers of the viruses infecting the so-called free society. Nor is the society truly free because the citizens are held in quarantine within the town walls. Beyond these walls, the epidemic is likely to spread. Mortality is everywhere, one can neither run nor hide from that common fate.

The "Council Chamber" scene offers a fine example of political satire. Six physicians (three men and three women), the medical advisors of the town, have called a meeting to chart the progress of the epidemic and discuss possible measures to check its progress. They will not admit that they are powerless. The Third Doctor declares:

> To say that scientific knowledge is powerless will lead to mysticism, which is outlawed. Or worse, to agnosticism, which is condemned by the medical association, the chemists, the physicists, and biologists, not to mention the public health administrators and the government.[59]

There is nothing "absurdist" about this pronouncement. It is a caricature of a policy once enforced in the Communist states. Only a couple of years ago, a research scientist seen in church during the high holidays or seeking baptism for his or her child was branded as retrograde, and cut off from the community. Reconciliation of science with Christian faith was considered an oxymoron. Ionesco carried his pointed satire to its logical conclusion when he had the Second Doctor declare that no one need die so long as they follow "the rules set down by the medical association."[60] People cannot be infected by any contagion "when imbued with the theory and practice of our credo."[61] Our credo is substituted for *the* credo, the state religion having replaced the church or temple.

A discordant note is sounded when the Fourth Doctor timidly ventures: "I believe there is such a thing as death."[62] This is dissident talk. By admitting the fact of human mortality, one opens oneself to contagion of the body and the mind. Nonbeing is a negative notion, subversive in the eyes of Kremlin ideologues. In June, 1983, at the party plenum, Konstantin U. Chernenko, at that time a Politburo member presiding over the arts, stated that "a young man needs an ideal embodying new goals in life, ideological convictions, industry, fortitude." The old Communist bureaucrat was raising again the standard of "the positive hero," builder of dams and factories, miner, welder, prospector, railroad worker, collective farmer. Such workers could not afford the decadent luxury of meditating upon death; they had no energy left for philosophizing. Above all, in both the fascist and the Soviet systems, citizens were supposed to watch out for the germ of doubt. To introduce such a notion was considered supremely subversive. Police control and censorship ensured that this would not take place.

As though destroyed by his own dissident thoughts, the Fourth Doctor drops dead among his colleagues. They register no surprise, having expected this punishment. What they did not expect, however, was their own doom despite their profession of scientific faith. The first to die is the First Doctor, just after he has made a daring statement: "It's a sickness that is contagious."[63] His peers chant: "You see!"[64] They will prove that death does not exist for them. As they exit, we hear from off-stage their words of warning to one another: "Don't fall,"[65] followed by the thump of each body as it drops to the ground. Petit or Grand Guignol? An amalgam of both. It reminds us that the grotesquely self-assured, cruel guignols, who hastened many men and women to an untimely end, could not escape from death behind the walls of their bunkers, or Kremlin suites. The Black Monk came for both Hitler and Stalin.

As the plague spreads through the city, politicians of the Left and the Right try to make use of people's fears to further their own ambitions. One orator suggests that the disease works in strange

ways, killing off potential enemies of the administration. The undertakers are accomplices of the ruling class and ought to be executed.
He would like to lead the mob to Town Hall and storm it. The crowd
is swayed, but at that very instant the orator drops dead.

The Second Politician speaks with dignity of the rights of the
survivors. Their condition will be much improved by the dwindling
of the population. He promises his audience a government of "men
who are as healthy as possible, and as immortal as the human condition will allow."[66] People applaud this idealistic realist. The meeting,
however, is broken up by two policemen, one of whom promptly
drops dead. Officers of the law are apparently not immune from the
presence of the Black Monk seen crossing the stage.

Chaos pervades the stricken city. The dying are left unattended,
the dead unburied. Every citizen lives for himself, and for the present
moment. The vignette entitled "Night Scene" presents the shocking
indifference on the part of neighbors to the plight of their fellow men
and women.

Each window opening upon the street is like a toy stage, each
reveals the drama within. A boy shouts that his father has attempted
to hang himself but is not dead; they need help. From another window voices answer derisively: "Quiet out there, people are trying to
sleep!"[67] At another window, an old man, holding a revolver to his
head, is ready to take his life. At yet another, we catch a glimpse of
a nurse strangling the old woman in her care in order to rob her. In
a few deft strokes Ionesco suggests the jungle of cities.

The town in *Killing Game* is a city under siege. All human relationships have been vitiated, all natural activities frozen. Husbands
and wives no longer meet freely, mothers cannot carry out wedding
arrangements for their daughters. The "state of war"—an expression
that was used in Poland after the abolition of Solidarity—has put an
end to the natural rhythms of life.

One of the most moving vignettes of the play takes place on a
stage split in two; it shows the simultaneous secret encounters of two
couples. Both men were out of town when the quarantine was insti-
tuted, both had to slip back past the militia in order to reach their
women. Despite the danger they are still running, both couples experience deep joy at being reunited. However, they will have to keep
to their apartments to go undetected.

The architecture of the two scenes is bold, and unusual for Ionesco: both couples speak simultaneously and the lines of the men and women are the same on each side of the split stage. The effect is musical. It is not what they say that matters but the impassioned tone of their voices, the feeling of urgency, of anguish mixed with tenderness. The pattern deviates slightly when one of the partners begins to feel nervous, to experience the need to step outside. In the case of the first couple, this is true of the woman, Jeanne; in the second it is the man, Pierre. Their partners notice a paleness, a restlessness. On each side of the stage, Jeanne and Pierre complain of a headache. They have difficulty breathing and their vision is clouded. Their mates attempt to calm them, until they realize that each of these two is afflicted by the dreadful illness. Whereas Jean clasps Jeanne in his arms, assuring her that he will never leave, the terrified Lucienne abandons Pierre in order to rush toward illusory safety.

This choral recitation, with overlapping voices echoing each other, serves to divert the public's attention away from the tragedy of a single couple. Ionesco suggests that multiple tragedies are playing themselves out all over the stricken city. *Killing Game* is not about individuals; it is a play about collective emotions.

In the midst of the total disarray of the plague-ridden city, where, as in Defoe's 1665 London, the bonds of human fellowship are sorely tried by the omnipresence of the invisible germ, Ionesco's spotlight falls on an aged couple, soon to be separated forever by the natural death of one of the partners. Although this event is unavoidable, it is hastened by the epidemic.

The two old people are much like the couple of *The Chairs,* except that the nearness of an end they do not seek precludes Ionesco's habitual use of irony. As in the Bérenger-Daisy scene toward the close of *Rhinoceros,* a lifetime is evoked in a brief vignette. As the husband and wife shuffle in, arm in arm, going in the direction of a bench, they converse in hushed tones, pursuing a single exchange carried on throughout their long life together. This is a modern version of Philemon and Baucis, as the haunted, sensitive husband admits to an unsatisfied wanderlust. His wife is touchingly open, fresh, full of wonder. (She is the Rodica Burileanu to whom Ionesco wrote a deeply touching public love letter in the form of his final journal, *La quête intermittente.*) She wishes her husband had been able to find what he was looking for, although, as in the case of Jean in *Hunger and Thirst,* happiness was there, in his own home. He knows of course that one cannot escape from one's self, but, as he explains to his lifetime companion, he cannot stop seeking:

> I go out in order to come back in. I come back in order to go out. Each time I've left it was only to come back. Returning, always returning, and each time to one's self.[68]

Now he has no strength left for wandering. As he holds onto his wife, he senses that she is about to fall. Her weakness is not that of age; the signs of the plague are unmistakable. No one will come near to lend a helping hand. The old couple is alone. Their final exchange is deeply moving:

> Old Man: Don't leave me. Don't leave me. You can't. I have you. I'll keep you. How could I not have understood you?
> Old Woman: We understand each other . . .
> Old Man: It's too late. The night will swallow us up. We had joy and I didn't know it. Come, my precious, take me with you into your night as I hold you.[69]

This *andante sostenuto* is Ionesco's own farewell to his loving wife. The coda can be found in his still untranslated journal:

> I tell my wife: most probably we'll be dead within three years' time. She shrugs her shoulders in silent resignation. She is infinitely more serene, far wiser. Rodica, my lucid little one, if we could only have two or three more years. . . . Alas, while we sit in this garden, enjoying its calm beauty, the whole world is nothing but a slaughterhouse.[70]

The structure of the final scenes of *Killing Game* mirrors this journal entry. The tender vignette is followed by a violent scene of looting, culminating in an Artaudian witches' sabbath, a cannibal feast. The end is a conflagration, a reminder of the Great Fire of London that engulfed the city the year after the plague.

As the old couple exits, he dragging his dying wife, four women enter. Indifferent and even angry, inured to such sights, they unmovingly watch the old people. Flanked by two undertakers, a death wagon appears, "pulled by two actors as 'horses.'"[71] The procession

is led by the Black Monk. The wagon has been summoned to remove
the corpses of a shopkeeper and his wife, "dead for at least two
days."[72] The onlookers have nothing kind to say about this couple.
In fact, the women form a mock chorus of mourners; their keening
is composed of derisive, envious comments:

> Fourth Woman: They were too rich.
> First Woman: They drank and ate too much.
> Second Woman: Drank and ate too much.
> Third Woman: They weren't friendly people.
> Fourth Woman: Nobody had to feel sorry for them.
> First Woman: They never thought of the poor for a second.
> Second Woman: Well, I guess now I don't have to pay them
> what I owed them.[73]

Now that the shopkeepers lie dead, their goods unprotected, the
occasion for looting is irresistible. At first the women hesitate; they
are not thieves, just ordinary citizens. Gradually it dawns upon them
that there is no one to stop them. Their longing for finery turns to
an orgy of consumerism. They grab what they see, adorning themselves with jewelry and feather boas. The Fifth Woman claims that
the shopkeepers were her cousins, that these goods are her rightful
inheritance. The other women jeer in the style of Dickens's *tricoteuses:*
"It's public domain now."[74]

Ionesco shows in capsule form the chaos unleashed by the
plague of revolutions and generalized social unrest. In its unbridled
fury, this scene comes close to being the perfect illustration of what
Artaud meant when he coined the suggestive term "theatre and the
plague."[75]

The next scene is even more Artaudian. It has been unaccount-
ably left out of the American translation. Since the play was originally
called *The Cannibals,* it is more than likely that this conclusion was
actually the point of departure for what became *Killing Game.*

Ionesco takes his play in the direction of ultimate horror. He
shows a poor neighborhood ravaged by the epidemic and ensuing
famine. The underprivileged creatures who roam through the deserted streets are no longer human beings; they have become wild
beasts driven by hunger. The rich were able to stock up provisions.
The others had no access to these reserves, no ready cash to fill their

cellars or attics. They attack an official, demanding that some staples be transferred to their neighborhood, but the bureaucrat hides behind legalistic language; clearly he will do nothing. At this moment something snaps. One woman points to the official, shouting: "Let's eat him!"[76] The man runs for his life, escapes, but the thought lingers in the minds of the starving masses. Two women grab the baby of a third: "Let's share the infant. Baby flesh is sweeter than that of an old clerk!"[77] In the ensuing melee, the mother is able to snatch her child away. Now we see men and women foraging for fresh corpses, preferably those of women since they are "more tender."[78] A vendor walks through selling meat pies. There is little doubt that these are stuffed with roasted human flesh. The cannibals' sole concern, however, is for hygiene, not morals; they wish to avoid feeding on victims of the plague. There are some "clean" corpses: suicides, murder victims, and those rare individuals who died of "natural" causes. Since these are few and far between, a man suggests that one need not wait for someone to die: "If you are driven by hunger, and a living person tempts you . . . don't hesitate. This has been common practice since time immemorial."[79] Words such as these give license for unchecked murder. The scene culminates in the capture of a healthy specimen, the mob's next meal!

If this scene seems exaggerated, one ought to keep in mind some of the stories told by concentration camp survivors. In her trilogy *Auschwitz et après,* Charlotte Delbo writes about the activities of some gypsy women prisoners. The latter were adept at stealing cigarettes out of the pockets of the SS. They would exchange them for a daily ration of bread. Once in a while, they came around offering a slice of roast meat, claiming that it had been filched from the SS mess hall. No prisoner ever admitted to accepting this tempting fare; they were certain the meat's provenance was the crematorium.[80]

The final scene of *Killing Game* starts on a hopeful note, the same as that of Camus's *The Plague.* An announcement is made that the plague is receding. However, Ionesco will not treat his audience to a happy ending. At the height of popular rejoicing, the assembled survivors realize that a fire has broken out, encircling the city. No one can hope to escape. "We're caught like rats in a trap,"[81] shouts a man. People scream, run to and fro. A figure stands to one side, observing the panic: the Black Monk. This is indeed "the triumph of death."

In both *Exit the King* and *Killing Game* Ionesco portrays death's ultimate victory. While the people have their health, they harbor the illusion that they are immortal, but, as their strength begins to ebb, they must face the metaphysical realization that they have enjoyed a stay in execution, that they are in fact living dead.

A vignette entitled "A Meeting in the Street" illustrates this particular *prise de conscience*. Two men enter simultaneously, one from stage right, the other from the left. They know one another but lost contact during the epidemic since they inhabit different districts of the city. They are each amazed to discover that the other is still alive. Each is supremely convinced that he owes his survival to the circumstances of his life, particularly to the fact that no one has yet been stricken in his family. Despite this reassuring fact, the men keep a safe distance between them.

Can one always avoid "the wrong people"?[82] This question is all the more poignant today, when the play can be read as a symbol for the AIDS crisis. The Second Citizen inquires: "And what if you were a doctor, a nurse, an undertaker's assistant, what would you do?" The answer comes without a moment's hesitation: "I would resign."[83] However, no one can claim, as the First Citizen does, that he or she is safely out of "harm's way."[84] In fact, the smug man who assumes that nothing will touch him was seen dining in a restaurant with a business acquaintance who just died of the plague. As the horror-stricken man lurches forward at the news, the Second Citizen pulls out a gun, ordering him to step back and keep his distance. The frantic man begs a passing nurse to examine him. She states coldly: "It's too late."[85] The First Citizen runs off screaming: "I'm a dead man! I'm a dead man!" Rushing after him, the Second Citizen fires his gun. The Nurse follows, echoing the First Citizen's cry: "And you're a dead man too! And I'm a dead woman."[86]

Hamlet's metaphysical exclamation: "Horatio, I am dead!" rings throughout Ionesco's two tragicomedies about death and dying. It conveys the dramatist's own apprehension: "I live like a dead man."[87] The playwright tells us that having spoken these words, he burst out laughing at the paradox.

Chapter 8

The Political Cartoonist

The Leader, Macbett, The Hermit, Oh What a Bloody Circus

In his heretofore untranslated 1979 journal, *Un homme en question* (A man questioned), Ionesco finally admits that, although he denied it before, he is a committed political writer. He states: "In my zeal to remain strictly apolitical, I indulged in political action. There is no doubt whatsoever that to be against politics is to act politically."[1]

What is Ionesco's political position? He is known to everyone as the writer who created the term *rhinoceritis* to describe the spirit of conformity, both of the Right and the Left. In France, he was long considered a conservative, despite the fact that he and his wife had fled a fascist regime. French politics, however, began to shift. The publication of Solzhenitsyn's *The Gulag Archipelago* made it impossible for intellectuals to ignore the fact that the Soviet Union was a conservative, brutally repressive society; it had killed some twenty or twenty-five million of its citizens in slave labor camps, prisons, and through mass deportations, "resettlement," and enforced collectivization.

Ten years before the publication of the first volume of *The Gulag Archipelago,* Ionesco began to denounce the scandal of the situation in Eastern Europe. The invasion of Czechoslovakia prompted an article in *Le Figaro Littéraire* (11/11/68), "La Tchécoslovaquie? Le seul pays d'Europe qui mérite son indépendance" (Czechoslovakia? The only country in Europe deserving of independence). Ionesco became the champion of the dissidents beyond the Iron Curtain as well as in Latin America and South Africa. The essays he wrote for *Le Figaro,*

L'Express, Il Giornale, Le Monde are collected in his 1977 journal *Antidotes* (Antitoxins), untranslated into English. Some of the titles of these essays reveal a clearly conceived political philosophy: "Le Fascisme n'est pas mort" (Fascism is not dead), "De Prague à Londres, la honte" (Disgrace from Prague to London), "La Chasse à l'homme" (The manhunt), "A bord de la nef des fous" (Aboard the ship of fools), "Si le monde était soviétisé" (If the world were under Soviet rule), "Agenouillé devant Mao" (On our knees before Mao), "La culture n'est pas l'affaire de l'état" (Culture should not be the business of the state), "Ces Américains anti-américains" (These anti-American Americans). These pieces testify to the dramatist's polemical bend.[2]

Ionesco's greatest political essay was published in 1979 in *Un homme en question,* under the title "Culture et politique" (Culture and politics). It was first delivered as a lecture at the School of International Affairs at Columbia University on Monday, October 16, 1978. Its original title was "Pour la culture, contre la politique" (For culture, against politics).

In this finely argued discourse, Ionesco states that politics and culture were once indissolubly connected, forming a harmonious system of ethics. Rulers, sovereigns, the democratic state turned to thinkers and artists for guidance. But, in the post–Marxist society, politics acquired an autonomous existence; it took precedence over all other manifestations of the mind. Revolutionary ideals gave way to the struggle for power, the lust of conquest. Thought became subservient to the project of *imperium mundi.* Instead of being in the service of humanity, politics grew into an organization for organization's sake. The State, an abstraction, claimed unquestioning allegiance of its citizens. Idealism vanished, replaced by ideological cant.

To establish a dictatorial hold over culture, every independent mind had to be silenced, every new artistic movement squelched: constructivism, surrealism, abstract expressionism disappeared into the storage rooms of museums when they were not destroyed. In the Soviet Union, a rash of tragic suicides ensued: Mayakovsky, Essenin, Blok, Tsvetayeva. Painters, sculptors, architects fled abroad. When revolutionary art and the Revolution parted company, the latter emerged as "an amputee of culture."[3]

Culture, Ionesco explains, is fundamental to the life process; it represents our continuity. Only by existing within a rich brew of culture (the French call it *un bouillon de culture*) are we able to develop as individuals, preserving at the same time a sense of solidarity with our fellow men and women. Besides, many great artists and thinkers have criticized their society, and, by so doing, assisted in its development. Artists cannot be the slaves of bureaucrats. Although Ionesco did not favor the student uprising of 1968, he says that he retained one of its slogans: "Il est interdit d'interdire" (It is forbidden to forbid).[4]

Above all, a dialogue must be established between the great minds of our time and those of the past. It is as though, having entered at night one of our great libraries, we overheard the whisper of books conversing with each other. This point is illustrated in the following passage:

> Culture is nothing if not a vast Parliament wherein Kant answers Plato, Plotinus enters into conversation with Meister Eckhart, Freud probes Sophocles' psyche, Hegel responds to Heraclitus by adopting his position, Karl Marx confronts Proudhon, Jacques Maritain clarifies the position of Thomas Aquinas, and Heidegger elaborates on Husserl.[5]

Ionesco claims art is a wondrous creature, at once archaic and modern. It is the reservoir of the unconscious. Unlike politics and its tool propaganda, art is unable to attempt or achieve a lie because the creative process takes place within depths unknown to the conscious mind of the artist. The artist is like a medium through whom art speaks. In a sense, even an artist's voice is not his or her own; various voices tear their way out of the human psyche, surfacing on his or her lips, transcribed upon the white sheet of paper. Art carries within its structure all of history and prehistory; "it unveils and signifies."[6]

Ionesco's "Culture et politique" is one of the most powerful manifestoes against totalitarianism issued by a contemporary writer of Western Europe. It is a call to counterrevolution, although by nonviolent means. Together with a group of intellectuals, Ionesco founded the Comité des intellectuels pour l'Europe des libertés (CIEL). CIEL is a self-appointed congress composed of people of good will, watchdogs who protest against any repressive act called to their attention. It concerns itself with heeding silenced voices. In Europe, where intellectuals carry great weight, a pressure group such as CIEL is able to sustain the hope of imprisoned, hounded, intimidated protesters, and convey to those who suffered inner exile that they are not bereft of friends.

For the past fifteen years, Ionesco's own isolation among the French intelligentsia of the Left has come to an end. With the dismantling of the Berlin Wall, the reunification of Germany, and the demise of the Ceaucescus, he has proved an early voice of reason. For years, during Jean-Paul Sartre's absolute "reign," the dramatist had been considered a mild lunatic, a verbal prankster who had no business making any pronouncements. Now, it has become clear that he needed to safeguard his independence from Western intellectuals who popped Marxism pills like uppers, a technique he perfected in Romania during the rise of fascism. Only in this manner was he able to develop his remarkable immunity to any form of "rhinoceritis."

While many espoused Maoism only to discover the excesses of the Cultural Revolution, and the existence of camplike reeducation farm communes, and denounced "American imperialism" at the very moment the Soviet Union was occupying Afghanistan, Ionesco remained true to himself. Of course, long before Sartre's death, the young readers of the *Gulag*, of Nadezhda Mandelstam, Eugenia Ginzburg, Amalrik, Grigorenko, Leonid Plyusch, Vladimir Bukovsky, Abram Tertz (Andrei Sinyavsky) began to wonder why the great pope of existentialism failed to denounce the proliferation of labor camps, psychiatric clinics where dissenters were held tight by means of a "chemical strait-jacket," and all manner of abuse against the individual. These young people realized that Ionesco was closer to Albert Camus's brand of humanism than to Sartre's intransigent leftism and his irascible anti-Americanism.

Among theater people, an unquestioning admiration for Brechtian theory had developed since the Berliner Ensemble came to the International Theatre Festival in Paris with their production of *Mother Courage* (1954). Young directors, such as Roger Planchon, met with Brecht and were influenced by his theory and above all his directorial skills. Only gradually did they see that Brecht's greatness did not lie in his didacticism, but in his impassioned portrayal of human misery. As for Ionesco, pressured by the critical establishment of the Left to place his talent in the service of an ideology, as Arthur Adamov had done, he turned for a long time against Brechtism, and even Brecht.

The controversy was played out among the British critic Kenneth Tynan (who had fought to make Ionesco known in England, but turned against him on the matter of politics), Ionesco himself, Philip Toynbee, Orson Welles, and readers of *The Observer*. The exchange appears under the title "The London Controversy" in Ionesco's *Notes and Counter Notes*. In his June 22, 1958, article "Ionesco: Man of Destiny?" Tynan wonders whether the dramatist's escape from realism might not be a flight into a vacuum. He also states that this kind of theater, although "pungent and exciting, remains a diversion."[7] Ionesco replied that the social plane is not the only reality, and went on to explain:

> The only worthwhile authors, those who are on the "main road" of the theatre, would be those who thought in a certain clearly defined way, obeying certain pre-established principles or directives. This would make the "main road" a very narrow one; it would considerably restrict the planes of reality (which are innumerable) and limit the field open to the investigations of artistic research and creation.
>
> . . . the authentic community is extra-social—a wider, deeper society, that which is revealed by our common anxieties, our desires, our secret nostalgias. . . . No society has been able to deliver us from the pain of living, from our fear of death, our thirst for the absolute.[8]

The balance of power was altered significantly with the emergence of the Nouveaux Philosophes, and the ideological shift of the influential journal *Tel Quel*. Ionesco started gaining new friends and admirers. He would even say with a sigh of relief: "I'm no longer alone, no longer *un maudit*." He proved once again that he does not run with the herd.

One of the most neglected aspects of Ionesco's oeuvre is that of the political cartoon. Some of his earliest works, as well as some of the most recent, fall under this rubric.

In August, 1953, Jacques Poliéri put together a cabaret spectacle of Ionesco's *Seven Short Plays*. It was an evening of light entertainment, a divertimento presented at the tiny theater of La Huchette. The seven sketches were written in Ionesco's neosurrealist style characterized by verbal inventiveness and an improvisational component. Yet, despite the surface spoofing, some of the dramatist's serious thoughts also emerged.

The plays were *Les grandes chaleurs* (The heat wave), the story of a gentleman whose conversation liquefies and evaporates under the burning rays of the summer sun; *La nièce-épouse* (The niece-wife), a "juridical sketch" in which an adulterous liaison between a viscountess and a baron is legalized by the viscount adopting his wife as his niece; *Le rhume onirique* (The dream head cold); *La jeune fille à marier* (Maid to marry), a mother's sales talk in praise of her daughter's qualities interrupted by the latter's arrival in the shape of a tall, mustachioed fellow; *Les connaissez-vous* (Do you know them?), a burlesque strip tease; *Le Salon de l'automobile* (The motor show), which shows a man's erotic attraction to a car; *Le Maître* (The leader), a denunciation of demagoguery. Three of the above have been lost: *Les grandes chaleurs, Le rhume onirique, Les connaissez-vous?*

The funniest and at the same time most serious of the above is *Le Maître.* It could be considered Ionesco's earliest political cartoon, a variation on Andersen's tale "The Emperor's New Clothes." It deals with mass psychosis and blind hero worship.

The play opens with an announcer standing at the center of the stage, his eyes glued in the direction of an invisible procession passing offstage. The Leader is coming. The crowd is represented by two "Admirers," a man and a woman. The Leader's every step is reported with mounting excitement by the Announcer, much in the style of radio reportage. It is also the speaker's responsibility to orchestrate the crowd's applause. The two Admirers jump up and down, shouting hurrahs. Suddenly an unscheduled development takes place: the Leader has changed his route. The Announcer dashes offstage, followed by the Admirers. They hope to catch up with the elusive Leader.

In the interval, the "Lovers" run in from two opposite sides of the stage. They have not yet met, and we will witness their first encounter. The space of love is not that of the political arena. For a while, we are allowed to forget the imminent arrival of the Leader. In this early play Ionesco compresses the time of flirting, courting, planning a future married life into a couple of minutes, a device he will use in *Rhinoceros* and *Killing Game.* In all these scenes, the emphasis is on the brevity of life; human beings live but an instant, like butterflies, then they must be engulfed by the boundless dark. This is also Beckett's message in *Waiting for Godot*. The young Lovers, however, are not yet aware of impending death; they flit offstage, eager for marital bliss.

They are replaced by the Announcer and the Admirers who return, still running. Their frantic exchanges translate their fear that they might miss the appearance of their hero. From a distance comes a great roar, that of the approaching mob. Once again the Announcer assumes his center stage position: his back is turned to the theater audience, his attention riveted to the meandering procession. His shouts of "Long live the Leader!" seem to bring the latter closer and closer, to summon him to this empty spot.

However, the Leader has had to make a stop along the way. The Announcer's running commentary allows the Admirers and the audience to follow in their mind's eye every twitch of their idol. These details are trivial, on the level of what we find in the pages of *People* magazine: the Leader knots his tie, reads the paper while sipping his morning coffee, climbs on a stepladder. An accident breaks the monotony of his existence when a parapet he leaned on caves in under his weight—this is the only indication we have of his great bulk—he falls, but phoenixlike, rises again. This list is no more absurd than the usual reports on a president's daily round of activities. What is absurd, Ionesco suggests, is to attach importance to trivia.

Once again the Leader has shifted his appointed route, which brings about another rout. The Announcer and Admirers dash off, leaving the stage free to receive the Lovers. The latter are now happily married, and on their way to market to purchase eggs (Ionesco's recurrent symbol for bourgeois marriage). They collide with the two Admirers, who run in again. The couples' elaborate bows and apologies are played out in marionette ballet style.

The play's rhythm now gains momentum, intensifies. The stage will not remain empty. As the married pair comes in contact with the crowd (symbolized by the two Admirers), their erstwhile harmony is shattered. A chase scene ensues, in the tradition of the silent film that is basic to Ionesco's dramaturgic aesthetic. The Admirers are chasing the Leader, the male Lover his bride. This *perpetuum mobile* is both farcical and sinister. It suggests a malaise, the contamination of the young couple's romantic oneness by mob psychology.

As the Leader approaches, the married couple begins to split up.

She flirts with the male Admirer, he with the female one. Ionesco telescopes the process of *désamour* (the falling out of love), culminating in betrayal. The latter, however, is intimately connected with the imminent presence of the Leader. The private world collapses under the impact of the public one.

As the figure of the much awaited and acclaimed Leader stands at last upon the stage, motionless, we see a headless man. Ionesco's point comes across with a wallop; most rulers do not deserve our unquestioning loyalty, our blind obedience, since they are only figureheads. So often we find that we are governed by headless statesmen.

What a political journalist says in an editorial, and a *philosophe* in many pages of prose, is expressed here in the briefest of sketches by means of a striking image. This technique is that of the cartoonist. From the start of his career as a dramatist, Ionesco reveals himself to be a political caricaturist. Today he might have worked in the popular French medium of *la bande dessinée*.

In January, 1972, Jacques Mauclair staged Ionesco's *Macbett,* a cartoon version of *Macbeth*. As Ionesco declared in *Le Figaro:* "My play concerns itself with genocide and treats the problem of political power."[9] Interviewed by Paul Cezan of *Les Nouvelles Littéraires,* he added: "My *Macbeth* is somewhere between Shakespeare and Jarry; it is close to *Ubu Rex*. . . . It was my friend Jan Kott's book *Shakespeare Our Contemporary* which showed me the way."[10] After the play's opening on January 27, Jacques Guilleminault of *L'Aurore* described it as "a mixture of Shakespeare and Tintin."[11]

Like Picasso's paintings based on Manet's "Le Déjeuner sur l'herbe," *Macbett* is art on art. Politics is Ionesco's concern in this play, as it was in *Rhinoceros,* but with a difference: in the latter, the dramatist presented the monstrous event as a moment of savagery, a regression to the beastly state, whereas in *Macbett* we witness the relentless, cyclic recurrence of political murder and destruction.

There are also revealing differences between *Macbett* and *Macbeth*. Shakespeare's tragedy opens on the mystery of evil as we are introduced to the three Weird Sisters and their familiars, Graymalkin the cat and Paddock the toad. Over these minor spirits hover the powerful Masters. Thus, the triad of witches is but the lower echelon of a three-fold hierarchy. The Satanic trinity in Shakespeare's tragedy suggests the three Parcae, and serves to set the mood for the entire play. In Ionesco's *Macbett,* the circularity of the mystic number three (three witches, three levels of spirits) is replaced by the binary split, and the disquieting, comical image of the double. This intention is inscribed in the spelling of two names: Shakespeare's Glamis becomes Glamiss, and Macbeth is spelled Macbett (it is also the way a French person pronounces the name of Shakespeare's hero). The number two stems from the original couple, Adam and Eve, but, in theological terms, it marks the start of division, that is, of the Fall of Man.

Macbett opens with the entrance of two characters who never appear in Shakespeare's play except as names: Glamis and Candor. They confide to each other their discontent with Duncan's reign and plot an uprising. The names Ionesco chose for his traitors are drawn from specific titles of nobility in *Macbeth:* Macbeth's initial name is Thane of Glamis. And Cawdor is the Scottish laird whose crown and land the brave Macbeth receives from King Duncan in gratitude for his heroic feats. In Ionesco's comedy, Cawdor becomes Candor, as though the middle consonant had been ironically turned topsy-turvy. In fact, the irony goes deeper since there is nothing candid about Macbeth or Macbett. By playing with the signifier, Ionesco leads us to the ambiguities of the signified.

In *Macbett,* Glamiss and Candor are dreadful twins, like Tweedledum and Tweedledee. They proclaim that right is on their side, and they must mete out justice to establish themselves on Duncan's throne. They sound like Jarry's Ubu and his wife, who is a caricature of Lady Macbeth. Ionesco's text is triple-layered with intertext: *Macbeth, Through the Looking Glass and What Alice Found There,* and *Ubu Rex.*

Following this capsule résumé of all revolutions and political plots, we watch the entrance of the two upholders of the existing realm: Banco (Banquo) and Macbett. The two conspirators fawn before the two generals loyal to the king. With two against two, the vaudeville routine changes into a sporting competition. Yet the doubling of the doubles is also disquieting; it opens the way for an exponential proliferation of corruption and murder. Also, as a mirror image of Banco, Macbett is stripped of Macbeth's horrifying gran-

deur; he becomes a comic book character. The nightmarish multiplication of grotesque-looking warriors suggests an organism gone
wild, a cancerous society.

What ensues is a great war. The sound of clashing arms and the
redness of the sky suggest the nearness of the field of battle. An armed
soldier crosses the stage, twirling his sword like a parade baton; for
him war is a glorious adventure. He is followed by a dishevelled
woman on the run, a poor peasant straight out of Picasso's *Guernica*.
A lemonade vendor plies his trade on this blood-soaked piece of
ground, advertising his drink as a universal panacea, good for healing
wounds, curing battle shock, and restoring failing hearts. (Ionesco is
having a bit of fun at the expense of Brecht's *Mother Courage*, the play
that established the German poet's reputation in France.)

Right after the lemonade peddler's sales pitch, Macbett walks
on, his sword dripping with fresh blood. Obviously the scratches he
has inflicted on his foe cannot be healed by lemon juice. The gentle
thane is brimful of blood-lust. His monologue, a mixture of horror
and delight, is a comic book version of Homer's *Iliad*, *The Song of
Roland*, Shakespeare's *Henry V*, and Rostand's *Cyrano:*

> The blade of my sword is all red with blood. I've killed dozens
> of them with my bare hands. Twelve dozen officers and men
> who never did me any harm. I've had hundreds and hundreds
> executed by firing squads. Thousands were roasted alive when
> I set fire to the forests where they'd run for safety. . . . Hun-
> dreds of thousands were drowned in the Channel in desperate
> attempts to escape. . . . There's not enough ground to bury
> them all. . . . They were all traitors of course. Enemies of the
> people. . . .[12]

This last phrase is a direct quote from the clichés of Communist
propaganda.

Clearly this is not a pretty war of the "Grande Illusion" type.
Ionesco's *Macbett* bears the stamp of World War II and the Holocaust.
The allusion to the Channel may be a reference to the encirclement
of the French troops at Dunkirk, where the British fleet efficiently
evacuated its trapped army, leaving their French allies to the tender
mercies of the advancing Germans. In another part of the same
monologue, Macbett speaks of women and children suffocating to

death in cellars, thus raising the image of bombing raids. The scale of the battle suggests modern technological warfare. The "burning forests" call to mind the use of napalm and the defoliation of the Vietnam underbrush. Macbett's soliloquy is a time capsule in which all wars, all atrocities from the beginning of time to our brutal present are contained in concentrated form.

The cruelty of the description is larded with bizarre humor à la Brueghel. Severed limbs acquire a will of their own as they continue to fight the enemy: "The severed heads of our enemies spit in our face and mock us. Arms shorn from their trunks go on brandishing swords and firing pistols. Amputated feet kick us up the backside."[13] The tone of the passage is Ubuesque, the acting style pure guignol. Yet the farcical expressions in no way diminish the horror of the scene. This is a battlefield such as we have seen in newspaper photographs, on our television screens, and more recently in the Kenneth Branagh version of *Henry V*. The bloated bodies, the piles of unburied dead are utterly familiar. Ionesco's grotesque and pitiful evocation of mass death leaves no doubt as to his own place in history, that of an artist haunted by our ceaseless wars, massacres, and genocides.

There is a curious innovation in *Macbett* that subverts the Shakespearian tradition of the soliloquy. The protagonist's monologue is followed at once by its double, a verbatim repetition by Banco. This echo emphasizes the comic quality of the discourse and reduces the "hero" to merely one of two. It is the logical extension into structural reflection of a level of discourse afflicted by the binary split. The mirror image or comic doubling constitutes the basic form of Ionesco's cartoonlike tragicomedy. The surprising result is that this device does not become monotonous. In fact, the repetition in another's voice of the very same bloody images deepens the mounting horror communicated to the audience. The same words, said over and over again, are heard differently each time. It is as though the dramatist were appealing for our full attention, the magnitude of the disaster being such that a single report would not convey it. Killing is monotonous, Ionesco suggests, and war is nothing if not the senseless reiteration of gratuitous, absurd cruelty.

Wars are made by rulers for the sake of strengthening their rule and expanding their empire. We will now be introduced to Archduke Duncan, as he is called in *Macbett*—this title of nobility is a reminder that on June 28, 1914, the Archduke Ferdinand was assassinated in the Bosnian town of Sarajevo, an absurd happening that precipitated World War I. The more recent violent, absurd destruction of the city deepens the irony of Ionesco's reference. Duncan is awaiting the outcome of the battle. Lady Duncan, the archduchess, is at his side, prompting him into battle if Macbett and Banco fail. Duncan, however, is as cowardly as Père Ubu, and as ruthless. Twice in the same short speech, he wonders where he may flee if his army is routed. He seems to have numerous enemies and, besides, the planet is shrinking for political refugees. Even wealth and powerful allies do not guarantee a dispossessed monarch a place in the sun (as the Shah of Iran discovered to his dismay). Ionesco's atlas is both ancient and modern; it takes Shakespeare's *Macbeth* far from prehistoric Scotland to some indeterminate, Jarryesque hybrid décor, a Nowhere that could be Everywhere. The Americas have been discovered, but are no longer conquered. One of Duncan's enemies is "the emperor of Cuba." (Might his name be Castro?) The archduke's predicament is far worse than that of the defeated Ubu, who sailed away on the Baltic, past "Cape Elsinore" and "the shores of the land called Germany, so named because it's exactly half way to Jermyn Street as the blow flies."[14] Hamlet would recognize this insane language of his making, as well as Duncan's justified fears:

> Where can I hide? The king of Malta is my enemy. So is the emperor of Cuba. *And* the prince of the Balearic Isles. And the kings of France and Ireland, and what's more, I've got lots of enemies at the English court. Where can I hide?[15]

Moreover, this undignified sovereign is divided in his feelings between his desire for victory and his fear of his own generals, who might exact a tribute after the battle. Today Ionesco's Duncan could be the twin of Saddam Hussein.

The silent, femme fatalish Lady Duncan demonstrates her true mettle when a wounded soldier stumbles onto the stage. This is a moment of blackest humor. The soldier, another escapee from Brecht, or from Voltaire's *Candide,* does not have the vaguest notion why he is fighting, or on whose side. Roped in by one party, then made prisoner, he was forced to fight for the other camp. Now he is bleeding to death. The archduke calls him a traitor, a deserter. But it is the archduchess, as unhesitant a murderess as Lady Macbeth, who draws a sharp dagger from under her bright green ball gown, ready to finish off the dying man. He assures her in a croaking voice that she need not trouble herself: "Oh, don't bother yourself, ma'am. I'll just crawl to that tree there and kick off."[16]

Blazing fanfares and joyous shouts announce the victory of Duncan's army. Having had a narrow escape, the sovereign's thoughts turn to vengeance:

Duncan: Did we win?
Macbett: The danger is over.
Duncan: Thank God. Has Candor been executed?
Macbett: No, my good lord. But we've taken him prisoner.
Duncan: Why haven't you killed him? What are you waiting for?
Macbett: Your orders, my good lord.
Duncan: You have them. Off with his head. Jump to it. What have you done with Glamiss? Have you torn him limb from limb?[17]

Following this triumph, Duncan is expected to pronounce a speech. His solemn utterance is full of pompous rhetoric and hollow clichés. Not content to honor the few who survived the battle, he addresses the dead, as though they would rejoice in having laid down their lives.

Thank you again, dead or alive, for having defended my throne, which, of course is also yours. [He does not suspect that by saying this he is prophesying his own demise.] When you return home, whether it be your humble villages, your lowly hearths, or your simple but glorious tombs, you will be an example to generations to come, now and in the future, and better still, in the past; they will keep your memory alive for hundreds and hundreds of years, in word and deed, voiceless perhaps but ever present, in fame and anonymity, in the face of an undying yet transient history. . . . [18]

This speech is a compendium of patriotic clichés. With the final reference to history, Hegel's legacy to the ideologues of our century, Ionesco's *Macbett* enters a new phase.

"La raison du vainqueur est toujours la meilleure"[19] (The victor is always right),[20] Candor's preexecution statement, is an ironic variation (in the French text) on La Fontaine's introduction to "Le loup et l'agneau" (The wolf and the lamb), a fable about the ruthlessness of power. Ionesco may be having his little joke, but, like La Fontaine, he proceeds to demonstrate the fundamental truth of this statement. These days it prefigures Klaus Barbie's cynical comment, reported in the French press at the time of his trial: "Had we won the war, we'd have been right." As for Candor, he is *dead* serious, or soon will be. His final words to the king, his lady, the generals, and the court are a confession of guilt, but with a twist:

> If only I'd won. But History was against me. History is right, objectively speaking. I'm just a historical dead end. I hope at least that my fate will serve as an example to you all and to posterity. . . . Historical reason is the only reason. I shall die happy. My life is an empty husk. . . . I'm a perfect example of what not to do.[21]

Candor has perfected the Stalin-trial style of public self-accusation. An obvious student of Marxism, he accepts his defeat and death sentence as part of the historical process. Has he swallowed enemy propaganda or been swallowed by it? He sees himself as Duncan/Stalin views him: "an empty husk." Ionesco, the cartoonist, is sketching here the essence of Stalin's purges.

The execution is performed as an entertainment for the royal family. A guillotine is erected as tea is served. Then many small guillotines appear, testifying to the fact that Candor's fate is not an isolated instance; it is part of a multiplicity of death sentences. Ionesco's typical proliferation device acquires here its full political coloration; it suggests, among other events, the year 1937, the bloodiest time in Soviet internal history.

However, since Ionesco does not wish to tie his play to a specific time or place, any more than Jarry did in his Ubu cycle, the tea ceremony brings us back to a traditional England, perhaps as a reminder that *Macbett* is a caricature of a British literary masterpiece. There is also a precise reference to Shakespeare's text when Lady Duncan is brought a wash basin, soap, and vials of perfume. In perfect Pilate fashion she washes her hands of the execution, then, having wiped them carefully, anoints them with "all the perfumes of Arabia."[22]

By means of this telling image, Ionesco strengthens his device of turning Shakespeare's Lady Macbeth into the Lady Duncan of *Macbett*. In this ironic cartoon version, Duncan's wife plots to seduce the shy general, as becomes obvious in the execution scene when Lady Duncan, sexually aroused by the rolling heads, moves closer to the hero of the day. *Thanatos* and *eros* may be commingled in this fiery creature, but the mix, in this context, is the essence of farce.

The cuckolded archduke is much too busy distributing land and titles to take notice of the hanky-panky going on under the tea table. As he turns to hand the timid Macbett his reward, his general answers in a strangled voice: "I'm all ears, my lord."[23] The organ of hearing is hardly the one in question at the moment.

While Macbett is being both assailed and assuaged, Banco finds his own hopes frustrated by Glamiss's flight. He is deprived of both land and title until the traitor is found. Weary of war, he confides in his companion: "We've got to start all over again!" Like a ridiculous operatic chorus, the two generals keep on repeating: "What a disaster!"[24]

Still looking like Tweedledum and Tweedledee, Macbett and Banco enter the forest in pursuit of Glamiss. A storm is brewing. Macbett, the brave general, is terrified: "What a storm, Banco. Terrifying. The trees look as if they're trying to pull themselves up by the roots. I just hope they don't topple onto our heads."[25] Could this foreshadow the moving of Birnam Wood toward Dunsinane? At this moment, the foot-weary thanes would gladly give up their imaginary kingdoms "for a horse."[26]

In Ionesco's comic play, these antiheroes settle for a lift in a peasant's cart. As Banco leaves to locate some other form of transportation, Macbett is assailed by the hovering voices of ambition, those of "the old hags"[27]—in the French text they are described as "old identical twins,"[28] thus stressing again the disquieting and grotesque doubling prevalent throughout the play. The scene is a clever amalgam of Shakespeare's two witch scenes (I.iii and IV.i). The clever twist in *Macbett* is that the two weird sisters are Lady Duncan and her lady-in-waiting, both in disguise. These fleeting and fleeing temptations lure the naïve soldier, impelling him to win his lady and his crown. When he hears he is fated to reign in his sovereign's place, his retort is not that the latter is still alive, but that he is possessed of a legitimate heir, his son Macol (Malcolm), a university student in

Carthage. (He will prove himself another Hannibal.) There is also a second son, Donalban (Donalbain), studying maritime commerce in Ragusa. Still virtuous, Macbett swings his sword at the two witches who promptly vanish, "changed into the wind and the storm."[29]

As Macbett rushes out in search of Banco, the latter is seen re-entering; he is also looking for his companion. This chase scene is reminiscent of a guignol play. The Second Witch is well aware of the grotesqueness of it all when she exclaims: "When they're not together, they're either following each other or looking for each other."[30]

The weird sisters now go to work on Banco. They inform him that Glamiss drowned. Duncan, displeased with Banco for having failed to capture the traitor alive, plans to seize the conspirator's estates, and hand his title to Macbett. The Second Witch intones: "Macbett is your rival. Your successful rival."[31] Thus, the poison of suspicion is poured into "the porches"[32] of Banco's ears.

When it comes to murdering Duncan, Macbett and Banco are like two bodies with one head. The scene mirrors Caesar's assassination in Shakespeare's *Julius Caesar*. Since the slaying is scheduled to occur while the king officiates at the traditional ceremony of the royal laying on of hands, the other source of the scene can be found in an incidental passage in *Macbeth*, Malcolm's description to Macduff of the King of England's miraculous cures. Edward the Confessor was said to have inherited the gift of healing scrofula, and James the First, for whom *Macbeth* was written, practiced a similar kind of cure. Malcolm's speech, a subtle praise of James the First, introduces the theme of restoration into Shakespeare's somber tragedy, foreshadowing the sound alliance between Duncan's heir and the brave Macduff. In Ionesco, the mock ritual serves to disguise Duncan's assassins, masked as a monk and two patients. Instead of presaging the state's recovery, and suggesting the intervention of divine grace, the ceremony in *Macbett* becomes a Black Mass in the course of which an unholy ruler is caught in his own sham.

One of the two murderers of the king is Lady Duncan. Standing over his dead body, the future Lady Macbett utters an ironically inverted form of the lines of Shakespeare's heroine: "Had he not resembled / My father as he slept, I had done't."[33] In *Macbett* it becomes: "Now that he's dead, he looks just like my father. I couldn't stand my father."[34] This is a Freudian Lady Macbeth, one who dares utter what the boy Eugène repressed in the depths of his wounded psyche.

The wedding of Macbett and his accomplice follows hard upon their deed. One might exclaim like Hamlet: "Thrift, thrift, Horatio. The funeral baked meats / Did coldly furnish forth the marriage tables."[35] However, in this case, a feast to outdo all former feasting is prepared. It is appropriately made up of 247 blood sausages and rivers of wine. Then the table realm is plunged in "swinish sleep."[36] During that time, another murder is committed, that of Banco.

While Macbett lies drunk, his bride and her lady-in-waiting proceed to a countertransformation. The queen casts off the crown and cross, spits out the host she held under her tongue, and clamors for the flask of "spiced and magic vodka."[37] When she adds that icons make her faint, we realize that Duncan/Stalin's erstwhile wife, more a Russian shaman than a Shakespearian witch, is as antiorthodox as the Soviet state used to be. But, as she slips back into her lice-infested dress, her white wig, her pointed nose, she becomes the incarnation of the poverty, ignorance, and malice Chekhov associated with Russian peasants.

Her mysterious disappearance following this metamorphosis parallels Lady Macbeth's suicide. In an outrageous spoof on myth and the supernatural, Ionesco has the "real" Lady Duncan materialize at the banquet where she reveals she was held prisoner in her own palace while the witch assumed her features and the sound of her voice. She adds she was kept informed of all the goings on by means of "the prison telegraph."[38] Her cell neighbors tapped out messages in code upon the wall. (Duncan's *oubliettes* seem to hold as many victims as the Moscow Lubyanka.) This mention of the Morse code—one of the ways in which prisoners still communicate today—testifies to the fact that Ionesco's farce is not merely a pastiche of Shakespeare's tragedy, nor a clever photomontage of *Macbeth* and Jarry's *Ubu Rex* (although this is its basic form), but that its author is also *signing* to us, his readers and audience. He lets us know that his deeper intent is to transmit a subversive political message masked as a romance, or a cruel fairy tale. These witches, goblins, familiars, these endless metamorphoses are but the trappings of woe. Ionesco uses the fantastic in order to lure us into the impenetrable forest of our unconscious, to guide us along the path of maturation. Yet, having retained the childlike sense of wonder, he knows that "the 'truth' of fairy stories is the truth of our imagination, not that of normal causality."[39]

One of the fascinating aspects of Ionesco's political cartoons lies in the *doublespeak* in which they are composed. This is the allusive and elusive vocabulary forged by dissident writers in Eastern Europe, South Africa, South America to skirt ever-watchful censorship. The Soviet bards (Alexander Galich, Vladimir Vissotsky, Bulat Okudzhava) made of this veiled language, transmitted throughout Europe by *magnitizdat* (cassette tapes) a powerful Molotov cocktail. The same was said of the malevolent double-punning of the philosopher-novelist Alexander Zinoviev, whose *Yawning Heights* has been compared to the works of former rebels: Rabelais, Swift, Voltaire. Ionesco, the champion of dissidents all over the world, often seems to address an audience other than the cultivated Western European. It is as though, in some fundamental way, he had never left his native Romania. But there is also something about his literary psychology that harkens back to his roots, to the Jewish *conversos*. Writing for him is hinting at something secret; it is a forbidden activity like keeping the Sabbath in the Toledo of the Inquisition. Although his coded language began as a dada-surrealist prank, it acquired its full harmonic resonance as his political imperative took over his whole being. In his case, secret communication is atavistic.

Interviewed by *Les Nouvelles Littéraires* about *Macbett*, the dramatist stated that one of the main sources in his rereading of *Macbeth* was Jan Kott's interpretation of that play in *Shakespeare Our Contemporary*. Kott's idiosyncratic reading springs from the events he witnessed in his native Poland during World War II and after the Communist takeover. Ionesco met Kott in Paris, when they were students at the Sorbonne. They kept in close contact after Kott returned to Poland, and resumed their friendship when the critic emigrated to Western Europe and the United States in the late sixties.

Macbett's blood-soaked atmosphere, where one killing leads to the next in an unbroken chain, owes a great deal to Kott's explications of Shakespeare. In a telling passage, the critic writes:

> *Macbeth* has been called a tragedy of ambition, and a tragedy of terror. This is not true. There is only one theme in *Macbeth*: murder. History has been reduced to its simplest form, to one image and one division: those who kill and those who are killed. . . .
>
> Macbeth has killed in order to put himself on a level with the world in which murder potentially and actually exists. Macbeth

has killed not only in order to become king, but to reassert himself. He has chosen between Macbeth who is afraid to kill, and Macbeth who has killed. But Macbeth who has killed is a new Macbeth. He not only knows that one can kill, but that one must kill . . . a man is he who kills, and only he. . . . It can be called "the Auschwitz experience."[40]

The greatest villain in *Macbett* proves to be Duncan's heir Macol. He describes himself as the issue of Banco and a gazelle metamorphosed into a woman. Thus, like Macduff in *Macbeth,* he is not of woman born. Brought up by Lady Duncan as her own son, since an heir to the throne had to be produced, Macol is a blend of Macduff, brought into the world by an early form of Caesarian section, and Malcolm, Shakespeare's rightful heir to the throne.

It is Macol's army that will finally defeat that of Macbett. This will not be achieved by magic, but by the lowest kind of ruse. As the two men meet in combat, Macol suggests that Macbett "look behind: in order to see the forest on the march."[41] It is a childish trap, but Macbett, mindful of the prophecy that he stands to be defeated when the woods begin to march in the direction of his castle, falls right into it. As a result, he is stabbed in the back by treacherous, cowardly Macol. As he falls to the ground, he utters a resounding *"Merde!"*[42] This is the final word of this caricatural version of Jarry's caricatural Ubu, whose initial word in *Ubu Rex* is *"MER-DRE!"* The latter is itself an expressionist caricature of what the French call *"le mot de Cambronne,"* turning the familiar expletive into a two-syllable, six-letter oath (it is also referred to as *"les cinq lettres"*), as inflated with the hot winds of bombastic rhetoric and rage as Ubu's "boodle."

Macol is another counterpart of Jarry's Ubu, a Macbett to the thirteenth power. The triumphant assassin is greeted by a delirious crowd, a mob of human rhinos. A soldier marches in with Macbett's head upon a pike. The crowd hoots in the style of the *tricoteuses,* and wishes the dead man further torments in hell. However, Macol stops them short; he will brook no disorderly conduct.

The new ruler states that he will assume the name of his real progenitor, Banco. His dynasty is represented by the sudden appearance of flat cutouts from the French comic strip *Les Pieds Nickelés:* Flochard, Ribouldingue, and Croquignol, unredeemably amoral gangsters. As the new leader addresses his people, "a forest of guillotines appears upstage."[43] Clearly, there will be a new rash of purges and executions.

It is Macol's soliloquy that is Ionesco's *coup de théâtre*. Lifted line by line from *Macbeth* (IV.iii.44–100), it mirrors Malcolm's speech to Macduff. However, in the Bard's tragedy it is a trick to test the honesty and loyalty of a potential ally. Ionesco made a major alteration in having Macol deliver the very same words in all seriousness at the very close of the play. Lines that often pass unnoticed in Shakespeare's tragedy assume an autonomous existence; they leap out in all their strangeness and horror. It is as though we hear them for the first time, although they are in fact a verbatim repetition. This device is also in perfect keeping with the structural pattern of doubling monologues that orchestrates Ionesco's somber cartoon. Ionesco ends his play on the same desperate note as Musset in his *Lorenzaccio*. Côme de Médicis and Macol are also twins.[44]

Macol's blood-curdling address reveals something essential about Shakespeare's text. Or rather it allows us to give it a modern rereading. Jan Kott writes that *Macbeth* is the deepest of Shakespeare's tragedies because it takes us to a threshold beyond which anything becomes possible and permissible. According to the Polish scholar, in *Macbeth* "the very concept of man has crumbled to pieces, and there is nothing left."[45]

Macol is a kind of Himmler, a murderous fanatic. What he promises the people is another version of the *Totenkopfverbände* (death's head units). His solution is "the Final Solution."

> Now I have power, I shall
> Pour the sweet mild of concord into Hell.
> Uproar the universal peace, confound
> All unity on earth.[46]

This is a declaration worthy of Himmler's promise: "Pitilessly we shall be a merciless executioner's sword for all these forces whose existence and doings we know . . . whether it be today, or in decades, or in centuries."[47] Ionesco extracted from Shakespeare's tragedy the theme of a passionate attachment to evil for evil's sake.

Macbett is an angry, witty, political cartoon, but it is also a serious examination of tyrannical power. It encourages us to reread Shakespeare's tragedy in order to see the many ways in which it can address itself to our situation. As in his first play, Ionesco uses flat characters, and is more than ever apsychological. The two-dimensional aspect of this dramatis personae allows the dramatist to demythologize the dream of conquest and mock the heroic stance. This is caricature upon caricature, a text tightly woven from intertextual strands backed by a powerful subtext. It elicits a bitter, bilious laugh since the joke is on us, on our predicament as men and women caught in the trap of History. "History is crafty," Lenin declared. Indeed, it is, when shaped by shrewd and unprincipled leaders. For the survivors, and for future generations, Ionesco's play provides a warning: we may laugh, but we must not laugh our fears away.

In 1973, the Mercure de France brought out Ionesco's first and only novel, *Le Solitaire* (The hermit). Although the title is followed by the definition *"roman"* (novel), this short narrative, written in the first person, belongs to a precise literary genre practiced in France with supreme refinement by André Gide, François Mauriac, and Albert Camus, *le récit* (a tale or an account). Its antecedents can be traced to Voltaire's *Contes philosophiques.*

Set outside of France, *The Hermit* is directly related to Gogol's novella "The Overcoat," to the opening chapters of Goncharov's *Oblomov* (which portray a slothful holy fool who keeps to his room and bed to avoid the empty bustle of daily life), and even more so to Dostoyevsky's *Notes from the Underground* and Kafka's *Metamorphosis.*

Ionesco's nameless antihero is "a sick man" if not "a mean man."[48] He describes himself in psychoanalytic terms as "a depressive."[49] Like the Underground Man, he has a mean office job he loathes, and office mates he despises. Also, like Dostoyevsky's narrator, this lowly scrivener benefits from an unexpected inheritance from a distant relative, money that allows him to take early retirement. His "mousehold"[50] is not unlike the "miserable and ugly corner, on the outskirts of the city"[51] where the Russian writer's jaundiced creature settles as soon as he comes into his six thousand rubles. More concerned with creature comforts, Ionesco's protagonist moves into "a solidly constructed building dating from 1865,"[52] the year following the publication of Dostoyevsky's *Notes.*

The Hermit enjoys living in a modest working-class Paris neighborhood, "not far from the Porte de Châtillon."[53] His back windows face a narrow street lined with villas and small gardens. His front view, however, is of an avenue rumbling with buses and trucks, traffic typical of the Gare du Nord district. This double exposure combines a bustling city life with something provincial, a reminder of the past; it is scaled to human beings, modest retirees. Thus, the Hermit's lodgings stand at the crossroads of the old and the new.

After his move from a small hotel, whose only advantage was to be within walking distance of his office, the Hermit is only too happy to shuttle between his apartment and a neighborhood restaurant where "his" table is kept for him at lunch and dinner time. The man's childlike helplessness appeals to the waitress, as it did in the past to two female office mates. He accepts passively the woman's interest and lets her move in with him. For a while, her presence relieves his anxiety.

His anxiety, however, proves to be something more than the result of a feverish imagination. The silent funeral processions he watches passing below his windows in the middle of the night, when this insomniac wanders from room to room, the red glow in the sky, the distant rifle shots and explosions, are harbingers of a suburban revolution fought by two bands of reactionaries, "one side backed by the Lapps, the other by the Turks."[54] Soon, the whole neighborhood, once so peaceful and safe, becomes an armed camp crisscrossed by barricades and cut off from Paris. During that time, other suburban communities are miraculously untouched by the upheavals of war.

Ionesco's 1973 story prophesies the Beirut of 1983, and the Baghdad of 1991. It also mirrors similar situations in the past: the Odessa of 1918 that kept on passing from the Whites to the Reds over and over again; the Warsaw ghetto of 1943, when a whole population was exterminated while the Poles watched the Jews struggle against their common enemy, never realizing that a year later they would be the next victims, watched in turn by the advancing Russian troops. Strange juxtapositions also took place in concentration camps where *kapos,* or prisoners on special duty, bathed in a swimming pool while their fellow prisoners were marched to the gas chambers. Across the ocean, North Americans strolled along their Main Streets, stopping for an ice cream soda on their way home.

Like his protagonist, Ionesco experienced the need to escape to a country free of "police encampments."[55] The final entry in *Present Past Past Present* yields one of the main keys to the proper reading of this *récit:* "The miracle has happened. For me at least. My friends in various ministries have gotten me a valid passport, with the proper visas. I am taking the train tomorrow. My wife is going with me. I am like an escaped prisoner who flees in the guard's uniform. I will be in France, in Lyon, Wednesday."[56]

As for the Hermit, he may be afflicted with "Oblomovitis" (the psychic illness of Goncharov's Oblomov); he may also be another "Underground Man," but unlike the two Russian nineteenth-century antiheroes (one must keep in mind that the term *antihero* was invented by Dostoyevsky in *Notes from the Underground*), he is unable to preserve his detachment. Since for him there is no escape abroad, he becomes a prisoner of his well-stocked apartment. Weary of the Hermit's mutism, his girlfriend leaves him for another. He is alone, like the Bérenger of *Rhinoceros.*

In his cell, or lair, close to the end of his life, the solitary man dreams of the past, his erstwhile colleagues and friends. His final vision is of a magnificent tree, visible only to him. It seems to have grown in the courtyard "in the space of a single night."[57] This is the archetypal tree of life, rising to the heavens. Suddenly the doors swing open, the walls seem to melt or grow transparent, as at the end of *Exit the King,* or in the 1964 play *Hunger and Thirst.* An immense universe crystallizes before the dazzled eyes of the dying man. Wars, revolutions, love affairs seem "a lot of fuss about nothing."[58] as Queen Marguerite tells the dying Bérenger Ier. The small room fills with the glow of a supernatural light, as though all the stars of the firmament were suspended from the branches of the marvelous tree. They were there all along, but flesh and fear had obscured their splendor.

The individual who cherished his solitary remoteness, the apolitical being who tried to safeguard his independence, will now take a step beyond passive resistance. He will welcome the mystic vision, taking it "for a sign."[59]

On November 14, 1973, Jacques Mauclair presented Ionesco's *Ce formidable bordel* (Oh what a bloody circus), which is based on the novel *The Hermit.* The staged version resorts to a device that is the opposite of the one used in the novel. Whereas in the latter all is seen through the narrator's eyes and heard through the inner voice that rises from his psychic depths, the play's protagonist is entirely silent. Incidental characters chatter, intrude on his privacy, make assumptions about his thoughts and reactions while he remains at the center of this turmoil, in his own zone of quiet.

The silent character is said to have been inspired by Buster Keaton, the silent-film actor used by Samuel Beckett in *Film* (1964). Both Ionesco and Beckett make of silence a positive presence, a way of resisting the easy superficiality of social intercourse. The Hermit and the Character are brothers of Watt, Murphy, Malone, and Worm. Moreover, as noted by Emmanuel Jacquart, this anonymous type of protagonist, the mirror image of his creator, has replaced the carefully described, vividly depicted character of nineteenth-century fiction. Like many of us, modern men and women, he finds it impossible to distinguish between reality and illusion. In Ionesco's play, lights and sound effects serve to stress the separation between public and private life. The louder the voices grow, the more obtrusive the gun shots sounding from the street, the more the central character seems to affirm through his stubborn mutism his rejection of meaningless turmoil. Only at the very end, when the ghosts from his past crowd around him, does he scream like a man possessed, chasing them away. The Character reveals Ionesco's readings in Eastern philosophy, particularly Zen Buddhism. In *Oriental Mythology* Joseph Cambell sums up the fundamental difference between Occidental and Eastern thought:

> The metaphysical *tremendum,* the deep awe before the great, unchanging truth, and the full submission of all human judgment to a mystery unnamed, which is infinite, impersonal, yet intimately within all human beings, all things, and in death too: these have been the sentiments that in the Orient have remained honored as the most holy. And from the point of view of the knowledge in rapture of that full void, the dedication of the Occidental mind to the merely personal affairs of men and women living in the world appears to represent only the loss of the fruit of life. . . . [60]

It is this magical fruit that the Character recaptures when he sees a wondrous tree fill the entire stage. This vision breaks his silence, and he bursts out laughing, and exclaiming: "I ought to have realized ages ago! What a joke! It's staggering! What a farce! Such a stupid practical joke! What a hoax! And I took it all to heart! . . . It's one colossal hoax!... Who could have imagined such a trick! What a circus! Hell's bells! What a bloody circus!"[61] This exclamation sums up Ionesco's views of politics, society, life in general.

A capsule version of Ionesco's weltanschauung is communicated by a tall gentleman, leaning on a cane, who seems to have found his way to the Character's apartment. In the Paris production, the Gentleman spoke with a Russian accent. These are some of the truths he throws at the silent man:

> Wars, I've had my fill of them. That's why I'm lame you see. Wounded in the war. We waged that war on people we didn't know and couldn't understand, because they spoke a different language.... I've stopped reading the newspapers, they upset me so.... Nothing but murders and massacres, floods and plagues, epidemics and earthquakes, holocausts, tyranny and genocide. Why do we hate each other so?[62]

There is no answer to this question; the Character's dignified silence is the only possible response. In *Antidotes,* Ionesco ventures: "The world may be a colossal trick God played on humanity."[63] This thought is followed by a revelation of what lies at the basis of a play so clearly Eastern in its mode:

> I must have been inspired by the story of a Zen monk who experiences an illumination on the threshold between life and death. After having spent every moment of his existence questioning himself and the mystery of creation, he casts a final look around him, but with new eyes. He shouts: "What a hoax!" and bursts out laughing.[64]

Having reached mature understanding, the brilliant political cartoonist views all of life as a series of tragicomic vignettes. The strangest discovery is that everything beautiful was always within reach from the beginning. The Character's final laughter raises the play's finale to the level of transcendent merriment, like that of Homer's gods rocking with gentle amusement at the sight of human follies.

Chapter 9

The Modern Classicist

Hunger and Thirst

On February 28, 1966, when Jean-Marie Serreau brought to the stage of the Comédie Française Ionesco's *La Soif et la faim* (Hunger and thirst) a Rubicon was crossed. Ionesco graduated officially from the status of a peripheral, Left Bank vanguardist and was raised to the rank of modern classicist, the descendant of Molière, Racine, Marivaux, Beaumarchais, and, closer to our time, Giraudoux. It was a veritable consecration for the enfant terrible of French letters. Four years later, he was elected to the Académie Française.

Ionesco himself never harbored any doubts about being *un classique*. Back in 1961, when he was in New York for the premiere of *Rhinoceros,* he made a funny little joke while being interviewed by a journalist at the bar of the hotel where he was staying, the Algonquin. After giving some straight answers to the first questions, he suddenly grinned—half naughty toddler, half aging clown—and inquired: "You do realize you are interviewing today's Sophocles?" In a more serious vein, Ionesco stated in the February 15, 1959, issue of *Bref* that he was "for classicism,"[1] and went on to explain:

> In the end I realized that I did not really write "antitheatre" but "theatre." I hope I have rediscovered intuitively in my own mind the permanent basic outlines of drama. In the long run, I am all for classicism: that is what the "avant-garde" is. The discovery of forgotten archetypes, changeless but expressed in a new way: any true creative artist is classical . . . the petit bourgeois is the person who has forgotten the archetype and is absorbed by the stereotype. The archetype is always young.[2]

The dramatist's faithful, precise definition of classicism—a return to the sources in ancient Greek literature—is confusing to the French who, when they hear the term *classique,* associate it with neoclassicism; that is, with baroque seventeenth-century literature, in particular the theater of Corneille and Racine. Ionesco enjoys the freedom of the "outsider" in France. He does not take Corneille for Aeschylus. When he mentions "the archetype" he is thinking of the origins of myth as analyzed by his friend Mircea Eliade in his *Cosmos and History: The Myth of the Eternal Return,* and he considers Jung's writings.

Jung meant by *archetype* the archaic remnants of primordial images. These may vary, but they issue from a basic motif or pattern. According to Jung, such images manifest an instinctive trend that is present all over the world; yet the origins of these images are mysterious, unknown, unknowable. They are symbols of creation, of death and rebirth, which resemble the teachings given adolescents in primitive initiation rituals. The ancient world believed that dreams were prophetic. Jung does not contradict this view, but he explains it by saying that the unconscious is already informed of something that the conscious mind has not yet formulated.

Ionesco himself experienced this phenomenon when, as a young man in Romania, he had a nightmare: he saw a woman engulfed by flames. In the dream, he was trying to save her, but was held back by a ring of fire. The following day, he found out that his mother died that same night, perhaps at the very moment he was having this dream. This vivid scene, reproduced in *Hunger and Thirst,* is only one example of the archetypal images Ionesco taps for his oneiric drama. Like Eliade, he is convinced that an object or an act becomes real insofar as it imitates an archetype. The poet-dramatist addresses his audience by means of these Platonic projections, shadows in the daytime, essences at night. In Jungian terms, he reaches out to the universal unconscious, speaking to all human beings on their deepest, most instinctive level.

One could say that this is precisely what Sophocles achieved in showing his audience the sinful, doomed marriage of a mother and her son. The myth of Oedipus is ever present in Ionesco's theater, but in the Jungian rather than a Freudian context. It would be a mistake to apply Freudian psychoanalysis to an Ionesco drama. He believes fervently that Freud is reductive, whereas Jung probes the complexities of the psyche without explaining them away. The dramatist's task is not to psychologize, but to recreate classical patterns.

In his essay "Ionesco's Classical Absurdity," Roy Arthur Swanson reaches the following conclusion:

> With proper qualification of the critical terms that bear application to Ionescan drama, it is feasible to conclude that Ionesco, well attuned to the absurdity exposed in Aeschylean and Sophoclean tragedy, has transmuted this exposure into true tragicomedy and has become the classical dramatist of the absurd.[3]

Swanson argues that Ionesco's absurdist theater, like that of Beckett, Adamov, and Pinter, possesses a weltanschauung that coincides with the one presented in Greek tragedy. He goes so far as to claim that "the theatre of the absurd is itself the recreation of Greek tragedy in a comic milieu."[4]

Swanson's essay is important because it removes once and for all from Ionesco's theater the vague and confusing label *avant-garde*, one that the writer himself objects to in his theoretical essays. In his "Talk about the Avant-Garde," Ionesco questions the term and proceeds to define it "in terms of opposition and rupture."[5] All true creators, he argues, are rebels; they must struggle against the ossification of thought and language. Yet each new author hopes to express not only his truth, but the truth as he sees it. All art is a probing, an adventure of the mind and heart, all artistic expression reaches for a form of transcendence, even of excess. Thus, realism initially sought "to extend the realms of reality,"[6] not to stay within the boundaries of the so-called real. Reality is not realist, Ionesco points out, it is simply a style, a school, a way of looking, writing, painting, singing, and dancing. Realism is a convention, like romanticism, symbolism, surrealism. Following the establishment of the realist mode, symbolism and surrealism sought a more vivid reality, or truth, in something hidden: the subconscious, the oneiric. Ionesco concludes:

> The question is simply for an author to discover truths and to state them. And the manner of stating them is naturally unfamiliar, for this statement itself is the truth for him. He can only

speak for himself. It is by speaking for himself that he speaks for others. Not the other way around.[7]

People are amazed when they see a huge, growing corpse on the stage, but they are no longer surprised by the gradual unfolding of a horrifying truth: a mother has become her own son's spouse and borne him four children. Yet, both Sophocles and Ionesco deal in their ways with what Swanson calls "the changeless mean of ignorance."[8] Both make use of words and images to convey an overwhelming sense of sin. Despite the absurdist idiom, the comic coloring associated with Ionesco's first phase, the playwright's mature dramaturgy moves closer to the Theban cycle than to high modernism.

In *Exit the King,* as discussed in chapter 7, we are shown a dying monarch, one whose final "exit" will be as dignified as that of the protagonist of *Oedipus at Colonus.* There is of course no grandeur about Bérenger Ier throughout most of the play; although terror and pity wring our hearts as we watch his anguish, recognizing in it our own fears, our senseless struggle against the unavoidable end, we cannot help but laugh at his clownish cringing and crying out, his scurrying to and fro, his circus pratfalls. However, when we laugh at Bérenger, we are laughing at ourselves, and this explosion of bitter merriment purges us, cleanses our spirit.

Is there anyone who has not experienced this blind terror? Tolstoy confessed that he woke up one night with the overwhelming apprehension that a day would come when he would no longer be among the living. He was still a young man when he had this clear vision of the death of his body and, with it, a vision of the universe alive in his mind, living through him because he was alive and conscious of being so. This thought propelled him out of his bed, and sent him running from room to room, until he came to a halt with yet another question: What was he racing away from? Death was not an exterior force he could outrun; it was waiting within his body, like a pit within the fruit.

Bérenger Ier discovers the same truth, and it also sends him running in his bare feet through the cobweb-covered throne room. He also experiences within his weakening flesh the verity of Pascal's *pensée* that all human beings are like prisoners condemned to capital punishment, awaiting that dreadful dawn in their cells. The only difference, Pascal pointed out, between the man in jail and the prisoner of his own mortal flesh, is that the latter does not yet know when his death has been decreed.[9]

Close to death, Bérenger acquires the dignity of the blind, old Oedipus who assumes a noble gait to enter alone the sacred grove of the Eumenides. There he will vanish from mortal eyes, much as Bérenger vanishes in the gray mist of the Void. The Messenger in *Oedipus at Colonus* reports that those who stood nearby saw the King "shading his eyes as if from something awful, / Then very quickly . . . do reverence / To earth and to the powers of air, / With one address to both."[10] Oedipus glimpsed death with the eyes of the spirit, the inner eye. Ionesco's Bérenger, led by one of the Eumenides, the transformed Queen Marguerite, treads step by step "the holy and funereal ground."[11] When he ascends the steps of his throne, and sits down, immobile, a stone statue of himself, he has become one of the immortals and, like Oedipus, "the patriarchal teacher of those who did not know that they did not know."[12]

The profound contentment, the acceptance of death as an integral part of life, raises the concluding scene of *Exit the King* to the level of classical stoicism. Both Sophocles and Ionesco have given us the ambivalent image of the human being as his or her "own beaten self."[13] Yet this ragged, suffering creature can also be the supreme boon, as indeed Oedipus became for King Theseus the gracious host who welcomes and protects him until his final moments.

As Swanson explains, classical Greek tragedy evokes calm by means of excitement and serenity through the experience of horror. A similar substitution takes place in the drama of the absurd, except that there humor constitutes the other term of the balance. The critic states: "In Greek tragedy the absurd is *exposed,* and in the theatre of the absurd it is *exposed to laughter.*"[14] When he was interviewed by Edith Mora for *Les Nouvelles Littéraires,* Ionesco admitted: "Laughter . . . laughter . . . certainly I cannot say I do not try to arouse laughter; however that is not my most important aim! Laughter is merely a by-product of a dramatic conflict that one sees on the stage . . . laughter comes as a reprieve: we laugh so as not to cry. . . . In my plays, the comic is often merely a stage in the dramatic construction, and even a method of constructing the play."[15]

This declaration reveals an entirely different view of the comic: there is no laughter for laughter's sake. Ionesco carefully points out that he does not think of himself as essentially a comic writer. For him, the comic device is a structural component of his dramaturgy. This emphasis on form testifies once again to Ionesco's classical aspect, his awareness of being *un classique*.

Ionesco believes that form survives beyond content, idea, message, even feeling. In his essay "The Play of the Passions," written for the *Times Literary Supplement* in 1972, he raises the following question: "Can we say of a statue, a temple, a cathedral or a symphony, an epic poem, that they are true or false? All we can do is acknowledge their existence, their reality; the fact of them."[16] Indeed, Greek temples are no longer used for worship, yet they still stand, survive, enclose something of the human spirit. We do not believe any longer in Poseidon, but we find a deep kind of joy at being in Sunium where we are able to admire the remains of his great temple rising at the edge of a promontory. A perfect structure continues to please; it corresponds to a necessity of the human spirit. Like Socrates, Ionesco might conclude that "the good cannot be beautiful, nor beauty good, if the two are not identical with one another."[17]

Of all of Ionesco's works, *Hunger and Thirst* is the most carefully structured and, thus, perhaps the most "classical." There is a good deal of humor in the play, albeit bitter, but this is a philosophical work, a kind of *summa* for the artist. Almost all of Ionesco's images and themes can be found again in this richly orchestrated drama. *Hunger and Thirst* also points beyond itself to the two magnificent dream plays that constitute the dramatist's final contribution to the theater.

A vast, autobiographical tone poem, *Hunger and Thirst* was originally divided into three parts rather than acts. However, Ionesco was not satisfied with the end product, so he turned his trilogy into a tetralogy. The additional scene, which in the final version becomes episode 3, was conceived in 1966. It was first staged separately at the Théâtre de Poche Montparnasse along with some other short sketches, then published in *La Nouvelle Revue Française* in July–December, 1976. The complete play, in four episodes, has at last been published in Ionesco's *Théâtre complet*.

Entitled "The Flight," episode 1 takes place within the protagonist's modest home. The stage represents a dark basement room, with two fan lights admitting a ray of dirty gray light. There is a

fireplace at the center of the rear wall, an old mirror on the right, and
a cradle to one side. This is the locus of the family life of three: Jean,
his wife Marie-Madeleine and their infant daughter Marthe. The
structure faithfully reproduces Ionesco's own family unit and the
names of the three characters are symbolic and biblical. Jean suggests
Ionesco—the Romanian name being the equivalent of our Johnson—
and evokes the figure of Christ's disciple, the author of the fourth
book of the New Testament, and the Book of Revelations, as well
as that of Saint John of the Cross, the mystic Spanish poet of the night
and the Void *(nada)*. Marie-Madeleine (Mary Magdalen) is one of the
women who witnessed Christ's Passion, and Marthe (Martha) is the
sister of Lazarus. Ionesco's dramatis personae are not allegorical
figures, but their names reinforce the biblical references throughout
the play, and the theme of the "hero path." Ionesco's symbolic tragedy moves from hope to despair. It ends in tragic imprisonment, be
it in a real jail, or the prison of the mind.

As the curtain rises, Jean reproaches his wife for having allowed
their moving back to a "funereal ground-floor flat."[18] He cannot get
used to having left a new building where they inhabited a top floor
with "windows all around, open to the sky . . . a gilded bal-
cony . . . space stretching all around."[19] Marie-Madeleine tries to reason with her husband. So far as she is concerned, she could be happy
anywhere as long as they are together. Jean brushes this simple wisdom aside. He is shivering with cold and anxiety. Their dwelling,
he maintains, is sinking into the wet, slimy ground. Nor is this vision
idiosyncratic. It is an expression of the poet-dramatist's apocalyptic
cosmology. Jean exclaims: "Streets and towns, whole civilizations
get swallowed up."[20]

The mud of Jean's apartment signifies both the sensuous attachment to daily living, and the disintegration of death; it is simultaneously what Queen Marguerite calls scornfully the "warm and
cozy . . . mud of life"[21] and the ooze of the passageway leading to the
underworld. Ionesco told Simone Benmussa that the basement apartment is a faithful recreation of a similar lodging rented by his mother
when she arrived for a visit to Bucharest. "My mother died before
she had a chance to move in," he reminisced, "but I believe she chose
these rooms because she sensed subconsciously that she was close to
death. It was on her part an acceptance of the grave; she was resigned

to dying. For me, this place where she never actually lived is the very
image of a tomb. Each time I dream of such a house I see my mother
in it."[22]

Indeed, the apartment is inhabited by a quaternity of anima
figures of a positive and negative kind. There is Jean's motherly,
selfless wife and their infant daughter—invisible in her crib—and
there are two female ghosts: a woman consumed by fire in the fireplace, like the dramatist's mother in his premonitory dream, and the
protagonist's maternal aunt, who comes striding through the mirror,
a stage device that reminds us of Jean Cocteau's beautiful figure of
Death in *Orphée*. However, there is nothing romantic about Aunt
Adelaide. Dressed in dirty tatters, yet walking with the nonchalant
grace of Giraudoux's Madwoman of Chaillot, she is an insane bag
woman. She refuses to acknowledge that she is dead, the otherworldly afterglow of the paranoia that characterized her last years of
life. As she chats with Jean and Marie-Madeleine, as casually as any
visitor, Adelaide's madness surfaces more and more. She harps upon
the subject of her family's lack of appreciation of what she did for
them, and of her achievements. Strangers, she states, honored her,
kissed her hand, wrote her love letters. They knew that it was she
who was the real author of "the treatise on medicine and surgery"[23]
signed by her husband. She insists on reminding the family that it
was she who helped her sister when she was abandoned by her husband. Though Aunt Adelaide's discourse is a bizarre mixture of fact
and fantasy, it is based on Ionesco's Aunt Sabine.

"I wish the character of Aunt Adelaide to appear simultaneously
as real and ghostly. The ambiguity must be felt all the time," Ionesco
explained to a group of friends who had come to join him in Stockbridge, Massachusetts in July, 1969. Having been invited for the
U.S. premiere of *Hunger and Thirst*, the Ionesco family was ensconced
in Heaton Hall, a stately hotel that has since been pulled down. The
Ionescos delighted in the European-looking reception rooms,
crowded with the kind of Victorian furniture with which they fur-
nished their own Paris apartment, the perfect décor for *The Bald
Soprano*. Looking happily at the immensely long hallways, the high-
ceilinged reception rooms, the large marble bathrooms, Ionesco
sighed: "Ces espaces sont vastes et mystiques!" (These spaces are vast
and mystical). While Rodica Ionesco walked in the woods behind

Heaton Hall, amazed by the plastic "wild" flowers planted in the moss, her husband met with actors and friends on the hotel porch. Swaying in a rocking chair, he told his listeners the story of Sabine:

> My mother's sister was married to a defrocked priest, a cultured man who spent the last years of his life in a monastery. Gustave Peytavi de Faugères was her third husband. Her own profession was dental surgery. It was she who came to our rescue when my father left for Bucharest. In 1958, twenty-two years after my mother's death, her sister suffered a mild cerebral hemorrhage. Her mind was affected. Although she enjoyed a comfortable pension, she began to dress like a *clocharde* (a homeless bum), and stood begging every day at the nearest metro station. Perhaps the memory of the years when she was the sole provider of a large family (her own father and mother, her sister, the sister's two small children) filled her with the dread of remaining destitute. There she was, wandering on the streets. Often some charitable soul walked her gently to the nearest police station. The officers on duty got to know her, and automatically released her, urging her to go home. On one occasion, however, she was driven to the mental ward of Sainte Anne Hospital, but they did not keep her there. She was a gentle lunatic. One day, however, she set fire to her own apartment. The firemen came and put it out at once. When they questioned her about how it had started, she told them some bizarre tale: her neighbor had stolen her keys and set fire to the place in her absence.

Ionesco stopped for a moment, and then added: "I have transcribed these details, without exaggerating a thing. Reality is very bizarre, one need not reach for strangeness."

The story of Aunt Sabine provides a very interesting key to much of Ionesco's absurd world. The firemen explain the peculiar intrusion of the Fire Chief in *The Bald Soprano*. But beyond this, an identification must have occurred in the writer's mind between himself and this peculiar woman, his second mother and the head of the family. In a sense, she is his negative anima, as she boasts of being a famous writer, a lecturer, the friend of many a head of state. Her old handbag bursts with medals, crosses, and ribbons she received for her published oeuvre. A caricature of the *femme de lettres,* she is the personification of the writer's psyche, the feminized projection of the future academician.

According to Jung, the most frequent manifestations of the malefic anima take the form of erotic fantasies. Despite her advanced years, Adelaide is convinced she is irresistible, a kind of Lorelei or Blue Angel. To prove she is no ghost, she opens her bodice and displays her breasts. Then, to demonstrate she has "lovely red blood" coursing through her veins, she removes her hat, "overloaded with artificial flowers and grapes," and, whipping out a knife hidden in her bodice, proceeds to slit open her own skull. This Flora/Pomona/ Dracula can only shed stage blood. Jean, who is not easily taken in by artifice of this sort, sets her straight: "It's not real blood. It's not liquid. And then it's too dark for blood. It's like jelly. Gelatine. Sticky! And it doesn't stain! A moment ago I had it all over my fingers: now it's vanished. . . . No, Aunt Adelaide, it's definitely not real blood. You're trying to mislead us."[24]

The blunt accusation acts as an exorcism. The offended spirit vanishes. Marie-Madeleine accuses her husband of having been unkind to "a near relation."[25] This cliché, applied to a ghost, is particularly comical. However, it precipitates a crisis. Jean realizes he can no longer linger in a haunted apartment. He will flee his home, his family. When his wife calls him a neurotic, he retorts: "I see things as they are. And that's *incurable.*"[26]

How does speaking to a ghost indicate that one sees "things as they are," that one is lucid, rational? Jean does not answer his wife's accusations directly; he is pursuing his own line of thought. Just as he freed himself from the negative anima by confronting the ghost with the brutal fact that she is a fake, a ham actress, he must now cut himself loose from the motherly woman, his wife. In so doing, Jean/ Ionesco follows in the footsteps of his own father.

In Jungian terms, severing this tie is an essential step in the ego's heroic act. Marie-Madeleine believes there is a cure for Jean's melancholia, that so long as they stay together they will find a line of treatment. By stating that lucidity is an incurable affliction, Jean is redefining neurosis as a positive force, a drive toward perfection. Jean's "hunger and thirst" are greater than a humdrum existence. The play's title, with its biblical echoes (Matt. 25:25), indicates that the author is going to present upon the stage his Everyman's quest, a spiritual voyage that will take him from the protective atmosphere of home to the rarefied air of a high plateau, and finally to the depths of the inferno.

The man who runs away from home is not yet a fully realized human being. Jean does not walk out in a decisive, dignified way. He makes his exit gradually, by playing a cruel game of hide-and-seek. Husband and wife are shown running around the stage, with Jean disappearing, reappearing, ducking behind pieces of furniture, like a naughty child. Marie-Madeleine scurries to and fro, at first with mild amusement, then with mounting annoyance. She becomes frantic, desperate. The audience catches glimpses of the elusive husband's head, of an arm, a leg; they do not seem to belong to the same body. (In performance, there are of course extra props: a head, separate limbs. A disquieting effect of dismemberment and ubiquity is achieved by this *commedia dell'arte* harlequinade.) However, the audience's laughter quickly dies on their lips. Their sympathy turns wholly to the flushed, breathless wife who has been drawn into this game, one in which she can only be the loser. As she seeks her invisible husband, echoing his haunting, taunting "Coucou! Coucou!" to locate his hiding place, the audience realizes that he will not return. Jean has succeeded in turning his kind, forgiving mother-wife into a bewildered, humiliated, cheated, tragically unhappy playmate.

This scene owes its heart-rending character to the fact that Ionesco dramatized in this absurdist, childlike form his father's desertion of his family. In *Present Past Past Present,* the dramatist speaks of his astonishment in discovering that his mother was, like him, nothing but a child, "a helpless puppet in [his] father's hands."[27]

Episode 1 of *Hunger and Thirst* reproduces the father's betrayal of the mother, transferring the act to the son. In a journal entry Ionesco writes: "I have taken my father's guilt upon myself."[28] The abandoned child in the crib is not a son (Eugène), but a daughter (Marie-France Ionesco). Although Ionesco has been a loyal husband, if not a faithful one, and a loving father, his own father's flight to Romania, which forced him, eventually, to leave France, remained alive in his mind. It represents an act he never committed, but one that he knew he was capable of.

Jean's quest will be that of the creative artist. In order to embark upon this voyage of discovery, he must first "tear this love from his heart."[29] In a poetic instance of symbolist staging, we are shown the protagonist uprooting a branch of briar rose growing from his chest. The branch, which metaphorizes his love for his wife and daughter, is then set upon the table. There is blood on it, for "the hero" must be ready to die before he is allowed to ascend to the next stage of the hero-path. When Marie-Madeleine runs back into the now empty room, she sees the lovely, blood-stained shoot. Faced with the evidence of her abandon, she grieves for the departed wanderer, never thinking of her own pain: "Poor Jean! How he must suffer! My poor little Jean's been hurt. He's leaving a trail of blood behind him on the road."[30]

Marie-Madeleine's piteous exclamation leads us into the folk tale world that is never far removed in Ionesco from everyday life. A moving story comes to mind, that of a mother's heart. It concerns a son who cut out his mother's heart in order to win that of a cruel beauty. As the matricide raced to join his lady love, bearing this dreadful offering, he stumbled and fell. The heart dropped to the ground and spoke: "Did you hurt yourself, my child?"

The "trail" motif is frequently used in fairy tales. "Hansel and Gretel" finds Hansel creating trails to mark his wanderings through the woods. The first time, white pebbles aid his return; the second, he foolishly uses bread crumbs, which are eaten by birds. The same fate befalls Little Tom Thumb. Marked by blood, the trail envisioned by Ionesco's anguished Marie-Madeleine is less that of a wandering child than Christ's *via dolorosa*. By giving his female character the name Marie-Madeleine (Mary Magdalen) Ionesco strengthens the comparison.

Ionesco's play provides what Mircea Eliade calls "an initiatory scenario." Jean must discover his identity and calling; he must explore the universe. Yet, in so doing, he assumes that every worthwhile endeavor lies ahead, away from home. The dramatist suggests that the magical universe need not be sought in remote regions, that it is present within the walls the child finds so confining.

Episode 1 ends with the back wall of the apartment growing transparent. It reveals a view of an inner garden rich with flowers, trees, birds. A silver ladder hangs from the heavens, its lowest rung resting in the center of the garden; it connects the earth to the firmament. Jean should not have left in search of wonders; like Marie-Madeleine, who is transported by this sight, he simply had to open his eyes, or perhaps that inner eye that would have allowed him to perceive what lay there, on the other side of his own wall.

At the end of *Hunger and Thirst,* Jean catches a glimpse of this magic garden in which his wife and their fifteen-year-old daughter are standing in the shade of the magic Tree of Life; it is a vision of paradise. By then, it is too late for the wanderer to join them. He has lost the Garden of Eden in his quest for perfection and has become the prisoner of a demonic monastic society into which he strayed in the course of his search. The simple joys of family life must remain a mirage, an oasis perpetually out of reach. This is his true punishment.

Although Ionesco's tragedy follows the archetypal patterns of myth, it must be seen as an anti-*conte-merveilleux*. The hero never reaches "his" kingdom, never attains the independence and maturity the fairy tale realm symbolizes. In fact, he reaches the place where the hero begins "at the mercy of those who think little of him and his abilities, who mistreat him and even threaten his life."[31]

Does Ionesco suggest that life is no fairy tale? In episodes 2, 3, and 4, the protagonist must endure a long and painful apprenticeship. He will discover many traps, disappointments, and defeats along the way. Perhaps it is his growing knowledge that constitutes Jean's particular realm. He becomes what he claimed to be at the start: an incurably lucid man.

Episode 2 is entitled "The Rendez-Vous." This meeting will never take place for it is not one with a real human being, but with an ideal, archetypal woman.

The set represents a high terrace, "hanging in mid-air."[32] The sky, dark at first, clears. Ionesco specifies in his stage directions that the light of the blue sky is a cold, "empty brilliance."[33] There is a hint of something lifeless about this spot, a quality that reminds Ionesco's readers or audience of the "radiant city" in *The Killer.*

Stranger still is the fact that the only building on this plateau, surrounded by arid mountains, should be a museum, protected by two guards in uniform. Jean's rendez-vous with a nameless woman is set for an indeterminate time at the museum entrance. The guards are neither friendly, nor aggressive. They tolerate Jean's presence, although he is clearly an intruder. Jean does not attempt to enter the museum. Inside the bland, anonymous walls, we imagine there may be tapestries and paintings representing mythological beasts, dragons slain by St. George, and scenes from the New Testament. Once, all

of these held significance for humanity, but they are purged now of
their magic power, or even the power to move one's soul. The gray
walls of the museum suggest a mausoleum holding the artifacts of the
past, objects grown meaningless in what Ionesco calls "une époque
désacralisée" (an epoch stripped of the sacred dimension). However,
a pattern is still discernable: the uniformed guards, guardians of humanity's cultural symbols, suggest the archetypal guardians at the
gate, the preservers of mysteries. Perhaps what Jean is looking for
lies within, but, like foolish Parsifal, he never inquires. Throughout
the scene he remains an innocent.

As the dream woman fails to materialize, Jean realizes that he has
sacrificed a tangible happiness for an illusion. Turning toward the
imperturbable keepers, he confesses:

> I wanted to escape old age, keep out of the rut. It's life I'm
> looking for! Joy I'm after! I've longed for fulfillment and all I find
> is torment. I had to choose between peace and passion, fool that
> I was!... Now the walls have collapsed. And here I am, de-
> fenceless, exposed to the blazing inferno of life, and in the freez-
> ing grip of despair.[34]

Jean, who had hoped to escape from the hell of his basement apartment, finds that he has wandered into another circle of Dante's inferno. His pilgrimage finally takes him into the Void.

In the definitive version of *Hunger and Thirst* episode 3 is "Le Pied
du mur" (The foot of the wall). A huge wall runs across the stage,
barring the way for the traveler. This is a rich metaphor suggestive
of Jerusalem's Western Wall, or Wailing Wall, and, closer to our
time, the now dismantled Berlin Wall. In a general sense it stands for
insurmountable obstacles in life. Ionesco's Jungian analyst taught him
to scale such a wall in his waking reverie.

Three related passages in *Fragments of a Journal* provide a key to
the decoding of the Kafkaesque episode 3. They are a faithful record
of dreams connected to the Jungian psychoanalysis Ionesco underwent in a Swiss clinic under the guidance of Doctor Ziegler. A constant in all of them is the image of a high church wall, an impassable
wall symbolizing the dreamer's inability to accept death. Ionesco begins by stating that the immediate problem facing him is "learning
how to die," the problem at the core of *Exit the King*.

In the first passage, the dramatist dreams of walking with his wife through a town square surrounded with ruins. In fact the square is a kind of abandoned "waste ground" full of brambles, brushwood, thistles. Before them rises an enormous church, or rather the high wall of that church, "like the wall of a great prison." The narrator-analysand now sees that the church is "a great vertical grave-yard . . . as it might appear to a bird, except for being upright." The dreamer tells his companion that this building, described by her as beautiful, is in fact "very ugly." Going back on her first opinion, she agrees with him. Since the wall is a graveyard, the incontrovertible fact of human mortality, the spouses cannot take pleasure in its archi-tectural beauty. They notice a tiny closed door, under the tower surmounted by a baroque cupola. The door leads into a crypt that is actually a kitchen. The image of death is reinforced by the appearance of a guide to the underworld, a dirty female cook in a black apron, surrounded by black kitchen utensils. In the dream, the Ionesco couple must pass through that grimy kitchen to issue from the verti-cal graveyard. They find themselves "in a sloping field covered with the same tangled, withered vegetation, under the same drab sky."[35]

In the second passage, which begins with the same description of a church wall and a small door down below, Ionesco seems to have progressed in his analysis. He is able to analyze the dream and himself:

> The wall, then, is the wall of a prison, of my prison. It is death since it looks like a graveyard from afar; the wall is a church wall, it separates me from a community; it is therefore the expression of my solitude, of noninterpenetration. I cannot reach others, and they cannot reach me. It is at the same time an obstacle to knowledge, it is what conceals life and truth. In short, what I am trying to pierce is the mystery of life and death, neither more nor less. Naturally such an undertaking seems impossible. But once again my dream contains my waking thoughts, the image being merely a visual résumé of this impossibility.[36]

He has come to the realization that he is cut off from himself, his deeper self unable to sustain his mind.

In the third passage, Ionesco calls the great wall "the wailing wall, the wall of separation."[37] Once again we are given a key to a figure in episode 3, that of the rabbi Schaëffer, with his flock of Yeshiva students walking in ranks to his imperious "Eins, zwei, eins, zwei, links, rechts, eins, zwei."[38] This is no gentle Hassid, but a Nazi *Gauleiter* shouting military commands in German, as though marching the children to the gas chamber. This wicked shepherd (this is the translation of the name Schaëffer) is also endangering the life of his flock by having them chant psalms in a country "where one is beheaded or dispatched to a penal colony for practicing one's religion."[39] Jean warns the rabbi: "You know where you are, in an officially atheistic country. . . . There are spies everywhere. You're in danger, and so am I, if people see us together."[40] It would be a major mistake to assume that Ionesco is criticizing Israel, a country for which he has the deepest respect and fondness. This passage can only be read by deciphering its subtextual message communicated in the doublespeak referred to earlier. The German-speaking rabbi belongs to the new religion, that of the supremacy of the State. The penal colony Jean mentions can be found on the map of the archipelago gulag, where slave labor camps are so many dots all over the preglasnost Soviet Union. Many believers were sent there for upholding their right to worship freely. In his essay "The Play of Passions" Ionesco praises the Russian heroes of conscience: Pasternak, Solzhenitsyn, Sinyavsky, Daniel, Akhmatova. They were able to "prevail over the powers of darkness." He writes:

> Books like *Cancer Ward* and *The First Circle,* where the passion
> for truth is as powerful as the truthfulness of passion, will bear
> witness down the centuries, as beautiful, solid, terrible and full
> of hope as cathedrals, to the greatness of man and the infamy of
> those monsters and tyrants who founded what are called "just
> and revolutionary" societies.[41]

Schaëffer is one of those monsters, indoctrinating the children in the new religion. He tells Jean: "Don't worry about me, or yourself. I managed to fix everything with the powers that be. The police will have nothing to say. It's all in order. Instead of singing psalms, the children chant passages I selected in *The Communist Manifesto.*"[42]

Ionesco's own political imperative surges powerfully in this scene in episode 3 of *Hunger and Thirst.* It makes itself even more manifest in the final act, "The Black Masses of the Good Inn," in which the wanderer reaches a kind of fortress. He knocks at the door, which is opened by Brother Tarabas (whose name rhymes with Barabbas). The monk invites the weary traveler to enter. This time Jean will not stay outside. He lets the guardian of the threshold usher him into the recesses of "the Good Inn." Sounding like a tour guide, Tarabas explains: "In the course of centuries these buildings may have been used as a prison, or a college, a monastery, a castle or a hotel."[43] The ambiguity of this polysemous definition has lingered on so that it is virtually impossible to tell what the place is now. But Jean is too famished to care. Shortly after his arrival, the Brother Superior appears. Ionesco specifies that he is "abnormally tall, dressed in white."[44] Under his flowing robes, he stands on stilts. This silent, awesome figure communicates by means of sign language.

Other monks file in, and the traveler is offered refreshments. This episode, an illustration of the play's title, is rooted in chapter 25 of the Gospel of Matthew, which describes the Son of Man dividing the blessed from the cursed according to the manner in which they treated their fellow men and women. Those who fed the starving, gave drink to the parched, clothed the naked, visited the sick and the prisoners in jail, are said to have given not only to strangers but to the Lord himself. Jean is the stranger who is given nourishment and drink, but, having accepted these, he will lose his freedom. The bread he receives is like that distributed by Dostoyevsky's Grand Inquisitor.

Although Jean is not given any warning about the debt he is incurring, he will have to pay for the hospitality he enjoyed by serving at the refectory table for the rest of eternity. This monastery is an anti-Christian society where Black Masses are celebrated, where tyranny reigns. Within its walls, people are starved, brain washed, forced to renounce their faith. It is a place of extorted confessions, inquisitions, bizarre reversals. Here Christ's teachings have suffered an extreme distortion. A hierarchical order is enforced, but one based on fear, not love. The aim of the community is to put everyone through a program of "unlearning."[45] Tarabas promises that one can be disintoxicated and reeducated in the space of thirty sessions. Following this program, freedom will no longer seem desirable. The monastery is an amalgam of the Soviet jail or psychiatric ward, and the Chinese reeducation farms.

In *Hunger and Thirst* Ionesco succeeded in blending his metaphysical and political visions. On the philosophical plane, he com-

posed his own version of Dante's *Inferno*. Jean's tragedy lies in that
he cut himself from salvation in the very process of looking for
Beatrice. The play is a stage poem, an allegory of the path followed
by artists, lovers, seekers of Good. But unlike Dante, who will eventually make his way up the silver ladder suspended in Jean's secret
garden, Ionesco's protagonist is captured by a corrupt society. It is
no longer one where "the Pope's man and the Emperor's man believed the same doctrine and took the Sacrament from the same al-
tar."[46] The Good Inn is neither good nor an inn; it is the frozen Lake
of Cocytus at the bottom of the Pit, in the Circle of the Traitors.

The most terrifying scene of episode 4 is a play within the play,
a "clown" entertainment offered by the Father Superior to his naïve
visitor. The two "clowns" are caged brothers, Tripp (the name in
French is pronounced "tripes," like the dish made from the lining of
the intestines), and Brechtoll, derived from Bertolt Brecht. Although
they are wheeled out on two separate platforms, they could be twins,
doubles. Dante's verses from Canto 32 come to mind:

> Their heads were bowed toward the ice beneath,
> Their eyes attest their grief; their mouths proclaim
> The bitter airs that through the dungeon breathe.
>
> My gaze roamed round awhile, and, when it came
> Back to my feet, found two shades so close pressed,
> Their hair was mingled on the heads of them.
> . . . .
> Both of them issued from one mother's belly.
> Nor shalt thou find, search all Caïna through,
> Two shades more fit to stand here fixt in jelly.[47]

The suffering of Tripp and Brechtoll is a public spectacle, observed by a huge audience of their fellow monks assembled on the
steps of an amphitheater erected in the Great Hall. The public is
divided into two groups: red on Tripp's side, black on Brechtoll's.
The colors may suggest the split between East and West, but what
becomes obvious is that neither group represents Good. One evil
confronts another, both faceless and hooded. Tarabas, the master of
ceremony and the Father Superior's *éminence grise*, leads the inquisito-
rial proceedings.

Tripp and Brechtoll have been denied food and drink for many days, with the intention of forcing them to reverse their initial positions: Brechtoll, the atheist, will be reduced to praying fervently for food; Tripp, a religious man, will deny his God. The smell of the steaming soup, the noise of the ladle against the side of the tureen, the incantation of Brother Tarabas will effect this double transformation, a mock conversion, an apostasy. By the end of the clown play, Tripp and Brechtoll will stand, as they did at the start, at diametrically opposite poles, but they will have switched beliefs, or at least will have been forced to so declare.

Ionesco once explained to a group of friends at dinner that extremists can always shift to another extreme position: a Communist can become a Fascist, a terrorist-killer may suffer a conversion and become a saint. The only thing that cannot happen, Ionesco said, is for an extremist to become a humanist.

The spectacle of the torture fills Jean with horror. He would like to leave the inn at once. However, he has incurred an obligation by drinking and eating. As he rummages through his pockets for some loose coins, he comes up only with a bit of earth and the blood he shed when he got caught on the brambles along the way. He realizes that in order to repay the monks he will have to work the rest of his life. In the distance, Marie and Marthe, a dual vision of the positive anima, call out to him from the secret garden, promising to await his return. He, however, must turn his attention to the Brother Accountant, who is chalking up his debt (in hours of work) upon a gigantic blackboard. As Jean serves the brothers, a chorus chants: "One, seven, three, six, nine, eight."[48] The absurd numbers echo Schaëffer's military exercises in the preceding episode. The rhythmic counting grows louder and Jean is forced to move faster and faster, like a mechanical marionette, or Rabbi Leib's Golem of Prague. He is now a lifer, a prisoner of the mechanism of power and tyranny. The twentieth-century Pilgrim's Progress ends in a man-made hell.

Hunger and Thirst was premiered at the Düsseldorf Schauspielhaus in December, 1964. It opened at the Comédie Française on February 28, 1966. The role of Jean was interpreted by the extraordinary actor Robert Hirsch, the brilliant Scapin of Molière's *Les Fourberies de Scapin* (1956). The critical response was mixed, although Hirsch himself received nothing but praise. The subscription audience, however, was up in arms, particularly that of *les mardis habillés* (dress night). Only the loyal Jacques Lemarchand detected the political message. In his review he spoke of the Tripp-Brechtoll scene's "ferocity of dogmatism," and praised the Comédie Française for having opened its doors to "the dramatist who represents throughout the world French theatre at its best."[49]

The most moving tribute came from the Catholic novelist François Mauriac. *Hunger and Thirst* awakened in Mauriac a profound meditation on the Holocaust. Mauriac was the first French writer to recognize Ionesco's post-Holocaust sensibility. He writes:

> One is seized with trembling at the sight of this world in which man is trapped . . . a world which, having decreed the death of God, became the theatre of a four-year massacre in the very country where God's death was proclaimed. This massacre took the lives of millions, including women and children. But bodies were annihilated in concentration camps only after the soul had been destroyed, after human beings turned into beasts. This is the crime of crimes.[50]

Although in his article Mauriac speaks of being shocked by the depth of despair in *Hunger and Thirst*—one wonders why he did not mention the silver ladder that represents the possibility of salvation, of the presence of God's grace in the world—the friend and admirer of Elie Wiesel, in whose eyes he recognized the expression of "the resurrected Lazarus,"[51] detected something essential in Ionesco's tragedy, a theme that brings to the fore our ferocious, dehumanized civilization.

With this somber parable Ionesco became a modern classicist, the author of an uncompromising tragedy, as lucid in its indictment as Sophocles' *Electra,* as dazzling in its ethical action and realism as the same writer's *Philoctetes.* As to Ionesco, when he is questioned today about the label "avant-garde," which he defended with wit and grace for many years, his answer testifies to the fact that for him there was never a shift, or fundamental change in the way he envisioned his oeuvre. The seeds of his classicism must therefore be sought and deciphered also in his early work. In a private conversation he explained:

> Any true creative artist is classical since he resurrects ancient archetypes that are forever young. We must invent myths for

our time. As myth-makers, we give rise to the kind of sacred, awe-struck theater that arose in the ancient world, in ancient Greece. When I write, I do not ask myself whether I'm being avant-garde or not. I'm just trying to describe the world as I see it and to transcribe my inner visions. To be avant-garde is not to be "far out," but to return to our origins, to reject traditionalism in order to find once again a living tradition.

Chapter 10

The Dream Plays

Man with Bags, Journey among the Dead

In a program note written by Ionesco for the November, 1975, staging of *L'Homme aux valises* (Man with bags), the dramatist states:

> Dream is theatre par excellence. We witness the surging of events, the birth of astonishing, utterly surprising *dramatis personae,* and yet these amazing creations come from us. Our secret self, unknown to our conscious mind, lies revealed to us. We discover our inner depth as well as some objective truths . . .
>
> . . . in *L'homme aux valises* I am trying to make use of elements drawn from dreams, dream images and situations expressed in an oneiric language. In short, I have tried to substitute for rational coherence another form which only appears to be incoherent in the face of rationality.[1]

L'Homme aux valises and *Voyages chez les morts* (Journeys among the dead) are both dream plays. Together they form a diptych in which dream material is transmitted raw, in a simple, direct manner. "These are family quarrels," Ionesco stated at a symposium held in his honor at the University of Southern California, "and although the contenders are no longer among the living and the contentions as dead as they are, the inveterate strife continues. Night after night I dream of the same members of my family, night after night the feud goes on."[2]

Nothing about the atmosphere of the dream plays is vague, unreal; it is characterized by that peculiar sharpness and vividness of detail inherent to the dream state. We are projected out of a linear universe onto the vertiginous spiral of the time-space continuum.[3] Ionesco believes that it is important to develop techniques of dealing with dream images, to be aware of the ideas they attempt to communicate. For the dramatist, the process is a familiar one since dreams are a form of dramatic enactment in which the dreamer plays many roles simultaneously: writer, director, lead actor.

In Ionesco's two dream plays—the conclusion to his dramatic oeuvre—we recognize many of the entries in Ionesco's journals: confessional admissions, *pensées* (patterned on Pascal's, and on Baudelaire's *My Heart Laid Bare*), meditations on politics and culture, anxiety attacks, illuminations. Concretized on the stage, states of mind and tropisms become universal effigies. In this sense, Ionesco's open form, that of free-flowing dreams, retains its "classical" roots.[4]

The myth of the visit to the underworld is as ancient as human consciousness; it is rooted in the universal unconscious. The spiritual quest of the First Man (the protagonist of *Man with Bags*) and that of Jean (the traveler of *Journeys among the Dead*) suggest Odysseus's encounter on the mist-enshrouded shores of the Cimmerians with Tiresias, the seer who reveals to him the way home. Nor was the author of the *Odyssey* the inventor of infernal voyages. He himself was the heir of an ancient tradition, remnants of which can be observed in the hypnotic trances of shamans, voodoo priests, and the "magic" healing of witch doctors. Cartographers of the Beyond have left their maps on sarcophagi. Nor are these explorations necessarily *katabases*.[5] In primitive cultures dead ancestors are periodically invited to visit the living and partake of a feast prepared in their honor. The way is always open for the dead and the living to make contact; the path can be traced through ritual and art. As W. H. Auden once said in the course of a lecture delivered shortly before he died: "Art is breaking bread with the dead."

Man with Bags: The Absolute Stranger

A man carrying luggage, a wanderer, is an eloquent symbol for the state of estrangement and spiritual exile that characterizes contemporary men and women. To roam aimlessly from country to country, continent to continent, exiled or self-exiled, losing one's roots, one's papers, one's name and identity, such is a common lot today. We are shadowless, like Chamisso's Peter Schlemihl, and if a shadow appears it is not cast by our bodies but by that of our doubles, spies, and police investigators. This is the century of displaced people and nations, an uprooted peasantry, genocidal class wars, religious persecutions, slaves, and hostages. No one understands this better than a dramatist born of a French-Jewish mother and a Romanian father, forced by his parents' separation and the rise of fascism to shift from one country to the other, and back again, driven by the war to hide in the French countryside, a man on the run shuttling between at least two cultures and two languages. *Man with Bags* is therefore Ionesco's personal myth, his life history set on the stage. It is also the story of twentieth-century Man as Wandering Jew, as Leopold Bloom-Ulysses.[6]

The First Man—he is never given a name so that he is both Man and Noman (Odysseus's tricky self-definition to fool the Cyclops)—is first seen walking out of nowhere, a valise in each hand. As the light gradually spreads over the stage, we see another man, sitting in front of an easel. With his blue beret and box of paints, he is the perfect cliché of the French Sunday painter, an occupation as peaceful and traditional as weekend fishing. In this wasteland one can hear nevertheless the lapping sound of running water, as though an invisible river flows across the stage. "That big river's called the Seine,"[7] the Painter tosses out, never turning to the traveler, yet assuming he is addressing a foreigner or a tourist.

A rumor of voices rises, wafting from the opposite bank. We are reminded of the dead crowding together to look at Odysseus. Something vaguely menacing fills the air: shouts, shots, imprecations. The First Man wonders whether this might not be some kind of organized public demonstration, even a revolution. The Painter wishes to reassure his interlocutor, but succeeds only in deepening his malaise.

> It's 1939, here.... Think of it: the Revolution's still going. That's why they're making their noise. The wind of 1789's still blowing on them . . . the gentle breeze of generosity. . . . You can thank God you didn't come in '44.[8]

The First Man and the audience have entered one of Ionesco's time capsules. *L'entre-deux-guerres* (the period between the two world wars) is squeezed in between the Reign of Terror and the Nazi occupation of France. The locus is also ambiguous: it is both Paris and Venice, twin cities joined together. A gondolier appears on the invisible Seine, as though the river became a canal. He extends a helpful pole to allow the traveler to jump in. Whether he hails from Venice, Paris, Ir, or Babylon, this voyager must cross the river, be it the Seine or the Styx.

Like Odysseus, the First Man will meet with dead friends, relatives, and even ancestors whose past is not clearly known to him. As for the living, his wife, son, and small daughter (the girl child is represented by an Egyptian doll, such as might have been found within a pyramid), they are on the brink of stepping into the Void to join the throng of the dead ready to welcome them.

Indeed, the line dividing the living from the dead is thin, often invisible, inexistent. Ionesco, the metaphysical writer, reminds us in this play, as he does also in *Fragments of a Journal,* that when we dream we cannot tell the dead from the living, so real do the absent ones appear. Upon awakening, we wonder how we endured the years of separation without feeling the sting of our loss at every instant of conscious existence. We take it for granted that we are still alive while those we loved have passed from our sight, our touch, our care. And yet, perhaps those who have joined the eternal crowd of their dead know peace and family warmth, a life more intense than that of the abandoned living. Such are the deeply disturbing questions raised by Ionesco's dream plays, philosophical musings of an artist drawing close to his own end.

In scene 5, the First Man seems to have reached, after long wandering, the *locus* of his maternal origins. He encounters a frail, aged couple: his maternal grandmother and grandfather. The couple sired twelve children, seven sons and five daughters, like Ionesco's own maternal grandparents. Another ghost, the Old Uncle, claims to have been the only successful businessman of the brood. Since he is at this point a shabby, dirty bum, his boast seems questionable. However, he states that it is best not to call attention to oneself in the country where they live. Could this mean that the mother's place of origin is now in one of the Communist countries of Eastern Europe, where it was important to hide one's bourgeois roots?

Scene 6 is even more puzzling. The First Man meets an Old

Woman who claims to be his wife. He, however, took her for his
mother. As in *The Chairs,* Ionesco suggests that with the passing of
years wives become their husbands' surrogate mothers. Again the
play parallels Ionesco's own family situation when in scene 2 the Old
Woman (the mother) tells the Woman (the wife) that she must now
take care of this man. In conversation, Ionesco confessed that his
mother had entrusted him to his fiancée in those exact terms.

The ghosts are not limited to the matrilineal line. Still in scene 6,
the First Man's father strides in. The protagonist begins to shout:
"I turn, you die. I look around, back here again . . . everybody's
gone . . . vanished . . . up in thin air . . . *whoosh!*" The Old Woman responds: "Your family's wiped out: mother, father, brothers, sisters,
cousins . . . the whole shooting match."[9] Certainly this utter annihilation does not suggest a "natural" death. Only our deadly twentieth-
century wars and holocausts can account for this mass slaughter. The
First Man wonders how he could have forgotten his grievous losses.
To forget is to die, to lose one's own self. Only in dreams can one
recapture what has vanished from the conscious mind. The First Man
says: "I never should've taken my head off the pillow to begin with!
When did I stop dreaming anyway."[10] This is the moment when the
wanderer through the realm of dreams finds his kin. When did they
all die? His father answers: "A year ago, a hundred years ago, no
matter."[11] Eternity is outside of time; it is spaceless timelessness.

In another scene we are shown an old scarecrow of a woman
seated in a wheelchair. At the sight of a radiant girl, the hag exclaims
joyfully: "Mommy! Mommy! Here!"[12] The girl clasps the bag of
bones against her glorious young chest. There seems to be complete,
unhesitating recognition. People may take it to be typical "Ionesco
nonsense," the absurd caricaturing itself, but in fact the dramatist has
never gone deeper into human truth, into the reality of memory and
sentiment. We realize that the aged invalid must have been separated
from her mother in early childhood, and the remembrance she has
cherished is that of a beautiful creature, vital, full of hope. Now that
she is close to senility, the old woman is as helpless as a baby; she
needs her "mommy" more than ever before. This moving recognition scene is one between the past and the present. The fact that the
ages of mother and daughter are reversed is all the more affecting.
Ionesco wishes us to meditate upon the implacable treadmill of time.

He is probably remembering his own mother, who died young, and from whom he was separated as an adolescent. It is a heart-rending scene, one that rises from the very core of the human condition.

Why did the mother disappear? There is no answer in the play, but one detects a hint that this dreadful secret might have a connection with her racial origins. The First Man is eager to find out the real name of his grandmother's mother. The ancestor's maiden name was changed, and it is now impossible to trace it. However, a clerk, when questioned, wonders whether this woman might not have belonged to one of the "persecuted ethnic categories." The First Man admits to some "suspicions" on his part. This encourages the Clerk to pursue with wicked glee:

> Ooooo! Maybe she was from a condemned race! Let's-wipe-out-those-filthy-little-this-or-that sort of thing! . . . The persecution could very well have some horrid side effects . . . unpleasant, maybe even nasty consequences for her lineage . . . for those who follow. You, for example.[13]

This talk about purity of blood, lineage, is strongly reminiscent of Hitler's racial laws. As Lucy S. Dawidowicz explains in *The War against the Jews 1933–1945*, by the end of 1937 Jewish professionals and civil servants had lost their jobs. In January, 1938, Göring initiated expropriation proceedings following a definition of what constituted "a Jewish firm." Camouflage of an enterprise (under an Aryan name for example) was punishable by imprisonment. The Jews were placed under complete control of the police. Dawidowicz explains:

> To simplify and clarify this procedure, a decree defining a "non-Aryan" was promulgated on April 11. A "non-Aryan" was anyone "descended from non-Aryan, especially Jewish, parents or grandparents." Descent was "non-Aryan" even if only one parent or grandparent was "non-Aryan." "This is to be assumed especially if one parent or grandparent was of Jewish faith." Thus, in cases of "racial" ambiguity, the religious affiliation would be decisive. Every civil servant had to prove "Aryan" descent, through submission of the appropriate documents— birth certificates and parents' marriage certificate. (Eventually, elaborate genealogical questionnaires had to be answered.) . . .

The Nazi definition was simple: a Jew is a Jew is a Jew—that is, down to the third generation.[14]

It is obvious that it would be more prudent for the First Man to desist from his line of inquiry. However, at this very moment, as though emerging from the protagonist's mind, his maternal ancestress materializes before his very eyes. In her lacy white frock, her straw garden party hat, she seems to have stepped out of a daguerreotype. The First Man is struck by her youth and beauty, but the Clerk offers a disquieting interpretation of these qualities: "It's because she changed her name. She got rid of the old name . . . and the name that was growing old. With a new young name, she herself became new and young."[15]

What is this name that is said to be growing old? Could it be a biblical one? And what about the "persecuted race"? Jews? Armenians? Gypsies? Ionesco does not provide an answer, but the question lingers on, puzzles the mind, like an unsolved riddle. In the economy of the play the lost name assumes a central function acting as a constant subtextual hint, an incomplete confession. This stems from Ionesco's own situation: his mother was probably the daughter of converted Jews, or of the descendants of *conversos.* In her family there was also a change of name. In his still untranslated final journal, *La quête intermittente,* published in 1987, Ionesco relates one of his most revealing dreams. It deals with the secret identity of his beloved mother, Thérèse Ipscar, ostensibly French but in reality a descendant of Sephardic Jews. In an entry dated "Canonica, November 20, 1986" he suggests at least part of the truth:

I dreamt of my mother last night. I so very rarely see her in my dreams. This time she was in the company of my father whom she was hoping to marry.

For this to take place, she had to reveal her name. She was hiding the name's real spelling: she was called, answered to, and wrote Artaux or Ateaux with an X. Why didn't she spell it like the great theatre man? What was so embarrassing? Such a lovely name. Mean people tried to force her to say her real maiden name. Curiously, one of them was my father's second wife. Also a high-ranking clerk of the town hall.

I wonder whether my mother did not avoid appearing in my

dreams since her death because she did not want to put me to shame.[16]

It is not possible from this entry to tell whether Artaux or Ateaux was the mother's "real" name, or whether it disguised another, one more typically Jewish. The capital X is part of the mystery since it is the sign of a hidden identity, or a substitution for the real one. What is unmistakable is the deep sense of shame attached to a foreign origin, probably a Jewish one. Not only did the young woman fear her fiancé's reaction, but her spirit, after her death, is conscious of a similar anxiety on the part of her son. As for the Clerk of *Man with Bags,* he haunts the dramatist eleven years later.

Although Ionesco is not a Jew, he might have been labeled as such in Nazi Germany. Recurrent patterns in his plays reveal that he identifies with the Jewish historical experience. As in the case of the English Jew Harold Pinter, there are telling allusions to "exclusion, expulsion, and literal and metaphoric extermination, coupled with a heightened sensitivity to alienation."[17] In her essay "The Weasel under the Cocktail Cabinet: Rite and Ritual in Pinter's Plays," Leslie Kane observes that in Pinter's dramas several characters have assumed names. These are not usually Jewish characters, but they share the Jew's uncertainty about his position in society; they are marginal, like Davies in *The Caretaker,* a man without identity papers, a man wearing the mask of a name that is not his own. The image of a "man with bags" tells us what the author has left unspoken: this haunted, hounded traveler, this eternal stranger is a Wandering Jew, a theme prevalent in both Ionesco and Beckett.

One of the striking phenomena of our epoch is the metamorphosis undergone by the myth of the Jew. Previously, the victims of the Diaspora were seen as the Other in the societies in which they settled. With the Holocaust, and its successive mass decimations and expatriations, the Jew has become the symbol of universal persecution, the essence of human suffering. The Russian dissident writer Andrei Sinyavsky chose a Jewish name as his nom de plume: Abram Tertz. Ionesco, a champion of the state of Israel, says that a world without Jews would be harder and sadder. It is good, he explains, to live with the vision of the New Jerusalem. Paradoxically, the Jewish people represent the deepest pain, the ultimate tragedy, but also the most radiant hope.

Hope is at the heart of every human being who has retained something of childhood's state of grace. As I have pointed out throughout this book, the childlike is crucial to Ionesco; it allows the adult to retain, or recapture, a sense of wonder. *Man with Bags* is an attempt to dramatize the search for the presentness of life. It is love of life that keeps the wanderer going, questing, surviving. When the First Man's relations try to tempt him to join them, to ride with them in a kind of tumbril, or a gigantic miner's wagon moving along invisible tracks toward an equally invisible Void, the protagonist backs away from the company of the dead. He is not ready for this final passage. As his ancestors and his dead children disappear in the wings, poured out by the wagon emptying its cargo into a shaft, or a mass grave, he picks up his two valises, shouting in their direction that he will let them know when the time comes.

The hope of survival on the brink of dissolution constitutes one of the leitmotifs of this play. The other, as we said earlier, is that of the loss of identity. Both of these amalgamate in act 2.

The protagonist's wanderings have taken him to a foreign country, somewhere behind the Iron Curtain. Although it is the country of his birth, the man is no longer able to read the street signs or find his bearings. Childhood friends appear; they have become pale-faced bureaucrats who fail to recognize their erstwhile companion, or pretend not to know him. After all, he is being closely watched by the police. Since he has misplaced his passport and lost his identity cards, he must contact the consul. This proves difficult. When it is finally accomplished, the protagonist finds a man on the brink of a break in diplomatic relations. He is willing to issue some papers, any papers in fact, to his frantic visitor, but it becomes increasingly obvious that these documents will be nothing more than paper. Nor does this empty shell of an official lose his diffidence when it becomes clear that his visitor has forgotten the name of his own father and mother. Nor does the traveler possess any clear notion of his age, size, or profession. The only description of himself that he is willing to offer is "one who exists."[18] When the consul draws his attention to the fact that he shares this quality with all living beings, he is happy to amend it to "one specialized in existing."[19]

There are of course countries in which this specialty is not easy to pursue. When the First Man, finally armed with worthless documents, reaches what he takes to be a hotel, he is surprised to see that his room has four beds, all of them occupied. The inn is actually a hospital, one much like the psychiatric wards in which dissident Soviet scientists, writers, and thinkers were held for "reeducation." In this particular clinic, patients are allowed to linger until one of the beds is needed. Then the occupant of the desired bed is dispatched from this world by virtue of a perfected system of euthanasia.

Mercy killing is to be practiced on one of the four patients, an old woman who complains that her flesh is being pierced by the branches of a tree growing within her body cavity. Ironically, for a dying person, the tree is an evergreen with needles for leaves. As the woman sits up in bed, arms stretched out in agony, as though crucified upon her inner growth, one of her companions seeks to reassure her. His wife, he explains, "suffered from Poplars." When the woman inquires whether this was fatal, the man responds ambiguously that she got over it. Then he adds: "Made her young again! You've got the old Spring-time Syndrome."[20]

The man is lying; his wife is dead. Yet, it is also true that the dead may look younger and at peace after the final agony. The lie covers this deeper truth. The tree-filled woman, who prefers suffering to dying, embraces the charitable lie. She is filled with dread when the "doctor" approaches her to administer the final injection. Even his promise that the drug will make her feel wonderful does not calm her. In an extraordinarily violent scene, the "doctor" kills the woman twice, first by injecting her with a poison, then, although she is clearly dead, by shooting her in the head for good measure.

The last week of the Paris run of *Man with Bags* coincided with the arrival of the Ukrainian scientist Leonid Plyusch. He had remained confined for three years in the mental clinic of Dniepropetrovsk. The press, the intellectual elite, as well as the French Communists had pressed for his release. He reached France at the time of the twenty-second Congress of the Communist Party. In the speech he gave at *Paris-Mutualité,* Plyusch disclosed the conditions of his internment following his arrest for "anti-Soviet propaganda." Drugged, held tight by the "chemical straight jacket," then brought to a comatose state by powerful doses of insulin, he was brutalized, beaten, and finally confined to Ward 9, among the criminally insane. He told of his progressive memory loss, of his sinking into apathy. Yet, all along he kept on struggling to hold on to the details of his torture in order to communicate them to the world at some future time. Ionesco's hospital scene in *Man with Bags* recreates upon the stage the experiments of Doctor Mengele, the death at Auschwitz of Father Kolbe, and the perversion of science in the preglasnot Soviet Union. The reports in the Paris press of Plyusch's revelations authenticated Ionesco's subtextual references.

The theme of madness pervades scene 6 of *Man with Bags*. The First Man has been wandering through a strange town, "sort of on the road to Poitiers," yet on the other side of the bridge one finds "Virginia Street" and on down "Saint James Bridge." Beyond the pond where a freckled girl likes "to swim naked," there is "Pucelle Street." Finally, the traveler will reach Ionesco's childhood village, La Chapelle-Anthenaise.[21] This is a dream map made up of bits and pieces of foreign excursions and local names ("La Pucelle" is Joan of Arc). This map is the successful culmination of Doctor Ziegler's Jungian treatment. Ionesco quotes him directly in *Fragments of a Journal:*

> Eastern thought, which we reject, is not understood in the West, for Eastern thinkers see things in a complex of correlations and meanings. It is clearly a different way of interpreting the world, any truth being merely the interpretation we may give of a thing, of things. To admit these phenomena which seem to us strange and absurd, we should simply have to substitute for our historic causal way of thought a spatial way of thought. We should imagine things spatially, not temporally. If we could abandon our historical point of view without assuming a spatial one, we should be even freer, we should have a different figuration of the world or rather, since any figure is in space, a non-figurative interpretation of the world.[22]

This passage is a key to the peculiar structureless structure of *Fragments of a Journal,* but it is also one that can open the two Dream Plays. The First Man is constantly wandering through atemporal spaces, scraps of his past, envisioned encounters with terror or the ideal. In *Man with Bags,* he is weighed down by his luggage, even as he walks through the puzzle of a city. Exhausted, he reaches a bar located in a beautiful park. He is much in need of rest and a drink. But this solace is refused to him unless he produces "a valid certificate of mental health." His flashing of credit cards is to no avail. The Bartender declares him "crazy."[23]

The play ends with a celebration, a fête, at once joyous, sensuous, and threatening. The action takes place in a large formal garden. There are fountains, fireworks, dance music, champagne. The First Man stumbles in with his suitcases, which seem to have grown heavier in proportion to his weariness. A magnificent-looking woman approaches the stranger, invites him to rest and partake of food and drink. She is larger than life, a dream creature, a sex goddess. The First Man is filled with expectation, a tremulous kind of desire. When the woman returns, she offers herself to him. The presence of the host, her husband, does not deter her; he will be the *mari complaisant*, turning his back to what is going on and watching the traveler's bags like a lackey. However, the park is crawling with spies. As the protagonist follows his forceful female partner, both of them describe ever-widening circles to the strains of Sibelius' "Valse Triste." There is no place for the would-be lovers to hide and consummate their passion. Armed men emerge from behind columnar trees, jump out of the thickets. Suddenly, the lady's husband appears. This time he is carrying the traveler's luggage. Time is running out. The park fills with dancing couples. Fireworks are set off; the stage is filled with laughter. However, the wanderer cannot join in with the general merriment. He has not traveled to this land to dance. Like most artists, he remains an observer in the midst of human folly.

The final image is of the First Man sitting on his valises at the core of a throng of revellers. Every one of the dancers turns into a traveler, each carrying a suitcase. The ballroom has changed into a railroad station. Some of the voyagers begin to pile up their luggage around the protagonist who does not move. He watches the hustle and bustle with a bemused smile. We recognize Ionesco's familiar device of proliferation, but used to a different end. The immobility of the man suggests contemplation. It is as though, after endless searching, he had reached the center of the mandala, perhaps after a final renunciation. The suitcases carried by the others contain their lives, much like the bundles carried by those herded into cattle trains that took them to the death camps. Some of the voyagers do not know that rushing only brings you closer to the end, to death. They run to and fro, impelled by some kind of senseless ambition. Others set down their existences at the feet of the sage. The First Man says softly: "I'll only dream when I'm awake. From now on that's the way it'll be. I understand now. I'll never waste my dreams by falling asleep. Never again. That's a fact."[24]

With the assistance of the brilliant actor-director Jacques Mauclair, Ionesco created a splendid image of the artist as the eternal Adam, a metaphor of Man as an inveterate dreamer (according to André Breton's definition) and perfect mediator. The play teaches us that to be fully present to oneself and to others, one ought to be of No Place and Every Place, to be Noman and Everyman. Only then can one create relationships based on mutual respect, reverence for the human spirit, even though the spirit is assigned to a grotesque and vulnerable dwelling, mortal flesh. As Ionesco declared in the course of an unpublished lecture delivered in March, 1976: "The reason for writing is to cast up to heaven our cry of anguish in order to let other men know that once we were here, we existed."

Journeys among the Dead: A Whispered Confession

Ionesco's final dream play, the second tablet of the diptych, is the most philosophical and personal of his tragicomedies. Were it rooted in ontological considerations alone, it would be abstract, were it predominantly confessional it might prove self-indulgent. Because the dramatist blended the two successfully, he created upon the stage the myth of the modern human being.

In *Journeys among the Dead* Ionesco "breaks bread with [his] dead." He comes to terms with long-buried feelings of remorse, feelings connected with the separation from his beloved mother, and his late identification with his father.

The main theme of the play is the quest for the absent mother. Little is revealed about her disappearance. We are told that one day she went to the railway station to purchase an upper berth in a one-way sleeping car. When Jean questions his father's ghost about this departure, the latter is unable to recall the train's destination. All he knows is that "she must have gone a long way. She got to a place where you can't see anyone any more, neither with your eyes nor by any other kind of technology." The father than concludes with a blatant lie: "She abandoned us."[25]

What then is this mysterious place where one can vanish out of sight and mind? It seems to belong neither to this planet nor to the underworld. It may be the locus of psychic transformations, the realm of the archetypal Feminine.

In *The Great Mother,* Erich Neumann speaks of "the formative power of the Feminine."[26] He explains that this power may start within the confines of the family, tribe, or clan, but that it must not remain in that sphere. The Great Goddess's central concern has to do with transcending the instinctual world of plants and beasts, in order to reach "the highest form of psychic reality."[27] It is a sublimation of the life force.

In *Journeys,* Ionesco blends the reality of his parents' separation with the mythical journey of the Mother Goddess of the Eleusinian mysteries. Death and disappearance stand at the core of these secret rituals. Stretched out upon the narrow sleeping-car berth, Jean's mother sails into eternity as though borne by an ancient Egyptian barge, or by the ships enclosed within Norman tombs. Having vanished, she is able to perform the magical transformations of soul that the Goddess is empowered to do. Meanwhile, Jean, a modern man, will rediscover what primitive people knew, namely that "in the generating and nourishing, protective, and transformative feminine power of the unconscious, a wisdom is at work that is infinitely superior to the wisdom of man's waking consciousness."[28]

After much questioning and searching, Jean finally reaches his mother. At first he fails to recognize her for she has grown as old looking as her own parents, who are by her side. When the protagonist expresses his dismay, his mother offers a logical explanation: "I've caught up with my parents' age. People age in the beyond, too. You get up to a hundred years old and then you stop. You'll age too, when you've joined us."[29] A woman who might be Jean's wife—he himself is not certain whether she is his wife, sister, or daughter—states that the mother's continued aging after death may be due to her feeling uneasy in the underworld. Those who age in the Beyond are people with unfinished business on this earth.

What is the nature of this "unfinished business"? Jean is to receive more than just an answer; all will be revealed to him when he reaches a deserted house where he encounters the effigy of a woman imprinted on his subconscious mind.

The friend with whom Jean enters the house claims to hear "weeping and wailing coming from the ceiling, and falling drop by drop."[30] Jean calls out to the woman he believes to be the mother he has been seeking; he begs her to come down. When the ghost finally answers his plea, it is no poetic apparition, no sweet angel from heaven; Jean faces a dishevelled hag, incoherent with rage and anguish. Images of decay fill her speech:

> I'm afraid, downstairs the floor's worm-eaten. Cockroaches have been born from my tears, there's a lot of vermin on the floor, the floor's worm-eaten, the grave is under the floor, I don't want to fall into it, all my relations are in it, turned to dust. Up here I was preserved from death and dust.[31]

Although the speaker is already dead, she does not seem to realize it. But the readers of Ionesco recognize in her lines one of the dramatist's recurrent images: a basement or ground-floor apartment sinking into slimy soil that smells like a freshly dug grave. Years before he wrote his dream plays, Ionesco's Jungian analyst explained some of these images to his analysand:

> Z. tells me that my dreams are archetypal. The wall is an archetype; the box, travelling through space, in which I am shut up in an almost foetal position, is equally archetypal.
> "Your distress in your dream is due to having left the earth. Earth, as you know, means the mother."[32]

However, later in life Ionesco reaches a different conclusion. He has come to realize that for him many of the symbols or archetypal patterns are reversed: the usually benevolent father figure is a monster, a tyrant; fire is not brightness but a premonition of death; water is not purity but mixed with soil, slime, and decomposition. Earth is not "a foster-mother," but decay. This is why all the spaces close to the soil are graves. Ionesco writes: "Cellars, the interiors of houses mean shelters for other people; for me they are tombs. When I dream of the inside of a house, it is always sinking down into the damp earth."[33] Gaston Bachelard would have called Doctor Z. "a psychologist of form," not one of "the imagination of matter." Ionesco, however, is an "authentic dreamer of the inner essence of substances." For him, a shadowy, dark corner evokes the terror of the vastness of night." He has experienced the *Dunkelschock* of the Rorschach test.[34]

In *Journeys,* Jean and his friend refuse to heed the ghost's request not to bring her down. They proceed to pull on an armchair whose underside can be seen from the room below. Slowly the decrepit, thronelike piece of furniture is lowered; it holds a tiny, white-haired creature, a wizened little girl hiding in the attic. As she begins to scream at the two men, Jean's friend, a reliable guide, points out that this hag could not be the gentle lady he remembers as Jean's mother; the ghost may be his grandmother, or even someone further back along the family tree, some ancient ancestress.

The armchair is a deep, brocade Victorian chair, almost a throne. Once again it is in Erich Neumann's book that one is able to discover a key to this image, one relevant to the structure of the play. Neumann writes:

> The seated Great Mother is the original form of the "enthroned Goddess," and the throne itself. . . . It is no accident that the greatest Mother Goddess of the early cults was named Isis, "the seat," "the throne," the symbol of which she bears on her head.[35]

Neumann goes on to state that the Magna Mater is frequently represented as sitting upon the earth. The seated mother embodies fertility. However, in *Voyages,* the ancestor is devoid of dignity, perhaps because she has been dispossessed in some fundamental way, one that will be uncovered at the end.

What could be the meaning of the ghost's ambiguous status: mother or grandmother, ancestress-figure? It goes to the very core of the archetype, the story of the unification of Demeter and Kore.

The unity of the virgin-mother (Demeter) and her daughter (Kore) was a central figure in the Eleusinian mysteries. These all-generating life principles were worshipped as one. They were symbols of fertility, resurrection, the cyclical aspect of nature. Kore (Persephone) was abducted by the king of the underworld and brought to live and reign with him in his dark realm. Demeter mourned and sought her daughter until she came to Eleusis. There, disguised as an old servant woman, she reared a male child Demophon. Then, putting off her disguise, she revealed her godhead to the Eleusinians. Hermes was dispatched to Hades to bring back Kore, but Kore's abductor had given his bride a pomegranate. To taste of this fruit means to have to return to the underworld. Such was the pact of the seasons. In the winter, Kore had to abide with her lord and master, but in the spring and summer she rose to join her mother and fructify the earth.

The reunion of mother and daughter is the essential motif of the mysteries. Mother and daughter were worshipped as one. In the steles, seals, and reliefs where they are depicted together, it is impossible to tell them apart, except that the younger woman holds a flower, and the matron a piece of fruit. Neumann concludes: "The true mystery, through which the primordial situation is restored on a new plane, is this: the daughter becomes identical with the mother; she becomes a mother and is transformed into Demeter . . . the mystery of the Feminine is susceptible of endless renewal."[36]

The fructifying mysteries were celebrated by men and women together. Often a young male is portrayed on the reliefs, standing between the two goddesses. He is the invested son, Triptolemus, the bearer of the golden corn, a "supraterrestrial grain whose mystery seed leads through death in the Great Mother to transformation and resurrection in the celestial meadows of the night sky, where the earthly male rises as an immortal gold-seed-star."[37]

In *Journeys among the Dead* Ionesco has recreated the myth of mother-daughter unity, and that of the education and initiation of the son. Jean, who is aware of the sacral symbol of the enthroned mother, promises the angry ghost a substitution for the hard, narrow, sleeping-car berth: "I'm going to take you away, clothed in purple. I shall put you in the most beautiful glass sarcophagus, like the ones of the Italian popes."[38] If the comparison with the popes is not devoid of irony, the passionate desire to honor the mother with a magnificent burial is very real. However, she is not to be placed in the earth, but perhaps sent to another planet, or into interstellar space. The glass sarcophagus is not unlike the "translucent packing-case" of Ionesco's dream in which he saw himself sitting within such a box, "possibly made of plastic," naked, "the size of a five- or six-year-old child" together with "a twin . . . [or a] double."[39] The artist preempts for himself the female oneness of Demeter and Kore when he returns to that moment in time when he had not yet suffered the separation from his mother.

At the end of the play, as Jean pursued his conversation with the ghost he took to be his mother, the latter's voice and manner are altered. The frightened, cowering hag turns into a harpy with immensely long, curved nails, veritable talons. She shrieks:

Where am I now? In the common grave, the pauper's grave, but
I was on the lookout and I hid above the ceiling, and that's why
this house hasn't fallen into ruin, in spite of its decrepitude. And
I shall make its foundations tremble, and I shall sow chaos in it.[40]

This twin sister to the mad Aunt Adelaide of *Hunger and Thirst*
orders a table covered by a black cloth brought in. Her throne is
placed behind it; it has become "the judge's bench."[41] A trial is
about to begin, but clearly this is no ordinary court of law; it is
nothing less than the Last Judgment. Jean is then invited to sit on
the right of the female judge, not unlike a young lord of the realm
of the dead.

It will be the Great Mother's task to put on trial the second
wife of Jean's father and that woman's entire family. On the pri-
mary level, one is aware of the autobiographical elements of these
dreams of revenge. Ionesco crystallizes here his own mother's grievances in regard to Helen Buruiana (Lola) and her brothers Costica
and Mitica, who appear in the play as the Captain and the Top Civil
Servant. Yet, the scene transcends the personal plane; it opens upon
the boundlessly wide and deep subject of "Man's inhumanity to
Man."

As the accused file in, the first to appear is the second wife,
Madame Simpson. She is now an ugly old woman dressed in the
provocative clothing of a young whore. The harpy threatens to sink
her talons into her rival's throat. Next comes the Captain, who is to
be judged for the murder of innocent people condemned on account
of belonging to a different race. Like Eichmann at his Jerusalem trial,
or Barbie in Lyons, the Captain claims that he merely followed orders. However, he adds that he feels proud of having helped extermi-
nate an inferior race. The woman judge draws herself up to her full
height, proclaiming: "I am Vengeance!"[42] Capital punishment will
not suffice as retribution for such black crimes against humanity.
Only the Old Woman/Supreme Judge may decide who is "ultra-
guilty—more guilty than guilty."[43] Although the Demiurge seems
to have forgotten the names of the combatants and the murderers,
and is having a good laugh at this Judgment, his representative, an
avatar of Nemesis, will invent punishment worthy of those inflicted
on Dante's "Traitors" in Nether Hell. Squeezing the Captain's throat,
she chants:

Your brains are all red and black. I'm going to smear them over your eyes, and stuff them up your noses and in your mouth. I'm going to shove my hand down your throat. Do you remember, handsome Captain, how you used to swagger in your beautiful, well-polished boots, and what a swashbuckler you were with your sabre?... I'm going to tear out your monocled right eye.... For a second, I'll leave your other eye open, so that you can see what's happening to you.[44]

The red and black colors of the brain suggest those of the Nazi emblem: a black swastika on a field of red. The shiny boots are also a reminder of the Iron Guard, or SS uniforms. The plays of Ionesco's mature years as a dramatist cannot be read innocently. His text is pregnant with subtext, almost every one of his words emit signals.

Thus, in the Old Woman of *Journeys* we recognize the Terrible Mother, who "devours her souls that have not withstood the midnight judgment of the dead in the underworld."[45] She may appear as the mistress of destruction, but it is through her purifying vengeance that rebirth can occur. As shaman, priestess, anima figure, she must uncover all hidden vices.

Having destroyed the man who had her family shot, the Old Woman turns her wrath upon the Captain's brother, the Top Civil Servant. (In real life, he was an official of the Ministry of Agriculture.) His crime lies in having persecuted defenseless farmers. This is a strong reminder of the violent *dekulakization* of 1930 in the Soviet Union, when peasants were driven off their land, deported, and often sent to slave labor camps. Ceaucescu took a page from Stalin's book, putting an end to private farming, razing farm houses, and resettling a stable, honest population in impersonal office-type buildings adjacent to arable land. Farmers were turned into agricultural slaves.

The Top Civil Servant's only hope of some kind of reduced sentence lies in the possibility that some of the farmers he spared might testify in his favor. However, they are all dead, turned to dust. As the accused man reaches inside his pockets for some scrap of evidence, he finds that they contain nothing but a bit of soil. The Old Woman/Supreme Judge intones:

Let the earth bear witness. That earth won't speak... it is no longer earth. Just look down at your feet; that earth isn't there.

There is no more earth, there is no more sky; there is no more world.[46]

The judgment is taking place in the Beyond. It is as though, by means of a shamanic trance, the trial had been lifted into eternity and infinity.

In that other world, wrongs are set straight and wrongdoers severely punished. The father's second wife, whose physical and spiritual ugliness were artfully disguised by a wig, make-up, fancy clothes, is revealed for what she is as the Old Woman tears off her hat, rends her dress, and rips off her fake nose. The young-looking woman is metamorphosed into an evil hunchback, while the erstwhile hag, her judge, grows in stature and beauty; they exchange roles.

The Last Judgment scene culminates in a *renovatio* (renewal). The Old Woman strips off her tattered clothing and emerges as a siren, singing in a voice of unearthly ecstasy. No longer Queen of Hades, she has become Ishtar, the goddess of life and fertility. Wronged by her husband, forgotten by him as well as by her son, Jean's mother, a component of the ancestress figure, is released and reunited with her repentant child.

On January 29, 1970, André Bourin of *Les Nouvelles Littéraires* interviewed Ionesco, who had just been admitted to the Académie Française a week earlier. The journalist asked the new academician a number of questions, among which one about his well-known habit of strolling to revisit places where he had lived. The answer Bourin received was extensive, and clearly related to the theme of the search for the mother, and beyond, to the quest of lost origins:

When I used to live in the Marais, the Saint-Paul district, I used to enjoy walking to Montparnasse. Now that I live in Montparnasse, I go for walks to the Marais. It's a neighborhood for which I feel a deep affection. I particularly like the rue des Rosiers, and the rue des Francs-Bourgeois. When I'm there, I feel I have reached another world. The rue des Rosiers is very beautiful. Walking along that narrow street I feel I've traveled a great distance. I go in search of the small hotel where I lived with my parents when I was four years old. Memories of things gone by, lost, surface in my mind. I sense that there is something utterly familiar about this place, although I don't quite know why.[47]

The ancient Jewish quarter of Paris, the rue des Rosiers, now an Arab neighborhood except for a couple of kosher restaurants and a handful of Holocaust survivors who returned to their modest homes, is indeed a strange universe, one that could be miles and eons away from Paris. The haunted, weeping house of *Journeys among the Dead* could well be standing on the rue des Rosiers, its moldy floor covering the entrance to the Kingdom of the Dead, peopled by those who were deported and died in the gas chambers of the Nazi death camps. In Ionesco's dream, the house and the mother have merged, become one, as indeed they are in all archetypal representations of "home."

Ionesco's dream plays depict the psychic inner space, the one in which the traveler finds no boundaries of time and place. In *Notes and Counter Notes* the dramatist evokes "the wealth of space there is within us." He wonders: "Who dares to adventure there? We need explorers, discoverers of unknown worlds, which lie within us and are awaiting to be discovered."[48] The voyage starts within, at the core of the self, but it takes the artist-explorer to the collective unconscious, that is from the part to the whole. The course of that journey does not run along a straight line; it is a spiralling perigrination.

Such a pilgrim is the hero-writer. Ionesco, the author of these dream plays, is another Triptolemus, the son brandishing the ear of the grain he must sow throughout the world. He has fulfilled the investiture transmitted to him through the matrilineal clan. In *Journeys among the Dead* Ionesco transcends the vengeance he portrays so forcefully on the stage. It is his own catharsis; he has forgiven if not forgotten. By recalling and communicating what he witnessed, he finally absolves himself.

Conclusion: Ionesco and His Critics

Improvisation or *The Shepherd's Chameleon*

"I do not think Mr. Ionesco is an important writer; I do not think he is any kind of dramatist; I do not hold him to be a thinker, not even a madman; in fact, I do not believe Mr. Ionesco has anything to say. . . . He is a fraud whose activities could best be summed up by the text of the following telegram: 'Fake surrealism not defunct. Stop. Ionesco follows.'" In this way did Jean-Jacques Gautier, the powerful reviewer of *Le Figaro*, dismiss *Jack or the Submission* and its author (10/17/55). Gautier's derision remained one of the thorns in Ionesco's flesh for many years to come. Nor was he alone in his debunking. J. B. Jeener of *Le Monde* showed his annoyance with *The Bald Soprano* when he wrote: "You laugh for the first five minutes, but are these five minutes worth an hour of boredom?" (5/13–14/50). Renée Saurel of *Combat* defined Ionesco's style as "burlesque," adding that "nothing happens on the stage since there is no dramatic situation, no action" (5/29/50). Having seen "Sept Pièces Courtes" directed by Jacques Polieri at the Huchette theater in August, 1953, Henry Magnon trumpeted in *Combat:* "I hate all this! Mr. Ionesco's humor is as desolate as the laughter of an exile" (8/11/53). (It is interesting to note that although Magnon rejects Ionesco he detected in the latter's wit the bitterness of being an exile, a stranger, a wanderer.) Magnon also states his dislike for Groucho Marx, and Ionesco's "pseudometaphysics." When *Victims of Duty* was created on a double bill with Charles Spaak's *Musique pour sourds,* most critics preferred the play of the screenwriter of "La Grande Illusion" and "La Kermesse Héroïque." Marcelle Capron had praise only for Mauclair's performance in the role of the Detective (*Combat*, 2/28/53). The emi-

nent philosopher Gabriel Marcel called the play "a cacoph-
ony... rehashed Strindberg" (*Les Nouvelles Littéraires,* 3/5/53).
Robert Kemp of *Le Monde* called *Victims* "a psychological cancan, a
frightful hotchpotch," adding that Ionesco's insight into the human
heart, social mores, and metaphysics "amounts to zero" (2/28/53).
Nor was the revival of the play in 1954 better received. Jean-Jacques
Gautier declared that "Ionesco, a man-circus, who makes of inepti-
tude one of the fine arts" was having "a good laugh at his audience"
(*Le Figaro,* 9/27/54). The playwright Jacques Audiberti described the
character of Nicolas d'Eu as "the vengeful ectoplasm of that inveterate, terrified tot Choubert" (*Arts,* 10/6/54).

Several journalists, however, while remaining cautious, began
to detect something important and new taking place. Upon seeing
The Lesson at the Théâtre de Poche, Guy Dumur, still one of the
most perceptive theater critics in France, stated firmly: "Rarely does
talent manifest itself from the start with such perfection. My greatest
regret is in having missed *The Bald Soprano* last spring, and I am also
sorry that the Théâtre de Poche is not giving that play in conjunction
with *The Lesson*" (*Opera,* 2/28/51). Dumur got his wish in October,
1952, when the double bill he envisioned was presented at La
Huchette where it is still running.

When it comes to early perspicacity, one critic stands out from
the start: Jacques Lemarchand of *Le Figaro Littéraire.* He was to become the champion of the new theater, and one of Ionesco's most
loyal supporters. Lemarchand was won over by *The Bald Soprano*
when he observed with amusement the audience's puzzlement and
rage. Having seen *The Chairs* he realized that the dramatist had tran-
scended his lighthearted dada-surrealist vein, that he was "a thinker
and a poet" (*Le Figaro Littéraire,* 5/3/52). About the double bill at La
Huchette he wrote wittily: "Within its walls, the theater holds a stock
of dynamite which might blow sky high every other theater in Paris"
(*Le Figaro Littéraire,* 10/18/52). But *Victims of Duty* moved him to
write his most impassioned praise: "It seems to me that with this play
Mr. Ionesco has come closer than he ever did before to bringing his
dramaturgy in line with his vision. His theater is not symbolist, psychological, poetic, surrealist, or social. For me, it is a theater of adventure, the inner adventure of the mind. . . . He is able both to wring
our hearts making us shed tears, and to have us collapse with laughter" (*Le Figaro Littéraire,* 3/7/53).

Ionesco's most enthusiastic endorsement came from his fellow writers, who came to the opening night of *The Chairs*. The ultimate accolade came from Jean Anouilh in 1956, when the play was revived at the Studio des Champs-Elysées. The boulevard dramatist's high praise capped a year of critical controversy, moves and countermoves unleashed by the provocative January–February issue of the scholarly, politically committed left-wing journal *Théâtre Populaire*.

The editors of *Théâtre Populaire*, Roland Barthes, Bernard Dort, Guy Dumur, Jean Duvignaud, Henri Laborde, and Jean Paris, decided that the time was ripe to present and discuss the dramaturgic theory of a writer unknown in France at that time: Bertolt Brecht. Brecht had come to the attention of the theater-going intelligentsia a year earlier, when the Berliner Ensemble performed *Mother Courage* at the Paris International Theatre Festival. Although Jean Vilar had staged a French adaptation of the same play, and Jean-Marie Serreau presented *A Man's a Man,* as well as the Marxist *The Exception and the Rule,* the Berliner's visit marked the start of a new awareness, a fascination with stylized production techniques that nevertheless featured realistic characters. Roger Planchon likes to recall how he traveled from Lyons to Paris in order to meet with Brecht and watch him rehearse his company. "Even more than a playwright, Brecht was a director of genius," he stated in private conversation. He added: "Brecht taught me everything I know." The year 1954 also witnessed the publication of René Wintzen's *Bertolt Brecht,* the first serious study of the German playwright in French.

Despite these first tremors, it was the special Brecht issue of *Théâtre Populaire* that accomplished what it had set out to do: it caused a groundswell, even a minor earthquake. The opening editorial's clarion call could not be ignored:

> For twenty-four centuries the European theatre has been Aristotelian. . . . It was considered good only if the audience was deeply moved, if it identified with the hero while the actor coincided with his role. Spectacle strove to be magical.

The translation into French of Brecht's "Short Organum for the Theatre," and its partial publication in the same issue, were meant to promote "a strong, coherent, stable system," to create a form of art anchored in society and history, one that would not address itself primarily to the senses or exclusively appeal to the emotions.[1] Art had to enter into discussion with the rational mind and answer society's quest for solutions to its ills. Brecht's manifesto and the editorial were further supported in this issue by the essays of Bernard Dort, Roland Barthes, Walter Weidli, and David Victoroff.

This battle cry begged for a response. It came in the form of a witty, ironic answer by Jacques Lemarchand. His essay "L'Ecolier Limousin et le Petit Organon" was published in the *Nouvelle Revue Française* (5/1/55). Tongue in cheek, the critic declared he was taken aback when he found out that twenty-four centuries of dramatic theory and praxis were founded on erroneous assumptions. Apparently, Aeschylus, Shakespeare, and Molière were set aside in this thirty-third year of the Brechtian era. The editorial of *Théâtre Populaire* decreed that the only theater deserving of any notice was political theater, drama concerned with class struggle. Its patron saint was Bertolt Brecht.

Lemarchand also criticized the discussion of *Verfremdungseffekt,* calling it unclear even in Brecht's own text.[2] But what was perhaps even worse, according to the learned critic, was that there was nothing new about this theory; much of the same ground had been covered by Diderot's "Paradoxe sur le comédien." Moreover, by comparing Dort and his fellow editors to Rabelais's grotesque jargon spouter, the Limousin "who spoke spurious French,"[3] Lemarchand suggested that they were a bunch of provincial pedants hoping to establish themselves as Parisian literati. Although, unlike Pantagruel, he did not bodily seize them by the throat, he let them know that they had better "steer clear of unusual words"[4] if they wished to retain their readership and a theatre audience for their deity.

As Julian H. Wulbern explains in his introduction to *Brecht and Ionesco,* although both dramatists "perceive the world about them in remarkably similar ways, their perceptions are, especially in their middle and late works, couched in dramas which differ profoundly in both form and philosophic statement. These differences arise partly out of the particular form of engagement with which each became identified: Brecht's overcommitment and Ionesco's unequivocal rejection of any form of political commitment."[5] For Ionesco, the Brecht issue of *Théâtre Populaire* was much more than the waving of a red flag (in more sense than one); he took it as a personal attack, the waving of the bull fighter's red cape, and he charged.

In the wake of his friend Lemarchand's lightly humorous essay, Ionesco composed *L'Impromptu de l'Alma* (Improvisation), a brilliant example of metatheater. Its subtext can be deciphered only by those who perused the Brecht issue of *Théâtre Populaire*. As the title indicates, the play is patterned on Molière's answer to the attack on *L'Ecole des Femmes*, his *Impromptu de Versailles*.

Like Molière in both the *Impromptu* and the *Critique de l'école des femmes*, Ionesco features himself as the protagonist of his satire of Parisian drama critics. He even considered following Molière's example all the way by playing his own persona on the stage. To further mark the Molieresque origins of his piece, Ionesco attributes pedantically doctoral Latin names to his caricatural dramaturges: Bartholomeus I, II, and III. In the initial production, the gowns worn by the puppetlike doctors were the flowing black robes characteristic of the scholar's gown of Molière's time; they echoed in fact the attire of Diafoirus and his simpleton of a learned son, the grotesque physicians dancing attendance upon Argan, the "imaginary invalid." Ionesco's medicine men are witch doctors who wish to cure maladies of style, form, and language. No doubt the dramatist found his inspiration in Roland Barthes's essay on the semiotics of costumology "Les maladies du costume de théâtre," initially given as a lecture for the "Amis du *Théâtre Populaire*" (5/8/54), then published as one of the key pieces of the Brecht issue.

In an interview with *Bref*, Ionesco admitted that the three Bartholomeus (the name is a Latinized echo of Barthes) were his "friends" Bernard Dort, Roland Barthes, and Jean-Jacques Gautier. The first two buffoons are mirror images of one another, marionettes echoing pedantic pronouncements as though these were prerecorded on some inner cassette tape:

Bart I: . . . For the more alienated you are . . .
Bart II: . . . the more involved you are . . .
Bart I: . . . and the more involved you are . . .
Bart II: . . . the more alienated you are. It's the electrical shock of alienation, or the Y effect.

The third vaudevillian, a caricature of the middle-of-the-road critic who panders to the bourgeois audience that flocks to commercial *boulevard* theaters, declares that his two companions indulge in "philosophistry."[6] They seem to have cultivated the fine art of contradiction honed by the young Ionesco in his Romanian dada essays collected in *Nu*. Echoing their creator's perverse literary practical jokes, they state that "the more truly false something is, the more falsely true it is. And the less truly false it is, the less falsely true." This brings them to the conclusion that "the false true is the true false, or the true true is the false false. . . . Opposites cancel out, *quod erat demonstrandum*." The actor playing the part of Ionesco sets things straight by rejecting this line of argument. For him opposites do not cancel out, they "exclude each other."[7]

By introducing a character whose interests are diametrically opposed to those of the first two, Ionesco widens his satire, taking it out of the sphere of intellectual jargon alone. He sketches a cartoon version of establishment stupidity, as common to intellectuals as to conventional minds.

There is, however, a frightening dimension to Bart III's rigidity and provincialism. In a scene in which the latter rejects Shakespeare on the grounds that he is not French—"he's a Russian . . . (or) Polish," according to the sacrosanct *Petit Larousse*[8]—the critic's xenophobia surfaces with a vengeance.

In 1956 the Pétain regime was not a distant memory. Ionesco, Beckett, and Adamov had all come under suspicion for being foreigners (Romanian, Irish, and Russian) and expatriates. In his essay "Du chapitre des *Chaises*" (On the subject of *The Chairs*) which came out two months after the premiere of *Improvisation,* Jean Anouilh wrote a self-deprecating, bitter praise of his competitors: "The young French theater bears the name Beckett/Adamov/Ionesco. There is nothing Breton or Perigordian about it. And here am I, an ancestor figure going back to 1932—was it a good year for wine?—an old guard dramatist, not even wholly respectable, a shame-faced *boulevardier* who never set foot inside Maxim's, nor enjoyed the forbearance granted an honest practicioner of *boulevard* theater. I feel full of trepidation at the prospect of having to deal with these young bucks from Central Europe . . . for indeed these three fellows borrowed my native tongue in order to have their plays performed in my village."[9]

What kind of "Central European" was Samuel Beckett? How provincial and stupid can one get? And yet Anouilh is no innocent babe; he knows exactly the nature of his audience and readership, and appeals to their ugly prejudices. His position is cleverly ambiguous.

Is he mocking the chauvinism of the petit bourgeois, or echoing the racism of the French Right? Could he be revealing under the mask of irony his own xenophobia? This bizarre sally echoes disquieting phrases commonly spouted under the German occupation by "true" Frenchmen and Frenchwomen: *"Les Allemands sont si corrects!"* (Aren't the Germans polite and well-behaved) or *"Les étrangers sont venus chez nous manger notre pain!"* (Foreigners have come here to take the bread from our mouths). There was also the threatening slogan, still alive in National Front circles *"La France aux Français!"* (France for the French). Ionesco must have had an earful of such declarations. No one who survived in Pétain's "Zone Libre" will ever forget them. Bartholomeus III sounds like an unregenerate collaborationist. Alas, he is only one of many as was made obvious in the film *The Sorrow and the Pity*.

Why "chameleon"? For Ionesco, the true chameleons are political extremists hiding under the protective black coloring of academic robes. They team up against independent thinkers in order to impose their own idiosyncrasies and ideologies. Although Ionesco never gave in to those pressures, preserving his independence at great personal cost, the befuddled protagonist of *Improvisation* seems, at one point, thoroughly brain washed:

> Bart II: (To Ionesco) You admit your mistakes?
> Ionesco: (With an effort) Why yes, Gentlemen . . . yes . . . my ignorance, my mistakes. . . . I'm very sorry . . . please forgive me . . . all I ask is to be taught what's right. . . . (He beats his chest) Mea culpa! Mea Maxima culpa![10]

Clearly the new religion is Brechtian Marxism. Ionesco, the dramatis persona of *Improvisation* has been questioned, tortured, purged; he has achieved a pathetic catharsis strongly reminiscent of the Stalin-era trials when the accused rushed to confess imaginary guilt. The protagonist will be saved in the nick of time by the one person who represents common sense, a Molieresque cleaning woman, Marie.

As Marie literally sweeps the doctors off stage, Ionesco remains alone. He will now be able to lecture about his ideas, addressing the audience. Before embarking on a mock-pedantic talk of his own, a rehash of his numerous interviews and essays, he declares that what his audience has just heard "was largely taken from the writings of the doctors."[11] Thus, Ionesco provides us with a clue that is supposed to send us back to the Brecht issue of *Théâtre Populaire*. All the absurdisms of Bartholomeus I and II actually issue from Bernard Dort's "Une nouvelle dramaturgie: Brecht ou l'anti-Racine," Roland Barthes's "Les maladies du costume de théâtre," Walter Weidli's "L'acteur de l'ère scientifique," and David Victoroff's "Le paradoxe du spectateur."[12] Some of the most extreme statements made by the critics appear in an almost unaltered form in Ionesco's cartoon of critical jargon.

Molière failed to express the social *gestus* of his age.[13]

The theatre is a lesson about some instructive happening, an event of educational value.[14]

The public's reactions are elementary. . . . Why do they clap their hands. The Romans called it *plaudere*. The Greeks used the verb *krotein*.[15]

The theatre is a lesson in things. . . . Every playgoer will be expected to come and see the same play several times and learn it by heart. . . . [16]

Do you realize you've got to learn everything from us? All about theatricality . . . costumology . . . historicization and decorology. . . . We will impart the basic elements of this new science.[17]

Nudity may also be considered a costume, as for example on the stage of the Folies-Bergères . . . costumologists are entrusted with the particular care of costume ailments; they are costumological physicians.[18]

We, the children of the scientific age, will learn how to distinguish the form of fire from its contents.[19]

There are a few simple rules for diagnosing whether a theater costume is ill or well. . . . Yours is suffering from hypertrophy of the historical function. . . . It's veridical. . . . Your costume is just an alibi. . . . It ought to be a sign.[20]

At this point in the *Impromptu,* an attempt is made to pull off Ionesco's trousers. An extra pair is pulled over them. He is crowned with a dunce's cap, much as Molière's Jourdain was crowned "Mamamouchi." The character Ionesco is also labeled "POET" on his back, and "SCIENTIST" on his chest. As the "Doctors" curb their patsy, he is made to bray and gambol. The utter lunacy of this scene suggests Molière's *Le Bourgeois Gentilhomme.* It also sends us back to Ionesco's early surrealist farces.

The doctors have been spouting axiomatic truisms, passing them off as dogma. In his final monologue, Ionesco advises: "The critic should describe, and not prescribe."[21] When the soliloquy turns into a sermon, Bart I comments: "You've fallen into your own trap."[22] No one can resist pontificating.

Ionesco's main objection to critical activity lies in the fact that literary critics in general, and drama critics in particular, are not satisfied with being faithful interpreters of a writer's work; they wish to guide, instruct, and assist him in formulating a program for his oeuvre, in short, to become tyrannical dramaturges and political gurus. In the course of a lecture delivered at the Sorbonne in March, 1969, Ionesco made the following point:

> And so the learned doctors wish to be obeyed. They are furious
> if they are disobeyed. They do not like you to be what you are,
> they would rather you were what *they* want you to be. They
> want you to play their game, accept their politics and become
> their tool. . . . Who are these doctors? They are the learned, the
> less learned and the not learned at all . . . those "engaged" or en-
> raged critics who positively refuse to accept you as you are.[23]

Given under the auspices of the Maison des Lettres, Ionesco's talk is a perfect explication of his *Improvisation.* It also refers to the very painful break that took place between Ionesco and his friend Arthur Adamov, a rift precipitated by pressures exerted by a group of politically motivated critics. Adamov took their suggestion to give up the writing of metaphysical plays in favor of a Brechtian theater. This choice did not prove a wise one; Adamov gained political allies, but lost his public. Ionesco continued to convey his own political thoughts under the absurdist mask. His fellow writer's worldwide success became unbearable for Adamov.

The political pressures that brought about the cooling of the Ionesco-Adamov friendship lie at the root of the play's mysterious subtitle. The latter is a clear reference to the chameleonic propensities of some writers, able and willing to change their coloring according to the ideological climate of the time. It is also rooted in the Brechtian theory of *Strassenszene* (street scene) that provides the protagonist with a key image for his play in progress. He describes such a scene to Bartholomeus I:

> It is the crucial scene of the play, the motive force. Once, in a large country town, in the middle of the street, during the summer, I saw a young shepherd, about three o'clock in the afternoon, who was embracing a chameleon. . . . It was such a touching scene I decided to turn it into a tragic farce.[24]

Ionesco, the writer of *Improvisation,* is mocking Ionesco, the protagonist of this impromptu, for finding a mock-bucolic scene "touching." In fact, however, the shepherd and his chameleon are not "absurdist," as has been assumed by numerous critics; this vignette is drawn from Brecht's statement that the epic theater ought to establish its model at a street corner.

> The epic theatre is a highly skilled theatre with complex contents and far-reaching social objectives. In setting up the street scene as a basic model for it, we pass on the clear social function and give the epic theatre criteria by which to decide whether an incident is meaningful or not.[25]

There is nothing bucolic or sentimental about Brecht's street scenes; they are tough, violent, pitiless urban vignettes raised to the level of poetry through language.

In his introductory note to his *Théâtre II,* Adamov seems to echo Brecht when he writes: "I discovered something extraordinary in the most common occurrences; street scenes could be turned into theatre scenes."[26] However, Adamov is careful to explain that he did not reach this illumination via Brecht but by reading Strindberg's *Dream Play:*

> I was struck with the passing parade of people who grazed each other without ever meeting, of the frightful diversity of casual

remarks which I caught walking by. It seemed to me that they constituted some kind of whole whose symbolic character rested upon their fragmentary nature.[27]

An incident he witnessed provided a basis for the kind of theater he wished to create:

> A blind man was begging; two young girls walked by without paying attention. They jostled him absent-mindedly while humming: "I closed my eyes, it was wonderful." The idea came to me to present human solitude on the stage in this concrete, highly visible way. In other words, I turned a phenomenon from real life into something metaphysical.[28]

The final word of this account of the genesis of Adamov's theater reveals the reasons for his original closeness to Ionesco. Both dramatists had simultaneously invented a new dramatic mode. No wonder the break between the two men was profoundly painful to both. Years ago, Ionesco went over what had occurred:

> A dogmatic critic, who had published a long essay about our theatre, approached us suggesting that the time was ripe to begin rebuilding, now that the past had been successfully destroyed. He meant that, as Marx had predicted, the capitalist bourgeois order had reached its end. We, the new dramatists, were expected to direct our plays to a new society, ready for a "positive" line.

What was this line supposed to be? Some of the above statements, made in private conversation in December, 1960, stem from Ionesco's Sorbonne lecture, delivered in March of the same year. The dramatist did not name the critic, but merely described him as "a young critic not so much learned as dogmatic." Apparently, this man had approached Ionesco to inquire whether the writer agreed that his plays criticized "the petite bourgeoisie." Ionesco answered that the petite bourgeoisie he had in mind was not "a class belonging to any particular society," and that for him the "petit bourgeois is just a man of slogans, who no longer thinks for himself . . . a manipulated man." The critic, who had associated Ionesco and Adamov in an article published by a weekly magazine, became the enemy of the first.

Ionesco adds that the line the "doctor-critic" wanted them to follow was of course his own. He adds:

> I did not follow the itinerary traced for me by this doctor. The other writer did; he was widely acclaimed along the primrose path; but I was reproached and excommunicated, hot coals were heaped upon my head . . . for only one kind of drama is permissible to them, co-existence is a word they do not understand.[29]

The "primrose path" turned out to be a *via dolorosa*. The last play in which Adamov reconciled the metaphysical and the social was *Le Ping-pong* (March, 1955), a bitter farce about two friends, Arthur, an art student (with the same first name as the author) and the medical student Victor, both of whom fritter their lives away playing a pinball machine at the misnamed café Espérance. The machine is a symbol for the workings of the capitalist system. It is the real protagonist of the play. *Le Ping-pong,* which Adamov directed for an Off-Broadway production, brought to a close the first phase of his career. As he veered from Strindbergian symbolism to an expressionist, Brechtian theater he became increasingly polemical. (With the exception of some Leftist intellectuals, Brecht was not appreciated in France, even after his visit with the Berliner.) Adamov found himself increasingly on the fringe. Sinking into obscurity, poverty, alcoholism, and ill health, he died in the small hotel room he had occupied all his life. It was rumored that he had taken his own life. Ionesco believed that his erstwhile companion was destroyed by the Marxist critics whose praise, followed by an evanescent support, robbed him of his independence. The importance of individualism is stressed in *Improvisation:*

> Bart I: Well, which are you to be, the shepherd or the chameleon?
> Ionesco: Oh no, definitely not the chameleon. I don't change color every day. . . . I'm not always being towed along by the latest fashion, like . . . I'd rather not say who. . . . [30]

Like Molière's *Critique de l'ecole des femmes* and his *Impromptu de Versailles,* Ionesco's *Impromptu de l'Alma* (Improvisation) is "a comedy of conversation."[31] If Molière's conceit was to have his Marquis and the pedantic poet Lysidas assume the traditional roles reserved for valets, Ionesco does much the same thing with his three critics. Again, like his illustrious predecessor, he reveals himself as a clever stager of public opinion. By following for once in the footsteps of France's premier jester, the leader of High Modernism won the comic war between writer and critic. Moreover, to pursue a parallelism emphasized by Ionesco's title for his play, if Molière's opponent—the writer against whom he had to measure himself—was the creator of French classical tragedy, Pierre Corneille, one might say that Ionesco's antagonist became the poet-dramatist Bertolt Brecht. This was due to the political pressures exercised by the reigning French intelligentsia. There is little doubt that Ionesco derived from Molière the strength of his ever-growing belief that the lowly genre of farce could be raised to compete with tragedy's depth of perception. By steeping farce in metaphysical thought, a third dimension was achieved, a genre was born that was neither farce, nor tragedy, but an amalgam of both.

Predictably, *Improvisation* was not a critical success. Robert Kemp wrote in *Le Monde:* "Ionesco is not fighting windmills, but the wind itself" (2/16/56). Max Favelli of *Paris-Presse-L'Intransigent* considered the play nothing but "an inside joke" (2/16/56). Claude Baignère of *Le Figaro* was negative, speaking of "general confusion" (2/16/56), as was André-Paul Antoine of *L'Information,* who called the play "typical Ionesco gibberish" (2/17/56). However, Morvan Lebesque in *Carrefour* spoke with irony of two young Marxist doctors, Barthes and Dort, who "undertook to teach theater according to the social map, as the *Précieuses* had instructed the men of their circle in the refinements of love following *la carte du Tendre*" (2/22/56). To be compared to Molière's "Affected and Learned Ladies"[32] could hardly have pleased Brecht's scholarly promoters.

No sooner did the *Théâtre Populaire-Improvisation* controversy begin to die down than a new storm arose in England. Kenneth Tynan, who had fought to establish Ionesco's reputation with the English-speaking public, began to have second thoughts about the revival of *The Chairs* at the Royal Court in 1958. On June 22, 1958, he published a scathing essay in *The Observer,* accusing "the ostriches of [the] theatrical intelligentsia" of seeking a new faith in their haste to shake off "the fetters of realism." Launching into praise of theater whose "characters and events have traceable roots in life (Gorky, Chekhov, Arthur Miller, Tennessee Williams, Brecht, O'Casey,

Osborne, and Sartre)," Ionesco's former champion denounced the antitheater for portraying a "world of isolated robots, conversing in cartoon-strip balloons of dialogue." Once again Brecht was singled out, held up as an example "for general emulation," in contrast to Ionesco's "blind alley . . . adorned with tachiste murals . . . a self-imposed vacuum."[33]

Ionesco's reply was surprisingly moderate and diplomatic:

> *The Chairs* is a plea, pathetic perhaps, for mutual understanding. As for the idea of reality, Mr. Tynan seems . . . to acknowledge only one plane of reality: what is called the "social" plane, which seems to be the most external, in other words the most superficial.

He concluded with specific advice for possible critical approaches:

> What, then, should the critic do? Where should he look for his criteria? Inside the work itself, its universe and its mythology. He must look at it, listen to it, and simply say whether it is true to its own nature . . . the work must be allowed to speak, uncolored by preconception or prejudice.[34]

Tynan answered. Orson Welles and Philip Toynbee intervened in the debate, the latter in defense of Arthur Miller whose simplistic realism Ionesco had decried. As to Ionesco's second reply, it was not published by *The Observer*. However, the French text was reproduced by *Les Cahiers des Saisons,* and is now part of "The London Controversy" as it appears in *Notes and Counter Notes*.

Ionesco's thoughtful answer is a meditation on the ways in which the renewal of language can bring about a fresh vision of the world. The dramatist comments on the pathetic lack of imagination characteristic of Socialist Realism as he observed it in the Soviet pavillion at the Paris International Painting Exhibition. Once again he stresses the fact that human beings ought not be considered as products of social structures, and that a fair, open, generous society must transcend "social machinery."[35]

That Brecht should have been thrust as an antagonist to Ionesco, both in France and England, must be viewed as an unfortunate accident. Marxist critics and scholars played a negative role in emphasizing the differences between the two writers when they might have brought to the fore many basic similarities. Despite Brecht's adherence to Communism, he never intended to become a propagandist for the party, and his independence from it became an embarrassment for the ideologues. When Brecht emigrated after Hitler came to power, he traveled across Russia to embark for the United States in Vladivostock. His acquaintance with the work of Mayakovsky, produced by Meyerhold, his admiration for the Russian dramatist's satirical plays *The Bedbug* and *The Bathhouse,* which were suppressed as formalist and ideologically confusing, led him to believe that he would not be allowed to experiment with new forms. He was cunning enough to seek asylum in neutral countries. Nor did he rush to East Germany after the war. As Julian Wulbern explains, he had to return to a German-speaking country to pursue and develop his work. Since he had been denied a visa to West Germany, he was left with little choice. Wulbern writes:

> . . . his application was ignored by the military government of the allied powers. This *de facto* denial left only three German-speaking countries from which to choose: Austria, Switzerland, and the Russian-occupied East-zone of Germany. One of his numerous Keuner stories expresses his inclination: Mr. K. preferred City B to City A. "In City A," he said, "I am loved, but in City B they are friendly to me. In City A I was used, but in City B they needed me. In City A I was invited to the table, but in City B they invited me into the kitchen." In short, while he was welcomed in Switzerland and would later be granted American citizenship, he felt needed in East Germany.[36]

With his Austrian citizenship, his publication contract with a West German company, and his prestigious appointment as general director of the Berliner Ensemble, Brecht enjoyed immunity from censorship. Under these circumstances, he could with impunity declare himself a practicing Marxist while remaining critical of the party and the regime. Politically, he was a gymnast, a genius of tightrope walking.

Since Ionesco speaks no German, and had little occasion to see Brecht's plays, except in French translation, his view of the German dramatist's theory and praxis came from the interpretation received

at the hands of Brecht's disciples. In France, as we said before, the
establishment became heavily Brechtian. In England, the discovery
of the Epic Theatre fed into the rise of the "Angry Young Men." As
Donald Watson explains, "it was in fact Brecht and Osborne between
them who probably prodded new British dramatists in a direction
more amenable to their traditions." Ionesco may have paved the
ground, freeing serious theater from "the dying embers of the poetic
drama of Eliot and Fry and John Whiting," but he was displaced as
the influential critics "led [the public] *away* from a full appreciation"[37]
of his work.

Ionesco's growing irritation with the Brecht phenomenon was
not alleviated by the estrangement he suffered between the late
fifties and the early seventies at the hands of the French liberal
establishment. He was labeled an archconservative despite his courageous rejection of fascism and his flight from Romania where he
made a brilliant start as a writer and teacher. As he continued to
denounce Soviet imperialism in *Le Figaro* and *Le Monde* he created
an unbridgeable abyss between himself and the post-1968 generation.

As to Ionesco's growing success, his numerous lecture trips
abroad, particularly to the United States, the performance of *Hunger
and Thirst* at the Comédie Française, and his election to the French
Academy, were interpreted as so many signs that the former vanguardist had become *une vieille barbe* (a doddering old fool).

In the late seventies things began to change. Solzhenitsyn was
awarded the Nobel Prize in literature, which he could not collect in
person. From June 8 to 12, 1973, a major Solzhenitsyn symposium
took place at the Centre Culturel of Cerisy-la-Salle. With the shatter-
ing publication of *The Gulag Archipelago* and the increasing number
of dissident emigrants, public opinion began to shift. Gradually, former Maoists, disenchanted *gauchistes,* even some members of the
French Communist party, began to question what they had taken for
a new kind of revelation. Ionesco was perceived as a man who had
seen things clearly, had denounced great evils thanks to his special
knowledge of Eastern Europe. Writers, scholars, thinkers, members
of the powerful journal *Tel Quel* started making overtures to the man
who diagnosed from the start a political plague as exportable as the
epidemic that ravaged Europe in the Middle Ages. Above all, the
United States was no longer perceived as the enemy, but was viewed

as an oasis, a bastion of democracy and freedom. Ionesco, who had remained throughout a friend of the United States, acquired the reputation of an astute political analyst. He had at last many friends and admirers.

Perhaps no occasion was happier than his eightieth birthday. Despite his fragile health, he had lived to witness the quiet revolution of 1989, the crumbling of the fascism of the Left, the demise of the Ceaucescus. He, who had never returned to Romania despite numerous official invitations, followed the developments with deepening emotion. He had stopped writing, having said what he had to say, but he could look back on a body of work in the form of plays, essays, journals that testified to his constant awareness.

Looking back at the considerable Ionesco oeuvre, it is obvious that he is one of the important political dramatists of our time. Yet his message is buried in the subtext, where it awaits many revisionist explications. He raises his cry of alarm without didacticism, for he is above all a symbolist poet of the stage. One can not agree with Wulbern when he says that "Ionesco remains socially and politically nihilistic."[38] A pessimist, a nihilist does not set pen to paper; for such a man there is no one out there he needs to reach, or hopes to enlighten. As Ionesco's translator Donald Watson explains in the concluding remarks of his Cardiff speech, pronounced on the occasion of Ionesco receiving the first International Writer's Prize from the Welsh Arts Council, Ionesco is an unregenerate humanist. This is why he remains vulnerable and perennially young. His writings address the young, and those who have retained the childlike quality of feeling wonder. Watson's words are wise and comforting:

> I do not see him as a fundamental pessimist, a purveyor of despair, but rather as a figure searching that same area of truth to which so many young people today are so strongly attracted. . . . Ionesco encourages us all to rethink our position and reassess our identity as we move into a strange new world.[39]

Chronology

1909

Eugène Ionesco is born in Slatina, Romania, on November 26 (November 13 according to the Orthodox calendar), the son of Thérèse Ipcar, a French national, and Eugen Ionescu, a graduate of the Bucharest University School of Law. (Later, Ionesco's father received his Doctorate of Law from the Paris *Faculté de Droit* [law school].) Ionesco's date of birth was until recently a mystery. The year appeared in every chronology, including that of this author for the Prentice-Hall *Ionesco*, as 1912. However, in a recently published translation from the Romanian of his early work *Hugoliade*, translated by Dragomir Costineanu "with the participation of Marie-France Ionesco" (Paris: Gallimard, 1982), the year of the dramatist's birth is listed as 1909. This was also confirmed by the findings of Professor Gheorgi Mihai, who "researched it in the archives of the city of Slatina." This research was published in the journal *România Literara*, 28 (1969). In the most recent chronology, heading the Bibliothèque de la Pléiade edition of Ionesco's *Théâtre complet*, the editor Emmanuel Jacquart explains what happened. Apparently Ionesco falsified his date of birth, making himself three years younger, when the critic Jacques Lemarchand greeted the "new generation of *young* dramatists ushering in the fifties." Jacquart speaks of "une *coquetterie* de l'auteur."

1911

The Ionesco family comes to Paris, where Ionesco's father starts his doctoral work. The parents of Thérèse Ipcar help the young family make ends meet. On February 11, Ionesco's sister Marilina is born.

1913

Birth of a third child, Mircea. The boy dies of meningitis when he is eighteen months old.

1916

Ionesco's father leaves Paris for Bucharest to fight in the war. Contact with his family in France is interrupted. Romania fights on the side of the Allies (August 28). Bucharest is occupied on December 6. On May 7, 1918, Bucharest signs a treaty. Believing that her husband was killed in action, Ipcar works to support her children. During that time, her husband asks for a divorce, claiming his wife's desertion of their home. In 1917, he will marry Helen Buruiana without informing her of his family back in Paris. The seven-year-old Ionesco is sent to an *internat* (boarding school) near Paris. He is very unhappy at being separated from his mother and sister.

1918
Ipcar and her children reside at a modest hotel rue Blomet (15th arrondissement). Ionesco is registered in the *école communale*. However, Ipcar worries about bombing raids. She decides to send her two children to the village of La Chapelle-Anthenaise in the Mayenne. These are very happy months for young Ionesco, despite the separation from his beloved mother. The village is evoked with nostalgia in the writer's journals, particularly *Fragments of a Journal,* and it appears in a number of his plays. Ionesco's film based on his novella "La Vase" (Slime), in which he plays the role of the traveling salesman, was made at La Chapelle-Anthenaise, as well as at his own country home near Paris, which is called "Le Moulin" in memory of the farm where he spent an important part of his childhood.

1922
Ionesco is called by his father to join him and his new wife in Bucharest. The thirteen-year-old boy is terribly unhappy to leave his mother. He will have to learn Romanian to enter the lycée Sfântul Sava. Marilina also joins her father and stepmother. Later on, Marilina will be allowed to live with her mother who moves to Bucharest.

1923
Ionesco writes a historical drama that he will later translate into Romanian.

1926
Ionesco leaves his father's home. He moves in with his mother, but the apartment is too small. He is also able to occupy a room in his aunt's apartment. His mother finds employment at the National Bank of Romania. The future dramatist discovers the work of Tristan Tzara, whom he will always consider as his literary ancestor. These are the years when he discovers the French surrealist writers: Breton, Soupault, Aragon.

1928
Ionesco receives his baccalaureate degree from the Craiova lycée. He begins to publish in the literary journal of the poet Tudor Arghezi, *Bilete de papagal*.

1928–33
Ionesco studies literature at Bucharest University. His degree will be in French literature.

1930

Ionesco publishes his first literary essay in the review *Zodiac*.

1931

Ionesco publishes *Elegy for Tiny Creatures*.

1929–35

Ionesco contributes to distinguished reviews such as *Azi* (Today), *Viata Literară* (The literary life), *România Literară* (Literary Romania), *Floarea de Foc* (Flower of fire), and *Critica* (Criticism). He writes political essays for *Vremea* (Times). These are also the years when Ionesco reads Faulkner and Proust. He discovers the Russian philosopher Lev Shestov, Dostoyevsky's greatest commentator. Shestov's quest for faith in the biblical God, the leitmotif of his thinking and writing in the last decades of his life, deeply influence Ionesco, as does his recognition that the supposedly universal laws discovered by science do not liberate human beings, but rather crush and destroy them. *Dostoyevsky and Nietzsche: The Philosophy of Tragedy* is one of Ionesco's favorite books. He also reads Spengler, Keyserling, Hegel, Schopenhauer. The philosopher he discovers at that time, and will continue studying throughout his life, is Plotinus.

1934

Publication of *Nu* (No), a volume of highly controversial essays. These are a sarcastic attack directed at the great luminaries of Romanian letters: Tudor Aghezi, Ion Barby, Camil Petrescu, and even his friend Mircea Eliade. Perhaps the most important essay in the volume is one devoted to the identity of opposites. The poet, influenced by Francis Jammes and Maeterlinck, gives way to a bold, sarcastic iconoclast. Ionesco acquires a notoriety due to the book's *succès de scandale*. However, the volume is also awarded a literary prize by a jury chaired by the literary critic Tudor Vianu.

1936

Ionesco marries Rodica Burileanu on July 8. His mother and sister attend, as well as his father accompanied by his second wife. Ionesco speaks of the enmity that pervaded the atmosphere. The newlyweds leave for a honeymoon in Greece. Ionesco's mother dies in October. Ionesco finds employment with the Ministry of Education.

1937

Ionesco teaches at the Bucharest lycée and publishes in the democratic weekly *Facla* (The torch), *Universul Literar* (The literary universe), and *Rampa* (The ramp), a daily covering the theater, literature, and the arts. He publishes an article on Van Gogh, an early indication of Ionesco's lifelong interest in art. Late in his life, Ionesco turns exclusively to his own painting and lithography.

1938

Ionesco receives a fellowship from the French Institute of Bucharest to write a doctoral dissertation on the theme of "Sin and Death in French Poetry." Ionesco plans to start with Baudelaire, and cover Verlaine, Rimbaud, Lautréamont, Mallarmé, and Valéry.

1939

Ionesco and his wife arrive in Paris. They pay a visit to La Chapelle-Anthenaise. Ionesco makes contact with the group of writers connected with the journal *Esprit*. He contributes to the prestigious literary and scientific monthly *Viata Româneasca* (Romanian life), whose editors are the philosopher Mihai Ralea and the literary critic G. Calinescu.

1942

The Ionescos move to Marseilles. They are poor refugees.

1944

The Ionescos' only child, Marie-France, is born.

1945

The Ionescos return to Paris in March and rent an apartment at 38, rue Claude-Terrasse (16th arrondissement), where they reside until 1960. Ionesco works as a proof reader in the Editions Administratives. He translates from Romanian the novel of Pavel Dan, *Urcan Batranu* (Father dan), and the works of Romanian poet Urmuz, a forerunner of Surrealism and of the Absurd.

1948

Eugen Ionescu dies in Bucharest. Ionesco writes in Romanian the first version of *The Bald Soprano*. Its initial title is *Englezeste fără profesor* (English without a teacher). He then composes *La Cantatrice chauve* (The bald soprano). Both versions issue from a conversation textbook used by Ionesco when he tried to learn English, *L'Anglais sans peine* (English without pain). Marie Saint-Côme, the daughter of Eugène Livinesco, introduces Ionesco to the director Nicolas Bataille.

1950

La Cantatrice Chauve is created at the Théâtre des Noctambules under the direction of Nicolas Bataille on May 11. Ionesco writes *Jacques ou la soumission* (Jack or the submission), *La Leçon* (The lesson), and *Les Salutations* (Salutations). He also plays in an adaptation of Dostoyevsky's *The Possessed* directed by Nicolas Bataille at the Théâtre de l'Oeuvre (in the role of Stepan Trofimovich).

1951

Ionesco writes *Les Chaises* (The chairs) and *L'Avenir est dans les oeufs* (The future is in eggs). He becomes a member of the mock-academy Le Collège de Pataphysique founded in 1948 by Emmanuel Paillet and Maurice Saillet, a specialist of the oeuvre of Alfred Jarry. According to Roger Shattuck, Proveditor-General

Propagator for the Islands and the Americas, Regent (by Transseant Susception) of the Chair of Applied Mateology, GMOGG, "the pataphysician looks at the world with imperturbability, in the manner of the child looking through a kaleidoscope or the astronomer studying the galaxy." Jarry, who welcomed "the fearless dynamism of the anarchists," invented "the science of imaginary solutions." "Pataphysics is the science of the realm beyond metaphysics." Ionesco was raised to the rank of "Transcendent Satrap," like Raymond Queneau, Boris Vian, Jacques Prévert, Marcel Duchamp, Michel Leiris, René Clair, Jean Dubuffet. The Collège de Pataphysique was Ionesco's favorite academy, the "in" group par excellence of the descendants of dadaism and surrealism. See Roger Shattuck, "What Is Pataphysics?" *Evergreen Review* 4, no. 13 (May–June 1960).

1952
The Chairs is created at the Théâtre Lancry. Ionesco writes *Victimes du devoir* (Victims of duty).

1953
Seven Short Sketches is performed. *Victims of Duty* is staged at the Théâtre du Quartier Latin under the direction of Jacques Mauclair. Ionesco writes *Amédée* at Cerisy-la-Salle as well as *The New Tenant*. *Théâtre I*, prefaced by Jacques Lemarchand, is published (Paris: Editions Arcanes).

1954
Amédée has its first performance. *Théâtre I* is published by Gallimard.

1955
"The Colonel's Photograph," the novella that will serve as the basis for *The Killer*, is published. Ionesco writes *L'Impromptu de l'Alma (Improvisation)*.
The New Tenant is created in Finland under the direction of Vivica Bandler.
Ionesco travels to London.

1956
The revival of *The Chairs* is staged together with *Improvisation*. Ionesco's novella "La Vase" (Slime) is published by *Les Cahiers des Saisons*.

1957
Ionesco writes *The Killer* in London. He writes *Impromptu pour la Duchesse de Windsor*, which is given privately in Paris. The short story "Rhinoceros" is published by *Les Lettres Nouvelles*. *The New Tenant* is created in France at the Théâtre de l'Alliance Française.

1958
Ionesco writes *Rhinoceros*. A public reading of the last act of the play is held at the Théâtre du Vieux Colombier. Gallimard brings out *Théâtre II*. The "London Controversy" occurs. John Calder brings out Ionesco's first volume of plays, translated by Donald Watson.

1959
There are meetings on avant-garde theater at Helsinki. *Rhinoceros* is staged at Düsseldorf, and published by Gallimard. The Ionescos move to 14, rue de Rivoli.

1960
Rhinoceros is staged by Jean-Louis Barrault at the Odéon and by Orson Welles at the Royal Court Theatre in London. In March, Ionesco gives a lecture at the Sorbonne, "Propos sur mon théâtre et sur les propos des autres."

1961
Ionesco writes "La Colère" (Anger) for the film *Les Sept Péchés capitaux* (The seven deadly sins). He travels to New York for the Broadway production of *Rhinoceros,* which is directed by Joseph Anthony at the Longacre Theater. Eli Wallach plays Bérenger and Zero Mostel plays the role of Jean.

1962
Ionesco writes *Délire à deux* (Frenzy for two), *Le Roi se meurt* (Exit the king), and *Le Piéton de l'air* (A stroll in the air). He lectures in May at the Collège Philosophique, "L'Auteur et ses problèmes" (The author and his problems). This talk is published later by *La Revue de Métaphysique. Notes and Counter Notes* is published. The public is informed at last that Ionesco considers hmself a "metaphysical" tragicomic dramatist.

1963
Gallimard publishes *Théâtre III.* A film of *The New Tenant* is made at the University of Bristol. Ionesco travels to Japan.

1964
Ionesco writes *La Soif et la faim* (Hunger and thirst). *Rhinoceros* is given in Bucharest. This is the first performance of an Ionesco play in his country. Two volumes of his plays are brought out by the Editions Pentru Literatura Universala of Bucharest.

1965
La Soif et la faim is published by *La Nouvelle Revue Française,* and *La Lacune* (The gap) by *Le Nouvel Observateur* (1/28/65). Three of Ionesco's plays are given in Bucharest: *The Bald Soprano, The Chairs,* and *Exit the King.* Ionesco travels to Saint-Gall in Switzerland.

1966
La Soif et la faim is presented at the Comédie Française, directed by Jean-Marie Serreau. Jean-Louis Barrault creates at the Odéon a spectacle entitled "Spectacle Beckett-Ionesco-Pinget." Directors and the public begin to realize that there is a new literary movement in contemporary drama, which I discerned and named "Metaphysical Farce" in 1959. Gallimard publishes *Théâtre IV.*

1967
Journal en miettes (Fragments of a journal) by the Mercure de France. Another episode of *La Soif et la faim*, "Au pied du mur" (One's back to the wall), is published by *La Nouvelle Revue Française*.

1968
Publication of *Présent passé passé présent* (Present past past present) by the Mercure de France. *The Killer* and *Victims of Duty* are given in Bucharest. The Ionescos travel to Mexico, Zurich, Israel, and the United States.

1969
Publication of *Découvertes* by Éditions Skira in Geneva. This is a journal illustrated by Ionesco. The original lithographs are exhibited by the Iolas Gallery of Geneva. In July, the Ionesco family travels to Stockbridge, Massachusetts for the rehearsals of *Hunger and Thirst*.

1970
Ionesco is elected to the Jean Paulhan Chair at the Académie Française. In Vienna he receives the prize of European Literature.

1971
Discours de réception d'Eugène Ionesco à l'Académie Française et Réponse de Jean Delay is published by Gallimard. German television presents the film *La Vase*, directed by Heinz von Cramer, with Ionesco in the main role.

1972
Ionesco delivers the opening address at the Salzburg Festival. He speaks of Mozart's message, the communication of an "inexplicable" joy, despite the fact that he died in poverty and pain. This talk is incorporated into *Un homme en question* (75–82).

1973
Macbett is published. Ionesco writes *Ce formidable bordel* (A hell of a mess).

1974
Gallimard brings out *Théâtre IV*.

1975
Ionesco writes *L'Homme aux valises* (Man with bags).

1976
Ionesco receives the Max Reinhardt medal at the 50th anniversary of the Salzburg Festival.

1977
Antidotes is published.

1978
"Décade Ionesco" at the Centre Culturel International de Cérisy-la-Salle, orga-
nized by Marie-France Ionesco and Professor Paul Vernois, the author of *La
Dynamique Théâtrale d'Eugène Ionesco* (Paris: Éditions Klincksieck, 1972). Most
Ionesco specialists participate, as does Ionesco himself (August 3–13).

1979
Un homme en question (A man is questioned) is published. Ionesco is invited as
"visiting professor" by the University of California at Santa Cruz.

1980
Ionesco lectures at Berkeley, San Francisco, and Santa Barbara. He is present at
a symposium organized by Professor Moshe Lazar at the University of Southern
California, where Ionesco spends the month of April as "artist in residence."
The papers delivered at the symposium (April 24–26) are published under the
title *The Dream and the Play: Ionesco's Theatrical Quest,* ed. Moshe Lazar (Malibu,
CA: Undena Publications, 1982). *La Nouvelle Revue Française* publishes *Thème
et variations: Voyages chez les morts.* The text of the play appears in three issues of
the journal: 324 (January 1, 1980); 325 (February 1, 1980); 326 (March 1, 1980).
An unpublished translation by Professor Daniel Gerould of the Graduate Center
of CUNY, directed by Paul Berman, is prepared for performance (September
22–November 2) at New York's Guggenheim Museum. Brilliantly directed and
acted, it fails to open on account of a difference of opinion between Ionesco and
the set designer Agam, a painter and sculptor from Israel. Ionesco travels to
Mexico and Chicago.

1981
Le Blanc et le noir (White and black) is published with 15 lithographs by Ionesco
(Saint-Gall, Switzerland: Erker-Verlag). This deluxe edition will be followed
by the Gallimard edition in 1985. Gallimard publishes *Voyages chez les morts*
(Journeys among the Dead) as *Théâtre VII.* Exhibition of Ionesco's paintings and
lithographs at the Erker Gallery in Saint-Gall, Switzerland (February 7–May 16),
then in Cologne (April 30–May 26). Ionesco is invited as "visiting professor"
by the State University of New York at Albany.

1982
Hugoliade is published. Exhibitions of Ionesco's paintings and lithographs are
presented in Lugano, Saint-Gall, Basel, and Athens. Ionesco writes his first opera
libretto, *Maximilian Kolbe,* with music by Dominique Prost. The libretto is
published for the first time in the English translation of Rosette C. Lamont by
Performing Arts Journal 17 6, no. 2 (1982). In December, Ionesco and his wife,
Rodica, act at the Centre Georges-Pompidou in Virginia Woolf's *Freshwater* (on
the centennial of Woolf's birth). Their fellow actors are Alain Robbe-Grillet,
Jean-Paul Aron, Florence Delay. The adaptation is directed by Simone
Benmussa. The play is also presented at New York University (October 20 and
21, 1983), then at the Théâtre du Rond-Point (November 7, 1983), at the River-

side in London (November 26 and 27), and finally at the Spoleto Festival (July 4 and 5, 1984).

1983
Roger Planchon presents at his theater in Villeurbanne (Théâtre National Populaire) a "Spectacle Ionesco," a "montage" of scenes from Ionesco's two final dream plays. The principal player is Jean Carmet. Planchon calls the spectacle "a theatrical autobiography in two parts." Art exhibitions are presented in Locarno (March 9–April 5), Munich (March 11–April 20), and Mannheim (October 29–November 20).

1984
Art exhibitions are presented in Berlin (March 18–April 17), Saint-Gall (April 28–June 2), Bologna (May 5–25), Zurich (September–November), and at the Paris Grand-Palais (October 20–28). The Ionescos travel to Austria, Germany, Italy, and the United States. Ionesco gives a lecture at Brown University.

1985
Le Blanc et le noir is published by Gallimard. The opera Le roi se meurt (Exit the king), with music by Suter Meister, is performed at the Munich opera house.

1987
Ionesco spends time painting at Saint-Gall. There is a celebration at the Théâtre de la Huchette of the 30th anniversary of the Spectacle Ionesco. Ionesco is honored in March with the "Médaille de la Ville de Paris."

1988
Gallimard publishes La quête intermittente (The intermittent quest). An exhibition of Ionesco's lithographs is presented at the Centre Georges-Pompidou (March 23–April 9). Ionesco participates in the first New York International Festival of the Arts by giving a lecture at Columbia University entitled "Does Anyone Still Need the Theater?" (June 15).

1989
The PEN Club jury, presided over by Ionesco, honors Vaclav Havel with the Freedom Prize. Ionesco and Samuel Beckett sign a petition in defense of Salman Rushdie.

1990
Ionesco publishes an article in Le Figaro (April 27) about the situation in Romania.

1991
Gallimard brings out Ionesco's Théâtre complet, annotated by Emmanuel Jacquart, in their Bibliothèque de la Pléiade.

Stage Productions

May 1950
La Cantatrice chauve (The bald soprano), directed by Nicolas Bataille at the Théâtre des Noctambules. Bataille played the role of Mr. Martin. The other actors were Simone Mozet (Mme. Martin), Claude Mansard (Mr. Smith), Paulette Frantz (Mme. Smith), Odette Barois (Mary, the maid), Henry-Jacques Huet (Fire Chief). Originally, the play was performed twenty-five times.

February 1951
La Leçon (The lesson), directed by Marcel Cuvelier at the Théâtre de Poche. Cuvelier played the role of the Professor. The Maid was played by a male actor, Claude Mansard. Rosette Zuchelli was the Pupil.

April 1952
Les Chaises (The chairs), directed by Sylvain Dhomme at the Théâtre du Nouveau-Lancry. Sylvain Dhomme played the Orator. Paul Chevalier and Tsilla Chelton played the Old Couple. Jean Tardieu's *Les Amants du métro* (Subway lovers) was the second one-act play on the bill.

October 1952
La Cantatrice chauve and *La Leçon* were given as a double bill at the Théâtre de la Huchette, where they are still running today.

February 1953
Victimes du devoir (Victims of duty), directed by Jacques Mauclair at the Théâtre du Quartier Latin. Mauclair played the Detective. Choubert was interpreted by R. J. Chauffard, and Madeleine by Tsilla Chelton.

August 1953
Sept petits sketches (Seven short sketches), directed by Jacques Poliéri at the Théâtre de la Huchette: *Les Grandes Chaleurs* (Great heat; after Caragiale), *Le Salon de l'automobile* (The motor show), *La Niece-épouse* (The niece-wife), *Le Maître* (The leader), *La Jeune Fille à marier* (Maid to marry), *La Connaissez-vous?* (Do you know her?), *Le Rhume onirique* (The dream head cold).

April 1954
Amédée ou comment s'en débarrasser (Amédée or how to get rid of it), directed by Jean-Marie Serreau at the Théâtre de Babylone. The role of Amédée was played by Lucien Raimbourg, that of Madeleine by Yvonne Clech. Music by Pierre Barbaud, sets by Jacques Noël.

October 1955
Jacques ou la soumission (Jack or the submission) and *Le Tableau* (The picture), directed by Robert Postec at the Théâtre de la Huchette. Jean-Louis Trintignant played Jacques. Some of the other actors were Tsilla Chelton (Jacques Mère), Reine Courtois (Roberte I and Roberte II). Music by George Delerue, sets by Jacques Noël.

Le Nouveau Locataire (The new tenant) had its world premiere in Finland under the direction of Vivica Bandler.

November 1956
The Bald Soprano and *The New Tenant,* directed by Peter Wood at the Arts Theatre, London.

May 1957
The Chairs, directed by Tony Richardson at the Royal Court Theatre, London. Joan Plowright played the Old Woman; George Devine was the Old Man.

L'Impromptu pour la duchesse de Windsor (Impromptu for the duchess of Windsor), with music by Pierre Boulez, was given at the home of an Argentinian gentleman living in Paris, Mr. Anchorena. The text of this sketch was misplaced.

June 1957
L'Avenir est dans les oeufs ou Il faut de tout pour faire un monde (The future is in eggs or it takes all sorts to make a world), directed by Jean-Luc Magneron at the Théâtre de la Cité Universitaire.

August 1957
The Future Is in Eggs, directed by George Devine at the Royal Court Theatre, London.

September 1957
Le Nouveau Locataire (The new tenant), directed by Robert Postec at the Théâtre d'Aujourd'hui (Alliance Française). Paul Chevalier played Le Monsieur, Graeme Allwright was the Premier Déménageur, and Claude Mansard the Deuxième Déménageur. Set by Siné.

February 1959
Tueur sans gages (The killer), directed by José Quaglio at the Théâtre Récamier. Jean-Marie Serreau played the role of the Architect, Claude Nicot that of Bérenger, and Nicolas Bataille was Édouard.

June 1959
Scène à quatre (Foursome) was premiered at the Spoleto Festival, played in French by Italian actors.

November 1959
Die Nashörner (Rhinoceros) was premiered at the Düsseldorf Schauspielhaus, directed by Karl-Heinz Stroux. Bérenger was played by Karl Maria Schley.

January 1960
Le Rhinocéros (Rhinoceros), directed by Jean-Louis Barrault at the Odéon, Paris. Barrault played Bérenger.

April 1960
Rhinoceros, directed by Orson Welles, was presented at the Royal Court, London. Laurence Olivier played Bérenger, Joan Plowright was Daisy.

Appendre à marcher (Learning to walk), a ballet choreographed by Deryk Mendel to a Ionesco scenario, with music by Malec, was given by the Ballets Modernes de Paris at the Théâtre de l'Étoile.

January 1961
Rhinoceros, directed by Joseph Anthony, was staged at the Longacre Theater in New York, with Eli Wallach in the role of Bérenger, Anne Jackson as Daisy, and Zero Mostel as Jean. This was Ionesco's first Broadway production.

March 1961
Les Chaises and *Jacques ou la soumission,* revived by Jacques Mauclair at the Studio des Champs-Elysées.

April 1962
Délire à deux . . . à tant qu'on veut (Frenzy for two or more), directed by Antoine Bourseiller at the Studio des Champs-Elysées. The role of Elle was played by Tsilla Chelton, Yves Penaud played Lui. This one-act sketch was given with two others by François Billetdoux and Jean Vauthier. The collective title was *Chemises de nuit* (Night shirts).

December 1962
Le Roi se meurt (Exit the king), directed by Jacques Mauclair at the Théâtre de l'Alliance Française. Mauclair played the role of King Bérenger Ier. Tsilla Chelton was Queen Marguerite. Reine Courtois played the young Queen Marie, the maid Juliette was played by Rosette Zucchelli.

Der Füssganger in der Luft (A stroll in the air), directed by Karl-Heinz Stroux at the Düsseldorf Schauspielhaus. World premiere.

February 1963
Le Piéton de l'air (A stroll in the air), directed by Jean-Louis Barrault at the Odéon. Barrault played Bérenger, Madeleine Renaud was Joséphine. French premiere.

August 1963
Exit the King, directed by George Devine at the Royal Court Theatre, London. Alec Guinness played King Bérenger Ier.

March 1964
Jean-Louis Barrault's production of *Le Piéton de l'air* is invited to New York's City Center.

Rhinoceros is performed in Bucharest. This is the first Ionesco play given in his native country.

May 1964
The New Tenant and *Victims of Duty,* directed by Michael Kahn at the Writer's Stage, New York City. Joseph Chaikin played the Second Furniture Mover in *The New Tenant* as well as the Detective in *Victims of Duty.* Charlotte Rae played the Concierge in *The New Tenant* and Madeleine in *Victims of Duty.*

December 1964
Hunger und Durst (Hunger and thirst), premiered at the Schauspielhaus under the direction of Karl-Heinz Stroux.

February 1965
The ballet *Le Jeune Homme à marier* (Young man to marry), an adaptation of *La Jeune Fille à marier* (Maid to marry) with the title role played by a male actor, was choreographed by Flemming Flindt and shown on Danish television.

La Lacune (The gap), premiered at the Centre Dramatique du Sud-Est.

The Bald Soprano, The Chairs, and *Exit the King* were presented in Bucharest.

February 1966
La Lacune, directed by Jean-Louis Barrault, was given at the Odéon. The three actors were Pierre Bertin, Jean Dessailly, and Madeleine Renaud.

La Soif et la faim (Hunger and thirst), directed by Jean-Marie Serreau at the Comédie Française with Robert Hirsch in the role of Jean. With this play Ionesco makes his entry into the repertoire of the Comédie Française, and becomes what the French call *un classique moderne.*

Jean-Louis Barrault, following in the footsteps of Antoine Bourseiller and Nicolas Bataille, stages *Délire à deux* at the Odéon.

May 1966
Le Pied du mur (One's back against the wall), later to be incorporated into *La Soif et la faim*, staged at the Théâtre de Poche by Antoine Bourseiller.

July 1966
Leçons de français pour Américains, directed by Antoine Bourseiller at the Théâtre de Poche.

November 1966
Mêlées et démêlés (ten sketches), directed by Georges Vitaly at the Théâtre la Bruyère.

December 1966
Revival of *Le Roi se meurt*, directed by Jacques Mauclair at the Théâtre de l'Athénée. New sets by Jacques Noël.

January 1968
Exit the King, directed by Ellis Raab at the Lyceum Theater in New York. Richard Easton played King Bérenger, and Eva Le Galienne was Queen Marguerite.

Tueur sans gages and *Victimes du devoir* presented in Bucharest.

July 1969
Hunger and Thirst presented for the first time in the United States at the Stockbridge Theater in Massachusetts. Ionesco traveled to Stockbridge to supervise the rehearsals.

January 1970
Das Grosse Massakerspiel (Killing game) premiered at the Düsseldorf Schauspielhaus under the direction of Karl-Heinz Stroux and Frantisek Miska.

September 1970
Jeux de massacre (Killing game), directed by Jorge Lavelli at the Théâtre Montparnasse. French premiere.

January 1972
Macbett, directed by Jacques Mauclair at the Théâtre Rive Gauche. Mauclair played the title role.

July 1973
Macbett, translated and directed by Charles Marowitz, staged at the Bankside Glove Playhouse, London.

November 1973
Ce formidable bordel (Oh what a bloody circus), directed by Jacques Mauclair at the Théâtre Moderne. Maurclair played the Character.

December 1975
L'Homme aux valises (Man with bags), directed by Jacques Mauclair at the Théâtre de l'Atelier. Mauclair played L'Homme; Tsilla Chelton (the Grandmother, the Mother, the old Vegetable Vendor, the hospitalized Second Old Woman with an Inner Tree); Mauclair's daughter, Monique Mauclair (a Nurse, the Sphinx, the Consul's Secretary); and André Thorent (the Painter, the Policeman, the Consul, the Doctor). Set by Jacques Noël.

November 1976
Man with Bags was given a stage reading at the Milwaukee Repertory Company. Ionesco and his translator Israel Horovitz were present at this performance.

September 1977
World premiere of Horovitz's adaptation of *Man with Bags,* directed by Paul Berman on the main stage of the Fine Arts Building at Towson State University, Towson, Maryland. The First Man was played by Dwight Schultz. The scenic design was by Wally Coberg.

June 1978
The Chairs revived by Jacques Mauclair at his own Théâtre du Marais.

January 1979
Jorge Lavelli directed *Le Roi se meurt* at the Paris Odéon. Michel Aumont was King Bérenger Ier, Catherine Fersen was Queen Marguerite, Tania Torrens was Queen Marie, Michel Duchaussoy was the Guard, Catherine Hiégel was Juliette, and François Chaumette was the Doctor.

September 1980
Journeys among the Dead, staged by Paul Berman at the Guggenheim Museum in New York. A number of previews were well attended, but this brilliant, elegant production failed to open because of a difference of opinion between Ionesco and his set designer, the Israeli painter and sculptor Agam.

February 1983
Spectacle Ionesco (a montage of scenes from *L'Homme aux valises* and *Voyages chez les morts*), directed by Roger Planchon at the Théâtre National Populaire at Villeurbanne. This amalgam of his two final dream plays was approved by Ionesco who traveled to Lyons for the premiere. The famous film actor Jean Carmet played the main role. *Voyages chez les morts* has not been given a major production in French as a separate play. However, *Voyages chez les morts* was heard over the radio station of France-Culture on September 23, 1982, under the direction of Claude Roland-Manuel. This slightly abridged version was read by Pascal Mazzotti, Henri Virlogeux, Roger Carel, Maria Meriko, and others.

April 1988
Revival of *Les Chaises,* directed by Jean-Luc Boutté with Pierre Dux and Denise Gence for the inaugural season of Jorge Lavelli's Théâtre National de la Colline.

October 1990
The Chairs, directed by Françoise Kourilsky, with Clement Fowler as the Old Man, Elizabeth Perry as the Old Woman, and Waguih Takla as the Orator, was given at the Ubu Repertory Theater in New York.

October 1992
Macbett, directed by Jorge Lavelli at the Théâtre National de la Colline.

Notes

Introduction

1. This redefinition of the Aristotelian concept of tragic catharsis is found in J. S. Doubrovsky's essay "Ionesco and the Comic of Absurdity," *Yale French Studies* 23 (Summer 1959): 3–10. The essay is reprinted in *Ionesco: A Collection of Critical Essays,* ed. Rosette C. Lamont (Englewood Cliffs, NJ: Prentice-Hall, 1973), 11–20. Doubrovsky writes: "This non-Aristotelian theatre presents us with a problem which Aristotle had not foreseen: that of pity and terror for which laughter is a catharsis." He goes on to explain that "if one goes further in the experience of absurdity, man becomes suddenly so unimportant that tragedy turns into farce, and an absurd laughter bursts forth."

2. Friedrich Dürrenmatt, "Problems of Theatre," *Tulane Drama Review,* 3, no. 1 (October, 1958): 20.

3. Ionesco, "Why Do I Write? A Summing Up," trans. Rosette C. Lamont, in *The Two Faces of Ionesco,* ed. Rosette C. Lamont and Melvin J. Friedman (Troy, NY: The Whitston Publishing Company, 1978), 18.

4. Ionesco, *Non,* trans. from the Romanian *Nu* and annotated by Marie-France Ionesco (Paris: Gallimard, 1986), 84.

5. Ionesco, "Why Do I Write?" 18.

6. The Assimil method of teaching foreign languages emphasizes the aural/oral approach. It comprises a textbook used in combination with a set of records, and now tapes. The student is introduced into a "typical" family (British, if you are studying English in France). The method claims to be based on a practical approach to the acquisition of a useful, everyday kind of vocabulary. Each lesson is read out loud and acted out in class by the students. It is interesting to note that *English Made Easy* is a method of teaching language by theatrical means. Yet, the situations in the book are ridiculously out of date, and the vocabulary antiquated and simpleminded. Ionesco was struck by these features of the text, and his mind turned away from the task of learning English to an exploration of absurdity through verbal play. This is what he means when he states that he became a dramatist "by accident." He had not written a play before, only poems and literary essays. One wonders what would have happened, or rather failed to happen, had he not attempted to acquire a foreign language, or met with the

director Nicolas Bataille, who had the genius to recognize that this strange sketch was the essence of theater.

7. For Ionesco's own description of his *prise de conscience,* see his 1958 talk delivered in Italy at the French Institute. It appears under the title "The Tragedy of Language," in his collection of essays, *Notes and Counter Notes,* trans. Donald Watson (New York: Grove Press, 1964), 175–80.

8. Ionesco, *Non,* 84. This quotation, as all subsequent ones from this book, my translation.

9. Ileana Gregori, "L'ironie dans *Nu,*" an afterword to the Gallimard edition of *Non,* 286.

10. Soren Kierkegaard, *The Concept of Irony,* trans. Lee M. Capel (Bloomington and London: Indiana University Press, 1986), 56.

11. Ibid.

12. Ibid., 77.

13. Ibid., 200.

14. A statement made to me by Ionesco.

15. Ionesco, *Non,* 195.

16. *Bardes dessinées* are book-length narratives done in comic strip form and designed for adult readers.

17. Ionesco, "Anger," in *Hunger and Thirst and Other Plays,* trans. Donald Watson (New York: Grove Press, 1969), 155.

18. Ibid., 163.

19. Ibid.

20. Ibid., 164.

21. Ionesco, *Non,* 86.

Chapter 1

1. Ionesco, *Fragments of a Journal,* trans. Jean Stewart (New York: Grove Press, 1969), 70.

2. Mircea Eliade, "Eugene Ionesco and 'La Nostalgie du Paradis,'" in *The Two Faces of Ionesco,* ed. Rosette C. Lamont and Melvin J. Friedman (Troy, NY: The Whitston Publishing Company, 1978), 22.

3. William Shakespeare, *Hamlet* (I.ii.133).

4. Richard Schechner, "*The Bald Soprano* and *The Lesson:* An Inquiry into Play Structure," in *Ionesco,* ed. Rosette C. Lamont (Englewood Cliffs, NJ: Prentice Hall, 1973), 25.

5. In his *Essays in Historical Semantics* (New York: S. F. Vanni, 1948), Spitzer states: "Not to deal with the meaning of learned words means simply to shy away from the whole semantic content of our civilization" (5).

6. Ionesco, *Fragments of a Journal,* 119.

Chapter 2

1. William Wordsworth, "My Heart Leaps Up when I Behold." In 1815 this short poem became the epigraph to Wordsworth's "Ode: Intimations of Immortality from Recollections of Early Childhood."

2. William Wordsworth, "Ode: Intimations of Immortality," in *The Complete Poetical Works of William Wordsworth* (Boston: Houghton Mifflin, 1904), 353–56.

3. Ibid., 1: 18.

4. Christopher Wordsworth, *Memoirs of William Wordsworth,* ed. Henry Reed (Boston: Ticknor, Reed, and Fields, 1851), 486.

5. Ionesco, *Découvertes* (Genèva: Editions Albert Skira, 1969), 80. My translation, as are all subsequent quotations from *Découvertes.*

6. Ionesco, *Fragments of a Journal,* trans. Jean Stewart (New York: Grove Press, 1968), 20.

7. Ibid., 10.

8. Ibid., 11.

9. Ibid., 8.

10. Ionesco, *Découvertes,* 55–58.

11. Ibid., 72–73.

12. Ibid., 83.

13. Ionesco, *Fragments of a Journal,* 20.

14. Richard N. Coe, "On Being Very Surprised . . . Eugène Ionesco and the Vision of Childhood," in *The Dream and the Play: Ionesco's Theatrical Quest,* ed. Moshe Lazar (Malibu, CA: Undena Publications, 1982), 9.

15. Ibid., 10.

16. Lewis Carroll, *Alice's Adventures in Wonderland* (New York: Random House, 1946), 8.

17. The reference is to William Blake's *Songs of Innocence.*

18. Ionesco, *Present Past Past Present,* trans. Helen R. Lane (New York: Grove Press, 1971), 20.

19. Ibid., 5.

20. Ibid.

21. Ionesco, *Découvertes,* 58.

22. See Mircea Eliade, *Cosmos and History: The Myth of the Eternal Return,* trans. Willard R. Trask (New York: Harper and Brothers, 1959).

23. Ionesco, *Present Past Past Present,* 159.

24. Ibid., 91.

25. Ibid., 51.

26. Ibid., 105.

27. Ibid., 33.

28. Ibid., 88.

29. Ibid., 137.

30. Ibid., 138.

31. Ibid.

32. Claude Bonnefoy, *Conversations with Eugène Ionesco,* trans. Jan Dawson (New York: Holt, Rinehart and Winston, 1971), 62.

33. Ionesco, *Present Past Past Present,* 166.

34. Ionesco, "Chronologie," *Théâtre complet,* edition présentée, établie et annotée par Emmanuel Jacquart (Paris: Gallimard, 1991), ciii. My translation.

35. Wordsworth, "Ode: Intimations of Immortality," 1: 34.

Chapter 3

1. Ionesco, *Hugloliade,* trans. from the Romanian by Dragomir Costineanu (Paris: Gallimard, 1982), 58. My translation from the French.

2. Ionesco, *Notes and Counter Notes: Writings on the Theatre,* trans. Donald Watson (New York: Grove Press, 1964), 175.

3. Ibid., 20.

4. Ibid., 27.

5. Jacques Lemarchand, "Préface," in Ionesco, *Théâtre I* (Paris: Gallimard, 1954), 9–10. My translation.

6. *Combat,* 5/29/50.

7. Ibid.

8. Richard Schechner, *"The Bald Soprano* and *The Lesson:* An Inquiry into Play Structure," in *Ionesco,* ed. Rosette C. Lamont (Englewood Cliffs, NJ: Prentice Hall, 1973), 37.

9. Ionesco, *Notes and Counter Notes,* 179.

10. Ibid., 180.

11. Ionesco, *The Bald Soprano,* in *Four Plays,* trans. Donald M. Allen (New York: Grove Press, 1958), 9.

12. Ibid., 8.

13. Ibid.

14. Ibid., 9.

15. Ionesco, *Notes and Counter Notes,* 103.

16. Richard Schechner, "An Inquiry into Play Structure," 22.

17. Ionesco, *Notes and Counter Notes,* 34.

18. Ionesco, *The Bald Soprano,* 19.

19. Ibid.

20. Ibid.

21. Ionesco, *Three Plays: Amédée, The New Tenant, Victims of Duty,* trans. Donald Watson (New York: Grove Press, 1958), 119.

22. Ionesco, *The Bald Sprano,* 36–37.

23. I am indebted to Issacharoff's reading of the Mary poem in his book *Le Spectacle du discours* (Paris: Librairie José Corti, 1985), 156–57.

24. Ionesco, *The Bald Soprano,* 40.

25. Ibid., 37.

26. Ibid.

27. Ibid., 30.

28. Ibid., 38.

29. Ionesco, *The Lesson,* in *Four Plays,* 46.

30. Ibid., 48.

31. Richard Schechner, "An Inquiry into Play Structure," 31.

32. Ionesco, *The Lesson,* 49.

33. Ibid., 50.

34. Ibid.

35. Ibid.

36. Ibid., 78.

37. Ibid.

38. Ibid., 77.

39. François Rabelais, *The Five Books of Gargantua and Pantagruel*, trans. Jacques Le Clercq (New York: Random House, The Modern Library, 1936), 3.

40. Ibid., 3–4.

41. Ionesco, *The Lesson*, 51.

42. Ibid., 53.

43. Charles Baudelaire, *Mon coeur mis à nu*, xxxiii. My translation.

44. Ionesco, *The Lesson*, 55.

45. Ibid., 55–56.

46. Ibid., 55.

47. Ibid., 59.

48. Ibid., 60.

49. Ibid., 61.

50. Ibid., 63.

51. Ibid.

52. Ibid., 64.

53. Ibid., 73.

54. Ibid., 72.

55. Elizabeth Klaver, "The Play of Language in Ionesco's Play of Chairs," *Modern Drama* 32, no. 4 (December 1989): 523.

56. Ionesco, *The Lesson*, 75.

57. Ibid., 78.

58. In France, the name *Jacques* (Jack) is an ancient term for peasant. "Faire le Jacques" is to play the fool. In 1358, a peasant uprising was called *Jacquerie;* the word is now applied to all peasant rebellions.

59. Ionesco, *Jack or the Submission*, in *Four Plays*, 82.

60. Ibid., 81.

61. Ibid., 82.

62. Ibid., 86.

63. Ibid., 87.

64. Ibid., 91–92.

65. Ibid., 95.

66. Ibid.

67. Ibid., 97.

68. Charles Baudelaire, "Hymne à la beauté," *Les Fleurs du mal*, in *Oeuvres Complètes* (Paris: Gallimard, Bibliothèque de la Pléiade, 1944), 1:37.

69. Ionesco, *Jack or the Submission*, 95.

70. Ibid., 103.

71. Ibid.

72. Ibid., 104.

73. Ibid., 105.

74. Ibid., 107–8.

75. Ibid., 109.

76. Ionesco, *The Future Is in Eggs or It Takes All Sorts to Make a World*, in

Rhinoceros and Other Plays, trans. Derek Prouse (New York: Grove Press, 1960), 131.

77. Ibid., 136.
78. Ionesco, *The Bald Soprano*, 13–14.
79. Ionesco, *The Future Is in Eggs*, 138.
80. *Le Figaro*, 2/5/90.

Chapter 4

1. Ionesco, *Notes and Counter Notes: Writings on the Theatre*, trans. Donald Watson (New York: Grove Press, 1964), 44–45.
2. I created this term to describe the dramaturgy of Arthur Adamov, Samuel Beckett, Eugène Ionesco, Jean Tardieu, and their followers, such as Fernando Arrabal, Roland Dubillard, Harold Pinter, Romain Weingarten. In the United States, the early works of Edward Albee and John Guare could be included. For a more detailed analysis see Rosette C. Lamont, "The Metaphysical Farce: Beckett and Ionesco," *The French Review*, 32, no. 4 (February, 1959), 319–28. Also Rosette C. Lamont, "Eugene Ionesco and the Metaphysical Farce," in *Ionesco*, ed. Rosette C. Lamont (Englewood Cliffs, NJ: Prentice Hall, 1973), 154–83.
3. Friedrich Dürrenmatt, "Problems of the Theatre," *Tulane Drama Review*, 3, no. 1 (October, 1958): 20.
4. J. S. Doubrovsky, "Ionesco and the Comic of Absurdity," *Yale French Studies* 23 (Summer, 1959), reprinted in *Ionesco*, 11–20.
5. Dürrenmatt, "Problems," 20.
6. *Le Figaro*, 4/26/52. My translation.
7. *Lettres Françaises*, 5/2–8/52. My translation.
8. *Le Figaro Littéraire*, 5/3/52. My translation.
9. These témoignages were published in *Arts*, 5/5–21/52. My translation.
10. *Combat*, 4/23/52. My translation.
11. Jean Anouilh, "Du chapitre des *Chaises*," *Le Figaro*, 4/23/56. My translation.
12. Ionesco, "Les deux mises en scène des *Chaises*," *Combat*, 2/10/56. My translation.
13. Ionesco, *Notes and Counter Notes*, 187.
14. Ibid., 191.
15. Ionesco, *The Chairs*, in *Four Plays*, trans. Donald M. Allen (New York: Grove Press, 1958), 116.
16. Ibid., 120–21.
17. Ibid., 121.
18. Henri Bergson, *Le Rire, essai sur la signification du comique* (Paris: Librairie Félix Alcan, 1930), 50.
19. Ionesco, *The Chairs*, 147.
20. Jean-Hervé Donnard, *Ionesco dramaturge ou l'artisan et le démon* (Paris: Minard, 1966), 57. Also see Emmanuel Jacquart, "Notes on *Les Chaises*," in

Théâtre complet, Ionesco (Paris: Gallimard, 1991), 1542. Jacquart speaks of a possible comparison, unconfirmed by Ionesco. He goes on to say that unlike Philemon and Baucis, the Old Man and the Old Woman will not die together, although they jump simultaneously from two opposite windows of their tower room. Their ultimate separation at that moment might be another way of drawing the viewer's attention to the absurdity of our universe.

21. Johann Wolfgang Von Goethe, "Open Country," in *Faust II,* V, trans. Walter Arndt (New York: Norton, 1976), 281.

22. Ionesco, *The Chairs,* 149.

23. Ibid.

24. Ibid.

25. Ibid., 150.

26. Since Donald Allen translates "ma crotte" as "sweetheart," I have used the original word here. See *Les Chaises* in *Théâtre complet,* 145.

27. Ionesco, *The Chairs,* 133.

28. Ibid., 153–54.

29. Ibid., 154.

30. Ibid.

31. Ibid., 156.

32. Ibid., 157.

33. Ibid.

34. Ibid., 158.

35. Ibid.

36. Ibid., 159–60.

37. Ionesco, *Notes and Counter Notes,* 190.

38. Ibid., 189–90.

39. Ibid., 191.

40. William Shakespeare, *As You Like It* (II.vii.174).

41. Ionesco, *Notes and Counter Notes,* 191.

42. Ionesco, *The New Tenant,* in *Four Plays,* 92.

43. Ibid., 96.

44. Ibid., 111.

45. Ibid., 108.

46. Ibid., 109.

47. Ibid., 111.

48. Ibid., 112.

49. Ibid.

50. Ionesco, *Notes and Counter Notes,* 217–19.

51. Joseph Campbell, *The Masks of God: Oriental Mythology* (New York: Viking Press, 1962), 96.

52. Ibid., 97.

53. Ionesco, *The New Tenant,* 115.

54. Ibid., 116.

55. Ibid.

56. This comparison between the walling in of the "new tenant" and the

burial of Egyptian pharaohs was made in the presence of Ionesco at the "Décade Ionesco" at the Centre Culturel International de Cerisy-la-Salle (August 3–13, 1978). The dramatist concurred with this interpretation.

Chapter 5

1. Ionesco, *Notes and Counter Notes: Writings on the Theatre*, trans. Donald Watson (New York: Grove Press, 1964), 162.

2. Ibid., 163.

3. Ibid.

4. Ibid.

5. Blaise Pascal, "Pensée 264 (63.) H. 3." in *Oeuvres complètes*, texte établi et annoté par Jacques Chevalier (Paris: Gallimard, Bibliothèque de la Pléiade, 1954), 1156–57.

6. Claude Bonnefoy, *Conversations with Eugène Ionesco*, trans. Jan Dawson (New York: Holt, Rinehart and Winston, 1971), 33.

7. Ionesco, *Three Plays: Amédée, The New Tenant, Victims of Duty*, trans. Donald Watson (New York: Grove Press, 1958), 132.

8. Ionesco, *Fragments of a Journal*, trans. Jean Stewart (New York: Grove Press, 1969), 56–57.

9. Ionesco, *Notes and Counter Notes*, 244.

10. William Shakespeare, *Hamlet* (I.ii.129–30).

11. Ionesco, *Victims of Duty*, 166.

12. Aristotle, *On Poetry and Style*, trans. with an introduction by G. M. A. Grube (Indianapolis, NY: The Bobbs-Merrill Company, The Library of Liberal Arts, 1958), 14.

13. Ionesco, *Victims of Duty*, 119.

14. Hugh Dickinson, *Myth on the Modern Stage* (Urbana: University of Illinois Press, 1969), 312.

15. This is Ionesco's own definition made in the course of an informal conversation with the author in New York in 1960.

16. Ionesco, *Victims of Duty*, 122.

17. Richard N. Coe, *Eugène Ionesco* (New York: Grove Press, 1961), 108.

18. Ionesco, *Fragments of a Journal*, 51.

19. Ionesco, *Victims of Duty*, 136.

20. Ibid., 135.

21. Ibid., 133.

22. Ibid., 134.

23. Dickinson, *Myth on the Modern Stage*, 330.

24. Vera Russell and John Russell, "Ionesco on Death," *Chicago Sun Times*, 9/15/63.

25. Ionesco, *Victims of Duty*, 150–51.

26. Ionesco, *Fragments of a Journal*, 92.

27. Ionesco, *Victims of Duty*, 158.

28. Ionesco, *Fragments of a Journal*, 60.

29. Ionesco, *Notes and Counter Notes*, 159.

30. Ionesco, *Amédée*, 14.

31. Charles Baudelaire, "Une Charogne," *Les Fleurs du Mal*, in *Oeuvres Complètes* (Paris: Gallimard, Bibliothèque de la Pléiade, 1944), 1:44.

> All of it sank, rose like the tide
> In spuming, effervescent sprays
> As though brimful of nameless breath
> The corpse revived and multiplied.
>
> Strange music wafted through the air
> Like running water, like the wind
> Or wheat within the basket tossed
> Yielding the winnowed fertile grain.

32. Ionesco, *Amédée*, 24.

33. Ibid.

34. Ibid., 28.

35. Ibid., 30.

36. Ibid.

37. Ibid., 28.

38. Ibid., 47.

39. Ibid., 47–48.

40. Ibid., 51.

41. Ibid., 50.

42. In *The Masks of God: Creative Mythology* (New York: Viking, 1970), Joseph Campbell describes alchemical processes: *nigredo* (blackness), characterized by decay *(putrefactio)*, reduces elementary matter *(prima materia)* to the undifferentiated state out of which the world came into being (279).

43. Ionesco, *Amédée*, 59.

44. Ibid.

45. Ibid., 62.

46. Ibid., 70.

47. Roger Shattuck, *The Banquet Years* (Garden City: Doubleday and Company, Anchor Books, 1961), 33.

48. Ionesco, *Amédée*, 73.

49. Bonnefoy, *Conversations with Eugène Ionesco*, 93. Jan Dawson translates Ionesco's "une Kermesse astrale" as "a merry-go-round of stars." I substitute a translation that is closer to the original: "an astral carnival."

50. This phrase was coined by Jean-Hervé Donnard in his book *Ionesco dramaturge ou l'artisan et le démon* (Paris: Minard, 1966). The chapter on *Amédée*, "A Caricatural Ionesco," was published in an English translation by Judith Kutcher in *Ionesco*, ed. Rosette C. Lamont (Englewood Cliffs, NJ: Prentice Hall, 1973), 38–54.

51. Ionesco, *A Stroll in the Air, Frenzy for Two*, in *Plays*, 6, trans. Donald Watson (London: Calder and Boyars, 1965), 46–47. I deviate slightly from the

Watson translation that reads: "Man has a crying need to fly. . . . It's an innate gift . . . so simple, so clear, so childish."

52. Ionesco, "The Marvelous Come to Life," trans. Rosette C. Lamont, *Theatre Arts*, 45, no. 9 (September, 1961): 19.

53. Loren Eisley, *The Immense Journey* (New York: Random House, 1959), 166.

54. Gaston Bachelard, *L'Air et les songes, essai sur l'imagination du mouvement* (Paris: Librairie José Corti, 1943), 157. My translation, as well as the others from the same book.

55. Shakespeare, *King Lear* (I.i.90).

56. Gaston Bachelard, *L'Air et les songes*, 20.

57. Ibid., 19.

58. Roger Shattuck, *The Banquet Years*, 33.

59. Ionesco, *Notes and Counter Notes*, 46.

60. Ionesco, *A Stroll in the Air*, 58.

61. Ionesco's one act opera *Maximilian Kolbe*, with music by Dominique Probst, was first performed at Rimini on August 20, 1988. It was directed by Tadeusz Bradecki and Krzysztof Zanussi. Subsequently, it was performed in France at the Cathedral of Arras, on June 18 and 19, 1989, and in Poland, on April 7 and 9, 1989, at Bytom and Katowice. My translation of the libretto was published with an introduction in *Performing Arts Journal* 17, 6, no. 2, 29–36.

62. Ionesco, *A Stroll in the Air*, 64–65.

63. Ibid., 67.

64. Lucy S. Dawidowicz, *The War against the Jews 1933–1945* (New York: Bantam Books, 1976), 176–77.

65. Ionesco, *Present Past Past Present*, trans. Helen R. Lane (New York: Grove Press, 1971), 52–53.

66. Ionesco, *A Stroll in the Air*, 67.

67. Ionesco, *Fragments of a Journal*, 92.

68. Ibid., 93.

69. Ionesco, *A Stroll in the Air*, 60–61.

70. Ibid., 69.

71. Ionesco made the following statement in an interview with Pierre Hahn: "Cette pièce continue mon pseudo-drame, *Victimes du devoir*." Quoted by Giovanni Lista in *Ionesco*, ed. H. Veyrier (1989), 72, as reported by Emmanuel Jacquart in his "Notes" on *Le Piéton de l'air* in *Théâtre complet* (Paris: Gallimard, 1991), 1718.

72. Ionesco, *A Stroll in the Air*, 65.

73. Ibid., 30.

74. Ibid.

75. Ibid., 31.

76. Ibid., 16.

77. Ibid., 17.

78. Ionesco, *Journeys among the Dead, Themes and Variations*, trans. Barbara Wright (London and New York: Riverrun Press, 1985), 34.

Chapter 6

1. Ionesco, *Present Past Past Present*, trans. Helen R. Lane (New York: Grove Press, 1971), 27.

2. Ionesco, "Selections from a Private Journal," trans. Rosette C. Lamont, in *The New French Dramatists*, special issue of *Yale French Studies* 29 (n.d.): 4.

3. Ionesco, *Present Past Past Present*, 55.

4. *Le Monde*, 2/13/59. My translation, as are all subsequent quotations from the French press.

5. *Le Monde*, 3/3/59.

6. *Arts*, 3/4/59.

7. *Carrefour*, 3/4/59.

8. *Nouvelles Littéraires*, 3/5/59.

9. *L'Express*, 3/5/59.

10. *Le Figaro Littéraire*, 3/7/59.

11. Ionesco, *Present Past Past Present*, 38.

12. Ionesco, *The Killer and Other Plays*, trans. Donald Watson (New York: Grove Press, 1960), 21.

13. Ibid.

14. Ibid.

15. Ibid.

16. Ibid.

17. Ibid., 64.

18. Ibid., 65.

19. Ibid., 70. The Killer's diary echoes the hunting log of Louis XVI, particularly on the day the Revolution broke out.

20. Ibid., 71.

21. Ibid., 77.

22. Ibid., 78.

23. Ibid.

24. Ibid., 79.

25. Ibid., 83.

26. Ibid., 99.

27. Ibid.

28. Ibid.

29. Ibid., 101.

30. Ionesco, *Present Past Past Present*, 52.

31. John Keats, "Ode to a Nightingale," in *Complete Poetical Works* by John Keats and Percy Bysshe Shelley (New York: Random House, The Modern Library, n.d.), 184.

32. Ionesco, *The Killer*, 101–2.

33. Ibid.

34. Ibid., 106.

35. Ibid., 107.

36. Ibid.

37. Ibid., 109.

38. Ionesco, *Present Past Past Present,* 67.

39. Ibid., 43.

40. Ibid., 116–17.

41. Ibid., 43.

42. Ionesco, *Rhinoceros and Other Plays,* trans. Derek Prouse (New York: Grove Press, 1960), 21–23. I have grouped together the elements of an exchange interrupted by comments made by bystanders.

43. Ibid., 25.

44. Ibid., 18.

45. Ibid., 19.

46. Ibid., 30.

47. Ibid., 30–31.

48. Ibid.

49. Ibid., 56.

50. Ibid., 66.

51. Mircea Eliade, *Shamanism, Archaic Techniques of Ecstasy,* trans. Willard R. Trask (Princeton, NJ: Princeton University Press, Bollingen Series 76, 1964), 95.

52. Ionesco, *Rhinoceros,* 80.

53. Quoted by Emmanuel Jacquart in his annotated edition of Eugène Ionesco's *Théâtre complet* (Paris: Gallimard, 1991), cvi.

54. Ionesco, *Rhinoceros,* 90.

55. Ibid., 103.

56. Ibid., 104.

57. Ibid., 107.

58. Ibid.

Chapter 7

1. Ionesco, *Exit the King,* trans. Donald Watson (New York: Grove Press, 1967), 50.

2. Claude Bonnefoy, *Conversations with Eugène Ionesco,* trans. Jan Dawson (New York: Holt, Rinehart and Winston, 1971), 79.

3. Samuel Beckett, *Waiting for Godot* (New York: Grove Press, 1954), 58.

4. Elisabeth Kübler-Ross, *On Death and Dying* (New York: Macmillan Publishing Company, Collier Books, 1970), 39.

5. Ionesco, *Exit the King,* 26. Marguerite and the Doctor press King Bérenger to "abdicate governmentally, morally and physically." The King orders the Guard to arrest them, and lock them in the dungeons. The word *dungeon* evokes the prison of the Bastille where prisoners were sent for crimes of "lèse majesté."

6. Ibid., 22.

7. Claude Bonnefoy, *Conversations with Eugène Ionesco,* 79.

8. Ionesco, *Exit the King,* 11.

9. Blaise Pascal, "Misère de l'homme, les puissances trompeuses," *Pensées,*

in *Oeuvres complètes,* ed. Jacques Chevalier (Paris: Gallimard, Bibliothèque de la Pléiade, 1954), 1137–48.

10. Ionesco, *Exit the King,* 37.

11. Monsieur Jordain is Molière's grotesque "Would-Be Gentleman."

12. Ibid., 46.

13. Ibid., 47.

14. Ibid.

15. Ibid., 70.

16. Jessie L. Weston, *From Ritual to Romance* (Garden City, NY: Doubleday Anchor Books, 1957), 59.

17. Ibid., 63.

18. Ionesco, *Exit the King,* 31.

19. Ibid., 17.

20. *Hamlet* (I.ii.255).

21. Ionesco, *Exit the King,* 39.

22. Ibid., 40.

23. Kübler-Ross, *On Death and Dying,* 50.

24. Ionesco, *Exit the King,* 31.

25. Ibid., 35.

26. Ibid., 39.

27. Ibid., 38.

28. Ibid., 45.

29. Kübler-Ross, *On Death and Dying,* 84.

30. Ionesco, *Exit the King,* 52.

31. Claude Bonnefoy, *Conversations with Eugène Ionesco,* 79.

32. Ibid., 54.

33. A detailed description of the Orphic Sacramental Bowl, and an illustration of it can be found in Joseph Campbell's *The Masks of God, Creative Mythology* (New York: Viking Press, A Viking Compass Book, 1970), 9–27.

34. Ionesco, *Exit the King,* 54.

35. Ibid., 55.

36. Homer, *The Odyssey,* trans. W. H. D. Rouse (New York: New American Library, Mentor Classic, 1949), 134.

37. Ionesco, *Exit the King,* 61.

38. Ibid.

39. Ibid., 62.

40. Ibid., 64.

41. *The Tibetan Book of the Dead,* trans. Francesca Fremantle and Chögyam Trungpa, with a commentary by Chögyam Trungpa (Boulder and London: Shambhala Publications, 1975), 1. The Bardo Thötrol is a Tibetan Buddhist scripture. It describes the projections of the mind as they appear immediately after death. It teaches recognition of these terrifying and at times seductive forms. Through recognition one is able to attain enlightenment. These texts, written down by the wife of Padmasambhava were buried in the Gampo hills in central Tibet. The texts were discovered by Karma-Lingpa. The transmission

of this knowledge was kept alive in the Surmang monasteries of the Trungpa lineage. Chögyam Trungpa says he received this transmission at the age of eight. He was trained in assisting dying people. In the summer of 1971, at the Tail of the Tiger Contemplative Community in Vermont, United States, Chögyam Trungpa offered a seminar on *The Tibetan Book of the Dead.* It was his hope to make this teaching applicable to students in the West. Ionesco claims to read and reread this work. That it has had a profound influence on his thinking is nowhere more obvious than in his play *Exit the King.*

42. Erich Neumann, *The Great Mother: An Analysis of the Archetype,* trans. Ralph Manheim (Princeton, NJ: Princeton University Press, Bollingen Series, 47, 1972), 149.

43. Ibid., 148–49.

44. Ibid., 216.

45. Ionesco, *Fragments of a Journal,* trans. Jean Stewart (New York: Grove Press, 1969), 59.

46. Mircea Eliade, "Eugene Ionesco and 'La Nostalgie du Paradis,'" in *The Two Faces of Ionesco,* ed. Rosette C. Lamont and Melvin J. Friedman (Troy, NY: The Whitston Publishing Company, 1978), 22–28.

47. Ionesco, *Exit the King,* 95.

48. Ibid., 92.

49. Ibid., 94.

50. Ibid.

51. Emmanuel Jacquart, ed., *Théâtre complet,* by Eugène Ionesco (Paris: Gallimard, Bibliothèque de la Pléiade, 1991), 1739.

52. Ionesco, *Exit the King,* 22.

53. Ionesco, *Killing Game,* trans. Helen Gary Bishop (New York: Grove Press, 1974), 3.

54. Ibid., 7.

55. Ibid., 8.

56. Ibid., 12.

57. Ibid.

58. Ibid., 26.

59. Ibid., 85.

60. Ibid., 86.

61. Ibid., 88.

62. Ibid.

63. Ibid., 90.

64. Ibid.

65. Ibid.

66. Ibid., 82.

67. Ibid., 69.

68. Ibid., 95.

69. Ibid., 98.

70. Ionesco, *La quête intermittente* (Paris: Gallimard, 1987), 69–70. My translation.

71. Ionesco, *Killing Game,* 98.

72. Ibid., 100.

73. Ibid., 99.

74. Ibid., 102.

75. Antonin Artaud, *The Theatre and Its Double,* trans. Mary Caroline Richards (New York: Grove Press, 1958), 15.

76. Ionesco, *Jeux de massacre,* in *Théâtre V* (Paris: Gallimard, 1974), 101. This quotation, as well as the subsequent ones from the original text, my translation.

77. Ibid.

78. Ibid., 102.

79. Ibid., 103.

80. Charlotte Delbo, "Le Misanthrope," in *Une connaissance inutile* vol. 1 of *Auschwitz et après* (Paris: Editions de Minuit, 1970), 122–23.

81. Ionesco, *Killing Game,* 108.

82. Ibid., 36.

83. Ibid.

84. Ibid.

85. Ibid., 38.

86. Ibid., 39.

87. Ionesco, *Fragments of a Journal,* 57.

Chapter 8

1. Ionesco, *Un homme en question* (Paris: Gallimard, 1979), 9. My translation, as are all subsequent quotations, from *Un homme en question.*

2. Ionesco, *Antidotes* (Paris: Gallimard, 1977). This volume contains one of Ionesco's most important essays of self-criticism, "Pourquoi est-ce que j'écris?" In it, the writer questions his reasons for writing. My translation of this essay, "Why Do I Write?" was published in *The Two Faces of Ionesco,* ed. Rosette C. Lamont and Melvin J. Friedman (Troy, NY: The Whitston Publishing Company, 1978), 5–19.

3. Ionesco, "Culture et politique," in *Un homme en question,* 49.

4. Ionesco, *Antidotes,* 151. My translation.

5. Ionesco, "Culture et politique," 55–56.

6. Ibid., 60.

7. Ionesco, *Notes and Counter Notes: Writings on the Theatre,* trans. Donald Watson (New York: Grove Press, 1964), 89.

8. Ibid., 91.

9. *Le Figaro,* 11/7/71.

10. *Les Nouvelles Littéraires,* 1/24/72.

11. *L'Aurore,* 2/2/72.

12. Ionesco, *Macbett,* trans. Charles Marowitz (New York: Grove Press, 1973), 14–15.

13. Ibid., 15.

14. Alfred Jarry, *Ubu Rex,* in *The Ubu Plays,* trans. Cyril Connolly and Simon Watson Taylor (New York: Grove Press, 1968), 73.

15. Ionesco, *Macbett*, 20.

16. Ibid., 23.

17. Ibid., 27.

18. Ionesco, *Macbett*, 28.

19. Ionesco, *Macbett*, in *Théâtre V* (Paris: Gallimard, 1972), 140. This is a takeoff on La Fontaine's "La raison du plus fort est toujours la meilleure."

20. Ionesco, *Macbett*, 30.

21. Ibid., 32.

22. William Shakespeare, *Macbeth* (V.ii.51).

23. Ionesco, *Macbett*, 35.

24. Ibid., 36.

25. Ibid., 37.

26. William Shakespeare, *Richard III* (V.iv.6).

27. Ionesco, *Macbett*, 38.

28. Ibid., 150.

29. Ibid., 43.

30. Ibid., 40.

31. Ibid., 42.

32. William Shakespeare, *Hamlet* (I.v.63).

33. Shakespeare, *Macbeth* (II.ii.13–14).

34. Ionesco, *Macbett*, 77.

35. Shakespeare, *Hamlet* (I.ii.180–81).

36. Shakespeare, *Macbeth* (I.vii.67).

37. Ionesco, *Macbett*, 85.

38. Ibid., 98.

39. Bruno Bettelheim, *The Uses of Enchantment: The Meaning and Importance of Fairy Tales* (New York: Alfred A. Knopf, 1976), 117.

40. Jan Kott, *Shakespeare Our Contemporary* (Garden City, NY: Doubleday and Company, 1964), 77–82.

41. Ionesco, *Macbett*, 101.

42. Ionesco, *Macbett*, in *Théâtre V*, 201.

43. Ionesco, *Macbett*, 103.

44. At the end of Musset's play, Côme de Medicis is the new ruler of Florence, following the assassination of the corrupt duke by his cousin Lorenzaccio. Musset shows clearly that Côme will be a ruthless tyrant, that the elimination of the corrupt duke has been useless because no republican leadership has stepped in.

45. Jan Kott, *Shakespeare Our Contemporary*, 86.

46. Ionesco, *Macbett*, 105.

47. Heinrich Himmler, *Die Schutzstaffel als antibolschewistische Kampforganisation*, quoted by Lucy S. Dawidowicz, *The War against the Jews 1933–1934* (NY: Bantam Books, 1976), 116.

48. Fyodor Dostoyevsky, *Notes from the Underground, White Nights, The Dream of a Ridiculous Man, and Selections from The House of the Dead*, trans. Andrew R. MacAndrew (New York: New American Library, Signet Classic, 1961), 90.

49. Ionesco, *The Hermit,* trans. Richard Seaver (New York: Viking Press, 1974), 107.

50. Dostoyevsky, *Notes from the Underground,* 120.

51. Ibid., 92.

52. Ionesco, *The Hermit,* 21.

53. Ibid., 29.

54. Ibid., 140.

55. Ibid., 14.

56. Ionesco, *Present Past Past Present,* trans. Helen R. Lane (New York: Grove Press, 1971), 192.

57. Ionesco, *The Hermit,* 167.

58. Ionesco, *Exit the King,* trans. Donald Watson (New York: Grove Press, 1967), 95.

59. Ionesco, *The Hermit,* 169.

60. Joseph Cambell, *The Masks of God: Oriental Mythology* (New York: Viking Press, Viking Compass Book, 1970), 131.

61. Ionesco, *Oh What A Bloody Circus,* in *Plays,* Vol. 10, trans. Donald Watson (London: John Calder, 1976), 95.

62. Ibid., 40.

63. Ionesco, *Antidotes,* 323–24.

64. Ibid., 324.

Chapter 9

1. Ionesco, *Notes and Counter Notes,* trans. Donald Watson (New York: Grove Press, 1964), 127.

2. Ibid., 131.

3. Roy Arthur Swanson, "Ionesco's Classical Absurdity," in *The Two Faces of Ionesco,* ed. Rosette C. Lamont and Melvin J. Friedman (Troy, NY: Whitston Publishing Company, 1978), 147.

4. Ibid., 137.

5. Ionesco, *Notes and Counter Notes,* 40.

6. Ibid., 43.

7. Ibid.

8. Swanson, "Ionesco's Classical Absurdity," 135.

9. Blaise Pascal, "Conclusion: Qu'il faut chercher Dieu," *Pensées,* in *Oeuvres complètes* (Paris: Gallimard, Bibliothèque de la Pléiade, 1954), 1180.

10. Sophocles, *Oedipus at Colonus,* trans. Robert Fitzgerald, in *The Oedipus Cycle* (New York: Harcourt, Brace and Company, 1941), 163.

11. Ibid., 159.

12. Swanson, "Ionesco's Classical Absurdity," 135.

13. Sophocles, *Oedipus at Colonus,* 112.

14. Swanson, "Ionesco's Classical Absurdity," 140.

15. Ionesco, *Notes and Counter Notes,* 117–18.

16. Ionesco, "The Play of the Passions," *Times Literary Supplement,* 10/6/72.

17. Plato, "Great Hippias," trans. Benjamin Jowett, in *The Collected Dia-*

logues, ed. Edith Hamilton and Huntington Cairns (Princeton, NJ: Princeton University Press, Bollingen Series 71, 1961), 1558.

18. Ionesco, *Hunger and Thirst and Other Plays,* trans. Donald Watson (New York: Grove Press, 1969), 9.

19. Ibid.

20. Ibid., 11.

21. Ionesco, *Exit the King,* trans. Donald Watson (New York: Grove Press, 1967), 36.

22. Simone Benmussa, *Ionesco* (Paris: Seghers, Collection Thèâtre de Tous les Temps, 1966), 10. This passage is translated by the author.

23. Ionesco, *Hunger and Thirst,* 17.

24. Ibid., 23–25.

25. Ibid., 24.

26. Ibid., 25.

27. Ionesco, *Present Past Past Present,* trans. Helen R. Lane (New York: Grove Press, 1971), 20.

28. Ibid., 21.

29. Ionesco, *Hunger and Thirst,* 33.

30. Ibid., 36.

31. Bruno Bettelheim, *The Uses of Enchantment: The Meaning and Importance of Fairy Tales* (New York: Alfred A. Knopf, 1976), 127.

32. Ionesco, *Hunger and Thirst,* 37.

33. Ibid.

34. Ibid., 46–47.

35. Ionesco, *Fragments of a Journal,* trans. Jean Stewart (New York: Grove Press, 1969), 52.

36. Ibid., 62.

37. Ibid., 66.

38. Ionesco, *La Soif et la faim,* in *Théâtre complet,* Édition présentée, etablie et annotée par Emmanuel Jacquart (Paris: Gallimard, Bibliothèque de la Pléiade, 1991), 842.

39. Ibid., 843. This quotation and the following ones from episode 3, "At the Foot of the Wall," are my translation. This act, or episode, has never before been translated into English, nor included in the English version of *Hunger and Thirst.*

40. Ibid.

41. Ionesco, "The Play of Passions."

42. Ionesco, *La Soif et la faim,* 843.

43. Ionesco, *Hunger and Thirst,* 54.

44. Ibid.

45. Ibid., 72.

46. Dorothy Sayers, "Introduction," in *The Divine Comedy, Hell,* by Dante, trans. Dorothy Sayers (Baltimore, MD: Penguin Books, 1949), 24.

47. Ibid., 272.

48. Ionesco, *Hunger and Thirst,* 105.

49. *Le Figaro Littéraire,* 3/10/66.

50. Ibid.

51. François Mauriac, "Préface," in *La Nuit,* by Elie Wiesel (Paris: Editions de Minuit, 1958), 12. My translation.

Chapter 10

1. Ionesco, "A Program Note: Toward a Dream Theater," in the program of *L'Homme aux valises* presented at the Théâtre de l'Atelier, November, 1975. My translation of this short text appears in its entirety in *Performing Arts Journal,* 1, no. 2 (Fall, 1976): 19–20.

2. Ionesco served as artist-in-residence at the University of Southern California in the spring of 1980. He participated in a symposium organized by Professor Moshe Lazar around his oeuvre, "The Dream and the Play: Ionesco's Theatrical Quest." This statement was made by the dramatist in the course of the symposium.

3. The "time-space continuum" is defined by Kenneth Steele White in his book *Einstein and the Modern French Drama* (Washington, DC: University Press of America, 1983) in the following way.

A continuum [as in space-time continuum] is an area that is continuous and self-same. . . . Einstein found that an accelerated frame of reference [coordinate system] and a gravitational field are really two aspects of the same thing. . . . Time and space are interrelated, as Einstein proved. The geometry of space is changing with time. Two of the most powerful concepts of our era, those defining space and time, have been shown by Einstein to intertwine, losing distinctiveness. . . . Integral to a certain number of important plays since 1896, it is embodied with wit and pungency in works by Ionesco, Beckett, Jarry, Apollinaire, and others. (54–68)

Kenneth Steele White explores the "analogy" that exists between Einstein's theory of relativity and the weltanschauung of the avant-garde dramatists. Nowhere is this more conclusively apparent than in Ionesco's dream plays.

4. The adjective *classical* is used here in the way it was in the preceding chapter where we pointed out that Ionesco consciously set about to recreate in his own theater the archetypal patterns of ancient Greek drama. Ionesco views himself as a "classical playwright," one closer to the great classicists of the ancient world than to the neoclassicists of the French seventeenth century. In this sense, the two last dream plays are even more classical than the well-structured *Hunger and Thirst.* However, a line can be drawn linking together all of Ionesco's confessional plays: *Victims of Duty, Hunger and Thirst, Man with Bags,* and *Journeys among the Dead.*

5. *Katabasis* means descent. Not every meeting with the dead takes place in the nether world. Dante's exploration of the Inferno is a gradual descent through the various circles of Hell. Odysseus, however, instructed by Circe, simply travels North. Once he has reached the deep stream of Oceanos on the mist-enshrouded shores of the Cimmerians he is able to meet with the dead.

Their realm is not below the earth, but at "the world's boundary" (Homer, *Odyssey*, book XI).

6. The image of the wanderer and the stranger in *Man with Bags* suggests a possible influence of the *Odyssey* as well as of Joyce's *Ulysses*.

7. Ionesco, *Man with Bags*, adapted by Israel Horovitz, based on a translation by Marie-France Ionesco (New York: Grove Press, 1977), 8.

8. Ibid., 9.

9. Ibid., 32.

10. Ibid.

11. Ibid., 33.

12. Ibid., 22.

13. Ibid., 28.

14. Lucy S. Dawidowicz, *The War against the Jews 1933–1945* (New York: Bantam Books, 1976), 78–79.

15. Ionesco, *Man with Bags*, 29.

16. Ionesco, *La quête intermittente* (Paris: Gallimard, 1987), 155–56). My translation.

17. Leslie Kane, "The Weasel under the Cocktail Cabinet: Rite and Ritual in Pinter's Plays," *The Pinter Review* 2, no. 1 (1988): 20.

18. Since Israel Horovitz "adapted" Ionesco's play, certain liberties were taken with the original. I regret the loss of Ionesco's term *"un existant,"* and therefore I have preserved it here. The reader may wish to check Ionesco's *L'Homme aux valises*, published originally in a single volume with *Ce formidable bordel* (Paris: Gallimard, 1975). Horovitz translates "un existant" as "I'm just a guy" (92), which eliminates the metaphysical nuance of Ionesco's term.

19. Once again Horovitz misses the point by translating the poetic and philosophical term *"un existant spécialisé"* as "kind'a special guy." As a result of this vulgar Americanism the most important aspect of Ionesco's definition—a definition that makes the fact of existence and survival the central theme of the play—is eliminated from the text. I cannot think of a more unfortunate betrayal. Also, it must be pointed out that Horovitz should never have made of the Consul an "Ambassador." The First Man is not dealing with a high-ranking diplomat. In fact, he has never been able to come close to anyone with real authority. This is an integral part of his sense of constant danger. I have carefully restored Ionesco's word *Consul* to this scene instead of Horovitz's erroneous and misleading *Ambassador.*

20. Ionesco, *Man with Bags*, 96.

21. Ibid., 116–17.

22. Ionesco, *Fragments of a Journal*, 112–13.

23. Ionesco, *Man with Bags*, 123–25.

24. Ibid., 134.

25. Ionesco, *Journeys among the Dead, Theme and Variations*, trans. Barbara Wright (New York: Riverrun Press, 1985), 13.

26. Erich Neumann, *The Great Mother: An Analysis of the Archetype*, trans. Ralph Manheim (Princeton, NJ: Princeton University Press, Bollingen Series 47, 1972), 280.

27. Ibid.

28. Ibid., 330.

29. Ionesco, *Journeys among the Dead*, 21.

30. Ibid., 55.

31. Ibid., 56.

32. Ionesco, *Fragments of a Journal*, 55.

33. Ibid., 133–34.

34. Gaston Bachelard, *La Terre et les rêveries du repos* (Paris: Librairie José Corti, 1948), 76. My translation.

35. Neumann, *The Great Mother*, 99.

36. Ibid., 307. Neumann explains in this passage "the transformative anima character of the Feminine," and "the world-governing unindividual love principle and sexual principle of life."

37. Ibid., 321.

38. Ionesco, *Journeys among the Dead*, 56.

39. Ionesco, *Fragments of a Journal*, 53–54.

40. Ionesco, *Journeys among the Dead*, 57.

41. Ibid.

42. Ibid., 58.

43. Ibid.

44. Ibid., 59.

45. Neumann, *The Great Mother*, 156.

46. Ionesco, *Journeys among the Dead*, 60.

47. "Moi et mes monstres, un entretien avec André Bourin," *Les Nouvelles Littéraires*, 1/29/70, 11. My translation. In the course of the Bourin interview, one becomes aware of Ionesco's maternal Jewish roots. His sensitivity can be dated back to an early version of *La Cantatrice chauve* consulted by Emmanuel Jacquart, the editor and annotator of Ionesco's *Théâtre complet* in the Gallimard "Bibliothèque de la Pléiade" edition of 1991. Jacquart reports that a manuscript of twenty pages exists in which a scene 2 corresponds to the present scene 7. The Fire Chief enters, and questions his hosts, the Smiths, about a possible fire in their apartment. As they continue conversing, the cases of two people are brought up: a Mr. Bok, who sells matches, and a Mr. Cook. Mr. Cook is not protected by municipal services such as the fire brigade because "his mother is of Jewish descent . . . and one is not allowed to put out fires in Jewish apartments or houses." This remark, Jacquart explains, alludes to the situation of the Jewish population in Romania during World War II. In the course of an interview granted by Ionesco to Jacquart on October 27, 1987, the dramatist talked at length about a Jewish professor he knew. The latter was assisted by one of his students, who helped him retain his government position by drawing his attention to the fact that a law existed on the books that declared that anyone whose father or grandfather had been a colonel or a medical officer during the war of 1870 was considered a full fledged Romanian citizen, despite his Jewish origin. Ionesco also declared that he had written this passage in 1943, during the war. Jacquart explains this passage in terms of the dramatist's fascination with the irrational, and his exploration of nonsense literature. It is my belief that Ionesco

did not take Jacquart into his confidence, and that the story of the Romanian professor is a mask for his own secret identity, and for his process of identification with the plight of the Jewish people. Although the dramatist's mother died before World War II, he realized that had she lived she might well have suffered racial persecution, and perhaps been sent to a concentration camp. According to Jewish law, the son of a Jewish mother is Jewish. Whether Ionesco knows this or not is irrelevant. The fact of the matter is that he has a special feeling for the Jewish people, an affection and admiration rooted in his devotion to his gentle mother. The Jewish question therefore is central to Ionesco's political imperative; it is at the very source of his *prise de conscience*. (See Emmanuel Jacquart, ed. *Théâtre complet* [Paris: Gallimard, Bibliothèque de la Pléiade, 1991], 1481–82.)

48. Ionesco, *Notes and Counter Notes*, trans. Donald Watson (New York: Grove Press, 1964), 231.

Conclusion

1. The word *organum* (Latin), or *organon* (Greek), means a tool, an instrument used to accomplish a certain task, physical or mental. In the wake of Aristotle, whose *Poetics* Brecht had rejected, Brecht is providing a "tool" for dramatic productions, and theatre criticism. Conceived in 1948, the theoretical essay "Short Organum for the Theatre" reveals a change of direction for Brecht. In this work he upholds the aesthetic pleasure principle he had denounced in connection with his didactic plays directed at an unmoved spectator. John Fuegi, in *Bertolt Brecht: Chaos, According to Plan* (Cambridge: Cambridge University Press, 1987), writes: "This new work represented a radical and largely irreconcilable shift from the strident *Mahagonny* notes of 1930" (66). Brecht's earlier hypothesis was based on the theory that "epic" form produces a cooler response than material offered in "dramatic" form. Fuegi writes: "Brecht himself came to abandon the term 'epic theatre' as he realized that it confused more than it clarified" (88).

2. In the spring of 1935 Brecht went on an exploratory visit to Leningrad and Moscow. In Moscow he was taken to meet the Russian aesthetician Schklovski, who created the term *"priem ostrannenija"* (making strange). Directly after this encounter, Brecht used the expression *"Verfremdung"* (see Fuegi, *Bertolt Brecht*, 82).

3. François Rabelais, *The Five Books of Gargantua and Pantagruel*, trans. Jacques Le Clercq (New York: Random House, The Modern Library, 1936), 181.

4. Ibid., 184.

5. Julian H. Wulbern, *Brecht and Ionesco: Commitment in Context* (Urbana: University of Illinois Press, 1971), 7–8.

6. Ionesco, *Improvisation or The Shepherd's Chameleon, Plays*, volume 3, trans. Donald Watson (London: Calder and Boyars, 1960), 117.

7. Ibid., 118.

8. Ibid., 120–22.

9. Jean Anouilh, "Du chapitre des *Chaises*," *Le Figaro* (4/23/56). My translation, as are all the quotations from the French newspapers used in this chapter.

10. Ionesco, *Improvisation*, 128.

11. Ibid., 149.

12. These articles appeared in the Brecht issue of *Théâtre Populaire*, no. 11, (January–February, 1955). Notes 11–18 reproduce the specific passages lifted by Ionesco from the various essays in order to satirize the pedantic language used by the critics.

13. Roland Barthes, "Les maladies du costume de théâtre": "C'est donc sur la nécessité de manifester en chaque occasion le *gestus* social de la pièce que nous fonderons notre morale du costume" (64). (We will base our costume ethics upon the necessity to manifest on each and every occasion the social *gestus* of the play.).

14. Bernard Dort, "Une nouvelle dramaturgie: Brecht ou l'anti-Racine": "Car ce théâtre, s'il est d'éducation, au sens fort du terme, n'est en rien didactique. La leçon n'est pas sur la scène. C'est à chaque spectateur de la tirer du spectacle—de la tirer pour et selon soi" (28). (For this theatre, though educational, in the strongest sense of the term, is in no way didactic. There is no lesson dramatized upon the stage. Each member of the audience must draw this lesson from the spectacle itself—to draw it for himself, according to his own lights).

15. David Victoroff, "Le Paradoxe du Spectateur": "La signification première des applaudissements nous est fournie par des considérations d'ordre étymologique. Alors que le latin possède un verbe spécial: *plaudere,* les Grecs n'avaient pas de vocable correspondant et se servaient du verbe *krotein* (de l'indo-européen *kret*—heurter), qui voulait dire: faire du bruit en entrechoquant" (81). (The original meaning of applause can be deduced from etymological considerations. While Latin possesses a special verb, *plaudere,* the Greeks had no corresponding equivalent. They used the verb *krotein* [from the Indo-European *kret*—to knock], which meant: to make a noise by knocking one object against another).

16. Bernard Dort, "Une nouvelle dramaturgie": "A la limite, on pourrait même prendre chacune des scènes en soi et l'étudier, la critiquer isolément des autres. Brecht l'indiquait même, dans une interview accordée à un journaliste du *Monde* lors de la création au Berliner Ensemble du *Cercle de craie caucasien* son public devait revenir plusieurs fois au théâtre, et, à chaque fois, s'intéresser à une autre scène, d'un autre point de vue . . . pour arriver, à la fin, à une compréhension totale de l'oeuvre qui serait la somme de ses interprétations successives" (32). (One might even take each scene separately and study it, criticize it as a separate entity. Brecht suggested in the course of an interview he granted a journalist from *Le Monde,* on the occasion of the Berliner Ensemble's creation of *The Caucasian Chalk Circle,* that his public ought to return to the theater more than once, studying each scene of the play from various points of view . . . in order to finally reach a total understanding of the work as the sum of successive interpretations).

17. Roland Barthes, "Les maladies du costume de théâtre": "Cette humanité du costume, elle est largement tributaire de son entour, du milieu substantiel dans lequel se déplace l'acteur. L'accord réfléchi entre le costume et son fond est

peut-être la première loi du théâtre . . ." (75). (The human quality of the stage costume depends to a major extent on the concrete environment in which the actor moves. Perhaps the basic law of theater can be found in this reflected harmony between costume and background).

18. Although Barthes does not mention nudity, he speaks of the extravagant, elaborate costumes favored by the "petits-bourgeois theaters such as Les Folies-Bergères, the Comédie Française, the Opéra and the Comique" (69). Ionesco must have been amused by this juxtaposition of the Folies-Bergères (where nude scenes alternate with highly costumed ones, or where panniered dresses are décolletées in front to a point below the breasts) with the "Maison de Molière," as the Comédie Française is often called, and the Paris opera houses. This must have led him to play with the concept that nudity ought to be considered as a kind of anticostume, therefore, in his view, a costume. This is the kind of typical philosophic contradiction Ionesco used in his early essays, collected in *Nu,* and as one of the devices in *Improvisation.*

19. This quote does not refer to a specific sentence but is inspired by Walter Weidli's essay "L'acteur de l'ère scientifique." In his own essay, published by the *Nouvelle Revue Française* (5/1/55), written in answer to the special Brecht issue, Jacques Lemarchand singled out for attack a sentence from Weidli's concluding paragraph: "Est-il besoin de dire que l'acteur de l'ère scientifique, s'il veut soumettre à la critique—d'une manière à la fois belle et intelligible—le comportement social de ses personnages, devra exercer intensément et continûment ses facultés d'observation et de réflexion?" (Is it really necessary to stress that the actor of the scientific era, if he intends to allow the social behavior of his characters to be scrutinized by critical judgment in a responsible and aesthetically pleasing way, will have to put to the test his faculties of observation and reflection?). Lemarchand writes that Racine must have given much the same kind of advice to his leading actress, La Champmeslé. Thus, neither Brecht nor Walter Weidli have discovered something radically new.

20. This quotation is an amalgam of a number of statements made by Barthes in his essay "Les maladies du costume de théâtre":

> . . . on sait les ravages épidémiques du mal vériste dans l'art bourgeois. (65)
> [. . . one is aware of the epidemic ravages wrought by the malady of excessive realism of bourgeois art.]
> Une deuxième maladie, fréquente aussi, c'est la maladie esthétique, l'hypertrophie d'une beauté formelle sans rapport avec la pièce. (67)
> [Another frequently encountered sickness is aestheticism, a hypertrophy of formal beauty without any connection to the play itself.]
> En somme, le bon costume de théâtre doit être assez matériel pour signifier et assez transparent pour ne pas constituer ses signes en parasites. Le costume est une écriture. (76)
> [In short, an appropriate theater costume ought to be concrete enough to signify, and yet sufficiently transparent so that its signs do not grow parasitical. Theater costuming is a form of writing.]

21. Ionesco, *Improvisation*, 149.

22. Ibid., 151.

23. Ionesco, *Notes and Counter Notes: Writings on the Theatre*, trans. Donald Watson (New York: Grove Press, 1964), 63.

24. Ionesco, *Improvisation*, 112–13.

25. *Brecht on Theatre*, trans. John Willett (New York: Hill and Wang, 1964), 128.

26. Arthur Adamov, "Note Préliminaire," in *Théâtre II* (Paris: Gallimard, 1955), 8.

27. Ibid.

28. Ibid. All three passages are my translation.

29. Ionesco, *Notes and Counter Notes*, 66–67.

30. Ionesco, *Improvisation*, 113.

31. Ramon Fernandez, *Molière ou l'essence du génie comique* (Paris: Grasset, 1979), 131. My translation.

32. Ionesco, *Improvisation*, 121.

33. Ionesco, *Notes and Counter Notes*, 87–89.

34. Ibid., 89–93.

35. Ibid., 108.

36. Wulbern, *Brecht and Ionesco*, 49.

37. Donald Watson, "Ionesco and His Early English Critics," in *Plays*, Vol. 10, by Eugène Ionesco (London: John Calder, 1976), 117–18; 132–33.

38. Wulbern, *Brecht and Ionesco*, 226.

39. Watson, "Ionesco and His Early English Critics," 134.

Bibliography

Works by Eugène Ionesco

Published as Collections at Gallimard

Théâtre I: La Cantatrice chauve, La Leçon, Jacques ou la soumission, Les Chaises, Victimes du devoir, Amédée ou comment s'en débarrasser. Préface de Jacques Lemarchand. Paris: Gallimard, 1954.

Théâtre II: L'Impromptu de l'Alma ou le Caméléon du berger, Tueur sans gages, Le Nouveau Locataire, L'Avenir est dans les oeufs ou Il faut de tout pour faire un monde, Le Maître, La Jeune Fille à marier. Paris: Gallimard, 1958.

Théâtre III: Rhinocéros, Le Piéton de l'air, Délire à deux, Le Tableau, Scène à quatre, Les Salutations, La Colère. Paris: Gallimard, 1963.

Théâtre IV: Le Roi se meurt, La Soif et la Faim, La Lacune, Le Salon de l'automobile, L'Oeuf dur, Pour préparer un oeuf dur, Le Jeune Homme à marier, Apprendre à marcher. Paris: Gallimard, 1966.

Théâtre V: Jeux de massacre, Macbett, La Vase, Exercices de conversation et de diction françaises pour étudiants américains. Paris: Gallimard, 1974.

Théâtre VI: L'Homme aux valises suivi de *Ce formidable bordel.* Paris: Gallimard, 1975.

Théâtre VII: Voyages chez les morts. Paris: Gallimard, 1981.

Théâtre complet. Édition présentée, établie et annotée par Emmanuel Jacquart. Paris: Gallimard, Bibliothèque de la Pléiade, 1991.

Published Individually in Gallimard's Manteau D'Arlequin Collection

Le Rhinocéros (1959); *Le Roi se meurt* (1963); *Jeux de massacre* (1970); *Macbett* (1973); *Ce formidable bordel* (1973); *Les Leçons de français pour américains* (1974), Appeared first in *Cahiers Renaud-Barrault* no. 54 (April, 1966).

Other Ionesco Texts at Gallimard

Special edition of *La Cantatrice chauve*, interprétation typographique de Massin et photographique d'Henri Cohen. Paris: Gallimard, 1954.

Notes et contre-notes (1962), and an expanded edition of the same in the Gallimard collection "Idées" (1966); *La Photo du colonel* (1962); *Discours de réception d'Eugène Ionesco à l'Académie Française et Réponse de Jean Delay* (1971); *Antidotes* (1977); *Un homme en question* (1979); *Hugoliade* (1982); *Le Blanc et le noir* (1985); *Non* (1986), translated by Marie-France Ionesco from the original *Nu* (Bucharest: Vremea, 1934); *La quête intermittente* (1987).

"Stories for Children under Three Years of Age." *Contes no. 1–4*. Illustrated by Étienne Delessert. Paris: Harlin Quist and François Ruy-Vidal, 1969–70. Reprint. Paris: Gallimard, coll. "Folio benjamin," 1983–85.

Published at the Mercure de France

Journal en miettes (1967); *Présent passé passé présent* (1968): *Le Solitaire* (1973).

Published at Albert Skira

Découvertes. Genève: Editions Albert Skira, coll. "Les Sentiers de la création," 1969.

Published in English

The Colonel's Photograph and Other Stories. Trans. Jean Stewart and John Russell. New York: Grove Press, 1969.

Exit the King. Trans. Donald Watson. New York: Grove Press, 1967.

Four Plays: The Bald Soprano, The Lesson, Jack or the Submission, The Chairs. Trans. Donald M. Allen. New York: Grove Press, 1958.

Fragments of a Journal. Trans. Jean Stewart. New York: Grove Press, 1969.

The Gap. Trans. Rosette Lamont. *The Massachusetts Review* 10, no. 1 (Winter, 1969): 119–27.

A Hell of a Mess. Trans. Helen Gary Bishop. New York: Grove Press, 1975.

The Hermit. Trans. Richard Seaver. New York: Viking Press, 1974.

Hunger and Thirst and Other Plays: The Picture, Anger, Salutations. Trans. Donald Watson. New York: Grove Press, 1969.

Journeys among the Dead. Trans. Barbara Wright. London and New York: Riverrun Press, 1985.

The Killer and Other Plays: Improvisation or The Shepherd's Chameleon, Maid to Marry. Trans. Donald Watson. New York: Grove Press, 1960.

Killing Game. Trans. Helen Gary Bishop. New York: Grove Press, 1974.

Macbett. Trans. Charles Marowitz. New York: Grove Press, 1973.

Man with Bags. Adapted by Israel Horovitz, based on a translation by Marie-France Ionesco. New York: Grove Press, 1977.

"The Marvelous Come to Life." Trans. Rosette C. Lamont. *Theatre Arts*, 45, no. 9 (September, 1961), 19.

Maximilian Kolbe. Trans. Rosette Lamont. *Performing Arts Journal 17* 6, no. 2 (1982): 32–36.

Notes and Counter Notes: Writings on the Theatre. Trans. Donald Watson. New York: Grove Press, 1964.

Present Past Past Present. Trans. Helen R. Lane. New York: Grove Press, 1971.

Rhinoceros and Other Plays: The Leader, The Future Is in Eggs or It Takes All Sorts to Make a World. Trans. Derek Prouse. New York: Grove Press, 1960.

"Selections from a Private Journal." Trans. Rosette C. Lamont. In *The New French Dramatists,* special issue of *Yale French Studies* 29.

A Stroll in the Air, Frenzy for Two or More. Trans. Donald Watson. London: Calder and Boyers, 1965.

Three Plays: Amédée, The New Tenant, Victims of Duty. Trans. Donald Watson. New York: Grove Press, 1958.

Ionesco on Art

Le Blanc et le noir. Lithographs by the author. Saint-Gall, Switzerland: Erker-Verlag. 1981. Reprint. Paris: Gallimard, coll. "Blanche," 1985.

Hommage à Fritz Wotruba. Saint-Gall, Switzerland: Erker-Verlag, 1975.

La Main Peint. Die Hande Malt. Gouaches by the author. Saint-Gall, Switzerland: Erker-Verlag, 1987.

Piero Dorazio. Text by Ionesco with lithographs by Piero Dorazio. Saint-Gall, Switzerland: Erker-Verlag, 1987.

"Pourquoi j'ai pris mes pinceaux." Preface to *Zouchy et quelques autres histoires,* by Jean Hamburger. Paris: Flammarion, 1989.

Ionesco on Himself (Interviews and Conversations)

Bonnefoy, Claude. *Conversations with Eugène Ionesco,* trans. Jan Dawson. New York: Holt, Rinehart and Winston, 1971. (First published as *Entretiens avec Eugène Ionesco.* Paris: Pierre Belfond, 1966.)

Lamont, Rosette C. "Entretiens avec Eugène Ionesco." *Cahiers Renaud-Barrault* 53 (February, 1966): 26–29.

———. "Eugène Ionesco." In *The Playwrights Speak,* ed. Walter Wager, with an introduction by Harold Clurman, 140–70. New York: Delacorte Press, 1967.

———. "An Interview with Eugène Ionesco." *Horizon* (May, 1961): 89–97.

———. "An Interview with Eugène Ionesco." *The Massachusetts Review* 10, no. 1 (Winter, 1969): 128–48.

Jacquart, Emmanuel. "Entretien avec Eugène Ionesco." *Stanford French Review* 3, no. 3 (Winter, 1979): 397–403.

———. "Interview with Ionesco." *Diacritics* 3, no. 2 (1973): 45–48.

Books about Ionesco:

In French

Abastado, Claude. *Ionesco.* Paris: Bordas, 1971.

Bachelard, Gaston. *L'Air et les songes, essai sur l'imaginaire du mouvement.* Paris: Librairie José Corti, 1943.

Benmussa, Simone. *Ionesco.* Paris: Seghers, Collection Théâtre Tous les Temps, 1966.

Bradesco, Faust. *Le Monde étrange d'Eugène Ionesco.* Paris: Promotion et Édition, 1967.

Corvin, Michel. *Le Théâtre nouveau en France.* Paris: Presses Universitaires de France, coll. "Que sais-je?" 1963.

Donnard, Jean-Hervé. *Ionesco dramaturge ou l'artisan et le démon.* Paris: Minard, 1966.

Hubert, Marie-Claude. *Langage et corps fantasmé dans le théâtre des années cinquante: Ionesco, Beckett, Adamov, suivi d'entretiens aved Eugène Ionesco et Jean-Louis Barrault, Préface d'Eugène Ionesco.* Paris: Librairie Corti, 1987.

Hubert, Marie-Claude. *Eugène Ionesco.* Paris: Contemporains-Seuil, 1990.

Issacharoff, Michael. *Le Spectacle du discours.* Paris: Librairie José Corti, 1985.

Jacquart, Emmanuel. *Le Théâtre de dérision.* Paris: Gallimard, coll. "Idées," 1974.

Kamayabi Mask, Ahmad. *Ionesco et son théâtre.* Paris: Caractères, 1987.

Laubreaux, Raymond, ed. *Les Critiques de notre temps et Ionesco.* Paris: Garnier, 1973.

Saint Tobi. *Eugène Ionesco ou à la recherche du paradis perdu.* Paris: Gallimard, coll. "Les Essais 177," 1973.

Sénart, Philippe. *Ionesco.* Paris: Éditions Universitaires, 1964.

Serreau, Geneviève. *Histoire du nouveau théâtre.* Paris: Gallimard, coll. "Idées," 1966.

Surer, Paul. *Le Théâtre contemporain.* Paris: SEDES, 1964.

Vernois, Paul. *La Dynamique Théâtrale d'Eugène Ionesco.* Paris: Éditions Klincksieck, 1972.

Vernois, Paul, and Ionesco, Marie-France, ed. *Situations et perspectives.* Paris: Belfand, 1980.

Wintzen, René. *Bertolt Brecht.* Paris: Editions Pierre Seghers, 1954.

In English

Burkman, Katherine H. *The Arrival of Godot: Ritual Patterns in Modern Drama.* Rutherford, NJ: Fairleigh Dickinson University Press, 1986.

Coe, Richard N. *Eugene Ionesco.* Writers and Critics Series. Edinburgh: Oliver and Boyd, 1961. Rev. ed. *Ionesco: A Study of His Plays.* London: Methuen, 1971. American rev. ed. *Eugene Ionesco: A Study of His Work.* New York: Grove Press, 1968.

Esslin, Martin. *The Theater of the Absurd.* London: Eyre and Spottiswoode, 1962. New York: Doubleday, 1969.

———. *Brief Chronicles.* London: Temple Smith, 1970.

Fletcher, John, ed. *Forces of Modern French Drama.* London: University of London Press, 1972. New York: Frederick Ungar Publishing Company, 1972.

Dickinson, Hugh. *Myth on the Modern Stage.* Urbana: University of Illinois Press, 1969.

Guicharnaud, Jacques. *Modern French Theater from Giraudoux to Beckett*. New Haven: Yale University Press, 1961. Rev. ed. 1967.

Grossvogel, David I. *Twentieth-Century French Drama* (Orig. *The Self-Conscious Stage in Modern French Drama*). New York: Columbia University Press, 1961.

———. *The Blasphemers: The Theater of Brecht, Ionesco, Beckett, Genet*. Ithaca, NY: Cornell University Press, 1965.

Jacobson, Josephine, and Mueller, William R. *Ionesco and Genet: Playwrights of Silence*. New York: Hill and Wang, 1968.

Lamont, Rosette C., ed. *Ionesco: A Collection of Critical Essays*. Englewood Cliffs, NJ: Prentice Hall, 1973.

Lamont, Rosette C., and Friedman, Melvin J., eds. *The Two Faces of Ionesco*. Troy, NY: Whitston Publishing Company, 1978.

Lazar, Moshe, ed. *The Dream and the Play: Ionesco's Theatrical Quest*. Malibu, CA: Undena Publications, 1982.

Lewis, Allan. *Ionesco*. World Authors Series. New York: Twayne Publishers, 1972.

Norrish, Peter. *New Tragedy and Comedy in France, 1945–70*. London: Macmillan, 1988.

Palumbo, Leonard, ed. *Spectrum of the Fantastic*. Westport, CT: Greenwood, 1988.

Pronko, Leonard. *Eugene Ionesco*. Essays on Modern Writers. New York: Columbia University Press, 1965.

———. *Avant-Garde: The Experimental Theater in France*. Berkeley: University of California Press, 1962.

Shattuck, Roger. *The Banquet Years*. Garden City, NY: Doubleday and Company, Anchor Books, 1961.

Steiner, George. *The Death of Tragedy*. New York: Hill and Wang, 1961.

Styan, John Louis. *The Dark Comedy: The Development of Modern Comic Tragedy*. Cambridge: Cambridge University Press, 1968.

Taylor, John Russell. *The Angry Theater*. New York: Hill and Wang.

Wellwarth, George E. *The Theater of Protest and Paradox*. New York: New York University Press, 1964. Rev. ed. 1971.

Wulbern, Julian H. *Brecht and Ionesco*. Urbana: University of Illinois Press, 1971.

Journal Issues with Special Sections on Ionesco

L'Avant-Scène Théâtre 373–74 (February, 1967).
Cahiers des saisons 15 (Winter, 1959).
Cahiers Renaud-Barrault 29 (February, 1960).
Cahiers Renaud-Barrault 42 (February, 1963).
Cahiers Renaud-Barrault 53 (February, 1966).
Cahiers Renaud-Barrault 97 (1978).
Esprit (May, 1965).
Tulane Drama Review 7, no. 3 (Spring, 1963).

Selected Journal Articles

Alvarez-Detrell, Tamara. *"Le Solitaire:* Ionesco's Ambiguous Answer to His Theatre."" *Language Quarterly* 24, nos. 3–4 (Spring–Summer, 1986): 51–53.

Burkman, Katherine H. "Opening Walls: Two Stories by Eugene Ionesco." *Midwest Quarterly* 21, no. 4 (Summer, 1980): 412–22.

Cismaru, Alfred. "Beckett and Ionesco: *Necessitas Scribendi." Antigonish Review* 48 (Winter, 1982): 95–100.

——. "Ionesco and His Theatre: L'homme en question." *Claudel Studies* 9, no. 2 (1982): 47–52.

——. "Ionesco at Eighty." *Texas Review* 10, nos. 3–4 (Fall–Winter, 1989): 62–69.

Coleman, Ingrid H. "The Professor's Dilemma: The Absurd Comic Principle in Ionesco's *La Leçon." Perspectives on Contemporary Literature* 7 (1981): 44–53.

Crichfield, Grant. "On ne badine pas avec les rhinocéros." *West Virginia University Philological Papers* 28 (1982): 140–45.

Dürrenmatt, Friedrich. "Problems of the Theatre." *Tulane Drama Review* 3, no. 1 (October, 1958): 19–24.

Edney, David. "The Family and Society in the Plays of Ionesco." *Modern Drama* 28, no. 3 (September, 1985): 377–87.

Féal, Gisèle. "La Mère Pipe et le tueur, ou la psychopathologie de la vie politique selon Ionesco." *French Review* 64, no. 2 (December, 1990): 317–25.

Frankel Gerrard, Charlotte. "Eugene Ionesco's Existentialist Recluse Twice Tried." *Symposium* 36, no. 3 (Fall, 1982): 195–206.

Gaensbauer, Deborah B. "Dreams, Myths, and Politics in Ionesco's *L'Homme aux valises." Modern Drama* 28, no. 3 (September, 1985): 388–96.

Galli, Gemma M. "Edifying the Reader: Ionesco's 'The Colonel's Photograph.'" *Modern Fiction Studies* 31, no. 4 (Winter, 1985): 645–57.

Greshoff, C. J. "Reflections on Some Plays of Ionesco." *Contrast* 13, no. 4 (December, 1981): 31–41.

Hagui, Adela. "Drame et langage chez E. Ionesco." *Anuar de Linguistică si Istorie Literară* 30–31 (1985–87): 45–52.

Harty, Kevin J. "Ionesco and Semiramis." *College Language Association Journal* 31, no. 2 (December, 1987): 170–77.

Jacquart, Emmanuel. "La Leçon d'Ionesco." *Travaux de Littérature* 1 (1988): 241–52.

Karampetsos, E. D. "Ionesco and the Journey of the Shaman." *Journal of Evolutionary Psychology* 4, nos. 1–2 (April, 1983): 64–77.

Klaver, Elizabeth. "The Play of Language on Ionesco's Play of Chairs." *Modern Drama* 32, no. 4 (December, 1989): 521–31.

Lamont, Rosette C. "The Metaphysical Farce: Beckett and Ionesco." *French Review* 32, no. 4 (February, 1959): 319–28.

Marie, Charles P. "Avant-garde et sincérité: Ionesco." *Revue d'Histoire de Théâtre* 38, no. 1 (1986): 39–66.

Piancentini, Gérard. *"La Cantatrice chauve* est-elle *La Cantatrice chauve?" Revue d'Histoire du Théâtre* 40, no. 4 (October–December, 1988): 344–56.

Pinkernell, Gert. "Eugène Ionesco's *Rhinocéros:* Erzählung (1957) und Stück (1958) als Reflexe der politischen Situation ihrer Zeit." *Archiv für Studium der Neueren Sprachen und Literaturen* 226, no. 2 (1989): 309–26.

Retford, Lynne. "Irony in Ionesco." *French Literature Series* 14 (1987): 174–77.

Schapira, Charlotte. "Destruction et reconstruction du langage dans le théâtre de Ionesco." *Les Lettres Romanes* 39, no. 3 (August, 1985): 207–17.

———. "Voltaire's Writings as a Possible Source of Ionesco's Absurd Drama." *French Studies Bulletin* 28 (Autumn, 1988): 12–14.

Simches, Seymour O. "The Mythic Quest of Ionesco's *Hunger and Thirst.*" *Journal of Evolutionary Psychology* 5, no. 3–4 (August, 1984): 237–43.

Tener, Robert L. "Scenic Metaphors: A Study of Ionesco's Geometrical Vision of Human Relationships in the Bérenger Plays." *Papers on Language and Literature* 23, no. 2 (Spring, 1987): 175–91.

Thibault, Jean-François. "Ionesco et l'avant-garde: Le jeu du Solitaire." *Journal of the American Romanian of Arts and Sciences* 13–14 (1990): 83–93.

Waite, Alan. "Les sens déviés de Ionesco." *Zeitschrift für Französische Sprache und Literatur* 96, no. 1 (1986): 1–11.

Index